DATE D

CONSCIENCE AND COMMUNITY

CONSCIENCE

AND

COMMUNITY

Revisiting Toleration
and Religious Dissent
in Early Modern England
and America

ANDREW R. MURPHY

The Pennsylvania State University Press
University Park, Pennsylvania

Library of Congress Cataloging-in-Publication Data

Murphy, Andrew, R., 1967–
Conscience and community: revisiting toleration and religious dissent
in early modern England and America / Andrew R. Murphy.
p.   cm.
Includes bibliographical references and index.
ISBN 0-271-02105-5 (alk. paper)
1. Religious tolerance—England—History—17th century.
2. Religious tolerance—Massachusetts—History—17th century.
3. Religious tolerance—Pennsylvania—History—17th century.
4. Liberalism—Religious aspects.   I. Title.

BR757 .M87 2001
323.44′2′09032—dc21
00-064977

CONTENTS

BIBLIOGRAPHIC ABBREVIATIONS
USED THROUGHOUT THIS BOOK

AJPS	*American Journal of Political Science*
APSR	*American Political Science Review*
Bloudy Tenent	*The Bloudy Tenent of Persecution* (London, 1644). In volume 3 of *The Complete Writings of Roger Williams*, ed. Samuel L. Caldwell. New York: Russell and Russell, 1963.
Clarke Papers	William Clarke, *The Clarke Papers: Selections from the Papers of William Clarke, Secretary to the Council of the Army, 1647–1649, and to General Monck and the Commanders of the Army in Scotland, 1651–1660.* 2 vols. (London, 1891, 1894). Edited by C. H. Firth. London: Royal Historical Society, 1992.
Cotton, *Letter*	John Cotton, *A Letter of Mr. John Cottons Teacher of the Church in Boston* (London, 1643). In volume 1 of *The Complete Writings of Roger Williams*, ed. Samuel L. Caldwell. New York: Russell and Russell, 1963.
Mr Cottons Letter	Roger Williams, *Mr. Cottons Letter Lately Printed, Examined, and Answered* (London, 1644). In volume 3 of *The Complete Writings of Roger Williams*, ed. Samuel L. Caldwell. New York: Russell and Russell, 1963.
HL	Henry E. Huntington Library, San Marino, California
HV	Quaker Collection, Haverford College, Haverford, Pennsylvania.
JEH	*Journal of Ecclesiastical History*
L	Thomas Hobbes, *Leviathan* (London, 1651). Edited by Edwin Curley. Indianapolis: Hackett, 1994.
Locke, *Letter*	John Locke, *A Letter Concerning Toleration* (London, 1689). Edited by James Tully. Indianapolis: Hackett, 1983.
NEQ	*New England Quarterly*

Penn, *Works*   *A Collection of the Works of William Penn.* 2 vols. (London, 1726). Reprint. New York: AMS Press, 1974.

PMHB   *Pennsylvania Magazine of History and Biography*

Locke, *PW*   John Locke, *Political Writings of John Locke.* Edited by David Wootton. New York, 1993.

PWP   *The Papers of William Penn.* Edited by Mary Maples Dunn, Richard S. Dunn, Richard Ryerson, Scott M. Wilds; asst. ed. Jean R. Soderlund. 5 vols. Philadelphia: University of Pennsylvania Press, 1981–86.

Rawls, IPE   John Rawls, "Introduction to the Paperback Edition," in his *Political Liberalism* (New York, 1996).

Rawls, *PL*   John Rawls, *Political Liberalism.* New York: Columbia University Press, 1993.

Rawls, *TOJ*   John Rawls, *A Theory of Justice.* Cambridge: Harvard University Press, 1971.

Reply   John Cotton, *A Reply to Mr. Williams His Examination* (London, 1647). In volume 2 of *The Complete Writings of Roger Williams*, ed. Samuel L. Caldwell. New York: Russell and Russell, 1963.

Somers Tracts   Walter Scott, ed., *Somers Tracts: A Collection of Scarce and Valuable Tracts, But Chiefly Such as Relate to the History and Constitution of These Kingdoms.* 2d ed. 13 vols. London, 1809–15.

SW   Friends Historical Library, Swarthmore College, Swarthmore, Pennsylvania

Winthrop's Journal   *Winthrop's Journal: History of New England, 1630–1649.* Edited by James Kendall Hosmer. New York: Charles Scribner's Sons, 1908.

WMQ   *William and Mary Quarterly*

WP   *Winthrop Papers.* 5 vols. Boston: Massachusetts Historical Society, 1929–47.

PREFACE

Conscience and Community is a work of historically informed political theory focusing on the development of religious toleration in early modern English and American political thought and practice. It is not, nor is it meant to be, a chronology of the development of religious toleration in the early modern world. Although I refer to historical events in the emergence of religious toleration, the historical narrative is neither exhaustive nor pursued for its own sake. Along the way, I refer the reader to sources whose main focus *is*, indeed, the historical chronology, and who lay out that chronology in all its important detail.[1] But this is not my primary aim, and in this project the historical references will be instrumental to the larger purpose of illuminating the emergence of an idea and its attendant political *practice*.

Second, this study is not an exhaustive account of toleration in England and America during the seventeenth century. The specific examinations I pursue—the English Civil War and Revolution, and the early histories of Massachusetts and Pennsylvania—represent just several loci of toleration during these years. I have chosen to focus on these periods because I view them as being of special importance to understanding the emergence of religious liberty in the early modern world. But they should be taken as illustrative exemplars from a wider universe.[2]

---

1. The classic source on toleration in the early modern world is Joseph Lecler, *Toleration and the Reformation*, trans. T. L. Westow (New York, 1960).
2. That wider universe is elaborated in great detail by W. K. Jordan, *The Development of Religious Toleration in England*, 4 vols. (Cambridge, Mass., 1932–40).

TOLERANCE, TOLERATION, LIBERTY OF CONSCIENCE: A NOTE ON DEFINITIONS

This book explores the emergence and development of religious toleration as a philosophical and practical phenomenon. The basic concept and practice I shall be examining is *religious toleration*, which I define as a governmental response to religious dissent or diversity in society, a response that eschews coercion and extends legal protections to adherents of non-mainstream religious groups. Such a definition is, I think, not controversial.[3] In its most restricted sense, religious toleration is a strictly "negative" liberty, fitting in well with classical liberalism and other traditions that stress liberty as the absence of constraint.[4] At the same time, we should not underestimate the demands that "negative" freedoms can put on regimes. Toleration may involve permitting unpopular forms of religious expression and protecting individuals' rights to engage in such activities. This is not *purely* negative, if negative refers only to the *absence* of something: regimes must guarantee that tolerated groups can gather without violence or harassment. Seen this way, toleration lies at the heart of early modern political thought, providing a benchmark or minimal condition of negative freedom from which any discussion of fuller liberty must begin.[5]

Many of the thinkers considered in this project, similarly, considered toleration as primarily a refraining from punishment. More recent scholars

3. Henry Kamen defines toleration as "the concession of liberty to those who dissent in religion" (*The Rise of Toleration* [London, 1967], 7); see also Preston King, *Toleration* (New York, 1976), 13ff. For some general discussions, see W. F. Adeney, "Toleration," in the *Encyclopedia of Religion and Ethics*, ed. James Hastings (New York, 1925), 12:360–69; Maurice Cranston, "Toleration," in *The Encyclopedia of Philosophy*, ed. Paul Edwards (New York, 1967), 8:143–46; and John Horton, "Toleration," in *The Blackwell Encyclopedia of Political Thought*, ed. David Miller (Oxford, 1991), 521–23.

4. On negative and positive liberty, see Isaiah Berlin, "Two Concepts of Liberty," in *Four Essays on Liberty* (New York, 1969).

5. Removal of criminal penalties constitutes a similar minimum in other areas of social and political life. Although such a minimum may eventually prove inadequate to secure evolving notions of liberty, basic toleration does set a standard from which further theorizing and action can proceed. See the following: on religious and cultural pluralism, Anna Elisabetta Galeotti, "Citizenship and Equality: The Place for Toleration," *Political Theory* 21 (1993): 585–605; on toleration and multicultural education, Peter Gardner, "Propositional Attitudes and Multicultural Education, or Believing Others Are Mistaken," in John Horton and Peter Nicholson, eds., *Toleration: Philosophy and Practice* (Brookfield, Vt., 1992); on campus intolerance, Jennifer Jackson, "Intolerance on the Campus," in the same volume; and on racial and sexual issues, the essays in John Horton and Susan Mendus, eds., *Aspects of Toleration: Philosophical Studies* (London, 1985).

often agree, but note further that "toleration" seems to carry an inherent note of condescension or indulgence, a grudging grant from the state that contains a hint of disapproval.[6] On this reading, the terms "liberty of conscience" or "religious liberty"represent more expansive notions than toleration and theoretically involve a claim of (natural or other) right as opposed to the mere "permission" associated with toleration. Anson Phelps Stokes calls toleration "a halfway house between an attitude by the state of ecclesiastical exclusiveness ... and ... freedom of conscience and equality of different religious organizations before the law."[7] Gordon Schochet's work on John Locke's theory of toleration, for example, provides the most trenchant contemporary argument about the distinction between toleration and religious liberty: while admitting that seventeenth-century thinkers evince no clear distinction between the two terms, he argues that Locke's *Letter Concerning Toleration* aimed far beyond mere toleration and "call[ed] for the end of the Anglican establishment."[8] In effect, Schochet argues that Locke was forced into the language of toleration by the terminology and discourse of his time, when in fact he was advocating something far more radical.[9] Rather than a "granted privilege" of toleration, Schochet suggests, we should view Locke as calling for "genuine 'religious liberty' as a matter of right."[10]

Regardless of whether the right to religious exercise is political or natural, arguments about such liberty are *always* situated in a political context and are *always* granted by state acquiescence. In seventeenth-century England, as Schochet admits, the political question focused on whether or not to tolerate

6. According to Richard Vernon, "Toleration involves the reluctant acceptance of things that one hates or despises" (*The Career of Toleration: John Locke, Jonas Proast, and After* [Montreal, 1997], 71). See also Jordan, *Development of Religious Toleration*, 1:17; Bernard Crick, "Toleration and Tolerance in Theory and Practice," *Government and Opposition* 6 (1971): 160; Edward B. Underhill, ed., *Tracts Concerning Liberty of Conscience and Persecution, 1614–1661* (London, 1846), 243; J. B. Bury, *A History of Freedom of Thought* (Oxford, 1952), 72; and Wallace St. John, *The Contest for Liberty of Conscience in England* (Chicago, 1900), 6.

7. *Church and State in the United States* (New York, 1950), 21.

8. "John Locke and Religious Toleration," in *The Revolution of 1688–1689: Changing Perspectives*, ed. Lois G. Schwoerer (Cambridge, 1992), 163.

9. Ibid., 150–51.

10. "Toleration, Revolution, and Judgment in the Development of Locke's Political Thought," *Political Science* 40 (1988): 84–96. Schochet makes the remarkable claim that "genuine 'religious liberty' as a matter of right was not seriously advocated until Locke published his *Letter Concerning Toleration*" (85), which overlooks such important works as Roger Williams's *Bloudy Tenent of Persecution* (London, 1644) as well as the English Baptist tradition. It is true, though, that the argument for religious liberty as a natural or prepolitical right was *not* a major strand of tolerationist thinking during the seventeenth century.

(generally, Protestant) dissenters. William Penn, for example, who usually employed the term "liberty of conscience" to denote his political aim, often used the term "toleration" as well, and sometimes in the same sentence.[11] This sort of linguistic or terminological interchangeability had a great deal to do with the political argument into which Penn (and many other advocates of religious liberty) entered: though some hinted at disestablishment of the Anglican Church, the political argument was by and large about whom to tolerate, and on what conditions, *alongside* the Anglican Church. Thus I do not find it helpful to differentiate between the two terms "toleration" and "liberty of conscience" when the historical sources on which my account relies do not do so consistently, and I shall use the terms "toleration" and "liberty of conscience" more or less interchangeably.[12]

Religious toleration represents, at the least, a *political* decision not to interfere with certain types of dissent, and throughout this book I shall understand religious toleration as a *political* phenomenon, as a legal or constitutional term denoting a political response to dissent.[13] Achieving religious toleration is a political goal, and the seventeenth century represents that era in which religious toleration became part of any "laundry list" of essential elements of legitimate government. This "laundry list" makes up the core elements of what we now call liberalism. At the same time, this study will amply document that most of those who participated in the theoretical articulation and political achievement of religious toleration during the seventeenth century were themselves deeply *religious* persons. Their worldview was Christian, more specifically Protestant; their arguments, audience, and indeed their opponents were almost exclusively Christian. This *political* principle, then, has to do with *religious* practices. Thus the complex and multifaceted nature of the phenomenon under consideration in these pages: religious toleration is a political value, an attribute of the interaction between a government and

11. Penn uses the two terms interchangeably in his *Proposed Comprehension Soberly, and Not Unseasonably, Consider'd* (London, 1672). See also the extended title to Penn's *Great Case of Liberty of Conscience* (London, 1670): "a general reply to such late discourses as have oppos'd a tolleration." In addition, Penn writes in his *Persuasive to Moderation* (1686) that the "subject of this discourse is . . . liberty of conscience to church-dissenters," while later referring to his "subject . . . a toleration" (*Works*, 2:729).

12. For a fuller discussion of these definitional issues, see my "Tolerance, Toleration, and the Liberal Tradition," *Polity* 29 (Summer 1997): 596–602.

13. Here I agree with Schochet's approach to Locke's *Letter* (and, in my extension, to the tolerationist literature more generally) as a *political* document. See Schochet, "John Locke and Religious Toleration," 148–49.

its citizens, that evokes the issues of ultimate meaning that have so often divided societies along lines of religion.

Generally speaking, I shall avoid using the term "tolerance" throughout this study. Elsewhere, I have argued that we may avoid some long-standing conceptual confusions by using "tolerance/intolerance" to refer to attitudes, and "toleration/antitoleration" to refer to institutional or behavioral phenomena.[14] Without making that argument here, I shall merely suggest that *no* set of attitudes is necessarily related to tolerationist outcomes in politics. Since this is a study in the history of political thought, I am most interested in ideas concerning what to *do* politically, rather than in elucidating the structure of (individual or social) attitudes toward religious dissenters. In this sense, my focus is similar to Bernard Williams's argument that the *practice* of toleration need not require individuals to exhibit a more substantive "virtue" of toleration.[15] Although John Horton has proposed denying the term "tolerant" to individuals who merely restrain unsavory prejudices, Michael Walzer illustrates a range of possible routes to tolerance—resignation, indifference, moral stoicism, openness to others, the postmodern celebration of difference—noting that "it is a feature of any successful regime of toleration that it does not depend on a particular form of this virtue."[16] Mutual respect might be "the most attractive attitude . . . but [it is] not necessarily the most likely to develop or the most stable over time."[17]

TOLERATION AND LIBERALISM: OVERCOMING THE "LOCKE OBSESSION"

In remarks concluding his recent exploration of early modern republican thought, Quentin Skinner called on scholars to "uncover the often neglected riches of our intellectual heritage and display them once more to view."[18] I

14. See my "Tolerance, Toleration, and the Liberal Tradition."

15. See Bernard Williams, "Toleration: An Impossible Virtue?" in David Heyd, ed., *Toleration: An Elusive Virtue* (Princeton, 1996).

16. "Not all those who rightly restrain themselves from acting so as to interfere with conduct to which they object act tolerantly . . . [since] there are some things it is inappropriate to tolerate because it is wrong or unreasonable to object to them in the first place" (Horton, "Toleration as a Virtue," in Heyd, *Toleration: An Elusive Virtue*, 41, 33); Walzer, *On Toleration* (New Haven, Conn., 1997), 10–12.

17. Walzer, *On Toleration*, 52.

18. *Liberty Before Liberalism* (Cambridge, 1998), 118–19.

hope that my account of toleration as it developed in early modern Anglo-American thought will contribute toward that worthy goal. The standard liberal story of toleration, of course, is a widely popular and rhetorically powerful piece of conventional wisdom. The "lessons" of the Reformation, so the argument goes, show that liberalism offered (and continues to offer) the most politically and philosophically adequate solution to the issue of religious difference.[19] The hasty equation of religious toleration with the liberal tradition—and, more specifically, the widespread obsession with the thought of one thinker, John Locke[20]—has often suggested, unfortunately and inaccurately, that toleration and liberalism arose, together and *de novo*, from the wreckage of medieval orthodoxy.[21]

Given the current debates that swirl around liberal theory and practice—and Locke's place as quintessential protoliberal—such a Locke obsession can cut two ways. Gordon Schochet, as noted above, celebrates Locke's purported reach beyond mere toleration into a full and robust religious liberty, a move from meek supplication for state benevolence to a confident claim of prepolitical or natural right. Those, on the other hand, who view modernity and liberalism as stalking-horses for relativism and rampant subjectivism, place much of the blame for contemporary ills on Locke. Glenn Tinder, for example, claims that "the principles on which Locke based his defense of toleration on the parts of governments became prominent among those on which there came to rest a broader idea—that all kinds of expression should be permitted, not merely religious ones, and that such tolerance should be practiced, not only by governments but by every power in society."[22]

Perhaps Tinder is right to claim that Locke's views did, over time, become popular among those with broader ideas about expression and social tol-

---

19. See, e.g., Rawls, *PL*; Jordan, *Development of Religious Toleration*; and King, *Toleration*.

20. John Christian Laursen and Cary Nederman rightly lament this "Locke obsession" in their general introduction to *Beyond the Persecuting Society: Religious Toleration Before the Enlightenment* (Philadelphia, 1998), 2–4.

21. I have also argued (in "Tolerance, Toleration, and the Liberal Tradition") that this inherent relationship between liberalism and toleration does exist; I have not argued, however, as have a number of liberal theorists (either implicitly or explicitly), that previous or nonliberal societies are by definition hostile to toleration. We are only recently getting away from viewing the medieval world through the lens of liberal triumphalism, and the stereotype cannot go away quickly enough.

22. *Tolerance and Community* (Columbia, Mo., 1995), 9–10. This volume is a revised reissue of Tinder's *Tolerance: Toward a New Civility* (Amherst, Mass., 1976).

erance (though I suspect that such people were equally as likely to find Locke constraining and excessively Protestant). If so, then Tinder should criticize them, not Locke. Paying careful attention to Locke's reasons for writing the *Letter* is not, as Tinder claims, "mere pedantry": it is an issue of fundamental interpretive importance.[23] Both Schochet and Tinder, I think, rely on a historiographically suspect principle in which the "real" meaning of Locke's theory of toleration—be it disestablishment or rampant individualist subjectivism— is to be found in something that Locke himself did not articulate. Whether Locke is the object of celebration or damnation, in either case the widespread obsession with his work only skims the surface of the contested terrain of toleration in early modern thought.

Any account of the development of toleration in theory and practice must acknowledge the European background of Reformation, Counter-Reformation, and religious war, not to mention the impulses toward toleration that appeared even in the medieval and classical worlds. Indeed, some of the most insightful research on toleration in recent years has explored just these alternate traditions and their tolerationist potentialities. Cary J. Nederman has forcefully argued—in his own work as well as through several volumes coedited with John Christian Laursen—for a recognition of the tolerationist possibilities inherent in medieval thought, and Gary Remer has pointed to Renaissance humanism as an alternative early modern account of toleration.[24] By drawing on a variety of materials—medieval interreligious dialogues, travel accounts, the rules of classical rhetoric—these scholars have broadened our understanding of the forms that toleration might take and painted a more complex and nuanced picture of the medieval and early modern world.[25] Even within the early modern world, new scholarship has explored previously overlooked tolerationist thinkers and their adversaries: Jonathan Israel has illuminated the important role played by Dutch tolera-

23. *Tolerance and Community*, 9.

24. Cary J. Nederman, *Worlds of Difference: European Discourses of Toleration, c.1100-c.1550* (University Park, Pa., 2000). See also the essays in Laursen and Nederman, *Beyond the Persecuting Society*; Nederman and John Christian Laursen, *Difference and Dissent: Theories of Toleration in Medieval and Early Modern Europe* (New York, 1996); and Gary Remer, *Humanism and the Rhetoric of Toleration* (University Park, Pa., 1995). See also Will Kymlicka, "Two Models of Freedom and Tolerance," in Heyd, *Toleration: An Elusive Virtue;* though compare Moshe Halbertal's critical comments (in "Autonomy, Toleration, and Group Rights") in the same volume.

25. For interreligious dialogue, see Nederman, *Worlds of Difference*, chap. 2; for travel accounts, see Nederman, *Worlds of Difference*, chap. 4; on classical rhetoric, see Remer, *Humanism*, 13–41.

tionists in English political thought and history, while the crosscurrents of European skepticism and toleration have recently been reexamined from a number of perspectives.[26]

Michael Walzer has also attempted to move scholars away from an excessive focus on liberalism as the sole route to toleration. Walzer points to a number of "regimes of toleration"—multinational empires, consociations, nation-states, immigrant societies—which embody various degrees and types of tolerationist commitments. Different sociopolitical arrangements, Walzer points out, do a better or worse job of safeguarding different kinds of diversity. Rather than seeking to "rank" systems (as Walzer puts it, "as if we could assign to each [regime] some quantity of moral value: seven, nineteen, or thirty-one and a half"), Walzer points us toward an appreciation of the myriad ways in which regimes have attempted to deal with ethnic, religious, and cultural differences.[27]

My approach in *Conscience and Community* shares this dissatisfaction with contemporary liberal-theoretical accounts of toleration; yet my focus is somewhat different. By examining seventeenth-century arguments in England and America—places often deemed to have given birth to "liberal" arguments about religious toleration—I attempt to show how different even these "familiar" arguments are from those of contemporary liberal theorists. On my reading, we ought not make the connection between early liberals like Locke and contemporary liberals like John Rawls and Bruce Ackerman too quickly. Locke and other Protestant tolerationists (e.g., Roger Williams, William Walwyn, William Penn) had far more in common with the Renaissance humanist defenders of toleration canvassed by Gary Remer,[28] even perhaps with Thomas Hobbes or Pierre Bayle, than they do with Rawls and Ackerman. In other words, not only have contemporary liberal theorists

26. See, for example, Jonathan Israel, "William III and Toleration," in Ole Peter Grell, Jonathan I. Israel, and Nicholas Tyacke, eds., *From Persecution to Toleration: The Glorious Revolution in England* (New York, 1991); idem, "The Intellectual Debate About Toleration in the Dutch Republic," in *The Emergence of Tolerance in the Dutch Republic*, ed. C. Berkiens-Stevelinck, J. Israel, and G. H. M. Posthumus Meyjes (Leiden, 1997); idem, "Toleration in Seventeenth-Century Dutch and English Thought," in *The Exchange of Ideas: Religion, Scholarship, and Art in Anglo-Dutch Relations in the Seventeenth Century*, ed. Simon Groenveld and Michael Wintle (Zutphen, 1994); Alan Levine, ed., *Early Modern Skepticism and the Origins of Toleration* (Lanham, Md., 1999); and Ole Peter Grell and Roy Porter, eds., *Toleration in Enlightenment Europe* (Cambridge, 1999).

27. *On Toleration*, 3; more generally, chap. 2.

28. Remer, *Humanism*, passim.

overlooked and devalued nonliberal arguments for toleration (as Nederman, Laursen, Remer, Levine, and others point out), but I argue that they have misunderstood and misconstrued the actual historical development of the arguments upon which they themselves rely. Thus a revisitation of the seventeenth-century debates that gave rise to "liberalism" (however we now construe it) will lead to a fuller understanding of, as I put it in the final chapter, both the limits *and* the promise of liberal toleration.

To my first, and best, four teachers:

JUDITH AND FRANCIS MURPHY

EMMA B. AND GEORGE EDWARD WISLER,

with love and gratitude

ACKNOWLEDGMENTS

I have benefited immeasurably from the rigorous and constructive criticism of a number of individuals over the course of writing this book; mentioning their names can only hint at my gratitude to them for their patience, time, and expertise. Foremost among these is Bernard Yack, who first saw this project sketched out as a brief doctoral dissertation prospectus at the University of Wisconsin-Madison and who guided it to fruition by offering just the right mix of autonomy and oversight. Bernie's unfailing generosity and support (not to mention his willingness to read successive drafts of the same chapter!) have improved this book immeasurably. Booth Fowler and Patrick Riley also served important roles on the dissertation committee and shared freely their considerable expertise on the variety of topics under consideration. Over the years, Bernie, Booth, and Patrick have offered constructive criticism as well as personal and intellectual support, and I am glad to call them friends as well as teachers and colleagues. I cannot imagine a more rigorous or congenial group of mentors.

I was also fortunate to have Charles Cohen and Johann Sommerville, both of the Department of History at the University of Wisconsin-Madison, on the original committee supervising the dissertation. Their contributions to the project have gone far beyond correcting errors of historical fact (though they certainly did that, and certainly some remain), broadening into conceptual and historiographical terrain and providing an interdisciplinary audience for what I hope remains an interdisciplinary project.

John Meyer and Sam Nelson have been constant sources of personal support as well as rigorous and constructive intellectual critics for close to ten years now; this book is a testimony to their friendship, and to their ongoing ability to offer criticism as constructive as it is critical. While at the University of Wisconsin-Madison, I received advice, criticism, and encouragement from a number of students and faculty, including Donald Downs, Brian Kroeger,

Laura Olson, David Siemers, Marion Smiley, Joe Soss, and Greg Streich. Kevin den Dulk read an early draft of Chapter 8 and helpfully provided me with a copy of his master's thesis on Rawls. I also owe debts of gratitude to the late Richard Ashcraft (University of California, Los Angeles) for an especially helpful conversation about Locke; James Farr (University of Minnesota) on early modern toleration; and Richard Dunn (University of Pennsylvania) and J. William Frost (Swarthmore College) on issues relating to early Pennsylvania and the Keithian schism. As this book was undergoing final revisions, Cary Nederman of the Texas A & M University offered helpful advice and graciously provided me with an advance copy of his *Worlds of Difference* (Penn State, 2000).

Material from this study has been presented at the annual meetings of the American Political Science Association, the Midwest Political Science Association, the Pennsylvania Historical Society, and the International Society of Political Psychology. In addition, portions have been presented to the Early American History Colloquium (Department of History, University of Wisconsin-Madison), the Huntington Library Colloquium series, and the Sawyer Seminar "Theories and Practices of Religious Toleration/Intolerance" at the Advanced Study Center of the International Institute, University of Michigan, Ann Arbor. I thank the participants in all these venues for their many helpful observations and would especially like to acknowledge the scholars who commented more formally on my work: John Francis Burke, Edwin Curley, Stephen Darwall, Catherine Holland, Robert Kraynak, Graham Maddox, Melissa Mathes, Jeff Polet, Thomas Rourke, Barry Shain, Brian Shaw, Beverly Smaby, Harry Stout, and Arthur Teicher.

The Institute for Humane Studies convened a Current Research Workshop at which I presented an earlier version of Chapter 8: I thank all involved—John Moser of IHS for arranging the events; Stephen Macedo, the workshop's chair; Jeremy Waldron and Jeff Spinner-Halev, my commentators; and participants Ingrid Creppell, Mark Graber, George Klosko, Alan Levine, and Joshua Mitchell—for their incisive and extremely helpful critiques on that occasion. At Villanova, I benefited greatly from conversations with Kevin Hughes and my colleagues in the Core Humanities Program; Tom Smith read and commented on a draft of Chapter 7 (and tactfully declined to take offense when I failed to return the favor due to a birth in our family).

Sandy Thatcher at Penn State Press, along with his staff, most notably Shana Foster, Cherene Holland, Patty Mitchell, and Jennifer Norton, has been unfailingly supportive of this book and indulgent of my many queries. Eldon Eisenach and Gary Remer read the entire manuscript for Penn State Press, and the final product is much improved as a result.

Throughout the research and writing of this book, I have been fortunate to receive generous financial support from a number of sources. The Huntington Library in San Marino, California, provided funds for travel and research, in the form of W. M. Keck Foundation and Robert Middlekauff Fellowships, during the summer of 1994. Additional support was provided by an Everett Helm Foundation Visiting Fellowship at the Lilly Library, Indiana University, Bloomington (March 1995); an Andrew W. Mellon Foundation Fellowship at the Library Company of Philadelphia (June 1995); and a Visiting Fellowship at the Advanced Study Center of the International Institute, University of Michigan (October 1997). For assistance in arranging and getting the most out of the above-mentioned research opportunities, I thank (respectively) Robert Ritchie, Ava Neal, James Green, and Stephen Darwall and Edwin Curley.

Research in historical archives and libraries, of course, represents only a part of the completed project. I was able to devote my time completely to writing during much of 1995 and 1996 thanks to fellowships from the Wisconsin Alumni Research Foundation (The Graduate School, University of Wisconsin-Madison) and the Institute for Humane Studies at George Mason University. The final phase of writing and revising the dissertation from which this book developed was made possible by a Summer (1996) Fellowship from the Pew Program in Religion and American History at Yale University.

Final revisions to this book were made possible by a senior fellowship at the Martin Marty Center of the University of Chicago Divinity School. I thank former Dean Clark Gilpin and current Dean Rick Rosengarten for facilitating my research at the Marty Center, and Sandra Crane for her help with innumerable technical details. Kirk Greer of the University of Chicago political science department proofread the manuscript one final time.

Finally, I thank a number of publishers and journals who have granted permission to reprint portions of this study that were previously published in their pages. They are as follows.

An earlier version of Chapter 7 was published as "Rawls and a Shrinking Liberty of Conscience," *The Review of Politics* 60 (1998): 247–76. I thank the *Review* and Notre Dame Press for permission to reprint it, slightly revised, here.

I thank Blackwell Publishers for permission to draw from my article "The Uneasy Relationship Between Social Contract Theory and Religious Toleration," *The Journal of Politics* 59 (1997): 368–92, in Chapters 2, 5, and 6.

I thank *Polity* for permission to draw on my article "Tolerance, Toleration, and the Liberal Tradition," which appeared originally in *Polity* 29 (1997): 593–623, in Chapters 6 and 8.

In addition to my parents and maternal grandparents, noted in this book's dedication, and my siblings Betsy and Matt, my most personal debts—to Beth, (later) to Peter, and (still later) to Sam—go beyond words and are, I think, best left there.

Chicago
February 2001

"A THEOLOGICAL SCARE-CROW" OR
"THE INWARD PERSUASION OF THE MIND"?

Conscience and Toleration in
Historical, Philosophical, and Political Perspective

Religious toleration appears near the top of any short list of core liberal values: theorists from John Locke to John Rawls have seen important interconnections between the principles of toleration, constitutional government, and the rule of law. Yet the topic has not received a great deal of historically informed scholarly attention in recent years. The standard account has tended to treat the emergence of toleration as a series of steps, beginning sometime in the sixteenth or seventeenth century and purportedly reaching its pinnacle in the political, philosophical, and constitutional instantiations of contemporary liberalism. Revisiting the historical emergence of religious liberty in Anglo-American political thought, however, reveals, not a series of self-evident or logically connected expansions, but instead a far more complex and interesting picture, one that helps correct traditional understandings of the historical development of toleration while at the same time offering new insights into toleration as it currently exists as a political value. It is that picture—which I shall often describe as representing a recurrent tension between conscience and community—that I seek to evoke in the pages of this book.

Toleration as a theoretical and practical concern—whether pertaining to religion or other divisive social issues—is hardly a historical curiosity. Indeed, several prominent scholars, drawing explicitly on seventeenth-century toleration debates, have suggested that toleration is somehow paradigmatic in American constitutionalism.[1] The issues raised by dissent, conscience, and diversity more generally continue to animate philosophical and political argument, speaking to contemporary issues of constitutional government, civil disobedience and the principled objection to specific laws, and the freedoms of speech, assembly, and press.[2] Scholarly research on "political tolerance" (the willingness of people to support civil liberties for unpopular minorities) explores public hostility to marginalized groups and often emphasizes the precarious nature of the basic liberal protections extended to them.[3] Contemporary societies face increasing levels and types of diversity, prompting intense debate about the acceptable extent, permissible limits, and conceptual foundations of toleration, as well as its relationship to multiculturalism and "identity" politics. Whether we are speaking of narrowly religious issues or the broader social dynamics of liberal societies, then, the phenomenon of toleration is centrally connected to the liberal tradition and retains a vital contemporary importance.

The years under consideration in this book represent a touchstone for nascent liberal ideas, a formative period in the tradition of Anglo-American constitutionalism. Scholars of early modern political thought agree that religious toleration represented a central political and theoretical concern for such important seventeenth-century thinkers as Locke, Milton, and Penn.[4]

    1. David A.J. Richards, for example, refers to toleration as the "central constitutional ideal," while John Rawls connects the settlement of seventeenth-century toleration debates with the "modern" societies for which his theory of justice is intended. See Richards, *Toleration and the Constitution* (New York, 1986), x; Rawls, *PL*, introduction and lecture 1. I address these ongoing implications of toleration in Chapters 7 and 8.
    2. See, on this point, Kant's "An Answer to the Question: What is Enlightenment?" in *Perpetual Peace and Other Essays*, trans. Ted Humphrey (Indianapolis, 1983). Although in Chapter 8 I argue against the idea that religious toleration is an endlessly extendable metaphor, Kant suggests that the refusal to dictate terms of religious belief and practice can function as part of a broader approach that fosters human freedom more generally. As he puts it, "The manner of thinking of a head of state who [allows men complete freedom in religious matters] goes even further, for he realizes that there is no danger to his legislation in allowing his subjects to use reason publicly and to set before the world their thoughts concerning better formulations of his laws, even if this involves frank criticism of legislation currently in effect" (45). More recently on the cluster of basic liberal freedoms, see L. T. Hobhouse, *Liberalism* (1911; Oxford, 1964), chap. 1, and Rawls, *PL*, lecture 8 ("The Basic Liberties and Their Priority"), esp. secs. 8–10.
    3. For just two examples of a voluminous literature, see John L. Sullivan, James Piereson, and George Marcus, *Political Tolerance and American Democracy* (Chicago, 1982), and George E. Marcus, John L. Sullivan, Elizabeth Theiss-Morse, and Sandra L. Wood, *With Malice Toward Some: How People Make Civil Liberties Judgments* (Cambridge, 1995).
    4. John Dunn refers to religious toleration as the "single most important application" of Lockean political theory, and Richard Ashcraft sees it as a *sine qua non* of the political movement

As my title suggests, I explore how such toleration debates evoke a tension between conscience and community, be it a tension between the several communities of conscience gathered within the boundaries of a single political entity, or the increasing assertion of the *individual* conscience against collective orthodoxy. Although I touch on a range of issues concerning early modern toleration within these parameters, I address myself more specifically to the English Civil War and Revolution and to the early histories of Massachusetts and Pennsylvania. These represent contexts in which arguments about toleration and religious dissent had especially significant repercussions for their specific participants as well as for subsequent developments in the broader Anglo-American tradition.

As evidenced by my subtitle, I argue throughout this book that we need to *revisit* this formative period in the history of religious toleration. When we do so, and attend closely to the political and philosophical developments that accompanied seventeenth-century toleration debates, we gain a renewed understanding of the *specificity* that made religious toleration such a divisive issue as well as the more *general* tension between conscience and community that continues to resonate in contemporary societies. We are left, I contend, with a more complex view of what happened and what it might have meant than is admitted by many contemporary liberal theorists (when they refer to historical developments at all, that is); a view that suggests that we should neither credit seventeenth-century thinkers for the subsequent successes, nor blame them for the subsequent shortcomings, of twentieth-century liberal theory and practice.

In approaching, or rather reapproaching, this familiar topic historically, I seek both to shed new light on the factors that contributed to toleration's rise and to correct conventional misunderstandings of the more specific debates on which I focus. The legacy of early modern tolerationists lies in an increasing theoretical and political reluctance to allow governmental imposition of a particular religious orthodoxy on individuals in society; in other words, a refusal to sacrifice conscience for the sake of community. The eventual success of tolerationist forces contributed to the emergence of

---

in which Locke played an important role, "a core problem . . . around which other related problems developed." See Dunn, "'Bright Enough for All Our Purposes': John Locke's Conception of a Civilized Society," *Notes and Records of the Royal Society of London* 43 (1989): 135, and Ashcraft, *Revolutionary Politics and Locke's "Two Treatises of Government"* (Princeton, 1989), 9. See also Mary Maples Dunn, *William Penn: Politics and Conscience* (Princeton, 1967).

societies we now call liberal, fundamentally different from the previously obtaining formulation in which a nation's religion necessarily mirrored that of its sovereign (*cuius regio eius religio*).[5] Early modern tolerationists sought to replace traditional notions of *religious* uniformity (as epitomized by cuius regio) with the notion of *political* or civil unity, in which members of various faiths could work together for the good of the polity even while holding different views on issues of ultimate truth. Tolerationist arguments were almost exclusively negative, seeking not social equality or even equal respect but merely the "negative" freedom to be left alone to worship as they considered most acceptable to God. Early modern tolerationists sought, quite literally, a *modus vivendi:* a way of living together without descending into the bloodshed that had traditionally settled religious differences.

Subsequent liberal thinkers have been attracted to toleration insofar as it embodies the idea of freely made choices, in which individuals voluntarily affirm the commitments that flow from their deepest ethical, moral, or religious beliefs. The early modern ideal of political or civil unity may seem minimal when compared with twentieth-century notions of equal concern and respect, and no less a liberal theorist than John Rawls claims that a *modus vivendi* regime represents an insufficient and unstable social arrangement compared with the shared sense of justice he seeks from citizens of his political liberalism (*PL*, 147–48). A firm commitment to equal protection of law, equal opportunity, and basic civil rights might indeed seem minimal against the background of calls for the celebration of difference and the more robust notions of citizenship championed by contemporary thinkers. But we should not be so hasty, I suggest in Chapter 8, to dismiss the value of a *modus vivendi*, or the basic toleration that historically accompanied it. This book seeks to provide a historically informed account of the central liberal principle that grew out of the efforts of early modern tolerationists, and to reflect more broadly on the ongoing tension between conscience and community implicated in these developments.

My claim that toleration possesses a continuing vitality, however, departs sharply from many contemporary theorists, who argue that the principles

5. In theory, of course, given propitious circumstances, *cuius regio* could lead to toleration; such circumstances, however, were not often the dominant ones in early modern societies. Furthermore, as we shall see, even when English kings desired toleration, they were often unable to effect it due to the opposition of Parliament. In Pennsylvania, explicitly founded upon notions of religious liberty, such toleration was put to a severe test when a schism erupted *within* the dominant Quaker community. I explore these developments in Chapters 4 and 5.

undergirding religious toleration can be generalized to account for the wide variety of ethnic, culture, and sexual differences that characterize twenty-first-century societies.[6] Close attention to the historical development of religious toleration suggests that the phenomenon itself and arguments in its favor are far more specific than such an expansive view would suggest. I do not claim, though, that early modern arguments are inaccessible, and I argue that the idea of "conscience" can be extended from its original, purely theological, meanings to deal with more general notions of belief. In this sense, the tension between conscience and community leads to a vibrant and vital debate, one very much alive in the twenty-first century, about the justification of *any* state power seeking to curtail an individual's liberty to act upon the basis of deeply held value commitments. Along these lines, Chapters 7 and 8 offer a sustained critique of many contemporary liberal theorists' appropriation of early modern toleration debates as a metaphor for solving a host of other social problems and some reflections on what a *modus vivendi* toleration might have to offer the twenty-first century.

REVISITING EARLY MODERN TOLERATION AND RELIGIOUS DISSENT: THE HISTORICAL NARRATIVE

In this study, I explore the emergence of religious toleration in seventeenth-century political thought, focusing on events in England as well as the colonies. This focus, of course, leaves out important aspects of the development of tolerationist ideas elsewhere in Europe, and I freely admit to sacrificing breadth for depth in my account. I shall refer the reader as I proceed to the works of other scholars whose work fills in the Continental backdrop to the Anglo-American developments on which I focus.[7] I do comment on the links between prominent thinkers as well as the intellectual history of the ideas considered herein, but in the main I confine myself to England and the early colonial American context. My concern in focusing on England and America is to elucidate the way tolerationist and antitolerationist arguments

---

6. Rawls, *PL*; Richards, *Toleration and the Constitution*. More specifically on the issue of gay rights, for example, see David A.J. Richards, *Identity and the Case for Gay Rights: Race, Gender, Religion as Analogies* (Chicago, 1999), introduction and chap. 3, and William N. Eskridge, *Gaylaw: Challenging the Apartheid of the Closet* (Cambridge, Mass., 1999), chap. 9.

7. See, for example, Levine, *Early Modern Skepticism*; Grell and Porter, *Toleration in Enlightenment Europe*; and more generally, Lecler, *Toleration and the Reformation*.

contributed to a developing and ongoing Anglo-American tradition, one that would later give rise to the revolutionary and constitutional achievements of the eighteenth century.

This study is bounded in time as well as space. I focus on the seventeenth century, for a number of specific reasons. First, the seventeenth century represents, in a real sense, America's founding era, the first sustained and systematic attempt to create English societies in this new land. During the seventeenth century, colonial founders articulated the social, legal, and political foundations by which their communities would be governed for years to come. Of course, colonists continued to think of themselves as English subjects, and would do so for some time. But the opportunities presented by colonization spurred a number of colonial founders to reflect upon the bases of governmental legitimacy, the rights and liberties of their people, and the role of government in the lives of ordinary citizens, all of which influenced debates over religious dissent and toleration. Second, the seventeenth century witnessed the most protracted and contentious attention to issues of religious liberty in all of English history, culminating as it did in the constitutional settlement of 1688, the accession of William and Mary, and the Toleration Act. Between roughly 1630 and 1690, the philosophical, pragmatic, theological, and political grounds of toleration were argued with a vigor—indeed, a ferocity—never witnessed before or since in England. In both the colonies and the mother country, then, religious dissent raised serious issues of order, obedience, authority, and resistance, and the political decisions rulers took influenced the course of events for years to come.

The historical narrative, in which I revisit and explicate the emergence of religious toleration in seventeenth-century political thought, constitutes Chapters 2 through 5 of this book. There was nothing preordained about the developments that took place between roughly 1630 and 1700, nothing teleological or logically necessary about the ascendancy of tolerationist ideas. Understanding what did happen, how religious toleration achieved a tenuous foothold in Anglo-American political thought and practice, is impossible without appreciating the many options that were *potentially* available to early modern regimes. The promise of comprehending, in the broadest and deepest sense, what toleration meant to these societies demands that we evoke its many *different* meanings for those whose lives were intimately bound up with the age's religious discord. Within the broad contours of this narrative, then, I focus most heavily upon Massachusetts and Pennsylvania in the colonial context, and the Civil War and Revolution in England, exemplars that epitomize the issues raised by toleration and religious dissent.

In my account of New England, I am primarily concerned with exploring the relationship between the intentions of the first settlers (informed largely by their experiences in England and the larger context of post-Reformation politics) and the first significant instances of religious dissent. In Chapter 2, I explore the religious dissent that arose in Massachusetts Bay, in the persons of Anne Hutchinson and Roger Williams, and the strife occasioned by the early Baptist and Quaker movements. The dissent that these groups raised went to the heart of Massachusetts Puritans' communal self-understandings, raising questions about their community's basic meaning and mission. This communal self-understanding prevalent among Massachusetts leaders necessitated certain limitations on the exercise of individual conscience. Hutchinson and Williams found these limitations unacceptable; and not surprisingly, the Puritan commonwealth viewed both as dangerous breeders of dissent, banishing each during the colony's first decade. Yet as far as we can tell, neither Hutchinson nor Williams articulated any theory of liberty of conscience at the time of their dissent in Massachusetts, making their careers in the colony highly ambiguous chapters in the story of American religious freedom.[8]

The banishment of Williams and Hutchinson represent both the end of one story—the career of religious dissent in Massachusetts Bay during the settlement's first decade—and the beginning of another. If the early suppression of religious dissent in Massachusetts represents a successful political and ideological opposition to toleration and religious dissent, then Rhode Island, as a colony committed to religious liberty, provides another view of the political implications of radical Puritanism. I explore the challenges faced by Williams and other members of the Rhode Island communities who sought to create civil order in a heavily religious culture while maintaining a nontheistic governmental sphere.

Moving from America back to England in Chapter 3, we see that English affairs during the 1640s and 1650s represent a significant locus of toleration

8. Williams, of course, played a key role in English toleration debates of the 1640s, and his efforts in the founding and early history of Rhode Island cemented his place in the history of liberty of conscience. Williams's position on religious liberty during the 1630s is far from clear, given the fragmentary nature of contemporaneous primary source materials. Claiming persecution does not, *ipso facto*, make one an exponent of religious liberty, nor does Williams's important role in founding Rhode Island necessarily tell us anything about his beliefs about liberty of conscience during the 1630s.

debate in their own right, perhaps the single most fertile period of English thought about religious liberty.[9] Religious issues, whether or not one gives them causal primacy in spurring the disputes that led to civil war, are crucial to understanding the strife of the 1640s: most English Dissenters remained in England (emigration to Massachusetts notwithstanding) to work for their ideals of a reformed church and society. Throughout that decade, debate over a religious settlement went hand in hand with the search for a political solution to the conflict between king, Parliament, and (later) the New Model Army. Oliver Cromwell's eventual ascendance led to the retention of a creedal state church, with a circumscribed parameter of official profession, along with wide latitude for Dissenting congregations outside this framework. Nonetheless, the fact that religious liberty resulted (however briefly) under Cromwell's regime tells us nothing about the intentions of those who initiated the conflicts of the 1640s. I stress that no major political or religious groups desired toleration during the run-up to the English Civil War, and that the Protectorate's extensive religious freedom was the unintentional, unintended result of Parliament's inability to control its own army.

Oliver Cromwell's regime did not long outlast his death in 1658, and King Charles II was restored in 1660. Charles attempted to implement toleration by royal decree. Parliament opposed the king on both procedural and substantive grounds, taking issue with his assumption of extralegal authority and suspecting (with some good reason) Catholic influences at court as the real forces behind tolerationist policies. Parliament enacted harsh penalties for Dissenters during the 1660s and barred Catholics and many Dissenting Protestants from holding office through the Test Act of 1673 (mandating oaths of allegiance and denials of Catholic doctrine by public officials). The association of sectarian Protestants with the religious enthusiasm of the Civil War and Cromwell's Protectorate cast toleration in a highly unfavorable light during the early Restoration: growing Whig concerns (especially during the Exclusion Crisis of 1679–81) about the possible reign of a Catholic king, while redescribing the perceived threat to English liberties, did not increase the prospects for toleration during those years either.

9. I shall refer to the events in England between roughly 1642 and 1649 as the "English Civil War" and the events of 1688–90 simply as "the Revolution." For the events between the two, I shall refer to the Commonwealth (1649–53), Protectorate (1653–59), or Restoration (1660–88). I find the term "Interregnum," though adequate for some scholarly purposes, less helpful for my purposes because of its inherently retrospective nature.

Chapter 4 explores the English Revolution of 1688, the upshot of the increasing tension between the Stuart kings and Parliament. The Toleration Act, passed in the following year, ensured Dissenting Protestants the right to assemble and worship publicly, contributed to an explosion in the number of Dissenting congregations, and is rightly considered a landmark in the history of liberty of conscience. Still, as I point out in Chapter 4, the Toleration Act granted considerably less religious liberty than either James II's Declarations of Indulgence (1687 and 1688) or Cromwell's Protectorate. Indeed, one of the key factors in the desertion of James II by English political and religious elites lay in his tolerationist efforts on behalf of English Catholics and Protestant Dissenters. On the philosophical level, the 1680s were entirely derivative: not one argument in favor of toleration was advanced during those years that had not been voiced during the 1640s and 1650s.

In 1681, against the backdrop of Restoration religious politics, concerns about a "popish plot" to impose Catholicism on England, and the Exclusion Crisis, Charles II granted William Penn a charter for Pennsylvania. Penn had figured prominently in Restoration religious debates: his apologia in defense of Quakerism and his attacks on religious persecution argue with great passion the value of toleration as a necessary component of legitimate government. Having spent time in prison for his Quaker activities, Penn saw in his colony the promise of a "holy experiment" for the cause of toleration. Chapter 5 examines the founding and early development of Pennsylvania, the degree to which Penn was successful in realizing his tolerationist commitments in actual practice. I highlight both the importance of Penn's achievement—a thriving colony in which adherents of many religious faiths lived together in relative peace—as well as the important issues of toleration raised by the civil prosecution of dissident Quakers during the Keithian schism of 1692–94. That episode, brief but explosive, was seized upon by Penn's opponents to discredit Quakers as incompetent, unjust, and hypocritical, and Pennsylvania politics assumed a place in the religious and political debates of England.

Consideration of developments regarding toleration on both sides of the Atlantic sheds light on the broader relationship between England and America, two societies whose fates have been inextricably linked.[10] For example, a

10. The most recent and ambitious, if somewhat overstated, treatment of this linkage between English and American development is Kevin Phillips, *The Cousins' Wars: Religion, Politics, and the Triumph of Anglo-America* (New York, 1999).

number of prominent individuals played important roles in both English and American toleration debates. The Puritan migration to New England was greatly influenced by the resurgence of heavy-handed Anglican ceremonialism under Charles I and Archbishop of Canterbury William Laud; and the hostility to Puritan ideas within the Church of England in the late 1620s and 1630s played a crucial role in spurring that migration. Several important Massachusetts Puritans (e.g., Roger Williams, Henry Vane), having lived in New England during the 1630s, returned to England to participate in the next decade's conflict, which (in their view) promised the rule of the godly for which they had striven so long. Such cross-Atlantic activity is not confined to the earlier cases: William Penn occupies a key role in the history of religious freedom as much for his efforts to gain toleration for Quakers in Restoration England as for his role in founding and governing the "holy experiment" of Pennsylvania. The nemesis of Pennsylvania Quakers, George Keith, came to prominence in Scotland and England, journeyed to Pennsylvania, returned to England where he converted to Anglicanism, and traveled back to Pennsylvania, once again engaging in religious and political debate with those whose views he found wanting.

This dialectical relationship between the mother country and its colonial offspring raises the more general question of how English theorists and actors viewed America itself. Colonial America was, in a sense, a great laboratory for English colonizers. The idea of a "fresh start," and the possibility of actually achieving what in England seemed impossible (be it Massachusetts's godly commonwealth or Penn's tolerationist community), animated many settlers to make the arduous ocean crossing. Clearly Pennsylvania and Massachusetts differed dramatically. In Massachusetts, the search for a better world was designed to unite that world under a common faith. In Pennsylvania, that search was animated by a commitment to toleration as a basic, intrinsic good. In both cases, however, plans for American institutions were formulated in response to problems identified in England. The success or failure of the ensuing institutions depended upon a host of factors often far removed and far beyond colonists' control. But the ideal of America (and its presentation in English debates) and the ideal of England (its usage in *American* debate) suggest the complex interplay of hopes and expectations that the new continent represented for the English and bears heavily on developments in the field of toleration.

WHY REVISIT? CORRECTING THREE MYTHS ABOUT RELIGIOUS TOLERATION

Anyone proposing, as I do, that we revisit a familiar topic, must provide at least the beginnings of an answer to the question of what is to be gained by such an exercise. In this section I suggest three primary insights gained by undertaking this study, each of which is addressed in much more detail throughout the book, most explicitly in Chapter 6. I present these general lessons in the form of three common myths about religious toleration, widespread misconceptions about this familiar topic that a revisitation will help correct.

Myth 1. Religious toleration is a self-evident and unqualified good; those who (historically) opposed it were either ignorant, narrow-minded, or concerned with preserving their own positions of social power. Renewed attention to early modern toleration debates engenders a renewed appreciation of the fear of civil war, anarchy, and religious violence that motivated *opponents* of toleration, and which provided perhaps the most formidable obstacle for tolerationists to overcome if they were to achieve their political goals. Antitolerationists were not dour, repressive killjoys dedicated to stomping out dissent at all costs, but individuals and groups deeply concerned about social order and the political, ethical, and spiritual consequences of tolerationists' ideas for their societies and fellow citizens.

Early modern toleration debates did not take place in a vacuum, where audiences selected the most persuasive arguments on the basis of analytic rigor or aesthetic appeal. Instead, they were (and in our time, *are*) political arguments, advanced in times of great social upheaval. Antitolerationists stressed the close association of religious and political dissent, as well as their concern for social order and unity, as often as they offered theological critiques of tolerationists' biblical interpretations. In the English Civil War, for example, armed conflict was animated by religious issues, and the concern for order and stability was hardly a "bloody shirt." The strenuous religious dissent of Roger Williams and George Keith occurred in the context of threats to the political existence of their respective colonies, and the debates occasioned by these two were, for the defenders of orthodoxy, inextricably connected with their communities' basic survival against enemies internal and external. We should not assume that antitolerationists were "crying wolf" or manufacturing straw figures when they warned repeatedly of a slippery slope into anarchy that would follow the granting of toleration to religious dissenters. I hope that this project begins a serious reconsideration of the subtle and coherent theological, political, and philosophical bases that often underlay antitolerationist arguments.[11]

Opponents of toleration were often accused by *their* opponents of setting up a "tyranny over the conscience," of injecting political power where God alone should rule supreme. By contrast, tolerationists were accused by their opponents of supporting policies that would lead to chaos, discord, faction, and anarchy. In Chapter 6, I offer an examination of Locke's emergent position on toleration as illustrative of the importance of political context. I do so, not simply to add one more entry to the voluminous literature on Locke, but rather to frame Locke as emblematic of the political evolution of an important segment of opinion in Restoration England.

This emphasis on order and the fear of anarchy, of course, calls upon scholars to take seriously the political circumstances that motivated individuals to take up the pen on one side or another of toleration debates. Religious dissenters asked their opponents, in a sense, to trust them that the severing of a centuries-old association between church and state would result, not in chaos and anarchy, but instead in a more peaceful social order. Given antitolerationists' understanding of historical events, the scriptural responsibilities placed upon godly magistrates, and Pauline emphases on the evils of schism, should it surprise us that they proved unwilling to extend that trust?

Myth 2. Religious toleration came about as a result of the efforts of skeptical Enlightenment rationalists—for example, Locke, Voltaire, Jefferson, Madison— who were generally religiously indifferent or moderate. We should not disregard how Christian early modern toleration debates were. Deeply religious Christians populated both sides of the argument, amassing impressive scriptural arsenals and deploying them vigorously. Seventeenth-century tolerationists, for example, attempted nothing less than a massive reconstruction

---

11. The history of early modern antitoleration remains to be written, and this project will only allude to its main contours. Such a work would immeasurably enhance our understanding of the dynamics of early modern religio-political debate and cannot appear too soon. For some good overviews, see Conrad Russell, "Arguments for Religious Unity in England, 1530–1650," *JEH* 18 (1967): 201–26, and Mark Goldie, "The Theory of Religious Intolerance in Restoration England," in Grell, Israel, and Tyacke, *From Persecution to Toleration*.

of what it meant to be a Christian, deemphasizing specific doctrines and liturgies and stressing basic virtues like piety, humility, charity, and purity of heart.

In this vein, this project will point toward a renewed appreciation of the importance of religious radicalism (sometimes intentionally, often not) in fostering religious freedom during the seventeenth century. Far from being the achievement of disinterested secular rulers, seventeenth-century toleration was embraced by religious extremists as the only way to rid their congregations of the corrupting influence of civil power. By and large, then, the figures who will play the most important roles in this book are not skeptical rationalists, not Thomas Jeffersons holding the Bible in one hand and scissors in the other, cutting and pasting together an ethical Jesus who preaches humility but makes no claims to divinity and does no miracles. Instead, they are radical Protestants concerned with the church's purity. Roger Williams and Anne Hutchinson are prime examples: for them, the possibility of even one unregenerate individual partaking in worship with the elect raised the dangerous possibility of spiritual "pollution." They found the broad and inclusive nature of Anglicanism (not to mention colonial Massachusetts, in Williams's view), in which the church and commonwealth were coterminous, simply unacceptable. George Keith also rebelled against the laxity and loose standards for membership in the Pennsylvania Quaker Meetings, going so far as to draft a Quaker catechism that he hoped would be administered to children and new members. In England, religious sectarianism in the New Model Army found its political corollary in a strong support for religious liberty. The Cromwellian settlement, and the toleration it offered, would have been impossible without army support.

The arguments made by seventeenth-century tolerationists were almost exclusively Christian in nature: the true Christian displays humility and forbearance toward those with differing views; Jesus commanded preaching and not coercion; belief is beyond the control of the will and can only be brought about by persuasion; true belief requires the possibility of acting upon those beliefs without the fear of penal sanctions. The rationalist and secular arguments for toleration that typified the eighteenth century are hardly irrelevant to the history of religious liberty in the Anglo-American tradition, and I do not mean to suggest approaching the subject in terms of seventeenth-century piety as contrasted with eighteenth-century rationalism, but I do seek to gain new insight on how early modern societies even reached the point at which religious liberty was considered such an important value, important enough to merit the later constitutional protections enshrined in, for example, the First Amendment to the United States Constitution. To get the fullest answer to that question, we cannot be satisfied with any inquiry that neglects the deeply religious nature of toleration debates, for any such inquiry misses a crucial element of the self-understandings of seventeenth-century thinkers.

If tolerationists were radically committed Christians, then we must reconsider the conventional associations between skepticism and toleration. Again, I do not claim that the two are unrelated. Skepticism of authority, whether epistemological, political, or ecclesiastical, clearly bolstered the increasing assertion of claims of conscience and calls for indulgence or toleration in the seventeenth century. Opposition to and skepticism about the authority claims of Catholic or Anglican ecclesiastical hierarchies drove Dissenters on both sides of the Atlantic to articulate notions of religious liberty and to construct new forms (both religious *and* political) to instantiate these ideas. Still, this connection between skepticism and toleration is not seamless, as the towering intellectual figure of Hobbes illustrates graphically. Hobbes and others like him, skeptical of traditional justifications of political and ecclesiastical authority, nonetheless rejected the claims of tolerationists that such skepticism required further extensions of liberty, especially religious liberty. For Hobbes, concerns for order in the wake of violent clashes between social and religious groups overrode epistemological reasons for distrusting theories of divine right. In Chapter 6, I examine Hobbes in more detail, as an embodiment of this tension between toleration and skepticism. Furthermore, some of the most important arguments for toleration, as we have seen in my attention to religious radicalism in the service of religious freedom, did not draw upon skepticism at all. Examples abound of tolerationists like Roger Williams who were at the same time radically Protestant—and anything but skeptical— in nature.

Myth 3. Religious toleration generalizes fairly easily and unproblematically to divisive contemporary social and political issues such as gender, race, ethnicity, and sexuality and provides a basis for multicultural and "identity" politics. Finally, my revisitation of toleration debates in the seventeenth century leads to an increased appreciation of what tolerationists were trying to accomplish, in concrete historical terms. Contrary to the grandiose claims of many contemporary liberal theorists, the legacy of early modern toleration debates lies not in the eradication of all pockets of social and attitudinal intolerance, the celebration of difference *per se*, or the articulation of broad notions of social equality and equal respect. Rather, appreciating that society would continue to be characterized by vast differences on religious and moral questions, tolerationists sought a way of living together in peace: a *modus vivendi*. This final observation may seem, from a twentieth-century perspective, minimal and largely negative. Far from minimizing such relevance, however, a clearer understanding of what toleration debates were really all about provides a *more* accurate assessment of relevance, a better understanding of how conscience and community continue to negotiate their uneasy relationship.

This study of toleration will remind us that in a key sense the legacy of early modern toleration debates is a very minimal one, the search for basic conditions of social peace that will permit society to maintain its cohesion despite deep divisions on issues of ultimate significance. Tolerationists did not expect that their fellow citizens would come to agree on religious issues, or that widespread hostility to Dissenters would be eradicated, or that religious dissenters would achieve broader social equality with members of more dominant faiths. (The Toleration Act, for example, ensured the Anglican monopoly on officeholding for another century and a half.) What tolerationists sought was a way of living together, a way of negotiating differences without resort to bloodshed. Indeed, given that the development and use of reason was a responsibility placed upon humans by God himself, many tolerationists claimed, one should not expect that all would reach the same conclusions about issues of ultimate significance, given the variety of human understandings and the different capacities of various individuals. Herein lies one of the great legacies of toleration for the history of liberal thought and practice: the recognition that, in John Rawls's words, societies would continue to be characterized, not just by pluralism, but by reasonable pluralism (*PL*, 36–37).

This admission of continued disagreement came to pass very gradually, of course, and we should not underestimate the degree to which "battle fatigue" and other, less lofty, factors were involved. This acceptance of continuing dissension within society will dissatisfy both those who are committed to strong theories of unified or uniform community and those who would have us celebrate difference *per se*. According to these standards, toleration may indeed appear minimal, a washing of one's hands with regard to pressing social problems. But as I hope to make clear, we should not underestimate the historical significance of the achievement of religious toleration. Minimal though the achievement may seem to twentieth-century audiences, tolerationists appreciated the variety of human understandings and sought a better way of conducting religious and political debate.

THE BROADER PICTURE: TOLERATION, CONTEMPORARY LIBERALISM, AND THE RETURN OF WHIG HISTORY

Growing out of seventeenth-century struggles to achieve religious liberty, religious toleration has emerged as a core liberal value, as political theorists and actors sought to build upon the successes of early modern religious dissenters and to articulate notions of responsible liberty and legitimate individual choice in spiritual matters.[12] For early modern advocates of religious toleration, as we shall see, choices about individual salvation, to be valid, required the free and voluntary assent of their adherents, not the imposed religious uniformity of a Christian commonwealth or the relentless attempt to suppress those who did not conform to an established faith. This emphasis on voluntarism and inward assent as a standard for legitimacy—what Will Kymlicka has subsequently called a life "led from the inside"[13]—has, in intervening centuries, figured prominently in the broader liberal commitment to individual choice as the barometer for judging a host of other individual attachments (e.g., civic associations, market structures, lifestyle decisions more generally).[14] As Charles Taylor has so ably explicated, the roots of such voluntarism lie squarely in the early modern period, in the notion (advanced by such thinkers as Descartes, Montaigne, and Locke) of the human subject as capable of reflexive self-understanding, rational self-control, and personal

---

12. In this sense, the overly narrow focus on liberalism as a route to toleration that I mentioned at the outset of this chapter and in the preface is not so much incorrect as incomplete. In other words, liberalism and toleration do have, I argue, a close and necessary relationship, but this does not make liberalism the only route to such toleration.

13. *Liberalism, Community, and Culture* (Oxford, 1989), 12. The notion that the modern self is based upon a specific sense of "inwardness" is also articulated in Charles Taylor, *Sources of the Self: The Making of the Modern Identity* (Cambridge, Mass., 1989), pt. 2.

14. Joseph Raz portrays the ideal of autonomy that toleration promotes as "a life freely chosen . . . opposed to a life of coerced choices," describing "the duty of toleration [as] an aspect of the duty of respect for autonomy" (*The Morality of Freedom* [Oxford, 1986], 371, 407).

commitment.[15] Contemporary liberalism, of course, has gone far beyond the wildest dreams of seventeenth-century thinkers in its seemingly *a priori* commitment to individual choice. Still, the core (contemporary) *political* claim remains analogous to the one articulated by early modern proponents of religious toleration: an imposed or coerced choice is no choice at all, and is presumptively invalid in any system claiming to foster moral personhood and human freedom.

This commitment to individual choice unifies a broad spectrum of contemporary liberal theory, a spectrum that includes broad disagreements about liberalism's philosophical and epistemological foundations. John Rawls claims that his political liberalism, in which overlapping consensus and public reason structure public debate, has its "historical origin . . . [in] the Reformation and its aftermath, with the long controversies over religious toleration in the sixteenth and seventeenth centuries" (*PL*, xxiv). A broad range of liberal theorists claim similar linkages between liberalism and toleration.[16] Empirical researchers into the phenomenon of "political tolerance" observe that the core practices of toleration, the allowance of things one opposes or rejects, represent the basis for a whole host of liberties closely associated with liberal democracies.[17]

Perhaps the most prominent (if controversial) school of liberal thought stresses the need for the liberal state to be neutral regarding the human good. On this view, recognition of human fallibility as well as the central importance

15. *Sources of the Self*, pt. 2.

16. Steven Kautz sees toleration as essential to the liberal tradition. See his "Liberalism and the Idea of Toleration," *AJPS* 37 (1993): 610–32, and his *Liberalism and Community* (Ithaca, N.Y., 1995), chap. 3. David A.J. Richards sees toleration as "the central or paradigm case of the rights that constitutionalism represents" (*Toleration and the Constitution*, x). Other authors refer to toleration as one of the "core practices of a liberal order" (Stephen Holmes, *The Anatomy of Antiliberalism* [Cambridge, Mass., 1993], 3); as a guarantor of "individuality, religious and social diversity, and commercial energy" (Stephen Macedo, *Liberal Virtues: Citizenship, Virtue, and Community in Liberal Constitutionalism* [Oxford, 1990], 9); or as "one of the central features of liberalism . . . a concern to allow individuals to pursue their own views of the good" (Robert Goodin and Andrew Reed, "Introduction," in *Liberal Neutrality* [London, 1989], 4). Edward Shils notes that both the autonomist and collectivist strands that characterize American liberalism support toleration ("The Antinomies of Liberalism," in *The Relevance of Liberalism*, ed. Research Institute on International Change [Boulder, Colo., 1978], 137–38). According to David Johnston, his "humanist" liberalism "would protect the basic rights and liberties that are associated with the ideas of constitutional government, the rule of law, and toleration" (*The Idea of a Liberal Theory: A Critique and Reconstruction* [Princeton, 1994], 188).

17. Sullivan, Piereson, and Marcus, *Political Tolerance and American Democracy*, chap. 1; Marcus, Sullivan, Theiss-Morse, and Wood, *With Malice Toward Some*.

of individuals as "self-originating sources of valid claims" requires that liberals privilege the right over the good, in the service of producing autonomous citizens.[18] Toleration is central to this approach, and scholars who advocate state neutrality generally see themselves as following in the footsteps of such earlier tolerationists as Locke and Mill.[19] For many liberal theorists, then, the centrality of toleration to the liberal tradition requires an official doctrine of state neutrality between competing conceptions of the good.[20]

Of course, not all liberals see the neutral state as a requirement of liberal theory. The important thing to note here for a study of toleration, however, is that *non-neutralist* liberals also affirm toleration's centrality to the liberal creed. Their difference with neutralists involves a disagreement over the *policy implications* or epistemological foundations of liberal principles, not a dispute over the primacy of toleration. Non-neutralists generally claim either that toleration does not require complete state neutrality, or that their respective liberalisms preserve toleration while avoiding the thorny justificatory problems presented by the concept of neutrality.[21] Liberal theorists of

---

18. John Rawls, "Kantian Constructivism in Moral Theory," *Journal of Philosophy* 77 (1980): 543. See also Rawls, *PL*, 191–94. For a representative sampling of neutralist writings, see Goodin and Reed, *Liberal Neutrality*; for an overview and critique of neutralism, see Susan Mendus, *Toleration and the Limits of Liberalism* (Atlantic Highlands, N.J., 1989), chaps. 4 and 5.

19. Ronald Dworkin's call for making political decisions "so far as is possible, independent of any particular conception of the good life," is rephrased by Bruce Ackerman, whose neutrality principle asserts that "nobody has the right to vindicate political authority by asserting a privileged insight into the moral universe that is denied the rest of us" (Dworkin, "Liberalism," in *A Matter of Principle* [Cambridge, Mass., 1985], 191; Ackerman, *Social Justice in the Liberal State* [New Haven, Conn., 1980], 10). For Jeremy Waldron, liberalism is essentially about allowing citizens to pursue their own conceptions of the good life, a claim that requires a neutral state and broadly tolerationist policies (*Liberal Rights: Collected Papers, 1981–1991* [New York, 1993], chaps. 2 and 7).

20. I leave aside John Gray's provocative claim that neutralism is fundamentally different from (and antithetical to) toleration: see "Toleration: A Post-Liberal Perspective," in *Enlightenment's Wake: Politics and Culture at the Close of the Modern Age* (London, 1995). Gray's argument helpfully points out important differences between contemporary and historical views of individual freedom, but ignores the fact that, for Rawls and others, the aim of seeking neutrality is similar to the aim of historical proponents of toleration: to vest authority for the most fundamental value decisions in individuals, not governments or church hierarchies. Gray's analysis works well as polemic, but misses this larger point. In fact, I agree with Gray that Rawlsian neutralism and the public reason it espouses, contrary to the claims of its defenders, actually betrays the history of liberty of conscience rather than extending it. See my "Rawls and a Shrinking Liberty of Conscience," *Review of Politics* 60 (Spring 1998): 247–76. I return to this discussion in Chapter 7.

21. William Galston calls for active state involvement in the moral formation of citizens, yet notes that "one of the most attractive features of liberal democracy is the wide opportunity it affords individuals to define and lead their lives as they see fit," and assures his readers (if in

all sorts, then, promote the centrality of toleration to their view of politics and society, although the specific implications of this value for political and legal institutions remain contested.

Critics of the liberal tradition, for their part, do not seem to disagree, seeing in liberalism a fundamental concern with toleration and individual choice.[22] Radical critics often argue that liberalism offers a sham toleration, masking more fundamental (and oppressive) structures of social power, whereas many conservatives accuse liberalism of an unsupported faith in progress as well as naïveté about the likelihood that individuals will exercise their capacity for choice in responsible ways.[23] Even those scholars who look

---

somewhat backhanded language) that his "purposive" liberalism "is not incompatible . . . with classic liberal commitments to freedom and individuality" (*Liberal Purposes: Goods, Virtues, and Diversity in the Liberal State* [Cambridge, 1991], 4–5, 9). Rogers Smith calls for the liberal state to foster "rational liberty" rather than neutrality or autonomy, noting that liberalism's most distinctive feature, "its insistence that government be limited . . . free[s] individuals to undertake private as well as public pursuits of happiness" (*Liberalism and American Constitutional Law* [Cambridge, Mass., 1985], 14; also chap. 8). Richard Sinopoli would allow non-neutral state actions so long as adversely affected citizens "recognize" that they are not being treated "as less valuable than others" (presumably to satisfy the liberal requirement of consent); elsewhere, Sinopoli argues for a "thick-skinned" liberalism, in which toleration is compatible even with official disapproval, since the search for truth that toleration purportedly fosters is not well served by an equation of all conceptions of the good. See his essays "Liberalism and Contested Conceptions of the Good: The Limits of Neutrality," *Journal of Politics* 55 (1993): 644–63, and "Thick-Skinned Liberalism: Redefining Civility," *APSR* 89 (1995): 612–20.

22. For Michael Sandel, "Liberalism describes a tradition of thought that emphasizes toleration and respect for individual rights," one that ultimately sanctions the demise of community and civic engagement. See Sandel, *Democracy's Discontent: America in Search of a Public Philosophy* (Cambridge, Mass., 1996), 4, and *Liberalism and the Limits of Justice* (Cambridge, 1982), esp. 154–66. See also William M. Sullivan, *Reconstructing Public Philosophy* (Berkeley and Los Angeles, 1986), 60–62. Ronald Beiner sees liberalism's elevation of individual choice to the highest good as "empt[ying] the concept of citizenship of all meaningful content," while the Straussian critique of liberalism focuses on the degenerative implications of liberal individualism for our concern to lead the good life. See Beiner, *What's the Matter with Liberalism?* (Berkeley and Los Angeles, 1992), 102, 22–25; for Straussian perspectives, see Kenneth L. Deutsch and Walter Soffer, eds., *The Crisis of Liberal Democracy: A Straussian Perspective* (Albany, N.Y., 1987), and Allan Bloom, *The Closing of the American Mind: How Higher Education Has Failed Democracy and Impoverished the Souls of Today's Students* (New York, 1987). Although liberalism itself has become just another tradition, Alasdair MacIntyre notes, its original appeal lay in its promise to free individuals from the weight of tradition and "enable those who espouse widely different and incompatible conceptions of the good life . . . to live together peaceably within the same society" (*Whose Justice? Which Rationality?* [Notre Dame, Ind., 1988], 335).

23. See, for the radical critique, Herbert Marcuse, "Repressive Tolerance," in Robert Paul Wolff, Barrington Moore, Jr., and Herbert Marcuse, *A Critique of Pure Tolerance* (Boston, 1967); for a conservative view, Tinder, *Tolerance*, chaps. 1, 2 (reissued as *Tolerance and Community*).

for nonliberal sources of toleration, whose work I briefly canvassed in the preface, do not seek so much to deny the connection between liberalism and toleration as to bolster the conceptual bases for toleration by adducing further support for its pedigree. Given the embattled state of liberal theory, they imply, we should not rest such an important value as toleration solely on liberalism's shoulders.[24]

As I have argued, toleration is generally recognized by scholars as intrinsically related to the liberal tradition. Indeed, those scholars seeking nonliberal routes to toleration rightly decry the predominant focus on liberalism by those writing the story of toleration. Even so, the historical development of liberal toleration, its emergence in seventeenth-century political thought and practice, remains poorly understood. The grand "Whig" narratives of the nineteenth and early twentieth centuries, which presented the history of (in this case, religious) freedom as part of the steady, almost inevitable rise of liberalism, democracy, and constitutional government from meager beginnings in the early seventeenth century through the present, are today largely out of fashion. Anachronistic and teleological readings of history persist, however, in the writings of some of the most prominent liberal theorists of our time.[25]

When contemporary liberal theorists refer to history at all, or to the history of liberal political thought, they betray such Whig sentiments surprisingly often. Scholars often (implicitly or explicitly) construct a stereotype of

24. Christopher Megone investigates the possibility of an Aristotelian approach fostering toleration in "Truth, the Autonomous Individual, and Toleration," in Horton and Nicholson, *Toleration: Philosophy and Practice*; on communitarianism and toleration, see Roger Crisp, "Communitarianism and Toleration," also in *Toleration: Philosophy and Practice*, and Tinder, *Tolerance*. See also the works by Laursen and Nederman, Remer, and Levine discussed in the preface.

25. One of the distinguishing characteristics of Whig history, according to its great expositor and critic Herbert Butterfield, is its "study of the past with direct and perpetual reference to the present" (*The Whig Interpretation of History* [London, 1931], 11). In this sense, Whig history presents an oversimplified version of the triumph of liberal ideals, viewed from the perspective of the author, who sits at the (normative as well as chronological) pinnacle of historical development. This perpetual reference to the present leads the historian on a "quest for origins" more interested in identifying supposed precursors to liberal ideas than in understanding, in all their richness and complexity, how various historical phenomena came to exist.

The classic critique of the Whig view of history is Butterfield's *Whig Interpretation of History*. See also Quentin Skinner, "Meaning and Understanding in the History of Ideas," *History and Theory* 8 (1969): 3–53, and R. G. Collingwood, *The Idea of History* (Oxford, 1946), pt. 4, sec. 1.

the history of toleration as the triumph of inherently superior ideas, the progress of which was impeded only by uninformed ignorance or by narrow-minded elites concerned with hoarding their own political, social, or economic power.[26] The former results in the historian lamenting the inability of earlier generations to understand the objective desirability of liberal ideals. The latter, conversely, implies that the superiority of liberal ideas is self-evident, and that those who (historically) failed to affirm it must have been purposely malignant. For example, if it is true that religious liberty represents "the logical conclusion of Protestantism and nonconformity," or that it is "logically the outcome of the Protestant belief that each individual (with God's assistance) could interpret Scripture for himself,"[27] the historian's task seems only to identify why it took so long for some people to realize this necessary logical or theological relationship. From the perspective of this project, such a view is both historically untrue (i.e., nothing in Protestantism is necessarily related to any substantive politics) and ignores the highly cogent philosophical, theological, and political reasons many had for *opposing* toleration.

John Rawls's *Political Liberalism*, perhaps the most powerful contemporary statement of the liberal ideal, represents one of the most prominent examples of contemporary Whiggism. Locating his political liberalism at the culmination of three hundred years of theorizing about the good society, with its roots in the seventeenth-century struggle for religious toleration, Rawls makes the grandiose and ambitiously ahistorical claim that "were justice as fairness to make an overlapping consensus possible it would complete and extend the movement of thought that began three centuries ago with the gradual acceptance of the principle of toleration and led to the nonconfessional state and equal liberty of conscience" (*PL*, 154). Embedded within Rawls's claims about political liberalism's normative superiority to other forms of liberalism are certain historical presuppositions that tend toward Whiggism, namely the idea that the acceptance of certain principles will somehow "complete" a complex and multifaceted historical process. Rawls's misconstrual of early modern tolerationists leads to his view of public reason

26. This is, unfortunately, the approach of Jordan's *Development of Religious Toleration in England*, which despite this major conceptual shortcoming remains the definitive reference on the subject.

27. Dunn, *William Penn*, 44; J. W. Gough, *John Locke's Political Philosophy*, 2d ed. (Oxford, 1973), 194.

and the limits of liberal political discourse as compatible with full liberty of conscience, about which I have more to say in Chapter 7.

A number of other noted and notable contemporary liberal thinkers display similar Whig sentiments. Maurice Cranston presents another view of the increasingly broad influence of tolerationist ideas. It is a familiar story. According to Cranston, toleration has proceeded in several distinguishable stages. Protestantism "led inexorably to the demand for toleration," and Locke's argument for toleration "eventually came to be regarded as common sense." Next, John Stuart Mill took up the issue in *On Liberty*, prizing toleration because "liberty, individuality, and variety were of the highest ethical value." Finally, twentieth-century totalitarianism and fears of communist subversion gave toleration "a new aspect": "the argument both for and against political toleration in the twentieth century cannot be said to have differed greatly from the debate concerning religious toleration that exercised the minds of earlier generations."[28]

Cranston's remarks represent an especially overt set of Whig suppositions. Other liberal thinkers express more muted, but substantively similar, sentiments. Jeremy Waldron claims the liberal neutrality is "only the most recent attempt to articulate a position that liberals have occupied for centuries," noting that although Locke and Mill did not use the precise term, neutrality represents "the latest expression of a view that liberals have always held about the attitude the state should take to the personal faith and beliefs of its citizens."[29] Bruce Ackerman argues that a liberal state in which "all other forms of social dependence are subordinated to the dialogic processes of Neutral Dialogue" is necessary to "create a *truly* liberal relationship between individual and community," implying either that previous formulations of liberal principles were not "truly" liberal or that a state of affairs exists that one can reasonably call "truly liberal" to the exclusion of all others.[30] In a dialogic liberal state, he argues, "Over time . . . the social life

---

28. Cranston, "Toleration," 12:144–46. This familiar story also appears in Sullivan, Piereson, and Marcus, *Political Tolerance and American Democracy*. In part, it results from an excessive focus on Locke and Mill, a much wider phenomenon among liberal theorists and their critics. For a cogent critique (that in some ways mirrors my critique of Rawls in Chapter 7), see Adam Wolfson, "Two Theories of Toleration: Locke versus Mill," *Perspectives on Political Science* 25:4 (1996) 192–202.

29. *Liberal Rights*, 143. Elsewhere, interestingly, Waldron argues that Locke's argument for toleration is largely ineffective and irrelevant to twentieth-century contexts. See his "Locke: Toleration and the Rationality of Persecution," in Susan Mendus, ed., *Justifying Toleration: Historical and Conceptual Perspectives* (New York, 1988).

30. *Social Justice*, 347 (emphasis added), 346.

of the liberal state will represent the full range of moral creation that lies within the grasp of citizens who confront one another without pretensions to moral dominion."[31] Viewing a particular (philosophic, historic) form of liberalism as paving the way for the "full range of moral creation," I suggest, is a claim akin to those of earlier Whig historians.

Although each eschews the more grandiose language of classic Whig historians, none of these theorists escapes the temptation to position his argument at the pinnacle of a historically progressive outlook on the nature and meaning of human freedom that is normatively superior to those that have gone before. Such theorists often seem intent upon establishing that "liberal" thinkers from the history of political thought either supported, or would have supported, concepts that they promote. Such historical assumptions, even in their most muted form, do nothing to help us understand how toleration developed, both as a philosophical element of the liberal creed and as a substantive, highly contested political reality.

Furthermore, by continuing to misconstrue the past as a pale striving toward the present, liberal theorists (who might more profitably remain silent on the question of history, if their real intention is to justify contemporary liberal ideals) misunderstand the present. To understand both past and present as they intersect with the history and career of toleration, we must attempt to reengage ourselves with the historical actors and ideas that accompanied the birth of Anglo-American toleration. Of course, it is true that the more successful (and more permanent) tolerationist victories did occur later rather than earlier in the seventeenth century, as much of the historical material presented in this project will show. Such progress, however, was not due to the inherent superiority of certain ("liberal") ideas or to iron laws of historical progress. Rather, it was the result of hard-fought political battles between equally articulate and coherent views of human society and the political good, along with the often-tenuous resolution of issues of social order and sovereignty.

What will emerge from this study, then, is an account of the philosophical and political emergence of religious toleration in early modern England and colonial America, one that is both historically grounded and comparative in context. The difficult task of forming and maintaining political societies often involved a tension between conscience and community, between the

31. Ibid., 23, 375.

claims of authority and increasingly vigorous calls for liberty. Understanding how these issues were explicated, debated, and eventually (if at times tenuously) resolved promises a fuller understanding of the resonance they still possess more than three centuries later.

PART ONE

Revisiting Early Modern
Toleration and
Religious Dissent

2

MASSACHUSETTS BAY

Puritanism and the Politics of Religious Dissent

> It is objected, that the magistrates may not appoint a minister of God, what
> he should teach: admit so much, yet he may limit him what he may not
> teach, if he forbid him to teach heresy or sedition. . . . Beside, every truth
> is not seasonable at all times.
>
> —John Winthrop, *Short Story*

> Consider . . . if the Lord Jesus were himself in person in Old or New
> England, what church, what ministry, what worship, what government, he
> would set up, and what persecution he would practice toward them that
> would not receive him?
>
> —Roger Williams, *Cotton's Letter Examined*

The Massachusetts Bay Colony has long been viewed as perhaps the quintessential example of a colonial regime that during its early years effectively
suppressed claims to religious toleration and liberty of conscience. The prosecution and expulsion of Roger Williams and Anne Hutchinson during the
1630s, along with the severe punishments inflicted upon Quakers and the
more or less successful resistance to increasingly widespread Baptist ideas
during the 1650s, it is argued, show how decisively and effectively colonial
leaders rejected religious freedom. Traditional interpretations of these disputes
have fallen along two main lines. Much scholarship, often bordering on the

hagiographic, highlights the troublesome, contentious nature of the dissidents and maintains that the punishments were a necessary, perhaps laudable, step to preserve the colony's very existence.[1] Other scholars, reacting against overly charitable interpretations of the suppression of religious dissenters, call Massachusetts an intolerant theocracy that punished those aspiring to liberty.[2]

I reject both of these views. Certainly punishment for political and social disruption, when such actions derive from religious commitment, raises *general* questions of religious liberty. Religious dissent in Massachusetts Bay was punished, often brutally. Neither Williams nor Hutchinson, though, sought toleration for themselves *qua* Dissenters, but as possessors of an objective truth claim. In this regard, both replicated earlier Puritan arguments about replacing error with truth, and neither advanced general theories of toleration at the time of their trials.[3] Quaker dissent, on the other hand, was

1. Hagiographic, that is, of the colony's founders. See John Adair, *Founding Fathers: The Puritans in England and America* (London, 1982); Stanley Gray, "The Political Thought of John Winthrop," *NEQ* 3 (1930): 681–705; Edmund S. Morgan, *The Puritan Dilemma: The Story of John Winthrop* (Boston, 1958); Samuel Eliot Morison, *Builders of the Bay Colony* (New York, 1930); Larzer Ziff, *The Career of John Cotton: Puritanism and the American Experience* (Princeton, 1962); and John Gorham Palfrey, *History of New England During the Stuart Dynasty*, vol. 1 (New York, 1858).

2. Brooks Adams, *The Emancipation of Massachusetts* (New York, 1887); James Truslow Adams, *The Founding of New England* (Boston, 1921); Richard Hildreth, *History of the United States*, vol. 1 (New York, 1849); Vernon L. Parrington, *Main Currents in American Thought*, vol. 1 (New York, 1927); George Bancroft, *History of the United States*, vol. 1 (Boston, 1834). This version of Massachusetts history is often hagiographic in its own way, a "hagiography of dissent" glamorizing religious dissenters as persecuted precursors of twentieth-century liberalism. For instance, according to Michael Zuckerman, "many men and women . . . were expelled from Massachusetts . . . by men who would admit neither laughter nor significant dissidence," and the "Puritan antagonism to festivity" is central to understanding the Puritan dispute with Thomas Morton ("Pilgrims in the Wilderness: Community, Modernity, and the Maypole of Merry Mount," *NEQ* 50 [1977]: 268, 273). Darren Staloff views the Puritan regime as a "mixed government of culturally dominant magistrates and representative laymen, both subject to the binding advice and admonition of the ministerial intellectuals," a "system of cultural domination" that exercised, in the Antinomian affair, "an unprecedented level of repression in the Bay" (*The Making of an American Thinking Class: Intellectuals and Intelligentsia in Puritan Massachusetts* [New York, 1998], 25, 39, 54).

See also Samuel Hugh Brockunier, *The Irrepressible Democrat, Roger Williams* (New York, 1940); Lyle Koehler, "The Case of the American Jezebels: Anne Hutchinson and Female Agitation During the Years of Antinomian Turmoil, 1636–1638," *WMQ* 31 (1974): 55–78; and Selma R. Williams, *Divine Rebel: The Life of Anne Marbury Hutchinson* (New York, 1981). Even Philip F. Gura's extremely valuable study *A Glimpse of Sion's Glory: Puritan Radicalism in New England, 1620–1660* (Middletown, Conn., 1984) does not entirely escape this trap.

3. Puritans in England had long argued that their views on church government more nearly approximated those of the primitive church (the touchstone for all Protestants) than did

often accompanied by highly disruptive public behavior, including public nudity and the intentional interruption of others' worship. Given that few in the seventeenth century extended toleration to disloyal political behavior, dishonoring magistrates, or the disruption of worship, these Dissenters may have little to do with religious freedom as it is generally understood, as part of the gradual unfolding of liberal democratic constitutionalism.

It is often assumed that Protestant theological individualism, growing out of Luther's notion of the "priesthood of all believers," is somehow essential to the history of religious liberty.[4] Puritans were, like all Protestants, fideistic theological individualists: one's salvation came neither through good works nor through church membership, but through faith and the inpouring of God's grace.[5] But this theological individualism was shared, to a large degree, by both Dissenters and their Massachusetts "persecutors," which reduces its power to explain developments in Massachusetts. Protestant theological individualism has no necessary connection with religious toleration because it does not rule out a strong sense of communal authority in a whole host of other spheres; indeed, the two (theologically individualistic voluntarism and communal uniformity) are intricately related in the Protestant experience.[6] In this chapter, and in the project as a whole, I seek a more

---

prevailing Anglican practice and thus should *prevail*, not merely coexist. If we refrain from reading the principles of Williams's *Bloudy Tenent* back into the events of the 1630s, Williams's banishment is a questionable test case for principles of liberty of conscience or toleration, since it is not clear that he himself viewed it that way at the time. W. Clark Gilpin notes that during his years in Massachusetts Bay Williams "gave scant evidence of the large-minded tolerance today popularly associated with his name" (*The Millenarian Piety of Roger Williams* [Chicago, 1979], 16).

4. G. G. Coulton, "A Protestant View of Toleration," *The Contemporary Review* 138 (1930): 310–19; M. Searle Bates, *Religious Liberty: An Inquiry* (New York, 1945); Dunn, *William Penn*, 44; Kamen, *Rise of Toleration*; St. John, *Contest for Liberty of Conscience*. In the English context, this theological individualism manifested itself in an emphasis on a preaching ministry as opposed to a sacramental priesthood.

5. To be fair, it is not clear that this theological individualism did in fact separate Protestants from Roman Catholics as significantly as Protestants thought. However, in a study such as this one, where I approach debates from the perspective of the participants, such a distinction is crucial.

6. For a cogent explication of this relationship, see Adam Seligman, *Innerworldly Individualism: Charismatic Community and Its Institutionalization* (New Brunswick, N.J., 1994), chaps. 1–2. Certainly many Protestants *did* claim a necessary connection between Protestantism and liberty of conscience; for the seventeenth-century argument, see Milton's *Readie and Easie Way to Establish a Free Commonwealth* (London, 1660): "The whole Protestant church allows no supreme judge or rule in matters of religion, but the scriptures, which necessarily infers liberty of conscience" (in *Areopagitica and Other Political Writings of John Milton*, ed. John Alvis [Indianapolis, 1999], 439), and Milton's *Treatise of Civil Power in Ecclesiastical Causes* (London, 1659).

historically aware and nuanced understanding of the relationship between Protestantism and toleration. The early history of Massachusetts Bay shows that debates about toleration and religious liberty often have very little to do with theology per se: they are arguments about communal meanings, solidarity, and survival. These questions *involve* theology, but in the end transcend it.

An exploration of the New England Way and its responses to religious dissent, in the context of a study of toleration, may illuminate the elements of a successful (ideological or political) *resistance* to religious dissent. By studying Massachusetts, we come to appreciate the strength of antitolerationist arguments and the obstacles that later tolerationists would have to overcome. This attention to early colonial history in Massachusetts will provide an important comparative perspective on the case of Pennsylvania, considered in Chapter 5. There, a theological dispute within the Philadelphia Quaker community spilled over into political and social unrest, and I consider how George Keith's dissent mirrors the upheavals brought about by Williams and Hutchinson.

Despite the remarkable success of "the New England Way" in maintaining a uniform public religious practice and the close relationship between church and state in Massachusetts, religious dissent was always present or lurking.[7] During the 1630s, Roger Williams and Anne Hutchinson were banished. Williams, besides preaching a Separatist doctrine of formal withdrawal from the Anglican communion in ecclesiastical affairs, objected to the administration of loyalty oaths and according to John Cotton, called the colony's patent "a national sin" (*Reply*, 47). Furthermore, he did this at a time when the Massachusetts Bay Company's enemies and rival English claimants to the New England territories were mounting a concerted attack at the royal court. Hutchinson, on the other hand, preached a radical grace theology that downplayed the importance of works to salvation; when questioned about these views by the General Court, she asserted an immediate revelation from God. Her followers included many prominent settlers (among them, Governor

---

7. The fact of almost-constant dissent does not, in my view, mean that we should cease to refer to a coherent "New England Way" in favor of, as Janice Knight puts it, "New England Ways" (*Orthodoxies in Massachusetts: Rereading American Puritanism* [Cambridge, Mass., 1994], chap. 1). Even Knight, who asserts that dissent afflicted the center and not just the margins of New England Puritanism, concedes that "these differences were as much matters of tone and sensibility as of doctrine," noting the "vast contours of shared doctrine" (32).

Henry Vane), and some of them disrupted services conducted by ministers they viewed as preaching false doctrine.

During the 1640s, Presbyterian sympathies of a number of Bay ministers caused concern among the orthodox ministers and magistrates. As we shall see, Massachusetts Puritanism sought a balance between (in their view) schismatic Separatism and anarchic Antinomianism on the one hand, and overly hierarchical Anglicanism on the other. Presbyterianism appealed to many Puritans in Massachusetts as it had in England, offering as it did a less hierarchical uniformity than Anglicanism yet still promising a degree of centralization that might bring order to the social chaos threatened by such groups as the Hutchinsonians.[8] Also during the 1640s, Samuel Gorton and his followers rained their insults on the Bay polity from their base at Shawomet, outside Massachusetts's borders. The Gortonists, Antinomians of a sort, were taken prisoner and held in Boston before being expelled from the colony. As the 1650s proceeded, growing opposition to infant baptism within the colony was abetted by visiting Baptists from other colonies. Also encouraged were the initial stirrings of Quakerism, especially in Salem, as Quaker missionaries descended on Massachusetts, setting off a series of confrontations that culminated in the execution of three Quakers in Boston in 1659 and, two years later, royal intervention to halt such punishments.[9]

8. The close relationship between Puritanism and Presbyterianism in England is well documented in Patrick Collinson, *The Elizabethan Puritan Movement* (New York, 1989).

9. Detailed accounts of these various Dissenting movements are outside the scope of this work. I highlight instead the issues and themes most salient to this project and refer the reader to more thorough secondary works. On Massachusetts and religious dissent during the early years, generally, see Thomas J. Curry, *The First Freedoms: Church and State in America to the Passage of the First Amendment* (New York, 1986), chap. 1; Gura, *Glimpse of Sion's Glory*; and David S. Lovejoy, *Religious Enthusiasm in the New World* (Cambridge, Mass., 1985). On Williams, see Edwin S. Gaustad, *Liberty of Conscience: Roger Williams in America* (Grand Rapids, Mich., 1991); Edmund S. Morgan, *Roger Williams: The Church and the State* (New York, 1967); Perry Miller, *Roger Williams: His Contribution to the American Experience* (Indianapolis, 1953); and Timothy L. Hall, *Separating Church and State: Roger Williams and Religious Liberty* (Urbana, Ill., 1998). On Hutchinson, see David D. Hall, ed., *The Antinomian Controversy, 1636–1638: A Documentary History*, 2d ed. (Durham, N.C., 1990), and William K.B. Stoever, *"A Faire and Easie Way to Heaven": Covenant Theology and Antinomianism in Early Massachusetts* (Middletown, Conn., 1978). On the Baptists, see William G. McLoughlin, *Soul Liberty: The Baptists' Struggle in New England, 1630–1833* (Hanover, N.H., 1991), and idem, *New England Dissent, 1630–1833: The Baptists and the Separation of Church and State* (Cambridge, Mass., 1971). On the Quakers, see Hugh Barbour and J. William Frost, *The Quakers* (New York, 1988).

In brief, then, the middle position that Puritans sought in their godly commonwealth provided fertile ground for critics, as Separatists and Baptists sought an ever purer church and Antinomians, Gortonists, and Quakers proclaimed the principle of inner revelation and the all-sufficiency of the Holy Spirit.

THE NEW ENGLAND WAY: PURITANISM AND ANTITOLERATION IN MASSACHUSETTS, 1630–1660

The 1640s were a time of synthesis and articulation for Massachusetts Puritans: with the difficult initial years (and the early Dissenters, Roger Williams and Anne Hutchinson) behind them, Massachusetts Puritans set about solidifying and buttressing their godly experiment.[10] The task of synthesis and argumentation fell largely to John Cotton, whose prominence on both sides of the Atlantic lent prestige to Massachusetts orthodoxy.[11] As the Civil War broke out in England, and the threat of episcopal and royal control over the colony receded, many Puritans looked forward to an era of godly rule in their homeland, one that could look to New England for insight into the operation of a holy commonwealth.[12] It soon became clear, though, that events in England were moving, politically if not theologically, in another direction. In England, because of the strong influence of sectarianism in the New Model Army and Cromwell's success in battle, the Independent program of toleration prevailed over the uniform Presbyterian settlement proposed by the Westminster Assembly and favored by Parliament.[13] While

10. Although his focus is on political and legal developments broadly conceived, and not strictly religio-political concerns, Robert Emmet Wall, Jr., refers to the 1640s as Massachusetts's "crucial decade." See Wall, *Massachusetts Bay: The Crucial Decade, 1640–1650* (New Haven, Conn., 1972).

11. Cotton, along with several other New England ministers, was invited to participate in the Westminster Assembly's deliberations: see *Winthrop's Journal*, 2:71–72. Although he eventually declined to go to England, the invitation illustrates Cotton's prestige in both English and American Puritan circles.

12. It is easy, however, to overstate the degree to which the Puritans themselves saw Massachusetts as an example for the world. In many ways, the ambitious language of Winthrop's "Model" is not borne out by the larger historical record, in which the idea of a refuge from God's wrath on England seems more dominant. See Theodore Dwight Bozeman, "The Puritans' 'Errand into the Wilderness' Reconsidered," *NEQ* 59 (1986): 231–51.

13. By referring to the Independents as tolerationists, I mean to make a relative statement, compared with traditional Anglicanism and the Presbyterianism prevalent in the Westminster Assembly. Avihu Zakai claims that Independents did not support toleration during the English

differing from the Assembly on issues of church government, New England Puritans did see merit in religious uniformity and in the suppression of overt heresies by civil magistrates. A vigorous assertion of religious uniformity figured heavily in Massachusetts thought and practice, and the Cambridge Platform of 1648 represents, in the words of one scholar, "the summa of the decade, indeed of the first thirty years of Puritanism in America."[14] How was this edifice constructed? How did it function in the thought and practice of New England magistrates?

Religion and Politics: Puritanism and Magistracy

Most of the prominent first-generation Massachusetts leaders journeyed to America during the early 1630s, and their vision of the relationship between church and state did not differ a great deal from the system they had left behind in England.[15] In other words, they desired a reformed national church, denounced Separatism as schismatic, and opposed toleration of dissent *qua* dissent while supporting their own version of church polity as more faithful

Civil War, rightly noting that they believed that the magistrate had power over religious matters and accepted the idea of a national church. Zakai also rightly notes that their opponents (e.g., Roger Williams) declined to distinguish between Independents and Presbyterians in their critique of the Westminster Assembly's proceedings. But Zakai seems to equate toleration with a complete rejection of magisterial control over religious affairs, and to imply that one either supported or opposed toleration in a dichotomous manner. In fact, a number of possibilities presented themselves during the 1640s, and for many toleration was compatible with a religious establishment. Toleration debates were not dichotomous, but rather concerned where to draw the tolerationist line, and whom to tolerate. Independent congregationalists supported a degree of toleration (for orthodox Protestants), while fuller liberty of conscience grew out of the sectarian and Separatist tradition. See Zakai, "Religious Toleration and Its Enemies: The Independent Divines and the Issue of Toleration during the English Civil War," *Albion* 21 (1989): 1–33; also see Margaret R. Sommerville, "Independent Thought, 1603–1649" (Ph.D. diss., Cambridge University, 1982). I deal with these issues in much greater detail in Chapter 3.

14. Stephen Foster, "English Puritanism and the Progress of New England Institutions, 1630–1660," in *Saints and Revolutionaries: Essays on Early American History*, ed. David Hall, John M. Murrin, and Thad W. Tate (New York, 1984), 29. This "New England Way" encompassed both church government and the relation between civil and religious power. In this project, I refer almost exclusively to the New England settlement as it related to toleration. For the more specific issues of church government, see Richard Mather's *Church-Government and Church-Covenant Discussed* (London, 1643) and John Cotton's *Way of the Churches of Christ in New England* (London, 1645).

15. Foster echoes this point in "English Puritanism" (5–6), though he further subdivides the migrants into early and late-1630s, seeing more Separatist influence among those coming to Massachusetts after 1636.

to the New Testament than its rivals. Toleration was not a part of the Puritan political or religious program during the 1620s or 1630s. At no time prior to the 1640s do we find any significant number of Puritan thinkers supporting toleration, nor do we encounter a principled defense of a general right to religious dissent. Instead, their primary aim in religious matters was to replace error with truth (the truth of the primitive church as outlined in the New Testament).[16] In order to achieve an opening for such truth, Jacobean Puritans had traditionally called for *their* toleration, i.e., that they should not be ejected from their positions in favor of Laudian Arminians or more moderate Anglicans.[17] When Thomas Dudley wrote to the countess of Lincoln that the origins of the Massachusetts Bay Colony lay in discussions about "the planting of the gospel there"[18] we can be sure that the gospel to which he refers is the *Puritan* gospel, the establishment of a biblically sound community. To tolerate a variety of discordant religious voices, Nathaniel Ward later said, was to show indifference to one's own beliefs, or confusion and apathy about the revealed will of God. "He that is willing to tolerate any religion, or discrepant way of religion, besides his own, unless it be in matters merely indifferent, either doubts of his own, or is not sincere in it."[19]

The first Massachusetts Bay settlers took exception to the exclusive use of the Anglican Book of Common Prayer and an ecclesiastical structure that allowed bishops to exert influence over gathered local congregations in matters of church discipline; however, they were not Separatists: indeed, they

16. Perry Miller, *Orthodoxy in Massachusetts, 1630–1650* (Boston, 1933), 279–84.

17. For example, in the debates over Arminianism during the Jacobean and Caroline periods, Puritans were not arguing that they should also be permitted latitude within the English church, but that Arminian errors should be purged from the church and replaced with Puritan doctrine. See, for example, the works of Henry Jacob listed in the bibliography; William Prynne's *Anti-Arminianism* (London, 1630), which calls for Parliament to "crucify" Arminians (epistle dedicatory); and William Ames, *A Fresh Suit Against Human Ceremonies in God's Worship* (Amsterdam, 1633), which compares the removal of "popish trinkets" from the Anglican Church to the removal of "whorish attire" from a virgin daughter (epistle dedicatory).

18. "To the Lady Bridget, Countess of Lincoln," in Everett Emerson, ed., *Letters from New England: The Massachusetts Bay Colony, 1629–1638* (Amherst, Mass., 1976), 70. Edward Johnson saw the aim of settling in New England as "to enjoy the liberties of the Gospel of Christ," specifically rejecting toleration: "now seeing it is the opinion of many," he wrote in 1651, "in these days of Reformation, that all sorts of sectaries (that acknowledge a Christ) should be tolerated by civil government, except the papist . . . this government, hath hitherto, and is for future time resolved to practice otherwise (the Lord assisting)." See Johnson, *Wonder-Working Providence of Sion's Saviour in New England* (1658), ed. J. Franklin Jameson (New York, 1910), 140, 144.

19. Nathaniel Ward, *The Simple Cobbler of Aggawam in America* (London, 1647), ed. P. M. Zall (Lincoln, Nebr., 1969), 10. All page references are to this edition.

considered themselves the *true* Church of England, keepers of Protestant doctrine even as those currently in control in England veered toward Arminian or crypto-Catholic "innovation" and "superstition." Although they remained nominally loyal to the English church, they left behind its elaborate ecclesiastical hierarchies and the rule by bishops and archbishops; although they clearly believed that the Anglican Church contained many blemishes, they did not view these impurities as so grievous as to deny its standing as a true church. Thus they considered their separation to be only local, a separation from the corruptions of the church but not from the church itself.[20]

Massachusetts Puritans, then, did not see the formal separation from communion with the Anglican Church as part of their religious intentions for the Bay plantation. Indeed, the responsibility of Christians in a church that contained error, according to Cotton, was not to withdraw but to work for its repair (*Reply*, chap. 2). Separatism was rejected for a number of reasons: it succumbed to the sin of schism, explicitly violating Pauline injunctions to unity;[21] it denied the authority of the magistrate to maintain and enforce the true faith, drastically reducing the scope of magisterial power at precisely the moment (the founding of a new political society) it was most needed; and it was contrary to English law. Referring to the Church of England as "our dear mother," the Puritans begged Anglicans to put away any hostility and to see the Massachusetts Company as "a church springing out of your own bowels."[22] Prior to his emigration to New England, Cotton chastised the Salem church for rejecting several prospective church members, fearing that such an action (erecting high barriers to church membership) might represent a prelude to Separatism. "Reject not the womb that bare you," he counseled.[23] When John Wilson was chosen teacher at Boston in July 1630, he received the laying on of hands "with this protestation by all, that it was only as a sign

20. Much of this debate centered on contested interpretations of Revelation 18:4. See Winthrop's "Reformation Without Separation," in *WP*, 3:10–14.

21. See especially Romans 14 and Philippians 3:16.

22. *The Humble Request* (London, 1630), 3, 6.

23. "John Cotton's Letter to Samuel Skelton," ed. David D. Hall, *WMQ* 23 (1965): 478–85. The letter was written in October 1630. Cotton did later revise his view on the actions of the Salem church: however, he revised his interpretation of what Salem had done (i.e., he no longer took their acts to be Separatist), rather than his view on Separatism, which remained negative. See Cotton's 1636 sermon at Salem, in *John Cotton on the Churches of New England*, ed. Larzer Ziff (Cambridge, Mass., 1968), 41–68.

of election and confirmation, not of any intent that Mr. Wilson should renounce his ministry he received in England."[24]

Practice, of course, was another matter. In every practical sense the great distance between the two made any enforcement of Anglican discipline virtually hypothetical; New England Puritans certainly knew this and used it to their advantage in pursuing the vision of church-state relations they believed most faithful to God's plan. As Edmund S. Morgan has noted, Massachusetts was "a place where Puritans could enjoy the advantages of separation without separating."[25] But crucially, in their own minds, they were not Separatists. Undeniably, the religious practices of Massachusetts departed widely from Anglican practices of the same period in their emphasis on gathered churches and the role of the covenant and profession of faith. John Winthrop pointed out in 1634 that certain aspects of Anglican polity were "not conformable to God's will revealed in his word"; although individuals might be justified in conforming to an imperfect ecclesiastical structure in England, "our case here is otherwise: being come to clearer light and more liberty . . . we may freely enjoy it" (*WP*, 3:132). However much English polemicists might have railed against Massachusetts practices as factious and Separatist, it seems more likely that Massachusetts Puritans looked forward to *reforming* the English church fully one day. Given that three thousand miles separated Massachusetts Bay from Canterbury and London, the practical importance of the distinction between Separatist and Nonconformist might seem rather small. The importance was crucial, however, to New England Puritans. One of the important differences between the two had direct bearings on the legitimate function of government in the religious realm, as became apparent in the case of Roger Williams.

Not being Separatists, Massachusetts Puritans granted the civil magistrate wide latitude in addressing vocal religious dissent. They did not advocate theocracy in the sense that church and state were merged; ministers did not

---

24. *Winthrop's Journal*, 1:52. Curiously, Hosmer notes this event as displaying "the rapid process of separation from old religious ties" (*Winthrop's Journal*, 1:51 n.1). Seligman also interprets the Puritans' intentions as Separatist from the beginning (*Innerworldly Individualism*, 52–58). Dudley specifically denies the charge of Separatism in his letter "To the Lady Bridget, Countess of Lincoln," in Emerson, *Letters from New England*, 78–79. Tom Webster emphasizes the nonseparating nature of congregationalism, citing the influence of William Ames: see his *Godly Clergy in Early Stuart England: The Caroline Puritan Movement, c. 1620–1643* (Cambridge, 1997), chaps. 15, 17.

25. *Roger Williams*, 25.

hold political office, nor did magistrates *qua* magistrates involve themselves in ecclesiastical disputes.[26] Rather, they sought theocracy in a much more fundamental sense, viewing church and state as "complementary instruments through which they hoped to defeat Antichristian governments and institutions and realize their pursuit of the millennium."[27] Civil magistrates were charged with preserving the common good and social peace necessary for the churches to flourish, and this responsibility included the punishment of heresy, sedition, and blasphemy where such became socially problematic. As Thomas Cobbet put it, "Corruptions in religion, outwardly breaking forth and expressed, may, yea and must be restrained and punished, by such as are called thereunto."[28]

This broad responsibility of Puritan magistracy derives from the important concept of the covenant in Puritan thought. Both the congregation and the civil community were conceived as based in the voluntary, consensual relations of believers. Under this understanding of community and authority, civil magistrates were permitted and indeed *required*, by God as well as the welfare of their subjects, to rule on public issues that threatened either the civil covenant that formed the basis of the Massachusetts settlement, or the covenant with God that provided rulers with a concrete set of social goals for a specifically *Puritan* society.

Virtually all Puritan leaders agreed that although civil government is instituted on earth by God (and thus of divine origin), and is necessitated by original sin, nonetheless, political power and the authority of magistrates arises from the voluntary consent of those governed. As Adam Seligman puts it, "The voluntary nature of the true Christian community was expressed in the covenantal or consensual nature of the ties assumed by its participants. This new community, based on a consensual notion of membership, was to

26. Winthrop was active in opposing the appointment of John Wheelwright, Anne Hutchinson's brother-in-law, to a post in the Boston church, but he did so as a member of the congregation and not as governor. Of course, his prestige as governor certainly caused many to support his position. But the distinction between temporal and spiritual power was important to Puritans, and fundamental to their understanding of the New England Way. See *Winthrop's Journal*, 1:195–97.

27. Avihu Zakai, *Exile and Kingdom: History and Apocalypse in the Puritan Migration to America* (Cambridge, 1992), 232. Elsewhere Zakai characterizes the Puritan view of church and state by noting that "they considered both as a means to the same religious end": see *Theocracy in Massachusetts: Reformation and Separation in Early Puritan New England* (Lewiston, Maine, 1994), 207.

28. *The Civil Magistrates Power in Matters of Religion* (London, 1653), 12.

be governed by elected officials whose authority was rooted in 'the general voice' of the community."[29] Cotton referred to "the people, in whom fundamentally all power lies."[30] Roger Williams agreed that "civil government is an ordinance of God" and that "the sovereign, original, and foundation of civil power lies in the people" (*Bloudy Tenent*, 249). Such widespread views also made their way into more formalized codes: the Massachusetts Body of Liberties, authored by Nathaniel Ward in the early 1640s, contains in its preamble the telling statement that the body politic has assembled these liberties "to ratify them with our solemn consent."[31] Perry Miller rightly points out that "the Puritan state was seen by Puritans as the incarnation of their collective will": in Alan Simpson's apt characterization, the social covenant represents the "tribalization of the Puritan spirit."[32]

This civil covenant was illustrated vividly to New England Puritans through the arduous journey they had undergone to reach Massachusetts Bay. Those who had made the Atlantic crossing saw Massachusetts as both a potential Promised Land and a dangerous wilderness.[33] The migration and the erection of institutional and political structures to facilitate communal life served as constant reminders of this social covenant, an agreement between individuals and families to live in harmony and to submit themselves to leaders chosen by representatives of the freemen of their settlement. Without an appreciation of the voluntary agreement between humans as the basis for the Massachusetts settlement, we lose the elements of congregational volun-

29. *Innerworldly Individualism*, 26.

30. *An Exposition upon the Thirteenth Chapter of the Revelation* (London, 1655), in Edmund S. Morgan, ed., *Puritan Political Ideas, 1558–1794* (New York, 1965), 175.

31. In Morgan, *Puritan Political Ideas*, 179.

32. Miller, *The New England Mind: The Seventeenth Century* (1939; Cambridge, Mass., 1954), 418; Simpson, "The Covenanted Community," in *Religion in American History: Interpretive Essays*, ed. John M. Mulder and John F. Wilson (Englewood Cliffs, N.J., 1978), 20.

33. Both of these are well summarized in Benjamin W. Labaree, *Colonial Massachusetts: A History* (Millwood, N.Y., 1979), 42–46. Noting that the Hebrew exodus was followed by forty years in the wilderness, Labaree adds that "Puritans were not sure whether the New England wilderness was a similar testing ground or the promised land itself" (44). For discussion of wilderness and the Indian threat associated with it, see John Canup, *Out of the Wilderness: The Emergence of an American Identity in Colonial New England* (Middletown, Conn., 1990); Alan Heimert's classic essay, "Puritanism, the Wilderness, and the Frontier," *NEQ* 26 (1953): 361–82; and Peter N. Carroll, *Puritanism and the Wilderness: The Intellectual Significance of the New England Frontier, 1629–1700* (New York, 1969). On the ocean crossing, see David Cressy, "The Vast and Furious Ocean: The Passage to Puritan New England," *NEQ* 57 (1984): 511–32.

tarism and popular political sovereignty so integral to understanding Puritanism in Massachusetts.[34]

The social covenant incorporated the Puritan commonwealth, it is true, but the substantive bases of law and social practice were supplied by another aspect of the covenant, the agreement to follow God's word. Perry Miller and Thomas H. Johnson describe Puritan government as "brought into being by the act of the people; but the people do not create just any sort of government, but the one kind of government which has been established by God."[35] In the Puritan view, both aspects of the covenant undergirded and had broad implications for the social, political, and religious life of the community, mitigating the potential individualism of Protestant theology.[36] Migration fused the organic holism sought in the primitive church with contractual ideas (the social covenant) into a communal bond incorporating both religious and political aims. Although both church and state were founded on the basis of consent, the laws of God applied to them equally. In the body politic, "every one (in his own admission) gives an implicit consent to whatever the major part shall establish, *not being against religion or the weal public.*"[37] As Winthrop explained it: "We are entered into a covenant with [God] for this work . . . and he will expect strict performance of the articles contained in it" (*WP*, 2:295). The future of New England would depend on the colonists' performance. If they failed to walk in the Lord's ways, disaster would surely befall them; but if they remained faithful, "men shall say of succeeding plantations: the lord make it like New England" (ibid.).

New England was to be the place where biblical principles were explored and implemented, as a reflection and an outgrowth of Puritan covenants.

34. By "popular sovereignty" I do not mean to imply that the Puritans were democrats. Rather, following orthodox Christian doctrine, Puritans held that the Fall made government necessary, but that the specific forms of political authority received their legitimacy through the consent of the governed. This was a wholly conventional political view. See, for example, Vitoria's "On Civil Power" (1528), esp. question 1, arts. 3–6, in which Vitoria argues that the essential cause of government is God, but that the material cause lies in the commonwealth (this is, more specifically, a sovereignty based in the *community* rather than in the individual). "On Civil Power" is reprinted in Vitoria, *Political Writings*, ed. Anthony Pagden and Jeremy Lawrance (Cambridge, 1991), 10–18.

35. Perry Miller and Thomas H. Johnson, eds., *The Puritans* (New York, 1938), 189–90. The New England Puritans "saw their emigration . . . as infused with a transcendent meaning of hastening the Kingdom of Christ on earth" (Seligman, *Innerworldly Individualism*, 60–61).

36. Seligman, *Innerworldly Individualism*; see also Christopher Hill, *Intellectual Origins of the English Revolution Revisited* (Oxford, 1997), chaps. 12, 14.

37. *Liberty and the Weal Public Reconciled* (London, 1637), 76, emphasis added.

Cotton saw a coherent plan of government in biblical texts and viewed the civil covenant as effecting what had not been possible in "Old" England.

> I am very apt to believe . . . that the word . . . of God [contains] a short . . . platform, not only of theology, but also of other sacred sciences. . . . It is very suitable to God's all-sufficient wisdom, and to the fullness and perfection of the Holy Scriptures, not only to prescribe perfect rules for the right ordering of a private man's soul . . . but also for the right ordering of a man's family, yea, of the commonwealth too, so far as both of them are subordinate to spiritual ends, and yet avoid both the churches' usurpation upon civil jurisdictions . . . and the commonwealth's invasion upon ecclesiastical administrations.[38]

Puritan rulers were assigned the special responsibility of making sure that the community discharged these covenantal obligations to God. As John Norton put it, "God hath armed the civil magistrate for the defense of religion."[39] Puritans were not only covenanting with one another, but with God, under a widely shared interpretation of God's requirements.

The restriction of the franchise to church members followed directly from the view that the community covenanted with God as well as each other: the saints, as the elect, were best able to discern scriptural truths and make wise decisions for the polity.[40] Limiting the franchise to church members was an essential element in seeking to bring together providential and mundane history, to point Massachusetts society toward godliness in its corporate actions. Thus the covenant obtained not merely between humans, but between humans and God. As Winthrop makes clear in his "Model," both aspects were to be operational in the minds of early Massachusetts settlers: he viewed them as "a company professing ourselves fellow members of Christ . . . we ought to account ourselves knit together by this bond of love. . . . [the work of settlement] is by a mutual consent through a special overriding providence

---

38. In Morgan, *Puritan Political Ideas*, 169.

39. *The Heart of New England Rent at the Blasphemies of the Present Generation* (Cambridge, Mass., 1659), 49.

40 See T. H. Breen, *The Character of the Good Ruler: A Study of Puritan Political Ideas in New England, 1630–1730* (New Haven, Conn., 1970), chap. 2, esp. 37–41. Cotton defends restricting the franchise in *A Discourse About Civil Government in a New Plantation Whose Design Is Religion* (Cambridge, Mass., 1663).

. . . to seek out a place of cohabitation and consortship under a due form of government both civil and ecclesiastical" (*WP*, 2:292–93). Winthrop considered the end of the colony "to improve our lives to do more service to the Lord . . . that ourselves and our posterity may be the better preserved from the common corruptions of the world" (2:293). Thus the *form* of the colony arose from the covenant among humans, its *substance* from the objective demands upon human endeavor made by God.

In the Puritan version of popular sovereignty, then, the people were obligated to obey the rulers they selected, who were in turn obligated to uphold and carry out the community's covenant with God: thus we might speak of the people as constituently, but not governmentally, sovereign.[41] The state, as Miller observes, "insert[ed] the terms of salvation into the political incorporation and . . . unite[d] the duties of civil obedience with the duties of Christian worship."[42] Consequently, Puritan Massachusetts had no place for claims of individual right or religious dissent; the Lord's business was demanding, and the community had pledged itself to doing it. In Cobbet's words, "*serve the Lord* (that is, Christ) is indefinite, and so extendable . . . but . . . forcible restraint and punishment of corruptions in religion, by the use of the temporal sword, is by command of God required of civil rulers."[43]

For Puritans, then, covenant theory and contractarian thinking implied neither democracy, liberal "rights," nor toleration, but rather the willing acceptance of God's rule by an earthly community.[44] Regarding democracy,

---

41. Of course, for Puritans (as, later, for John Locke), God was the only sovereign truly worthy of the title. Winthrop reconciled popular sovereignty with New England political forms by an analogy of delegation: in choosing magistrates, individuals "take [men] from among [themselves] . . . that we shall govern you and judge your cases by the rule of God's laws and our own, according to our best skill" (*Winthrop's Journal*, 2:238). This distinction between constituent and governmental sovereignty clarifies how, for Puritans, political authority could originate in the people, yet the expectation flowing out of this understanding remain one of absolute obedience to the activities of rulers. For a helpful discussion of these two senses of sovereignty, see Samuel H. Beer, *To Make A Nation: The Rediscovery of American Federalism* (Cambridge, Mass., 1994), chap. 10, esp. 314–15, 338. The distinction echoes one between "delegation" and "authorization" theories of sovereignty, going to the question of whether the people, in forming sovereigns, only delegate a power they retain, or whether they part with that sovereignty altogether. On this distinction, see Johann P. Sommerville, *Politics and Ideology in England, 1603–1640* (New York, 1986), 22–27.

42. *New England Mind*, 412.

43. *The Civil Magistrates Power*, 23.

44. Compare Hobbes on Israel's covenant with God (*L*, chap. 35).

Cotton found no scriptural precedent,[45] and Winthrop rejected it with a Great Chain of Being argument about natural hierarchy.[46] In Puritan thought we find no civic republicanism, no Lockean state of nature in which reasonable individuals create politics to safeguard temporal interests while theological duties remain in a distinctly separate sphere of life. Puritans like Cotton and Winthrop saw the religious responsibilities of individuals, gathered churches, and societies as immediate and overriding.

Ultimately, the community would be judged in light of its success or failure in building a godly commonwealth, and rulers saw great danger in allowing vocal heresy or dissent. If true Christianity lay in the simplicity of the early church, and the covenant into which Massachusetts had entered required the community to follow the ways of the Lord, where in the early church was a permissive attitude toward religious division and dissent sanctioned? Was not toleration of religious dissent more likely to be "toleration of the works of the devil"?[47] In Seligman's words, "Rule by holy ministers and sainted magistrates ensured the proper exercise of God's ordinances and so the establishment of a social order under the direct auspices of God's authority."[48] The governor who allowed error to flourish, who failed to carry out his twofold duty (to humanity and to God), violated God's requirements of magistrates and potentially brought judgment upon not only himself but the entire community. Nathaniel Ward turned talk of toleration on its head, stating simply, "I dare aver, that God doth no where in his word tolerate Christian states, to give toleration to such adversaries of his Truth, if they have in their hands to suppress them. . . . [p]oly-piety is the greatest impiety of all."[49] John Norton, echoing these sentiments, turned toleration into an issue of public responsibility for allowing sin to flourish, drawing on Old

---

45. "Democracy, I do not conceive that ever God did ordain as a fit government either for church or commonwealth" (in Morgan, *Puritan Political Ideas*, 169. For Cotton, democracy denoted direct popular involvement in political decisions and was likely to deteriorate into mob rule and anarchy. Instead, he saw theocracy as preferable: not, that is, rule by priests, but the explicit recognition by a community's leaders that they were following the laws of God. See Cotton, *An Abstract of the Laws of New England* (London, 1641), chap. 1, and *Book of Laws and Liberties* (Cambridge, 1648), which notes that church and state "each do help and strengthen each other" (1). For a helpful summary, see Zakai, *Exile and Kingdom*, chap. 7.

46. See Winthrop's "Model," in WP, 2:292ff.

47. Cobbet, *The Civil Magistrates Power*, 92.

48. *Innerworldly Individualism*, 66.

49. *The Simple Cobbler*, 6, 8. Cobbet also saw the danger of God's punishment if Massachusetts tolerated religious heterodoxy: see *The Civil Magistrates Power*, 96–97.

Testament lessons. "The not bearing testimony against iniquities to be punished by the Judge by meet execution of justice, renders Israel from time to
time, both guilty and scandalous in respect of such sins. Commission of evil
makes it the sin of the delinquent; irregular permission thereof, makes it the
sin of the state."[50]

If responsibility for securing compliance with the terms of the covenant
fell to Puritan leaders, then clearly they possessed wide latitude and broad
discretion in seeking to create conditions in which the covenant could be
fulfilled.[51] The Puritan theory of sin, influenced as it was by Augustine and
Calvin, located depravity within the human heart through original sin, but
simultaneously sought to create an environment in which godliness could be
promoted and sinfulness mitigated.[52] Winthrop distinguished between civil
(political) and natural liberty, noting that granting excessive liberty to Dissenters, given fallen human nature, merely invited depravity. The equation
of natural liberty with human sinfulness strengthened the argument against
toleration. In the covenant, humans *renounced* natural liberty and accepted
the rule of God, and godly informed consent represented the ideal of civil
liberty; a godly community granting its voluntary consent to godly leaders,

50. *The Heart of New England Rent*, 50.

51. Cobbett insists that the magistrate should call a synod for guidance on doubtful points
of theology, but grants him the leeway to follow the synod's rulings more or less as he sees fit (*The
Civil Magistrates Power*, 67–79).

52. Here my view departs from those of Andrew Delbanco and Jesper Rosenmeier. Consider Delbanco's description of the migration: "The journey to America was an effort to conserve
what was left of the conviction that sin, rather than being an entity implanted in the soul, was . . .
a temporary estrangement from God. Behind . . . the Puritan journey lay an utterly un-Calvinist
hope . . . that Englishmen were not so much depraved as victims of a distorting experience. The
Puritan social critique, as Richard Hooker had understood, carried a wistful hope that the fault
lay not with man but what had been done to man" (*The Puritan Ordeal* [Cambridge, Mass., 1989],
79–80).

Consider also Rosenmeier's description of the New England idea: "The elders had made the
exodus from England convinced that a return to Adam's innocence in the Garden of Eden would
be the final state of Christian redemption for the individual as well as for the world. . . . The
paradise Adam had lost, they would regain" (438). See his "'New England's Perfection': The Image
of Adam and the Image of Christ in the Antinomian Crisis, 1634 to 1638," *WMQ* 27 (1970):
435–59.

I find no mention in any orthodox New England Puritan writing that sin was conceived of
as "temporary" or due merely to "experience." Certainly such views were expressed by Dissenters
and those who challenged the corporate "errand" New England represented, but orthodox
Puritanism seems implacably hostile to such sentiments. At the same time, Delbanco and
Rosenmeier are certainly right to point out the importance Puritans placed on the importance of
a godly environment in allowing individuals and communities to mitigate and minimize the effects
of sin in corporate life.

to carry out the society's covenant with the Lord. Winthrop thus supported "a liberty to that only which is good, just, and honest."[53] As Perry Miller points out, this understanding of godly magistracy places Massachusetts leaders in a position of authority relatively similar to that of other seventeenth-century magistrates in terms of the types of power wielded over their subjects and the aims for which that power might be exercised.[54]

This responsibility of Puritan magistracy might entail excluding individuals or groups from residing within the colony's borders, as Winthrop extrapolated from the compact theory of society during the Antinomian crisis.

> The essential form of a commonweal or body politic such as this is ... the consent of a certain company of people, to cohabit together, under one government for their mutual safety and welfare. . . . From the premises will arise these conclusions.
>
> 1. No commonweal can be founded but by free consent.
> 2. The persons so incorporating have a public and relative interest each in other, and in the place of their co-habitation and goods, and laws, etc. . . . so as none other can claim privilege with them but by free consent. . . .
> From these conclusions I thus reason.
> 1. If we here be a corporation established by free consent, if the place of our cohabitation be our own, then no man hath right to come into us etc. without our consent. . . .
> 3. If we are bound to keep off whatsoever appears to tend to our ruin or damage, then we may lawfully refuse to receive such whose dispositions suit not with ours and whose society (we know) will be hurtful to us.[55]

Cotton compared the banishment of heretics and other troublemakers to excluding someone with the plague or other infectious disease, while Norton saw laws against Quakers as a form of communal self-defense.[56] They would not pursue heretics through the wilderness, Puritan magistrates claimed, but

---

53. In Morgan, *Puritan Political Ideas*, 207.
54. *New England Mind*, 457.
55. "A Declaration in Defense of an Order of the Court Made in May, 1637," in *WP*, 2:422, 423.
56. Cotton, *Reply*, chap. 1; Norton, *The Heart of New England Rent*, 54.

would deal firmly with those within their borders who threatened their godly commonwealth. As Ward put it, "All Familists, Antinomians, Anabaptists, and other such enthusiasts shall have free liberty to keep away from us, and such as will come to be gone as fast as they can, the sooner the better."[57]

The leadership of Massachusetts sought to reinforce social cohesion and focus the community on its collective task. The banishments during the settlement's first decade clarified the limits of acceptable public belief and set the stage for religious dissent to come.[58] In New England, magistrates viewed religious dissent as a threat to civil sovereignty, whether the threat came from Williams's challenge to the colony's basis of existence, Hutchinson's challenge to the ecclesiastical structures and social harmony deemed necessary for human salvation and security, or the broader but no less vehement challenges by the Baptists and Quakers that echoed these concerns. In addressing these threats, Massachusetts leaders attempted to construct *new* ways of integrating new questions into the ongoing "errand" of Puritan New England, including the jeremiad sermon, with its evocation of a link between past and present generations, and other institutional attempts to break down the increasingly distant relationship between church and society as the seventeenth century progressed.[59]

Scripture, Primitivism, and New England as Refuge

At a deeper level, Puritan opposition to toleration sprung from a belief in the unity of Christian truth and an intense, quintessentially Protestant search for the primitive (New Testament) church. Puritan theology and practice were predicated upon recapturing the simplicity and purity of the ancient church: in fact, the ancient church was a powerful rhetorical commitment shared by orthodox Massachusetts Puritans, Roger Williams, and Anne Hutchinson,

57. *The Simple Cobbler*, 6. Massachusetts magistrates did, however, use a bit of subterfuge in the Gorton incident, persuading several Indian sachems well outside the bounds of their patent to place themselves under the colony's jurisdiction. When these sachems complained that Gortonists had defrauded them of land, Massachusetts magistrates seized them and brought them to trial in Boston.

58. "The response of the Bay colony to first the Quakers and later the Baptists was shaped by its previous experience in dealing with the criticisms of Anne Hutchinson, Roger Williams, and the Presbyterians of old and New England" (Carla Gardina Pestana, *Quakers and Baptists in Colonial Massachusetts* [New York, 1991], 2).

59. Seligman, *Innerworldly Individualism*, chap. 5. On the jeremiad as an enduring cultural and rhetorical form, see Sacvan Bercovitch, *The Puritan Jeremiad* (Madison, Wis., 1978).

as well as earlier generations of Puritans protesting against Anglo-Catholic "innovation."[60]

Epistemologically and cosmologically, the context for New England Puritanism remained the context of the Protestant Reformation more generally: the drive for religious truth looked, not forward, but to a pristine past. As Perry Miller puts it, "Puritan theory . . . was only in a slight degree progressive; it was for the most part the elaborate restatement of a medieval ideal."[61] The further Reformation in New England represented "a drive toward origins," to use Theodore Bozeman's phrase, a move forward in providential history by seeking a primitive purity. One must not stray too far from God's revealed plan, since "the presumed right to contrive new structural or theological forms not found among the first was the opening wedge which had admitted the myriad errors of popish religion."[62] Biblicism joined with primitivism in opposing both diversifying tolerationist impulses in religion and the human inventions of the Anglican and Catholic traditions. Joseph Lecler, in describing early English Puritans, could have been describing New England Puritans: "[They] were not so much defenders of conscience as champions of the Bible."[63]

60. In his letter to Winthrop of 24 October 1636 Williams claims only to seek the simplicity of Christ and the early church (*The Correspondence of Roger Williams*, ed. Glenn W. Lafantasie [Hanover, N.H., 1988], 1:65–69). Hutchinson justified her theological discussions from "a clear rule in Titus, that the elder women should instruct the younger" ("The Examination of Mrs. Anne Hutchinson at the Court at Newtown," in Thomas Hutchinson, *The History of the Colony and Province of Massachusetts-Bay*, ed. Lawrence Shaw Mayo [Cambridge, Mass., 1936], 1:368). John Wheelwright argued that "we must first contend for the faith once delivered to the saints," exhorting his hearers that "if the Philistines fill [the well of the Gospel] with the earth of their own inventions . . . the servants of the Lord must open the wells again" ("Sermon Preached at Boston in New England upon a Fast Day, the 16th of January 163[7]," in *John Wheelwright: His Writings* [Boston, 1876], 162, 163).

61. *New England Mind*, 429. Avihu Zakai presents an alternative vision of Puritanism in England and New England, one in which primitivism plays a lesser role than forward-looking millenarian radicalism. See *Theocracy in Massachusetts*, chaps. 1–2; also see Gilpin, *Millenarian Piety*, chaps. 1–3.

62. Theodore Dwight Bozeman, *To Live Ancient Lives: The Primitivist Dimension in Puritanism* (Chapel Hill, N.C., 1988), 14, 51. Much of my discussion in this section is influenced by Bozeman's careful and highly nuanced exposition of Puritanism. See also Bozeman's "Biblical Primitivism: An Approach to New England Puritanism" and C. Leonard Allen's "Roger Williams and 'the Restauration of Zion,'" chaps. 1 and 2 in *The American Quest for the Primitive Church*, ed. Richard T. Hughes (Urbana, Ill., 1988).

63. Joseph Lecler, *Toleration and the Reformation*, trans. T. L. Weston (New York, 1960), 2:391. Given the orthodox understanding of conscience, Puritans did not see the two as conflicting.

According to the Puritans who made the migration to New England, the opportunity to live out this biblicism and create a biblically sound community was sadly lacking in England. Many voiced a yearning for the biblical community as a primary reason for coming to America; Michael Walzer notes English Puritanism's "attack on the traditional political world" as one of the movement's defining characteristics.[64] Internationally, Protestantism had fallen on hard times in the opening decades of the seventeenth century, and Puritans (as steeped in the providential view of history as any of their contemporaries) saw in these events signs of God's displeasure at the failure to purify "Romish" elements in English church liturgy and government. Many early Massachusetts leaders, while still in England during the 1620s and 1630s, suggested that England was provoking God's wrath; that because of its failure to reform its church fully, as well as the broader corruption in social life and mores, England was due for divine punishment. Thomas Hooker, in his farewell sermon to England, pointed out England's social problems, corruption, "popish" influences, poverty, and the general turning-away of the nation from God. He exhorted the faithful to repentance:

> As sure as God is God, God is going from England . . . God begins to ship away his Noahs . . . and God makes account that New England shall be a refuge for his Noahs and his Lots, a rock and a shelter for his righteous ones to run unto. . . . Tell me, are there not as great sins amongst us as were in Jerusalem . . . ? Are we better than other brethren and neighbor nations, that have drunk so deeply of God's wrath?[65]

64. *The Revolution of the Saints: A Study in the Origins of Radical Politics* (Cambridge, Mass., 1965), chap. 5.

65. *Thomas Hooker: Writings in England and Holland, 1626–1633,* ed. George H. Williams, Norman Pettit, Winfried Herget, and Sargent Bush, Jr. (Cambridge, Mass., 1975), 244, 246, 250. See also Christopher Hill, *The English Bible and the Seventeenth-Century Revolution* (London, 1994), chaps. 12, 14, and Zakai, *Theocracy in Massachusetts,* 129: "For the Puritans of the migration, only the overseas prospect held out hope; England was no place for true reformation."

In addition, one might construe the idea of refuge as, not from God's wrath on England, but from something much more immediate to home parishes. John T. Horton explored the difference in emigration from two dioceses (one with a lenient Anglican bishop, one with a more orthodox Laudian bishop), finding much higher levels of migration from the latter. See Horton, "Two Bishops and the Holy Brood: A Fresh Look at a Familiar Fact," *NEQ* 26 (1953): 361–82; also see "Migration and the Rhetoric of Persecution," pp. 40–48, in Zakai, *Theocracy in Massachusetts.*

Such sentiments also appeared repeatedly in Winthrop's writings. As early as May 1629, after reciting a litany of European Protestant defeats, he told his wife that God was "turning the cup towards us also . . . I am verily persuaded, God will bring some heavy afflictions upon this land, and that speedily." He expressed his faith, however, that the faithful will be preserved: "[God] will provide a shelter and a hiding place for us" (WP, 2:92–92). In the "General Observations for the Plantation of New England," Winthrop lists God's coming judgment on England and the potential for New England to serve as a refuge for the faithful just below the general religious consideration of serving God's church and providing a bulwark against Jesuit influence in the New World (WP, 2:111). These ideas about divine retribution for failure to follow God's word, as we have seen, operated in New England as well, when Puritans there were faced with strident religious dissent.

Of course, one could put a happier face on the issue of refuge from God's wrath, as Richard Saltonstall wrote to John Winthrop, Jr., in 1633: "Corruptio unius est generatio alterius; and God makes the ruins of one church to be the raising of another. The Lord give you long to enjoy those happy times that you see now."[66] Having journeyed so far, and undergone such hardships, to erect their godly community and escape the coming judgment on England, Edward Johnson warned, "Let none wrest [power] from you under pretense of liberty of conscience. . . . sure you were not made for tolerating times."[67] The colony as a refuge from the wrath of God figured heavily in the thinking of this first generation of Massachusetts Puritan leaders, and such a refuge would not be one in which a multiplicity of religious perspectives would be welcomed.[68]

Liberty of Conscience and Erroneous Conscience, Order and Anarchy

Massachusetts magistrates vigorously denied that they persecuted individuals for the sake of conscience. Williams, Gorton, Hutchinson, Clarke, and others insisted just as vigorously that they did. In a sense, the two sides were arguing past each other, for each used the term "conscience" in specific and often incommensurable ways. The idea of "cases of conscience" reaches well back

66. Robert E. Moody, ed., *Saltonstall Papers* (Boston, 1972), 1:121.
67. *Wonder-Working Providence*, 29, 30.
68. On the apocalyptic and eschatological dimensions of the refuge Puritans saw in Massachusetts, see Zakai, *Exile and Kingdom*.

in the Puritan tradition, to the Reformation disputes over the *adiaphora*, or indifferent things of worship.[69] As Massachusetts debates show, however, deep divisions remained upon the specific boundaries and definitions of conscience itself. Cotton's view of conscience mirrored the orthodox Christian view, which will be elaborated further in Chapter 3's examination of antitolerationist argument in England during the 1640s. The magistrates' expulsion of Roger Williams, Cotton claimed, did not constitute persecution, which lay in "the affliction of another for righteousness' sake" (*Reply*, 26). Persecution thus contained an objective element. Individuals might be sincerely mistaken, Cobbet admitted, but in the end "the highest rule, to which all are in conscience bound, is the very word of God."[70] If one asserts an erroneous theological

69. The category of "indifferent" things, or *adiaphora*, played a central role in early modern toleration debates, generally (though not exclusively) utilized by tolerationists to argue against compulsion on matters not central to Christian doctrine. As opposed to clear biblical imperatives like the Ten Commandments or Christ's teachings, for example, "indifferent" things referred to such matters as dietary restrictions, family, and marriage, that were considered morally or salvifically inefficacious.

The concept of adiaphora was elaborated by Erasmus, and further developed by Melanchthon: see especially his *Loci Communes* (1555), chaps. 34, 35. Initially, the term referred to rituals that do not appear in the New Testament; later it was broadened to demarcate fundamental articles of faith from matters that do not reach to the essence of salvation. Early modern tolerationists often reduced these fundamental articles further, to general precepts of ethical behavior, as we shall see in the work of William Walwyn, considered in the next chapter. Walwyn asserted that compassion, helping the poor, and feeding the hungry were far more central to Christ's teaching than rituals and intricacies of doctrine. See Walwyn, *A Still and Soft Voice from the Scriptures* (London, 1647), 10, and *The Power of Love* (London, 1643), "To every reader."

The best recent discussion of indifferent matters, especially in their elaboration by Erasmus, is Remer, *Humanism*, 50–101. As Remer rightly notes, this issue could cut both ways in toleration debates: "The concept of adiaphora . . . permits the humanist to argue for a more comprehensive Church on the ground that differences between denominations are not essential to faith. But the concept of adiaphora can also be used to argue for greater state intervention in religious matters. By characterizing a practice as nonessential, it becomes possible to limit that practice while still claiming that no one's religious freedom has been infringed" (140).

See also Bernard J. Verkamp, *The Indifferent Mean: Adiaphorism in the English Reformation to 1554*, Studies in the Reformation, vol. 1 (Athens, Ohio, 1977). On the historical role played by Melanchthon, see Clyde L. Manschreck, "The Role of Melanchthon in the Adiaphora Controversy," *Archiv für Reformationsgeschichte* 48 (1957): 165–81. Puritans leaned heavily on the works of William Ames: see Ames's *Conscience with the Power and Cases Thereof* (London, 1639). On cases of conscience and the casuistic tradition in English Puritanism, see Keith Thomas, "Cases of Conscience in Seventeenth-Century England," in *Public Duty and Private Conscience: Essays Presented to G. E. Aylmer*, ed. John Morrill, Paul Slack, and Daniel Woolf (Oxford, 1993), 29–56.

70. *The Civil Magistrates Power*, 98–99.

position, one cannot, logically speaking, be righteous, or persecuted for righteousness' sake.

For Cotton, one who erred on fundamental points of religion endangered his own soul and the well-being of the community, "sinning against his own conscience": thus could Cotton assert that his interpretation of "liberty of conscience sets the conscience at liberty."[71] True liberty was Christian liberty, the liberty of believers to follow the Gospel: understood this way, it could only bolster godly individuals in their Christian lives, and not divide families, congregations, and communities. As John Norton put it, "If you ask what liberty is? you may look at it as a power, as to any external restraint, or obstruction on man's part, to walk in the faith, worship, doctrine and discipline of the Gospel. . . . When you hear men plead for liberty, see that it be not liberty falsely so called."[72] Edward Johnson urged Massachusetts leaders to oppose "such as would have all sorts of sinful opinions upheld by the civil government . . . that our Lord Christ might reign over us, both in churches and commonwealth."[73]

To understand the Puritan idea of erroneous conscience, we must understand the subtle and highly differentiated series of theological and social distinctions that constituted it. Theological differences (errors, in Puritan eyes) might concern fundamentals or nonfundamentals. Fundamentals consisted of a fairly routine list of Protestant views: the "foundations of Christian religion . . . [e.g.] the doctrine of salvation by Christ, and of faith in his name, repentance from dead works, resurrection from the dead; and the like."[74] Errors in fundamentals kept to oneself and nonfundamental errors held in a meek or humble manner fell outside the jurisdiction of the magistrates' authority.[75] In addition, erroneous opinions held out of ignorance, or by individuals who seemed likely to be persuaded of their mistakes, called

71. Cotton, *The Controversie Concerning Liberty of Conscience in Matters of Religion* (London, 1646), 8; idem, *The Bloudy Tenent, Washed, and Made White in the Bloud of the Lambe* (London, 1647), 3.

72. *Three Choice and Profitable Sermons* (Cambridge, Mass., 1664), 7–8. Cotton "readily grant[ed] . . . that liberty of conscience is to be granted to men that fear God indeed" (*The Controversie*, 14).

73. *Wonder-Working Providence*, 140, 145.

74. *Cotton, Bloudy Tenent Washed*, 5. Cotton specifically excluded issues of church polity from this list: in these, he said, "Toleration might more easily be allowed" (6).

75. *Platform of Church Discipline* (Cambridge Platform), chap. 17, sec. 2; Cobbet, *The Civil Magistrates Power*, 12–14; Cotton, *The Controversie*, 8.

for lenience. As Winthrop put it, "Seeking to pluck out of the fire such as there may be hope to be reduced out of error and the snare of the devil, do seem to require more moderation and indulgence of human infirmity where there appears not obstinacy against the clear truth."[76]

Errors of any sort held "with a boisterous and arrogant spirit, to the disturbance of the civil peace," however, impinged upon both the churches' peace and the civil magistrates' charge to preserve order.[77] Anne Hutchinson's claim to immediate revelation brought her examination by the General Court to a swift and (to her) unfavorable conclusion. The court accused Quakers of "tak[ing] upon them[selves] to be immediately sent of God and infallibly assisted by the spirit to speak and write blasphemous opinions, despising government and the order of God in church and commonwealth . . . reproaching and reviling magistrates and ministers."[78] On another occasion, the court accused Quakers of viewing themselves as "pure and without sin," and "show[ing] contempt against [civil magistrates] in their outward gestures and behavior."[79] Even when erroneous conscience issued forth in tumultuous civil behavior, though, Cobbet argued that magistrates could distinguish between leaders of such discord and followers. "Some are seducers, and ringleaders in the offenses and abuses, some seduced; neither all errors, nor all erring persons, are of equal guilt, and justice must *suum cuique tribuere.*"[80]

Cotton, for his part, insisted that he was advocating neither hasty nor drastic punishments for nonessential differences in theology or church practice. He admitted that many in the colony shared Williams's views and were not banished. Such individuals, he claimed, were "tolerated not only to live in the commonwealth, but also in the fellowship of the churches."[81] Separatism as a set of strictly religious commitments, Cotton implied, was not itself incompatible with membership in the Massachusetts community. But no society could be expected to sanction the active undermining of its own

76. *Winthrop's Journal*, 2:260–61.

77. Cotton, *The Controversie*, 8–9; Cobbet, *The Civil Magistrates Power*, 15.

78. General Court, 14 October 1656, reprinted in Richard P. Hallowell, *The Quaker Invasion of Massachusetts*, 4th ed. (Boston, 1887), 133. See also the court's pronouncement of 19 October 1658, also in Hallowell, *Quaker Invasion*, 138.

79. "To vindicate the justice of this court's proceedings in reference to the Quakers," in Hallowell, *Quaker Invasion*, 144, 147.

80. Cobbet, *The Civil Magistrates Power*, 16.

81. *Reply*, 44. Clarke disputed this claim: see *Ill Newes from New England* (London, 1652); reprinted in *Massachusetts Historical Society Collections* (Boston, 1854), ser. 4, vol. 2, p. 64.

foundations; and Williams's opposition to loyalty oaths and his references to the colony's patent as a "national sin" attacked the very foundations of the colony as constituted. After repeated disputations, attempts at persuasion, and ministerial and civil conferences, Cotton wrote, Williams not only refused to see the error of his ways but also to stop spreading them publicly. Ejecting one holding and preaching such views from the country was not persecution (not, that is, punishment for righteousness' sake), but more along the lines of excluding someone with plague or other contagious fatal disease from one's borders, in order to safeguard the population.[82]

Allowing considerations of conscience to override civil laws and public order invited anarchy: as Nathaniel Ward would later write, "The state that will give liberty of conscience in matters of religion, must give liberty of conscience and conversation in their moral laws, or else the fiddle will be out of tune."[83] When Anne Hutchinson asked, "Must not I then entertain the saints because I must keep my conscience,"[84] Winthrop refuted her by analogy: if one's brother had committed treason, he asked, would Hutchinson claim that conscience excused her concealing him from the magistrates? The implication was clear: she certainly would not; or if she would, she was not fit for Massachusetts society. Although both John Wheelwright and Anne Hutchinson claimed conscience in their defenses, it seems doubtful whether these claims involved any sort of "liberty of conscience" argument more generally. The General Court told Wheelwright that "this case was not a matter of conscience, but of a civil nature," making the important distinction between purely religious matters and those having an impact on public order.[85] His fast-day sermon had spread the "heat and contention and uncharitable censures," and because of his words, "all things are turned upside down among us."[86] Clearly these disputes transcended theology. Sedition was a civil penalty, "a going aside to make a party . . . so as [the people] fall to take part one against another."[87] In other words, disputes fall within either the sphere of conscience *or* the civil sphere, and issues having a deleterious effect on civil peace leave the realm of conscience in their very essence. Thus *by definition*

82. *Reply*, 27; also *The Controversie*, 14.
83. *The Simple Cobbler*, 10.
84. "The Examination," in Hutchinson, *The History*, 1:366.
85. John Winthrop, *A Short Story of the Rise, Reign, and Ruine of the Antinomians, Familists and Libertines* (London, 1644), 46.
86. Ibid., 24, 46.
87. Ibid., 52–53.

one cannot claim conscience in defense of one's violation of a civil law (recall, too, the broad nature of civil offenses, as Williams had pointed out, which included the First Table of the Ten Commandments).[88]

Despite these careful distinctions regarding fundamentals, nonfundamentals, and disruptive behavior, it seems that clear that Massachusetts Puritans generally were highly suspicious of religious dissent and suspected it of fomenting social and political subversion virtually wherever it appeared. Williams's Separatism had denied the settlement's legitimacy, and Hutchinson had divided families and congregations against one another with her claim to have had an immediate revelation from God. Gorton mocked the colony's pretensions to godliness, while Quakers engaged in erratic and disruptive behaviors, including public nakedness.[89] Thus it might be more accurate to say that the social and political *consequences* of various theological positions, not necessarily the theology itself, were at issue.[90] The two, of course, were not inseparable for either side in these debates. Looking back over the strife, Thomas Shepard drew lessons for the colony's inhabitants in his 1638 election sermon:

> Because the kingdom of God is not divided against itself, if therefore any usurp any government over that state which God hath set, 'tis not of God but of Satan. . . . Let us learn us what to judge of those that may come to usurp over the churches here or state here; however they may have sheep's clothing, yet if they can come in by their faction, you will then find them to be brambles; ambitious, base, and bloody.[91]

Immediately after banishing Anne Hutchinson, the General Court ordered that all Hutchinsonians be disarmed, overtly connecting them with radical Anabaptists and the Muenster commune. "There is just cause of suspicion,"

---

88. The First Table of the Ten Commandments lists one's duties to God; the Second Table, one's duties to others.

89. Pestana, *Quakers and Baptists*, 39–40. Hallowell denies these charges. See *Quaker Invasion*, chap. 4.

90. Edward Winslow emphasizes the civil nature of the charges against Gorton, namely, the social and political division Gorton spread wherever he went, in *Hypocrisie Unmasked* (London, 1646), passim.

91. "Thomas Shepard's Election Sermon, in 1638," *New England Historical and Genealogical Register* 24 (1870): 364.

the order read, "that they, as others in Germany, in former times, may, upon some revelation, make some sudden eruption upon those that differ from them in judgment."[92] The Muenster revolt had firmly established "Anabaptist" as a term of abuse among Protestants, and its rhetorical effectiveness continued a century after the fact. In 1534–35, a number of Anabaptists created a communistic regime in the city, confiscated the property of those they considered heretic, expelled the aged and sick, and executed those who criticized their behavior. Eventually the regime was overthrown by an army of Catholics and Lutherans, and the repression that followed was far more brutal than the regime it replaced, but the incident as a whole branded Anabaptists as revolutionaries. The Hutchinsonians, who evoked the shadow of Muenster to Massachusetts magistrates, were not merely a Dissenting theological faction: they were armed and, to their opponents, possessed a pedigree of license and lawlessness.

Gorton and his followers presented, to Massachusetts Puritans, a prime example of the sort of contentiousness to which Antinomianism would necessarily lead. Everywhere he went, it seemed, dissension followed: Plymouth, Portsmouth, Providence, elsewhere in Rhode Island. Indeed, in Providence Gortonists caused such strife that a number of the inhabitants there petitioned Massachusetts to intervene and help restore civil peace.[93]

The claim that tolerating religious dissent would lead to chaos, irreligion, and anarchy was repeated again and again by Massachusetts leaders. Cotton saw in the English disturbances of the 1640s the lawlessness and heresy that would always accompany toleration and referred directly to the English Civil War and its religio-political issues in his *Reply* to Williams. In a stunning polemic, he viewed Williams's making their quarrel public at such a time part of the

dreadful justice of God . . . in such a season, when the spirit of error is let loose to deceive so many thousand souls of our English nation:

92. Nathaniel B. Shurtleff, M.D., ed., *Records of the Governor and Company of the Massachusetts Bay in New England, 1628–1686* (Boston, 1853–54), 1:211. In "The Examination," Dudley notes that "these disturbances that have come among the Germans have been all grounded upon revelations, and so they that have vented them have stirred up their hearers to take up arms against their prince and to cut the throats of one another, and these have been the fruits of them, and whether the devil may inspire the same into their hearts here I know not, for I am fully persuaded that Mrs. Hutchinson is deluded by the devil" (Hutchinson, *The History*, 1:388).

93. These disputes are outlined in Winslow, *Hypocrisie Unmasked, and Wall, Massachusetts Bay,* chap. 4.

so that now their hearts are become as tinder, ready to catch and kindle at every spark of false light . . . for these are the days of vengeance, when the Antinomians deny the whole law; the anti-sabbatarians deny the morality of the fourth commandment; the papists deny the negative part of the second commandment. It is a woeful opportunity that God hath left Mr. Williams to, now to step in, and deny the affirmative part of it also.[94]

Since religious uniformity and orthodox religion underlay ethical behavior and civic responsibility, it became easy for New England magistrates to suspect calls for toleration of inherently threatening the peace and stability of their society. "Such a liberty . . . carrieth the mark of anarchy in the state," wrote Cobbet.[95] To recall Ward's words, "The state that will give liberty of conscience in matters of religion, must give liberty of conscience and conversation in their moral laws, or else the fiddle will be out of tune."[96]

Godly lives and godly communities cannot be created or sustained in the absence of a secure civil order, John Norton pointed out. This order (and the civil government required to maintain it) was of divine origin. "Order is a divine disposal, of superior and inferior relations, in human or Christian societies, distributing to each one respectively, what is due thereunto . . . [and] is necessary in man's fallen estate."[97] Those who undermine order, namely, for Norton, the Quakers, work in the devil's cause. Appealing especially to the poor and discontented, he went on, Quakers portray their revelations as infallible, and their toleration threatens New England with murder, confiscation of property, and loss of liberty: "Witness their doctrine and practice in Munster. . . . [T]hey held . . . it was lawful for the people to depose their magistrates being unbelievers, and they counted all unbelievers who were not of their mind."[98] A petition circulated in 1658 in favor of even severer penalties against Quakers noted that the Quaker activities in Massachusetts "daily increaseth rather than abateth our fear of the spirit of Munster, or John of Leyden revived."[99]

---

94. *Reply*, 22–23. See also Cotton, *Bloudy Tenent Washed*, chap. 45.
95. *The Civil Magistrates Power*, 89.
96. *The Simple Cobbler*, 10.
97. Norton, *The Heart of New England Rent*, 30.
98. Ibid., 4; also 38–43.
99. Petition reprinted in Hallowell, *Quaker Invasion*, 155.

SEPARATISM, MYSTICISM, BAPTISM, AND QUAKERISM: CRITICS OF MASSACHUSETTS ORTHODOXY AND THE ORIGINS OF RHODE ISLAND, 1630–1660

The two prominent banishments of the first decade, Williams and Hutchinson, prefigure in interesting ways the two later and more durable Dissenting movements that came to fruition during the 1650s and 1660s: the Baptists and Quakers. These "critics of Massachusetts orthodoxy" constituted two main camps, characterized by (in the case of the Baptists) an insistence on a pure church and (in the case of the Quakers) a reliance upon an inner spiritual principle or revelation.[100] All of these Dissenting groups or individuals can be seen as sorts of "perfectionists" dissatisfied with the compromises and halfway steps toward reformation that they saw in the Massachusetts polity.

Separatism, Baptism, and the Search for a Pure Church

Although the Massachusetts settlement's religious aims were not monolithic, they did require a unified public vision of godliness and the human responsibility for supporting each other in the fulfillment of God's commands. We have already seen that New England Puritans, though emphasizing individual responsibility for salvation, restricting church membership to visible saints (those who could provide a confession of faith and evidence of conversion),[101] and criticizing the moral laxity of English parishes, nevertheless identified congregation and township in the English way. The Puritan meetinghouse, both physically and figuratively, anchored the Puritan town, and restriction of the franchise to church members after 1631 cemented the close association of godliness and civic responsibility.[102] Like Puritans in England, those in Massachusetts held that congregations, not distant bishops, should exercise ecclesiastical discipline, and that individuals unable to furnish evidence of conversion should not be admitted to communion.

Williams's Separatism challenged the congregational project in precisely the same terms that congregationalists had taken issue with Anglicans in

---

100. These are general tendencies, not mutually exclusive or dichotomous categories, as will become more clear as I present them.

101. See Edmund S. Morgan, *Visible Saints* (Ithaca, N.Y., 1963).

102. See Harry S. Stout, *The New England Soul: Preaching and Religious Culture in Colonial New England* (New York, 1986), chap. 1, esp. 13–15.

England; namely, that a church based upon geographic, rather than spiritual, boundaries necessarily involved godly individuals in worship with the unregenerate, and that this was dangerous to the spiritual health of the saints.[103] Thus in the interest of godliness the monopoly of impure congregational churches had to be broken and the true saints, repenting of all former ungodly associations (e.g., Anglican Church membership), erect their own purified congregations. For Separatists, the congregation should be based not on geography but on election. In this sense, Williams rightly argued that New England Puritans agreed with Anglicans in upholding a national church.[104] Unfortunately for Williams, his Separatist commitments flew in the face of Winthrop's "Model of Christian Charity," which evoked the social covenant in which the settlers were to "be knit together as one man" to do the Lord's work (*WP*, 2:294). Had the Separatist project succeeded in Massachusetts, it would have represented, at the very least, an explosion in sheer numbers of congregations and, to the magistrates, a severe breach in the unity of the New England church.

The Baptist movement, although originally appearing in isolated instances of opposition to infant baptism,[105] coalesced late in the 1650s into a coherent position arguing against the increasingly lax standards for church membership (including, eventually, the Halfway Covenant adopted in 1662, which extended membership to church members' grandchildren). Now these increasingly lax standards did not appear overnight or by accident, but were themselves part of a conscious attempt to bridge the widening gap between church and people, between visible saints and the unregenerate. Indeed, one scholar has seen the efforts of the late 1630s–1660s as an effort to reintegrate authority and community in light of the *failure* of the Puritan "errand" as originally understood.[106] Critics, however, were not appeased: Baptist church polity was even more restrictive and exclusive than was the congregationalist. Like Separatists before them, they called upon congregationalist church leaders to

---

103. "The principle which gives coherence to the quarrels between Williams and the authorities is the determination of the separatist, in the interest of religious truth, to purify the church from all pollution. . . . The real sufferers from the doctrine of forced worship have always been the saints" (Alan Simpson, "How Democratic Was Roger Williams?" *WMQ* 13 [1956], 56, 57).

104. See Roger Williams, *Mr Cottons Letter Lately Printed, Examined, and Answered* (London, 1644), in *The Complete Writings of Roger Williams*, ed. Samuel L. Caldwell (New York, 1963), 1:326–27.

105. See, e.g., *Winthrop's Journal*, 1:270; 2:126, 177.

106. Seligman, *Innerworldly Individualism*, chaps. 4–5.

weed out unregenerate members even more vigorously than they already did. Despite Massachusetts churches' claim to the simplicity of the early church, Baptists argued, the continued baptism of infants incorporated a practice without sanction from Christ, one that allowed as members individuals who could provide no evidence of conversion.[107] As Carla Pestana describes the Baptist position, "The children of saints—whether infant or adult—had no place in the Baptist church until they experienced conversion themselves."[108] As Williams had argued twenty years previous, so Baptists argued in the 1650s and 1660s: the church must be kept pure, membership must be restricted to visible saints, and human "innovations" without clear scriptural warrant must be kept out. Anything less (or more) polluted the church.

Furthermore, at the heart of the political disputes raised by such issues as infant baptism and church membership lay the fact that Separatist (and later Baptist) congregations acknowledged no earthly authority but themselves in matters of church doctrine and discipline. Separatism admitted neither the authority of any other church over a gathered congregation of saints nor the authority of magistrates in church affairs. Although, as we have seen, Puritans saw church and state as distinct entities with different aims, they *did* allow magistrates to take action to suppress heresy and blasphemy, and to enforce the First Table. Williams's denial of this crucial (for virtually all seventeenth-century Christians, that is) aspect of governmental power thus struck at the very formation and legitimacy of the New England state as constituted. It also struck at the conventional seventeenth-century understanding of the legitimate function of government and provided early Rhode Islanders with an enormous challenge, that of creating civil order in a heavily religious culture while maintaining a nontheistic governmental sphere, a task at which Rhode Island (and, by implication for observing Massachusetts Puritans, Williams's ideas about church and state) did not always succeed.[109]

This insistence by Williams, and later the Baptists, on a pure church also leads to a radical dichotomization of the civil and spiritual realms, to strong claims about the separation of church and state. All of the critics of the New England Way affirmed, in one way or another, the radical distinction between

107. See Clarke, *Ill Newes*, 12–15, 36–37.
108. *Quakers and Baptists*, 69.
109. Williams himself admits the difficulty in creating and maintaining public order in a letter to Winthrop [before 25 August 1636], in *WP*, 3:296–98.

temporal and spiritual power that represented a legacy of the English Separatist and sectarian traditions, against the interweaving of the two that Puritanism (along with its Anglican critics) considered essential to the preservation of a godly community. Both Baptists and Separatists, for example, often cited the parable of tares and wheat in their arguments for toleration.[110] The impulse for separation of church and state in the interest of a pure church appears throughout Williams's and Clarke's analyses of Massachusetts' shortcoming and their own hopes for Rhode Island.

For Williams, political interference in church affairs necessarily corrupted the church: as he put it, "Christianity fell asleep in Constantine's bosom."[111] Williams posed a sharp dichotomy between spiritual and political power, conceptualizing the church as "like unto a corporation, society, or company of East India or Turkey merchants": only when the health of the whole state is threatened by the activities of one of these "companies" is the magistrate justified in intervening in their affairs.[112] Clarke framed the distinction in similar terms: "That one may be called an earthly, and outward administration, which suits the outward man . . . and is managed by an outward and visible sword of steel . . . which being diligently attended to tends to the peace, liberty, and prosperity of a civil state . . . [the other power and state of man is] heavenly and spiritual, it being that which suiteth with, and principally is exercised about the spiritual, or hidden part of man, to wit, his spirit, mind, and conscience."[113]

Williams argued that coercion was proper in civil affairs, whereas religious issues could be settled only by persuasion. The example of ancient Israel, in which political rulers possessed broad authority over the community's religious affairs, proved nothing, being only a typological fore-

110. For the wheat and tares, see Matthew 13:29. The parable is cited by Williams in *Bloudy Tenent*, chap. 24, and by Clarke in *Ill Newes*, 8.

111. *Bloudy Tenent*, 184; *The Bloudy Tenent Yet More Bloudy* (London, 1652), 72–73. The criticism of Christianity's alliance with the Roman Empire and the related critique of the church's assumption of temporal power was a long-standing one and is, of course, not unique to Williams. It stretches back through the long tradition of English anticlericalism, and indeed to the roots of the Reformation itself. See Luther's *Address to the Christian Nobility* (1520); also see Dante's critique of the supposed "Donation" of Constantine, in *De monarchia* (c. 1312–13), bk. 3, chap. 9–10, and *Inferno*, canto 19, lines 115–17.

112. *Bloudy Tenent*, 73. See also *Bloudy Tenent*, 224–25, and *Bloudy Tenent Yet More Bloudy*, 29.

113. *Ill Newes*, 6. The distinction between the earthly and the spiritual can be traced back to Romans 8:5–9.

shadowing of Christ's heavenly kingdom.[114] Williams put it most succinctly in his preface to *The Bloudy Tenent*, maintaining that "all civil states . . . are proved essentially civil, and therefore not judges, governors, or defenders of the spiritual or Christian state and worship" (3).

Mysticism and Immediate Revelation: Anne Hutchinson, Samuel Gorton, and the Quakers

Winthrop's journal entry for October 21, 1636, records the heresies advanced by Anne Hutchinson in her meetings with the women of Boston: that the Holy Spirit has "personal union" with the regenerate person, and that one's sanctification (the internal and behavioral transformation of a godly individual) provides no evidence whatsoever of one's justification (God's imputation of righteousness to believers).[115] The Hutchinsonians, then, effectively held that godly behavior (this includes following moral law, something they condemned as a "legal" rather than gospel) represented only a "covenant of works" and no sign of grace, providing no evidence of one's status as a saint. By condemning this basic element of Puritan theology as a mere "covenant of works," the Hutchinsonians privileged the inward spiritual experience over the "mere" outward practice of Massachusetts church polity. During the 1640s, Samuel Gorton and his followers echoed Hutchinson's earlier critique of Massachusetts ministers as under a covenant of works, criticizing Puritan doctrine as "bent only to maintain that outward form of worship which they had erected to themselves, tending only to the outward carriage of one man to another" and placing

114. On Williams's typological interpretation of Scripture more generally, see Perry Miller, "Roger Williams: An Essay in Interpretation," in *The Complete Writings of Roger Williams*, vol. 7 (New York, 1963), 5–25, and idem, *Roger Williams*.

115. *Winthrop's Journal*, 1:195. Puritans never considered works irrelevant to a godly life, but only wished to put them in their rightful place in the process of salvation, secondary to faith. The Puritan emphasis on faith, of course, represents a standard Protestant reaction against perceived Catholic abuses of the role good works could play in the process of salvation, a reaction that animated Luther's original critique.

Charles Cohen helpfully explicates the concepts of justification and sanctification: "Bound into a 'spiritual relation' with Christ by faith, [the saints] are justified—accounted righteous—for the Savior's sake. . . . [The] physical consequences [of justification] issue in sanctification, the lifelong process of restoring the faculties from the 'filthiness of sin, to the purity of God's image.' . . . Peace of conscience follows forgiveness of sin through justification, and sanctification manifests itself in the zeal to accomplish God's commands." See Cohen, *God's Caress: The Psychology of Puritan Religious Experience* (New York, 1986), 95, 102. For another helpful discussion, see Stoever, *"A Faire and Easie Way to Heaven,"* 63–77.

restrictions on truly godly individuals filled with the Holy Spirit.[116] These claims caused Massachusetts leaders to view Hutchinsonians and Gortonists, literally, as "Antinomians," individuals whose assertion of inner spirituality entailed a rejection of conventional laws of (individual, social, and political) morality. Scholars have variously viewed the Hutchinsonian controversy as "the first encounter of a Puritan commonwealth with its own radical offspring," a debate over preparation for salvation or the mortality of the soul, an extended argument about the realms of nature and grace, or an episode in the uneasy place of mysticism within the Puritan family.[117] Whichever of these we choose to highlight, the Hutchinsonian debates again show clearly the political implications of theological debates in a community such as Massachusetts Bay. Proclaiming Massachusetts practice as akin to "your ancestors the Papacy," Gortonists compared the whole idea of preparation for salvation (the idea that an individual could in any way effect God's salvation) to sex before the wedding day and referred to church ordinances as "man's inventions."[118]

116. Gorton, *Simplicities Defence Against Seven-Headed Policy* (London, 1646), in *Collections of the Rhode Island Historical Society* 2 (1835): 46.

117. For these various interpretations, see the following. On "radical" offspring, see Stoever, *"A Faire and Easie Way to Heaven,"* x, and Gura, *Glimpse of Sion's Glory,* chap. 9. T. H. Breen put the same sentiment a bit more tamely, calling the affair "a family quarrel" (*Character of the Good Ruler*, 37). Preparation for salvation is stressed by Perry Miller, "'Preparation for Salvation' in Seventeenth-Century New England," in *Nature's Nation* (Cambridge, Mass., 1967), and Norman Pettit, *The Heart Prepared: Grace and Conversion in Puritan Spiritual Life,* 2d ed. (Middletown, Conn., 1989). Pettit further distinguishes between an Antinomianism that rejects preparation on account of human helplessness and depravity (Cotton's) and one that rejects preparation because of divine illumination a la Hutchinson (chap. 5). Hutchinson is connected with the mortalist heresy by James Fulton Maclear, "Anne Hutchinson and the Mortalist Heresy," *NEQ* 54 (1981): 74–103. Nature and grace makes up the bulk of Stoever, *"A Faire and Easie Way to Heaven,"* chap. 1. For Puritanism and mysticism, see Maclear, "'The Heart of New England Rent': The Mystical Element in Early Puritan History," *Mississippi Valley Historical Review* 42 (1955–56): 621–52, and Marilyn Westerkamp, "Anne Hutchinson, Sectarian Mysticism, and the Puritan Order," *Church History* 59 (1990): 482–96.

Because of the important theological elements of the Hutchinsonian controversy, those interpretations of the debate failing to take theology into account tend to be the least convincing. See, for example, Anne Fairfax Withington and Jack Schwartz, "The Political Trial of Anne Hutchinson," *NEQ* 51 (1978): 226–40, who view the affair as wholly political, or Williams, *Divine Rebel,* and Koehler, "American Jezebels," both of which infuse the affair with twentieth-century feminism. Amanda Porterfield skillfully weaves together gender and religious considerations in her *Female Piety in New England: The Emergence of Religious Humanism* (New York, 1992), 95–106.

118. Gorton, *Simplicities Defense,* 64, 12; Winslow, *Hypocrisie Unmasked,* 5. Gorton also criticized infant baptism and swearing oaths (*Simplicities Defense,* 76, 84–85), illustrating that the two categories into which I have placed Massachusetts religious dissenters must be seen as suggestive, not exhaustive.

As the Puritan magistrates saw it, Hutchinson was as great a threat to the survival of their community as the Pequots or Narragansetts. Indeed, deteriorating relations with the natives formed the background of the Antinomian disputes. Hutchinson's sympathizers refused to serve in expeditions against the Pequots, further conflating theological disputes with suspect civil behavior.[119] The implications of her claims were clear to all concerned: a claim to personal divine revelation (by a woman, no less) coupled with a denial that any act (even the act of *faith* or public repentance) was necessarily connected to a godly lifestyle, was being brought to bear against the judgment of the community.[120] Hutchinson's theological claims about the disjuncture between sanctification and justification and the nature of the relationship between the Holy Spirit and the believer worried colonial magistrates far less than the (real or expected) social and political implications of Antinomianism.

In confronting the Antinomian disturbances, then, Massachusetts authorities saw individuals claiming immediate revelation from God, from which they taught that the overwhelming majority of society's political, religious, and social leaders were Antichrist and should be opposed with spiritual warfare. Wheelwright's language in his 1637 fast day sermon was striking and provocative: "We must all prepare for battle and come out against the enemies of the Lord . . . we must kill them with the word of the Lord."[121] Although he claimed to be speaking metaphorically, Wheelwright freely admitted that his words might "cause a combustion in the church and the commonwealth."[122] These immediate revelations were not subject to the review or discipline of any authority, ecclesiastical or political, and the Spirit-filled individual, as Massachusetts leaders understood the term, was a law unto him- or herself. Consequently, "the threat perceived by ministers and magistrates in these doctrines was of the dissolution of their own moral authority and, in essence, the breakdown of the moral bonds of community."[123]

119. Winthrop, *Short Story*, 25; see also Edmund S. Morgan, "The Case Against Anne Hutchinson," *NEQ* 10 (1937): 638.

120. Wheelwright had attempted to play down these implications of the Hutchinsonian theology: "Let us have a care to show ourselves all manner of good conversation . . . let us not give an occasion to those that are coming on, or manifestly opposite to the ways of grace, to suspect the way of grace, let us carry ourselves, that they may be ashamed to blame us . . . let us have a care that we give not occasion to others to say we are libertines or Antinomians, but Christians" ("Sermon," 174–75).

121. Ibid., 161, 166

122. Ibid., 169.

123. Seligman, *Innerworldly Individualism*, 84.

Antinomianism was connected in many minds to the radicalism and savagery of the Muenster commune, and Massachusetts Puritans vigorously asserted the authority of civil power and the churches' role in preserving general social peace. Hutchinson's radical distinction between justification and sanctification, furthermore, implicitly threw into question the issue of church membership, which formed the basis of political participation in the colony. Along with all of this, of course, went questions of gender, social hierarchies based on education (especially an educated ministry, a hallmark of Puritanism from its earliest days),[124] and the notion that the godly were bound to some ethical law or set of injunctions of Christian behavior.

Although fewer systematic writings have survived from the early Quaker missionaries in Massachusetts, it seems safe to say that Quaker theology similarly emphasized the importance of the Spirit-filled individual. The general tenor of Quaker thought emphasizes personal experience of revelation: as William Robinson wrote to the Massachusetts General Court before he was put to death in 1659, "The Word of the Lord came expressly to me," telling him to go preach in Boston.[125] In addition, Quakers took issue with church structure, ritual, and liturgy, as well as such basic Protestant doctrine as the Trinity; and self-consciously undermined conventional social deference to magistrates and social superiors by, for example, refusing to remove their hats in their presence.[126] With such an inward, spiritual focus, it is not surprising that Quakers emphasized the necessity of inner conviction and the inner cognizance of God's call to the individual as an argument against compulsion in matters of faith. As Daniel Goold put it, "Concerning religion, let everyone be fully persuaded in his own mind and worship according as God

124. Winthrop pointed this out most clearly, saying that "all this while there is no use of the ministry of the word nor of any clear call of God by his word, but the groundwork of her revelations is the immediate revelation of the spirit and not the ministry of the word" ("The Examination," in Hutchinson, *The History*, 1:387).

125. Robinson's paper reprinted in George Bishop, *New England Judged* (London, 1661), 95.

126. For Quaker denials of the Trinity, see Francis Howgill, *The Popish Inquisition Newly Erected in New England* (London, 1659), 53. On social deference, Howgill claims that New England magistrates punished Quakers because "they will not complement (like flattering courtiers . . .) and use flattering titles to men who are in unbelief, who seek respect and honor one of another (which is below)" (49). Quakers Christopher Holder, John Rous, and John Copeland were sentenced to have their ears cropped in 1658, and Massachusetts Governor Endecott was incensed by their insistence upon calling him by his given name rather than his title (Howgill, *The Popish Inquisition*, 22). More generally on Quakers and social deference, see Hugh Barbour and J. William Frost, *The Quakers in Puritan England* (New Haven, Conn., 1964), chap. 6.

shall persuade his own heart, and if any worship not God as they ought to do and yet liveth quietly and peaceably with their neighbors and countrymen . . . is it not safer for you to let them alone to receive their reward from him who said, I will render vengeance to mine enemies. . . . Let God alone be Lord of the conscience, and not man."[127]

Perfectionism, Church, and State

What these movements share is a tendency that I shall call "perfectionism."[128] Although an extreme version of such perfectionism apparently took place in Hugh Bewett's claim to be free from original sin,[129] I use the term to illustrate a more widespread phenomenon among religious dissidents in New England. Williams's perfectionism, for example, was directly related to his Separatism. The two "stumbling blocks" Cotton listed as responsible for Williams's separation from the Massachusetts Bay churches—that New England churches did not require specific repentance for members' previous Anglican fellowship, and that they did not insist on formal separation—illustrate Williams's dissatisfaction with the imperfections remaining in "reformed" Massachusetts churches. Williams, Cotton reported, objected that the Bay churches timidly "walk betwixt Christ and Antichrist" (*Letter*, 308). For Williams, imperfection or unrepented sins in any church member "polluted" the saints therein, and his Separatist perfectionism led him to denounce basic elements of the Massachusetts community as understood by its leadership. As Perry Miller puts it, Williams would countenance no moderation when issues of salvation were at stake: "He demanded the real thing or nothing at all."[130]

A deep disagreement with this perfectionism lies at the root of Cotton's rejoinder to Williams; as he puts it, Williams's obsession with church purity

127. Goold's letter of 1660 is reprinted in Hallowell, *Quaker Invasion*, 90. This emphasis on inner convincement and the inefficacy of force was also voiced by Clarke (*Ill Newes*, 6, 12), and James Cudworth, whose letter is also reprinted in Hallowell, *Quaker Invasion*, 165. For more on Quakerism, see Chapter 5.

128. I use the term "perfectionism" in a similar (though not identical) sense to McLoughlin (*Soul Liberty*, 107); and I expand on the term in my comparison of George Keith, Roger Williams, and Anne Hutchinson in Chapter 6. The term as McLoughlin uses it is more appropriate to Hutchinson than to these other two, but (as I explain in Chapter 6) I seek to relax the parameters of McLoughlin's definition to denote a more widespread phenomenon in colonial religious dissent.

129. *Winthrop's Journal*, 2:17.

130. Miller, *Roger Williams*, 28. See also Gaustad, *Liberty of Conscience*, chap. 2.

makes the church covenant a covenant of works all over again, a reinvention of "popery" as opposed to the Puritan emphasis on grace (*Reply*, 158–59). As in all religious debates, New England Puritans stressed their attempts to strike a middle ground between factious Separatism and conformity to Anglican (or later, Presbyterian) error. In the words of Timothy Hall, Massachusetts Puritans "were simply more interested in spiritual harmony than in Roger Williams's fantastic demands for exacting ecclesiastical purity. . . . For the sake of spiritual and civil unity the Puritans were ready to tolerate a fair amount of dirt on the robes of righteousness."[131] This was not timidity or "trimming," they claimed, but judicious faithfulness to the role of the church in an imperfect world. "It is not surgery, but butchery, to heal every sore in a member with no other medicine but abscission from the body," Cotton wrote (*Letter*, 309). Williams's exhortation to Winthrop to "abstract yourself with a holy violence from the dungheap of this earth"[132] was bound to fall on deaf ears. The project of Massachusetts was based upon the idea that although God demands the utmost striving of human beings toward godly life, perfection simply is not possible in a fallen world, and that insisting on such perfection (in church or state) to the exclusion of all else would lead to dire consequences for social solidarity and spiritual well-being. In the words of Winthrop's biographer, "Williams would not learn the lesson which Winthrop had taught himself so painfully before he left England, that there was no escape from the dung heap of this earth; and that those who sought one or thought they had found it acted with an unholy, not a holy, violence."[133]

By framing Separatism as the logical extension of Puritanism,[134] Williams raised the possibility that others within the Massachusetts community would do likewise in the future. The emergence of indigenous Baptist congregations during the 1660s shows that this threat was not an idle one. As we have seen, the Baptist opposition to infant baptism was grounded squarely in the desire for a pure church. Membership should be limited solely to those who could provide clear evidence of justification, a standard that by definition excludes infants. Of course, it goes without saying that a pure church could take no doctrinal order from a civil magistrate either, since as Williams put it, the

131. *Separating Church and State*, 24.
132. Williams to John Winthrop, 24 October 1636? in *Correspondence*, 1:68.
133. Morgan, *Puritan Dilemma*, 130. See also David S. Lovejoy, "Roger Williams and George Fox: The Arrogance of Self-Righteousness," *NEQ* 66 (1993): 199–225.
134. *Mr Cottons letter*, 422ff. See also Hall, *Separating Church and State*, 22.

collaboration between Roman emperors and the Christian church had spelled the end of true Christianity.

It also seems clear that Anne Hutchinson represented a brand of perfectionism in the religious life of the colony, akin to yet far surpassing that proposed by Roger Williams. Recall that the Separatist claims made by Williams questioned the purity of the Massachusetts *congregations*; the Separatist solution, like the congregational one, involved recongregating, rebaptizing, and remaking the covenant, approximating as nearly as possible the visible and invisible churches.[135] Of course, the Separatist (and later Baptist) project went beyond the orthodox Puritan one in its insistence on an exclusive, pure church: the Puritan impulse was directed against both the inclusive Anglican model and the exclusive Separatist extreme. In their general emphasis on congregations as explicitly covenanted gatherings of saints, though, both Puritans and Separatists agreed: thus the religious radicalism of Williams's Separatism was tempered by a highly social and communal understanding of the church experience, and the essential role of the congregation in that experience.

Hutchinson's teaching, however (although she did not, apparently, advance this claim), potentially rid the believer of the necessity of belonging to *any* congregation, in effect denying the necessity of a church at all, and removing the believer from the sphere of any disciplinary ecclesiastical framework whatsoever.[136] In essence, as David D. Hall puts it, "the performance of moral duties was unrelated to divine mercy."[137] The believer was (potentially) his or her own congregation, and that individual's actions were difficult to reproach, since inward revelation justified all actions. This was a form of separation far more radical, far more individualistic, than anything proposed by Roger Williams or those who objected to infant baptism. Perfectionism, the insistence on a pure church, and the stress on immediate revelation eroded the close relationship between church and commonwealth that Massachusetts Puritans had worked so hard to create, and which they saw as integral to the success of their godly community. Still, the Hutchinsonians did not see themselves as rampant individualists. In their rejection of "traditional" social ties in favor of charismatic,

135. The visible and invisible churches are elaborated in Morgan, *Visible Saints*.
136. See Charles E. Park, "Puritans and Quakers," *NEQ* 27 (1954): 53–74, esp. 55–58. Although the essay addresses the Puritan response to Quakerism and not the Hutchinsonians, it notes, significantly, that the major division between Puritans and some of the radical sects in New England involved the necessity of the church itself.
137. *Antinomian Controversy*, x.

emotional ones based on grace, the Hutchinsonians resembled both the early Puritans in England and their Separatist and Baptist critics in New England. Although the protest against Puritan orthodoxy in Massachusetts made clear the "existence and, indeed, the growth of a populace beyond the confines of the church," in each case such theological protests aimed not at a social or political individualism but at the making of new social and communal bonds, offering "an alternative model of community to that of the covenanted church."[138]

Liberty of Conscience in Practice: The Origins of Rhode Island

After his expulsion from Massachusetts, Roger Williams played an important role in the founding of Rhode Island. Although we cannot infer a commitment to liberty of conscience on the basis of Williams's experiences in the Bay colony, it seems clear that such a commitment motivated his actions in founding Rhode Island. It also seems clear that this commitment caused immense difficulties in the early years of that colony. Williams described his aims in founding Providence, "I desired it might be a shelter for persons distressed of conscience," and the town's arbitrators reported in 1640 that "we agree, as formerly hath been the liberties of this town, so still, to hold forth liberty of conscience."[139] The General Court of Newport "ordered . . . that none be accounted as delinquent doctrine, provided it not be directly repugnant to the government or laws established."[140] Under the colony's first charter in 1647, this liberty was enshrined as fundamental law in the colony: "[Laws shall be promulgated] to the end that we may each to other (notwithstanding our different consciences, touching the truth as it is in Jesus, whereof, upon the point we all make mention), as good and hopeful assurance as we are able, touching each man's peaceable and quiet enjoyment of his lawful right and liberty."[141]

Without an established church as a touchstone for social solidarity and moral influence, Williams and his cohabitants were navigating in uncharted

---

138. Seligman, *Innerworldly Individualism*, 76, 95. On the connection between theological individualism and tightly bound communities see also Walzer, *Revolution of the Saints*, 12ff., and Michael Zuckerman, "The Fabrication of Identity in Early America," in *An Almost Chosen People: Oblique Biographies in the American Grain* (Berkeley and Los Angeles, 1993), chap. 1, esp. pp. 43–47, 50–54.

139. John Russell Bartlett, ed., *Records of the Colony of Rhode Island and Providence Plantations, in New England* (Providence, 1856–64), 1:22, 28.

140. Ibid., 113; reaffirmed 1641 (1:118).

141. Ibid., 156–57.

waters. Massachusetts Puritans, for their part, saw in the early history of Rhode Island proof positive of their assessment of Williams's views. Theodore Dwight Bozeman notes the chronic problem of disorder in early Rhode Island, and the assumption of the time that religious and political radicalism went hand in hand:

> It was largely through efforts to establish an effective mastery over . . . civil disorder that Rhode Islanders hoped to justify their experiment in religious toleration. . . . The task of Rhode Island was the almost impossible one of eclipsing the ready memory of Munster by providing a . . . demonstration that violent chaos was not the necessary result of a departure from the established model of religious uniformity.[142]

Massachusetts polemicists were not the only ones who pointed out that dissension and faction characterized Rhode Island's civic life: Williams himself bewailed these divisions and the ammunition they gave to opponents of religious liberty elsewhere. Almost immediately, the difficulty of abandoning a centuries-old practice that (albeit imperfectly) had equated church membership with civic duty and ethical behavior became apparent. Barely six months after Williams's flight from Massachusetts, he wrote to Winthrop asking advice about dealing with some contentious young men in Providence. "We have no patent," he wrote, "nor doth the face of magistracy suit with our present condition."[143] Dissension was endemic during the settlement's early years. On another occasion, Williams complained of townsmen "who openly in town meeting more than once professed to hope for and long for a better government than the country hath yet," and who had apparently gone so far as to threaten an appeal to England.[144] During the 1640s Samuel Gorton briefly settled in Providence. Proclaiming, in Phillip Gura's words, "the all-sufficiency of the Holy Spirit in the true Christian," Gorton and his brand of Antimonianism split the town and caused some inhabitants to petition Massachusetts for aid.[145] "Almost all suck in his poison," Williams wrote

---

142. "Religious Liberty and the Problem of Order in Early Rhode Island," *NEQ* 45 (1972): 45, 57; also see Hall, *Separating Church and State*, 80–81.

143. Williams, *Correspondence*, 1:53.

144. Ibid., 154.

145. "The Radical Ideology of Samuel Gorton: New Light on the Relation of English to American Puritanism," *WMQ* 36 (1979): 86. The appeal to Massachusetts is reprinted as an appendix to Gorton's *Simplicities Defense*.

Winthrop.[146] As the 1640s closed, Williams told John Winthrop, Jr., that once again "our colony is in civil dissension."[147] Disputes among towns were widespread as well, and Williams repeatedly condemned these divisions, news of which was so widespread that even Sir Henry Vane in England wrote to admonish Rhode Islanders.[148] One scholar has described Rhode Island during the 1640s as facing "an acute identity crisis, which in turn entailed a fundamental crisis of authority."[149]

In fact, liberty of conscience itself was implicated in political debate. In 1638 Joshua Verin was denied the franchise in Providence for "breach of a covenant for restraining liberty of conscience."[150] Although we know very little about this incident, Verin's offense appears to have involved preventing his wife from attending worship services, actions which he apparently saw as compatible with the biblical subjection of wives to husbands and the responsibility of heads of households for the spiritual well-being of those entrusted to their care. As Winthrop observed, Verin *himself* had acted out of conscience (in seeking to prevent his wife from falling into theological error).[151] Such a dispute illustrates how difficult it often was for Rhode Islanders to find common ground upon which to base their civil deliberations.

CONCLUSION

We should see in New England the endeavor to reconstruct and recapture a communitarian whole, a reformed church in a Christian society, that had become corrupted by layers of human tradition. What differentiated New England Puritans from their English brethren as the seventeenth century progressed is the former's reflection of Jacobean and early Caroline emphases on uniformity and a national religious structure, elements of Puritanism which became ever more hotly contested in the 1640s in England, and which

146. Williams, *Correspondence*, 1:215.
147. Ibid., 26.
148. *Records of the Colony of Rhode Island*, 1:285–86.
149. G. B. Warden, "The Rhode Island Civil Code of 1647," in Hall, Murrin, and Tate, *Saints and Revolutionaries*, 140.
150. *Records of the Colony of Rhode Island*, 1:16.
151. *Winthrop's Journal*, 1:286–87. For his part, Roger Williams called Verin a "boisterous and desperate" wifebeater: see his letter to John Winthrop, 22 May 1638, in *Correspondence*, 1:156.

many jettisoned entirely during that decade. The importance of this national religious structure was not lost on their critics. Roger Williams noted the close association between his banishment from the colony and his religious dissent as proof "that the commonweal and church is yet but one" (*Mr Cottons Letter*, 377). Samuel Gorton united the critique of a national church with the earlier-mentioned Puritan aversion to human innovation, saying that "the spirituality of your churches is the civility of your commonwealth, and the civility of your commonwealth is the spirituality of your churches, the wisdom of men being the whole accomplishment of them both."[152] Those who were unsuccessful in achieving their religious agendas in Massachusetts Bay in many ways foreshadowed the course of English religious politics, and such figures as Williams, Cotton, Hutchinson, and Gorton epitomized the bitter strife that intensified during the Civil War years and into Cromwell's reign.

The differences that appeared between English and New England Puritans in the 1640s derive their bitterness, in part, from these shared understandings of and commitments to Reformation principles. The 1630s represent "a decade of challenge and trial, overturning settled practices and assumptions and forcing fissures between apparently like-minded men on issues of ceremonial conformity and emigration. . . . The harshest words were reserved for the 1640s: this decade saw the godly scattered across the face of the world, speaking different languages."[153]

When we combine the Puritan understanding of the "distinct and due administrations" of church and state with Cotton's distinction between a rightly informed, erroneous conscience and errors held "with a boisterous and arrogant spirit, to the disturbance of the civil peace," we begin to see the outlines of the New England Way, which in effect mirrored the Reformation view of the godly ruler and his responsibilities.[154] They considered it no accident that neighboring Rhode Island, having done away with the close and mutually supportive relationship between church and state, was afflicted with frequent eruptions of civil strife and political chaos.

152. *Simplicities Defence*, 62; also reprinted in Winslow, *Hypocrisie Unmasked*, 10.
153. Webster, *Godly Clergy*, 286.
154. *Platform of Church Discipline*, 65; Cotton, *The Controversie*, 8. For the Reformation view, see Quentin Skinner, *The Foundations of Modern Political Thought* (New York, 1978), vol. 2, chap. 1. Luther and the Puritans shared an Augustinian perspective (Miller, *New England Mind*, chap. 1), reinforcing the impact of Romans 13 and the strict doctrine of nonresistance to civil authority.

The first thirty years of the Massachusetts Bay Colony illustrates *a* pathway of Puritanism. But others sharing many theological positions with Massachusetts Puritans proposed *other* paths.[155] Religious dissent in early Massachusetts encountered a number of obstacles. Subtle, coherent antitolerationist arguments drew on the common background of Puritan theology and widespread views about the role of the church in society. As the 1640s and 1650s progressed, Massachusetts Puritans explicitly defined their "New England Way" in opposition to the rising tide of toleration under Cromwell's regime in England, holding firm against Baptist criticisms on the issue of church membership as well as the Quaker "invasion" from neighboring Rhode Island, while at the same time seeking to rearticulate the bases of communal meaning that such dissent had threatened.[156] For Massachusetts Puritans, there was simply no way to separate theology from the community's social and political organization, and claims to strident, public dissent from established religious practice undermined the very bonds of society. In any community, such dissent would have had a difficult time succeeding. In one struggling to survive in a forbidding physical and cultural environment, perched on the edge of a continent three thousand miles from the mother country, it had almost no chance. Religious freedom in Massachusetts did not begin to emerge until the 1660s, and it did so as a result not of the efforts of courageous Dissenters like Williams or Hutchinson or the "success" of theories of toleration, but rather as a result of political changes in England and popular uneasiness about the harsh penalties exacted on Quakers.[157]

Eventually, of course, toleration came to Massachusetts Bay. The Quaker missionaries of the 1650s and the Baptist congregations of the 1660s represent externally and internally originated threats to the orthodoxy created in

155. I do not mean to imply that all these groups were, in some sense, Puritans or hyper-Puritans, and I wholeheartedly agree with the increasing scholarly reluctance to characterize Quakers as such (see Melvin B. Endy, Jr., "Puritanism, Spiritualism, and Quakerism: An Historiographical Essay," in *The World of William Penn*, ed. Richard S. Dunn and Mary Maples Dunn [Philadelphia, 1986]). My point is that most of these groups did see themselves as, in some sense, "true Protestants," or at least truer than their Massachusetts interlocutors.

156. See Seligman, *Innerworldly Individualism*, chaps. 4–5; on the symbiotic relationship between community and deviance generally, and New England in particular, see Kai T. Erikson, *Wayward Puritans: A Study in the Sociology of Deviance* (New York, 1966).

157. Quakers survived brutal persecution in Massachusetts only by the grace of King Charles II early in the 1660s, and Baptists benefited from popular revulsion at this brutality as well as their theological similarities with orthodox Puritans. These developments are documented in Pestana, *Quakers and Baptists.*

the colony's first several decades. The dynamics of New England shifted considerably with the entrenchment of Rhode Island to the south as well as the ever fluid political situation in England.[158] But the relationship between the eventual success of religious dissent in Massachusetts and the earlier episodes involving Williams and Hutchinson, for example, remains highly ambiguous.

In dealing with Roger Williams and Anne Hutchinson, then, Massachusetts Puritans did not see themselves as opposing "further reformation" as Williams put it, or the election proclaimed by the Antinomians, or any form of toleration understood as the freedom of Christian believers to pursue God's ordinances. They saw themselves as opposing persistent, public, divisive, erroneous doctrines that undermined the settlement's foundations, set the people against each other, and distracted the community from its primary purpose of living out a godly life. Conscience, rightly informed, presented no problematic social consequences. Variant opinions held discreetly or concerned with (doctrinal or liturgical) matters of lesser import, also deserved toleration. However, vocal and disruptive dissent on fundamentals chipped away at the holy awe necessary for the fulfillment of covenantal obligations and thus directly threatened the state the Puritans were building. In the magistrates' view, Williams attacked the legality and legitimacy of the settlement itself. Hutchinson divided families, churches, and magistrates against each other on the basis of unchallengeable immediate revelation. The rise of toleration among the English Puritans just showed, to Puritans in New England, how deep the corruption ran in the Old World. Yet of course their own communities were hardly immune from such notions: faced with the "continual growth of alternative loci of membership and authority among sectarian and protesting groups, such as Baptists and Quakers," Massachusetts Puritans sought continually to rearticulate and reconceive their "fundamental tenets of collective meaning and purpose."[159] As we shall see, the tolerationist and

---

158. On these issues, see H. Frank Way, "The Problem of Toleration in New Israel: Religious Communalism in Seventeenth-Century Massachusetts," in Laursen and Nederman, *Beyond the Persecuting Society*, 268–72. Way's attempt to substantiate the growth of toleration in Massachusetts by quantifying the legislative activity of the General Court between 1628 and 1686 is less helpful, I think, than his nuanced discussion of contextual changes in and around Massachusetts that allowed toleration to gain a foothold.

159. Seligman, *Innerworldly Individualism*, 101.

Dissenting influences that bedeviled Massachusetts Puritans were part of a broader context of Anglo-American religio-political agitation, a series of struggles that would prove vital in the difficult establishment of religious toleration in seventeenth-century thought and practice on *both* sides of the Atlantic.[160]

160. This comparative context is articulated, if in somewhat overly ambitious fashion, in Phillips, *Cousins' Wars*.

3

THE ENGLISH CIVIL WAR,
COMMONWEALTH, AND PROTECTORATE

Unintentional, Unintended Toleration

Carnal and profane men desire nothing more than that they may not be compelled to any religious duty, but permitted to do what seem good in their own eyes. . . . [L]iberty of heresy and schism is no part of the liberty of conscience which Christ hath purchased to us at so dear a rate.

—George Gillespie,
Wholesome Severity Reconciled with Christian Liberty

So long as I must not act, according to the freedom of my own spirit and power within me, but must be guided by others without me, and punished for such actions. . . . I am then in bondage, and my eyes are put out.

—Gerrard Winstanley, *Fire in the Bush*

Unlike the relatively successful resistance to toleration in colonial Massachusetts, the Puritans of mid-seventeenth-century England were obliged to forge a different relationship between Puritanism and religious freedom. In Massachusetts, a unified conception of the requirements of ordered society and the dangerous social and political consequences of toleration survived well into the settlement's third decade, in reaction to the dissent that threatened to undermine the community's sense of divine mission. In England, divisions between congregationalists and Presbyterians as well as disputes between

Puritans and more radical sectarians led to a much more contested political battle, and a very different outcome, regarding toleration. We understand the dynamics of Puritanism's development on both sides of the Atlantic more richly when we consider the differing courses of arguments concerning dissent and toleration in England and America.

There are two conventional views of the English Civil War, Commonwealth, and Protectorate. The first asserts that England during the 1640s and 1650s provides one of the first and most significant examples of the political acceptance and success of tolerationist arguments.[1] These years set the stage for later developments in England (culminating in the Toleration Act of 1689), as well as liberal democratic theory and practice more generally (Rawls, *PL*, xxiv). The successful (if relatively short-lived) achievement of religious toleration, a bedrock value of liberal theory, makes the 1640s and 1650s stand out as a rich source of tolerationist arguments and a case example of the triumph of early liberal ideas.

The second view is a corollary of the first. One of the major factors contributing to this tolerationist victory, it is claimed, was the increasing prominence of epistemological skepticism among many seventeenth-century thinkers, which undermined ecclesiastical and other forms of authority. Skepticism purportedly fosters toleration in the following way: since we cannot be certain regarding our claims about truth, we are never justified in imposing our (possibly mistaken) notions on others.[2] This argument would later appear

---

1. The literature on this subject is extensive. Such a claim is often connected to a "Whig" view of history, to which many would claim that historians and political theorists no longer subscribe. Still, the underlying assumptions of such an approach remain strong. See, for example, Adeney, "Toleration," 12:363–64; Jordan, *Development of Religious Toleration in England*: Kamen, *Rise of Toleration*; and Phillips Brooks, *Tolerance: Two Lectures* (New York, 1887), 39ff. See also the introduction to A.S.P. Woodhouse, ed., *Puritanism and Liberty* (Chicago, 1950), [11–100]; Charles Blitzer, *An Immortal Commonwealth: The Political Thought of James Harrington* (New Haven, Conn., 1960), xi; Christopher Hill, *God's Englishman: Oliver Cromwell and the English Revolution* (New York, 1970), 13–14; idem, *Society and Puritanism in the Pre-Revolutionary England*, 2d ed. (New York, 1967), esp. chap. 14; F. D. Dow, *Radicalism in the English Revolution* (New York, 1985), 73; Gerald R. Cragg, *Freedom and Authority: A Study of English Thought in the Early Seventeenth Century* (Philadelphia, 1975); Joseph Frank, *The Levellers: A History of the Writings of Three Seventeenth-Century Social Democrats, John Lilburne, Richard Overton, William Walwyn* (Cambridge, Mass., 1955), chap. 1; and Ernest Barker, "The Achievement of Oliver Cromwell," in *Cromwell: A Profile*, ed. Ivan Roots (London, 1973), 13.

2. The sources on this claim often relate emerging science to tolerationist commitments: see Cragg, *Freedom and Authority*, chaps. 2, 9. Christopher Hill claims that "conservatives were frightened by the skeptical implications of the new scientific method, its refusal to accept traditional authority, its readiness to test everything by reason and experiment." See Hill, *The Century of*

in John Locke's *Letter Concerning Toleration*, not to mention John Stuart Mill's nineteenth-century call for broader tolerance of social nonconformity and individualism. As Mill put it in *On Liberty*: "All silencing of discussion is an assumption of infallibility."[3]

I argue that the first of these two conventional views of mid-seventeenth-century England is largely wrong, and the second, though suggestive, needs to be severely qualified. With regard to the first, I argue that tolerationist arguments did not "win" in any popular or intellectual sense during the 1640s or 1650s. None of the parties who instigated the rebellion against Charles I had any intention of tolerating religious dissent for its own sake, nor did they articulate general theories of religious liberty. In an atmosphere of lapsed censorship, tolerationist claims were pressed with increasing vehemence as the 1640s progressed. The breakdown of royal authority, however, and the climate that allowed such claims to be made, also strengthened the rhetorical and political position of antitolerationists, who were concerned about the threat of anarchy, licentiousness, and the collapse of social order. As in first-generation Massachusetts, claims for toleration in England encountered subtle, coherent arguments opposing such freedom and had to address fears of political radicalism often associated (for good reason) with religious dissent. The victory of the New Model Army, not the noble nature of tolerationist ideas or the mean-spirited obstinacy of their opponents, ensured the "success" of tolerationist arguments. The army's assault on Parliament in 1648 cleared the way for the imposed religious liberty of the Cromwell regime of the 1650s. There may be a lesson about religious freedom to be gleaned from these years, but it has more to do with the possibilities of enlightened sovereignty and military rule than the slow, steady march of liberal ideas.

What about the second view, regarding skepticism and toleration? Here the link seems, at first, more credible. The proto-Millian argument was used by a number of thinkers during the 1640s.[4] Conversely, attacks on *toleration*

Revolution, 1603–1714, 2d ed. (New York, 1980), 79; also see Hill, *The World Turned Upside Down: Radical Ideas During the English Revolution* (New York, 1972), 89–90, chap. 14.

On early modern skepticism and toleration, see the essays collected in Levine, *Early Modern Skepticism*. But Richard Tuck, in "Scepticism and Toleration in the Seventeenth Century," in Mendus, *Justifying Toleration*, 21–36, challenges too ready a connection between skepticism and toleration.

3. On Liberty, ed. Elizabeth Rapaport (1859; Indianapolis, 1978), 17.

4. See, e.g., Jeremy Taylor, *Theologike Eklektike; or, A Discourse on the Liberty of Prophesying* (London, 1647), chaps. 3–9, and the Large Petition of the Levellers, which argues that none should be molested on account of conscience "by judges that are not infallible but may be mistaken as well as other men in their judgments" (in Woodhouse, *Puritanism and Liberty*, 321).

often took the form of attacks on skepticism as disguised unbelief or "trimming."[5] However, the example of such thinkers as Thomas Hobbes and the more general influence of Erastianism[6] in English politics should give pause to those who would make the skepticism/toleration connection too readily. The skeptical tolerationist, we must remember, advances an argument consisting of two statements: (1) we know Truth only partially, and incompletely; therefore (2) we should tolerate. One might plausibly (as, for example, Hobbes did) accept the first premise and deny the consequence. Alternately, one might adopt the tolerationist platform *independently* of any skeptical epistemology, as Roger Williams did both in England and in Rhode Island.[7] In other words, given the understanding of human nature professed by Hobbes (and many others), the implications of extensive individual liberty, and the experience of England's Civil War, toleration did not necessarily follow from skepticism.

The 1640s were, undeniably, a period of intense ferment in the area of religious dissent, toleration, and debate over church government. My claim that such ideas did not "win" does not detract from their importance in the least. As we shall see, tolerationist ideas, if not popular among the Parliamentary opposition or in the kingdom at large, did prevail among the individuals who had been victorious on the battlefield, and thus were highly politically significant during the Civil War years. This military success became part of the ideological background against which future toleration debates took place. Attention to this ideological background, to the actors, events, and ideas of the decade, will illuminate my claim that the army and its *overthrow* of representative government was responsible for the religious liberty of the late 1640s and 1650s, and that toleration was actually *opposed* by those who instigated the Civil War.

5. The great example here is Samuel Rutherford's *A Free Disputation Concerning Pretended Liberty of Conscience* (London, 1649), 32–38.

6. Erastianism is the theory that power over ecclesiastical affairs is vested solely in the civil sovereign. Erastus's original critique concerned the power of excommunication and whether clergy might exercise such a power independently of the civil magistrate. In its more general historical (and polemical) usage, "Erastianism" denotes an aggrandizement of civil at the expense of ecclesiastical authority. For helpful discussions, see Johann P. Sommerville, *Thomas Hobbes: Political Ideas in Historical Context* (New York, 1992), 127–34; idem, *Politics and Ideology*, 203–8, on the English theory of royal supremacy; and Mark Goldie, "The Reception of Hobbes," in J. H. Burns and Mark Goldie, eds., *The Cambridge History of Political Thought, 1450–1700* (Cambridge, 1991), 610–15.

7. Williams typifies what I call "intolerant tolerationism": see my "Tolerance, Toleration, and the Liberal Tradition," 610–15.

THE CONFLICTS OF THE 1640S: PRIMARY ACTORS AND ISSUES

Background: Religious Grievances and the English Civil War

Without entering into an extensive debate on the causes of the English Civil War, I briefly elaborate in this section the main religious issues that led up to the conflict between Charles I and Parliament.[8] Doing so will highlight my claim that toleration *per se* played little or no role in the tension that led to the outbreak of armed conflict. Those opposing Charles and Archbishop of Canterbury William Laud did not see themselves as "radical"; and in a sense, the original aims of the English Civil War were conservative through and through. Puritans and Parliamentarians sought to recover England's Calvinist heritage and return Parliament to a meaningful role in the country's governance after Charles's eleven-year personal rule (his refusal to call a Parliament between 1629 and 1640). As Robert Ashton has put it, "Conservation and tradition . . . is the keynote of the attitude of most of the principal opponents of royal policies in the 1630s and 1640s."[9] Both sides in the Civil War saw themselves as upholding the established faith and protecting English orthodoxy from innovation. Indeed, according to John Morrill, "those who denounced 'Arminianism' did so for impeccably conservative reasons: to protect the English church from innovation and subversion."[10]

Toleration and liberty of conscience played no role in the Parliamentary or Puritan opposition to Charles and Laud, nor was it proclaimed as a principle

8. These religious grievances have been well articulated elsewhere by John Morrill. See "The Religious Context of the English Civil War," *Transactions of the Royal Historical Society,* ser. 5, no. 34 (1984): 155–78; "The Attack on the Church of England in the Long Parliament, 1640–1642," in *History, Society and the Churches: Essays in Honour of Owen Chadwick,* ed. Derek Beales and Geoffrey Best (Cambridge, 1985), 105–24; and "The Church in England, 1642–9," in *Reactions to the English Civil War 1642–1649,* ed. Morrill (London, 1982), 89–114.

9. Robert Ashton, *The English Civil War: Conservation and Revolution, 1603–1649,* 2d ed. (London, 1989), 17; see also chap. 6. For David Underdown, the Parliamentary revolutionaries of 1642 were "moderate reformers in both church and state," while Austin Woolrych points out that "most of them wanted no more than a moderate reformation within the traditional framework of episcopacy and a Book of Common Prayer." See Underdown, *Pride's Purge: Politics in the Puritan Revolution* (Oxford, 1971), 23, and Woolrych, "Oliver Cromwell and the Rule of the Saints," in *Cromwell: A Profile,* ed. Ivan Roots (London, 1973), 51. Even after Pride's Purge, it remains unclear how "radical" Parliament really was: although the Rump Parliament left behind after the Purge authorized a regicide, Woolrych argues that they "were a far from revolutionary body of men" (*Commonwealth to Protectorate* [Oxford, 1982], 5).

10. Morrill, "Attack on the Church of England," 106–7.

by any of the major parties during the 1630s and early 1640s.[11] Although tithes, for example, had long been unpopular with Separatists and sectarians (who rejected a national church altogether) and would continue to serve as a lightning rod for critics of the Anglican establishment, a broad consensus among English elites supported the continuance of a publicly supported ministry.[12] If we often hear the terms "reformation and liberty" used to describe Parliamentary aims during the 1640s, we should remember that the preponderance of Parliamentary efforts were directed at the former, even if in later years the second purpose seemed briefly to overshadow the first.[13] Although Jacobean Baptists had called for disestablishment, that was not a dominant, or even a significant minority, position.[14] English elites opposed toleration for a number of reasons: it undermined the unity they held to be part and parcel of Christianity; it threatened the institution of a unified church, which they saw as fostering nascent English nationalism and deemed necessary for a united society; and it weakened religious orthodoxy, which they considered essential to ties of obligation and contract. Among influential elements of the Parliamentary coalition, as Conrad Russell puts it, "The ultimate fear was of a society of unfettered consumer choice in religion."[15]

11.   As I noted in Chapter 2, toleration did occasionally arise in Jacobean church debates, but the primary aim of those raising it involved replacing error with truth. Jacobean Puritans often argued that they should not be ejected from their ministries. Such claims rested on the biblical justification for their positions, not on a theory about inherent rights to dissent. See, for example, William Stoughton's *Assertion for True and Christian Church-Policy* (1604; London, 1642), and the works of Henry Jacob listed in the bibliography. See also Miller, *Orthodoxy in Massachusetts*, 279–84.

12.   See Margaret James, "The Political Implications of the Tithes Controversy in the English Revolution, 1640–1660," *History* 26 (1941): 1–18.

13.   William Haller, *Liberty and Reformation in the Puritan Revolution* (New York, 1955); Arthur E. Barker, *Milton and the Puritan Dilemma* (Toronto, 1942). Of course many critics saw a *rapprochement* with Rome and vigorous enforcement of Anglican uniformity as threatening English *liberty* as well. See, e.g., John Goodwin, *Anti-Cavalierism* (London, 1642), which claimed that cavaliers were ready "to fall upon us, and our lives and liberties, both spiritual and civil, upon our estates, our gospel and religion" (3). This work is reprinted in William Haller, ed., *Tracts on Liberty in the Puritan Revolution*, 3 vols. (New York, 1934), 2:217–69.

14.   "Until the beginning of the English Civil War, few voices called for separatism as a workable principle": see Eldon J. Eisenach, "Hobbes on Church, State, and Religion," *History of Political Thought* 3, no. 2 (1982): 231. For the earlier (Jacobean) Baptists, see *Persecution for Religion Judged and Condemned* (London, 1615); *A Most Humble Supplication of Many of the King's Majesty's Loyal Subjects* (London, 1620); and Leonard Busher, *Religion's Peace, or a Plea for Liberty of Conscience* (London, 1614). Of course, more radical religious dissent stretched back to the English Reformation and further, to the Lollards in the fourteenth century. I am speaking here of views broadly influential among English elites.

15.   *The Causes of the English Civil War* (Oxford, 1990), 70. For a comprehensive overview of early modern arguments against toleration, see Russell, "Arguments for Religious Unity in England."

The religious disputes between Charles and Parliament can be summarized in the term "church reform."[16] During the early 1640s, those opposing the Laudian church, with few exceptions, desired a unified, comprehensive, Calvinist national church duly authorized by Parliament; that is, a more fully reformed version of what they already had, as opposed to the "popish" and autocratic church under Charles and Laud or the Separatist tendencies that (in their minds) threatened spiritual chaos. The broad rubric of "church reform" encompasses several commitments, each vital to understanding the broader context of the Civil War.

First, church reform implied a reform in *theology*. Eradicating "popish" Arminian error from the English church represented one of the primary aims of those opposing royal religious policy, since Arminianism suggested a movement away from the orthodox Calvinist theology that had historically been the English church's mainstay.[17] Recall from Chapter 2 that many prominent New England divines had left England because they opposed the increasing prevalence of Arminianism under Laud, and the persecution and ejections of nonconforming ministers that went along with it. A broad swath of English Puritanism sought, quite simply, a return of the national church to its Calvinist roots.

16. Of course, in seventeenth-century England, social, religious, and political commitments intermingled, since where the civil government maintains an established church, church reform necessarily carries broad social and political implications. Indeed, considering the tradition of apocalyptic thinking in England, reform of the church held potentially eschatological and cosmological significance. See Paul Christianson, *Reformers and Babylon: English Apocalyptic Visions from the Reformation to the Eve of the Civil War* (Toronto, 1978). Still, these religious dissidents and opposition political figures clearly did not intend the toleration of heterodox opinions when they initiated the Civil War.

17. My discussion of Arminianism largely follows that of Nicholas Tyacke, in his *Anti-Calvinists: The Rise of English Arminianism 1590–1640* (New York, 1986). Tyacke uses the term to denote a coherent, spreading body of thought that reacted against the dogmatism of the Reformation, was philosophically skeptical of Calvinism, and defended ecclesiastical hierarchy against Calvinist egalitarianism (244–45). During the reign of Charles I, Arminianism came to be associated with the monarchy, while Parliament remained heavily influenced by the English Calvinist tradition.

For a critique of Tyacke, see Peter White, "The *Via Media* in the Early Stuart Church," in *The Early Stuart Church, 1603–1642*, ed. Kenneth Fincham (Stanford, Calif., 1993), 211–30. William Lamont has argued that Arminianism only really became an issue in English political debate during the 1650s. See his "Arminianism: The Controversy That Never Was," in *Political Discourse in Early Modern Britain*, ed. Nicholas Phillipson and Quentin Skinner (Cambridge, 1993).

Anti-Arminianism served as a broad rubric that could include anything from opposition to "popery" and "idolatry" or elaborate ceremonialism to generic anti-episcopal sentiment.[18] Such fears of "popery" were, in John Morrill's words, "widely believed and not wholly foolish."[19] Theoretically, of course, the principle of the divine right of the monarchy had its origins in antipapal defenses of civil sovereignty.[20] But English Puritans and Parliamentarians saw in Laudian Arminianism, with its claims to a divine right for the episcopacy and its alliance with royal power, a real danger of creeping Catholicism and the surrender of English sovereignty to papal influence. William Prynne wrote of the "heretical and grace-destroying novelties which have of late invaded, affronted, and almost shouldered out of doors the ancient, established, and resolved doctrines of our church." Calling for reestablishment of the "ancient, orthodox, and dogmatical conclusions which the Church of England, since her Reformation, hath always constantly embraced, ratified, and defended as her own," Prynne exhorted Parliament to "crucify" the Arminian heresy.[21] John Pym, proclaiming that "the greatest liberty of the kingdom is religion," lamented the "manifold innovations lately introduced into several parts of the kingdom, all inclining to popery."[22] William Ames compared "popish" ceremonies to "whorish attire" on a young maiden.[23] Laud's support for liturgy, ceremonialism, and ornate church restoration, not to mention Charles's Catholic queen and her retinue of priests, looked to skeptical observers like sure signs of a growing Catholic influence around the throne.

18. Russell, *Causes of the English Civil War*, 75–82.

19. Introduction, *Reactions to the English Civil War*, 15. My point here is not that Laudian episcopacy *was* actual or crypto-Catholicism, but that it was seen as such by a growing body of Puritans and Parliamentarians. Hugh Trevor-Roper (*Catholics, Anglicans, and Puritans* [London, 1987] and "Archbishop Laud in Retrospect," in *From Counter-Reformation to Glorious Revolution* [Chicago, 1992], 131–50), makes an impassioned case that Laud was in fact *returning* to the roots of English Reformed thought, while Caroline Hibbard explores the conflict over "court Catholicism" in *Charles I and the Popish Plot* (Chapel Hill, N.C., 1983). We must also keep in mind the broader context of English anti-Catholicism as a backdrop to these fears of popery. See Robin Clifton, "The Popular Fear of Catholics During the English Revolution," *Past and Present* 52 (1971): 23–55.

20. J. N. Figgis, *The Divine Right of Kings* (Cambridge, 1914). See also the comment by the Fifth Monarchist, Lieutenant-Colonel Goffe of the New Model Army: "Tis true the kings have been instruments to cast off the pope's supremacy, but we may see if they have not put themselves into the same state" (*Clarke Papers*, 1:282).

21. *Anti-Arminianism*, epistle dedicatory.

22. "A Declaration of the Grievances of the Kingdom, c.1640," in *Somers Tracts*, 4:392, 394.

23. *A Fresh Suit*, epistle dedicatory.

James I had always managed to effect a balance, if a precarious one, among the various factions within the church, but Charles proved politically less adept than his father. Nicholas Tyacke argues that "the unwillingness of Charles unambiguously to repudiate the policies which he and his advisers had been pursuing since the late 1620s is central to the failure to reach a settlement in the years 1640 to 1642."[24] Opposition to Arminianism as a stepping-stone to popery became a siren-song of English Puritanism under Charles, and both English and Scottish critics attacked Laud mercilessly.[25] But Parliamentary and Puritan opposition did not hinder the archbishop from using his influence to promote allies to powerful church positions and to harass Puritans out of their ministries.[26]

A second element of "church reform," no less contested, involved church *structure and government*: growing anti-episcopal sentiment in Parliament made a drastic revision in the role of bishops almost inevitable. This sentiment reflected concerns about Laud as well, since Laudians claimed that the episcopacy existed by divine right.[27] Opposition to such claims (as well as specific opposition to the political influence that bishops wielded in the House of Lords) drew on a long tradition of English anticlericalism dating back to the Lollards in the fourteenth and fifteenth centuries and congregationalist and Presbyterian sympathies among Puritans.[28] Parliament and Puritans opposed divine right episcopacy for different reasons: for Parliament, it represented an infringement on its own Erastian claim to ecclesiastical supremacy; while for many Puritans, it conflicted with their own *jure divino* claims about church

24. *Anti-Calvinists*, 243.

25. Bulstrode Whitelock blamed Laud for the dissolution of Parliament in 1640 (*Memorials of the English Affairs* [1682; Oxford, 1853], 1:99), and Scottish attacks on the archbishop reached a fever pitch from 1638 on. See [Harold Blair], "Novations in Religion . . ." (HL Manuscript EL 7001), a blistering attack on Laud, which asserts that "if the pope himself had been in [Laud's] place, he could not have been more popish" (6). This document is reprinted in slightly altered form as "The Charge of the Scottish Commissioners," in *Somers Tracts*, 4:415–31.

26. Laud's policies, Tyacke argues, eroded the "shared Calvinist middle ground" that had previously (if sometimes uneasily) encompassed both Puritans and the church hierarchy (*Anti-Calvinists*, 223). For a detailed study of some notables punished during Laud's tenure, see Stephen Foster, *Notes from the Caroline Underground: Alexander Leighton, the Puritan Triumvirate, and the Laudian Reaction to Nonconformity* (Hamden, Conn., 1978).

27. For an excellent overview of Laudianism, see Anthony Milton, *Catholic and Reformed: The Roman and Protestant Churches in English Protestant Thought, 1600–1640* (New York, 1995); for Laud's own words, see his *Speech Delivered in the Star-Chamber, at the Censure of John Bastwick, Henry Burton, and William Prynne* (London, 1637).

28. See A. G. Dickens, *The English Reformation* (New York, 1964), chap. 2.

government, be they Presbyterian or congregationalist. Parliament summoned the Westminster Assembly of Divines in 1643 to address the questions of church theology and government, and the convening of the Assembly represented Parliament's commitment to overseeing the reformation of the national church. These differences between Parliamentary and Puritan approaches to the location of ecclesiastical authority would become glaring and overwhelming after victory over royalist forces was achieved later in the 1640s.

Voices for Unity and Reformation: Parliament, the Scots, and the Westminster Assembly of Divines

Parliament, the Scots, and the Westminster Assembly, though not strictly unified, represent the forces most strongly committed to pursuing religious reform. Each had its own agenda, which made agreement ultimately unattainable, but the breakdown of central authority, virtual collapse of the established church, and proliferation of radical religious rhetoric and agitation during the 1640s cemented their claims to represent established political and ecclesiastical structures for achieving the aims of the rebellion (and conversely, for *restricting* the conflict to those areas of contention over which the resistance was initiated). Parliament, the Scots, and the Assembly operated on the assumption that negotiating a settlement with the king, returning in some way to the "ancient constitution" in which king and Parliament shared responsibility for governance, remained the ultimate goal of the rebellion.[29]

Any such settlement would involve both political and ecclesiastical elements. The idea of calling a "national synod" to chart the course of the English church was not an entirely new one. In 1641, Charles had proposed that "if the Parliament should advise him to call a national synod he should consider of it, and give them due satisfaction in it."[30] Parliament summoned the

29. The shared commitment to rule of law and limited monarchy allowed these actors to engage in ongoing negotiations with moderate royalists over the nature of a post–Civil War settlement. Indeed, although numerous obstacles remained (chief among them the structure of the English church), the fear that such "moderate" settlement would emerge led Cromwell and the army to move against Parliament in 1648. For a good overview of this moderate position, see David L. Smith, *Constitutional Royalism and the Search for Settlement, c. 1640–1649* (Cambridge, 1994).

30. Clarendon, *History of the Rebellion and Civil Wars in England*, ed. W. Dunn Macray (Oxford, 1888), vol. 1, bk. 4, sec. 82, p. 437. For Parliament's petition for a national synod, see the Grand Remonstrance, in Samuel Rawson Gardiner, ed., *Constitutional Documents of the Puritan Revolution, 1625–1660*, 2d ed. (Oxford, 1906), 152.

Westminster Assembly of Divines in 1643 to pursue, in Robert S. Paul's words, a "theologically viable and ecclesiastically workable system of church government."[31] After preliminary debates concerning the Thirty-Nine Articles (the doctrinal core of Anglicanism), Parliament directed the Assembly to speedily "tak[e] in hand the discipline and liturgy of the Church."[32]

Church discipline related directly to church government and toleration: congregationalist Puritans (Independents) sought to locate discipline and admonition within local congregations, and the imposition of civil penalties for ecclesiastical offenses was one of the religious dissenters' primary grievances. Sectarians and Separatists (e.g., Roger Williams, William Walwyn), viewed *all* members of the Westminster Assembly as implicated in a process that *prefigured* an opposition to toleration, or that hedged in such a toleration so severely as to fall short of being meaningful.[33] But no member of the Westminster Assembly dissented from the idea that there should be a Calvinist national church, and no Separatists or sectarians were seated as members. Years later, Milton would observe that

> most [of the members of the Westminster Assembly] were such as had preached and cried down with great show of zeal the avarice and pluralities of bishops and prelates. . . . Yet these conscientious men, ere any part of the work for which they came together, and that on the public salary, wanted not impudence to the ignominy and scandal of their pastor-like profession and especially of their boasted reformation. . . . while they taught compulsion without conviction (which not long before they so much complained of as executed unchristianly against themselves) their intents were clear to be no

31. *The Assembly of the Lord: Politics and Religion in the Westminster Assembly and the "Great Debate"* (Edinburgh, 1985), 2. Paul's book is the most recent, comprehensive, and balanced study of the Assembly. See also Morrill, "Attack on the Church of England," and John Lightfoot, *Journal of the Proceedings of the Assembly of Divines, in The Whole Works of the Rev. John Lightfoot*, vol. 13, ed. John Rogers Pitman (London, 1824), 120.

32. Lightfoot, *Journal*, 17.

33. Even the Dissenting Brethren, those members of the Westminster Assembly who sought the widest latitude for individual congregations, were not pleading for toleration, but for Protestant unity and an expanded role for the congregation in disciplinary decisions *within* a national church. Presbyterians opposed such an expanded role, or at least feared the lengths to which it would extend, fearing collusion with heterodox and potentially blasphemous views, and a slippery slope into the tolerationist abyss.

other than to have set up a spiritual tyranny by a secular power to the advancing of their own authority above the magistrate.[34]

Indeed, Assembly debates concerning church government would remain highly muted compared to those raised by the army, Levellers, and sectarians.[35] Of course, Presbyterian and Independent understandings of what the national church should look like differed dramatically.[36] Severe and bitter disagreements would soon appear within the Assembly concerning the church's theology, uniformity, and indulgence toward "tender consciences."

The Westminster Assembly's work was altered by the Parliament's Scottish alliance in 1643: the Solemn League and Covenant pledged to "endeavor to bring the churches of God in these three kingdoms to the nearest conjunction and uniformity in religion."[37] Because of their religious disputes with Charles and Laud, and the crippling effect a Parliamentary victory would have on

34. The selection "Character of the Long Parliament," from Milton's *History of England* (1670) is reprinted in Milton, *Areopagitica and Other Political Writings*, 451–52.

35. Not to mention highly *protracted*: Scottish Commissioner Robert Baillie referred to the Assembly's deliberations as "Trent-like" (*The Letters and Journals of Robert Baillie, A. M., Principal of the University of Glasgow*, ed. David Laing, 3 vols. [Edinburgh, 1842], 2:164).

36. In Presbyterian eyes, Independents effectively did away with a national church by removing the national synod's disciplinary power. Independents, for their part, sought religious uniformity in a national structure that left discipline and decision making largely to local congregations. Separatists and sectarians, who rejected a national church entirely, claimed that differences between Presbyterians and Independents were merely ones of *degree* rather than of *kind*. At the same time, the differences between Independents and Presbyterians did have enormous significance for the way those two parties viewed the conflict, and it is that perspective I wish to highlight.
I use the terms "congregationalist" and "Independent" interchangeably. Although this is as risky as any other generalization, the term does identify a group of divines with recognizably congregationalist leanings who nonetheless rejected sectarianism and Separatism. Although it is true that on some points "Independent ecclesiology closely resembled that of the Separatists" (Sommerville, "Independent Thought," iii), and certainly as the 1640s progressed the anti-Laudian alliance between Presbyterians and Independents broke down, important differences between Independents and Separatists remained. Independents were, for example, more restrained in the toleration they were prepared to grant.

37. *A Solemn League and Covenant, for Reformation, and Defense of Religion* (Edinburgh, 1643), 3. The English would attempt to retain some flexibility in matters of church government by stressing another passage in the Covenant, one that tied English reformation to "*the Word of God*, and the example of the best reformed churches" (*A Solemn League and Covenant*, 3, emphasis added).
Lawrence Kaplan, *Politics and Religion During the English Civil War: The Scots and the Long Parliament, 1643–1645* (New York, 1976), remains the best study of the course and dynamics of the Scottish alliance.

future attempts to impose Anglicanism on Scottish Presbyterians, the Scots saw in the alliance with Parliament a chance for communal self-defense as well as a means for spreading their version of Reformed church polity.[38] Scottish hopes for religious uniformity, then, would be played out through the unification of forces on the battlefield, and there was reason for optimism that a settlement acceptable to both sides might result from successful prosecution of the rebellion. Parliament had expressed guarded support for a moderate Presbyterian system as early as 1641, and a degree of Presbyterian sympathy had long existed among English Puritans.[39] Eminent Scottish divines attended the Westminster Assembly: from the outset, relations were tense,[40] but the importance of defeating a common foe enabled this tenuous alliance to hold for several years. Still, for many English the Scots would always remain meddling outsiders, taking a heavy toll in English independence for their aid in defeating Charles.[41]

This general issue of Presbyterianism and the structure of the English church led to the first major disputes in the Westminster Assembly. The battle was touched off by the publication of *An Apologeticall Narration*, which

38. Military losses had threatened to doom the Parliamentary cause shortly after the outbreak of hostilities. Parliament found a ready and willing ally in the Scots. Religious dissension between Charles and Scottish Presbyterians dated back to the late 1630s, when Laud had attempted to impose the English Book of Common Prayer on Scottish churches. Rioting ensued, resulting in a Scottish occupation of northern England.

39. Whitelock reports that the Commons had "agreed that every shire should be a several diocese, a presbytery of twelve divines in each shire, and a bishop over them. . . . To have a diocesan synod every year, and every third year a national synod" (*Memorials of the English Affairs*, 1:135). In a remark that contained forebodings of difficulties to come, he added that "[the national synod] to make canons, *but none to be binding till confirmed by parliament*" (1:135, emphasis added). This system is clearly not the Scottish form of church government, but it does contain general Presbyterian elements.

The definitive reference on the Presbyterian sympathy in English Puritanism remains Collinson's *Elizabethan Puritan Movement*.

40. Baillie claimed that the English primarily sought a civil alliance, the Scottish a religious one (*Letters and Journals*, 2:90). In this observation, we see the seeds of later misunderstanding. For Baillie, the aim of the Solemn League and Covenant "was the propagation of our church discipline to England and Ireland" (2:103), and "the fruit of our victory is the advancement of religion" (2:152).

41. William Shaw claims that "the English Parliament, under the pretense of necessity, had forfeited its future freedom of action in the matter of church reform" (*A History of the English Church During the Civil Wars and under the Commonwealth, 1640–1660* [New York, 1900], 1:144). The loss of Parliamentary "freedom," in my view, came not with the Scottish alliance, but with the rise of Parliament's own New Model Army, and ended once and for all with Pride's Purge.

was quickly followed by responses from Scots and others.[42] The "great debate" that followed pitted the Independents, or "Dissenting Brethren" (who advocated a system that would extend more autonomy to individual congregations), against the advocates of Presbyterian uniformity and the authority of the national synod.[43]

This "great debate" between Presbyterians and Independents was not, strictly speaking, a toleration debate at all. The Westminster divines often spoke of "accommodation," an attempt to split the difference between congregational autonomy on the one hand, and a more centralized Presbyterianism on the other.[44] Accommodation addressed the degree of autonomy

42. Thomas Goodwin, Philip Nye, Sidrach Simpson, Jeremiah Burroughes, and William Bridge, *An Apologeticall Narration* (London, 1643); also reprinted in Haller, *Tracts on Liberty*, 2:307–39. The responses and counterresponses to the *Narration* constitute a literature far too extensive to be considered here. For a few examples, see the following: [Alexander Henderson], *Reformation of Church-Government in Scotland Cleared from Some Mistakes and Prejudices* (London, 1644); [Adam Steuart], *Some Observations and Annotations upon the Apologeticall Narration* (London, 1643); Thomas Edwards, *Antapologia; or, A Full Answer to the Apologeticall Narration* (London, 1646); and [Alexander Forbes], *An Anatomy of Independency, or a Brief Commentary on the Apologeticall Narration* (London, 1644).

Robert S. Paul sees the *Narration* as the functional equivalent of a plea for toleration (*Assembly of the Lord*, 231). Despite the uproar in the Assembly after the *Narration*'s publication, though, the word "toleration" does not appear in the work at all, and the term "tender consciences" appears only once. Clearly one can evoke a claim for toleration without using the specific words, but my point here is that the *Narration* contains no mention of any of the conventional justifications for toleration.

Paul also states that "[the Independents] had asked to be granted toleration and having made that request for themselves, they could not deny the same principle to others, especially to those who were risking their lives in the ranks of Cromwell's troopers" (231), a statement that in my view confuses historical fact with "logical" necessity. If those in Cromwell's ranks were not orthodox Protestants, many Independents would indeed have denied them toleration and seen no contradiction in their position. See Sommerville, "Independent Thought," chap. 5. See also Zakai, "Religious Toleration and Its Enemies," although Zakai seems to equate toleration with a complete rejection of the magistrate's power over religion. Separatists who sought full liberty of conscience did tend to reject any magisterial authority over religious affairs, but most tolerationists accepted the system of tithes and allowed the civil magistrate to promote general religiosity. Robert Ashton notes that Independents were much more inclined to allow some sort of modified episcopacy, given certain guarantees of toleration for Protestant dissenters: see his *Counter-Revolution: The Second Civil War and Its Origins, 1646–1648* (New Haven, Conn., 1994), 274.

43. This "great debate" was of key importance, although it is unlikely that the conflicts between Presbyterians and Dissenting Brethren "proved ultimately the main cause why the . . . Assembly failed to accomplish all the good which had been expected from its important deliberations" (W. M. Hetherington, *History of the Westminster Assembly of Divines*, 4th ed., ed. Robert Williamson, [Edinburgh, 1878], 189). The debate did, however, illuminate sharp disagreements over congregational independence that divided England's political and religious elites.

44. "Accommodation" played on the desire for Protestant unity, a powerful rhetorical device in a society steeped in anti-Catholicism. As George Gillespie said, "I wish that instead of

individual congregations should be permitted to exercise *within* the national church structure, not the liberties of congregations outside the established church.

In another sense, though, these Assembly debates became increasingly moot, since Parliament remained in firm control of the political situation. Paralleling the "great debate" over church government was the political struggle with Parliament over the location of sovereignty over the church.[45] Parliament had summoned the Assembly, appointed its members, and set its agenda, in order that the Assembly might, as William Haller has noted, "not . . . establish, but . . . advise Parliament in the establishment of a Reformed church."[46] Responding to a sharply worded Assembly petition asserting the divine right of Presbyterianism, Parliament sent a delegation to remind the divines that "by [Parliament's] power you now sit," and that "amongst [Parliamentary] privileges none more essential than this: that in them resides the power of making laws. . . . You are not to make use of the public character the Houses have put upon you, to contradict their votes."[47] Parliament concluded this rebuke by noting that "it is the doctrine of the Pope to take from princes the power that God committed to them."[48] The Westminster Assembly had no independent base of power, and Parliament made its own position clear: systems of church government were not established by Scripture (as the Scots and congregationalists claimed),[49] but by the civil magistrate, whose legitimate authority encompassed establishing religion, supporting the true faith, and suppressing heresy. Prynne argued that civil magistrates might create whichever form of church government they deemed appropriate, assuming that such a system did not expressly contradict Scripture.[50] Thus

---

toleration, there may be a mutual endeavour for a happy accommodation . . . since God has promised to give his people one heart and one way" (Rev. Alex F. Mitchell and Rev. John Struthers, ed., *Minutes of the Sessions of the Westminster Assembly of Divines* [Edinburgh and London, 1874], 28); see also Gillespie, *Wholesome Severity*: "I had rather go two miles in an accommodation, than one mile in a toleration" (36).

45. See Paul, *Assembly of the Lord*, chap. 13.

46. Haller, *Tracts on Liberty*, 1:48.

47. Mitchell and Struthers, *Minutes*, 452, 449, 451.

48. Ibid., 455.

49. In the Assembly debates over church government, both Presbyterians and their Dissenting colleagues made *jure divino* claims. Both claimed that their systems of church government were derived directly from Scripture. See Paul, *Assembly of the Lord*, 102.

50. *Twelve Considerable and Serious Considerations Touching Church-Government* (London, 1644); [Prynne], *Diotrephes Catechised*, 2d ed. (London, 1646).

Parliament's Presbyterian church would remain under the control of civil magistrates: Baillie lamented this "lame Erastian presbytery."[51]

As noted previously, Parliament, the Assembly, and the Scots were highly suspicious of claims for toleration. Their embodiment of established political and ecclesiastical channels, even while in rebellion against the king, associated them with ordered reformation and opposition to the radical tendencies of the sects.[52] The three did not always agree on either the justificatory or substantive elements of religious politics during the early and mid-1640s. But Parliamentary Presbyterianism, firmly under civil control, provided many potential benefits: a broad theoretical appeal in a country with a tradition of established religion, a means for redressing the shortages of ordained ministers throughout England,[53] a corrective to the excessive power of bishops and archbishops under the old system, and an antidote to the increasing prevalence of religious radicals and sects that had mushroomed in the breakdown of central authority. Just as many of the Assembly debates were rendered moot by Parliamentary assertions of sovereignty, however, so did factors external to both Parliamentary and Assembly deliberations doom this Parliament-approved church system. For just as Parliament voted Presbyterianism into effect, the Parliament's creation, the New Model Army, was overtaking its creator as a political entity and power base of its own.

Liberty and Toleration: the Army, Levellers, Sects, and the Overthrow of Parliament

While Parliament and the Westminster Assembly were charting a religious settlement for the kingdom, forces were in motion outside their halls that

---

51. *Letters and Journals*, 2:362. To their critics, Parliamentary assertions of sovereignty differed little from those made by their royalist adversaries. As Michael Mendle puts it: "The old question endured. If an old priest lurked within the new presbyter, was the old king to be found in the new parliament?" See Mendle, "Parliamentary Sovereignty: A Very English Absolutism," in Phillipson and Skinner, *Political Discourse in Early Modern Britain*, 119.

52. The attempt at representing lawful authority even while in rebellion against the king was usually accomplished by stressing that the lawful sovereign was not simply the monarch, but rather "the King-in-Parliament"; not, that is, the whim of an absolute sovereign, but the balanced monarchy evoked by the traditional understanding of the ancient constitutions. See, e.g., HL Manuscript EL 6874, an extract of a sermon by Calibut Downing; and, for a fuller explication, Sommerville, *Politics and Ideology*, 38–45, 176–77.

53. See, e.g., *The Humble Petition of Many Well-Affected Freemen and Citizens of the City of London* (London, 1646).

would not only prevent the Presbyterian system from coming into existence, but would radically alter the course of English religious politics and lead to Charles's execution in 1649. The New Model Army, created by Parliament in 1645, won impressive victories and soon came to have a political life of its own. Because of its emergence as an independent (and armed) power base and its religious radicalism, the army represented a serious challenge to Parliament's conduct of the war and control of the ensuing settlement.

It is important to note that this developing rivalry between the army and Parliament was not simply a case of a military authority intimidating a civilian one. The New Model Army saw itself as a popular institution akin to Parliament, "not a mere mercenary army, hired to serve any arbitrary power of a state, but called forth and conjured by the several declarations of Parliament to the defense of our own and the people's just rights and liberties."[54] "The Army's commission [was] derived from Parliament" and invested with Parliament's power to defend popular liberties, claimed John Goodwin.[55] "If we measure the lawfulness of parliamentary judicature by the call of the people thereunto," he continued, "the Army . . . hath every whit as lawful a constitution to judge who are enemies of the peace and safety of the kingdom as the Parliament itself hath."[56]

Relations between the army and Parliament originally began to sour over pay and concerns about possible decommissioning and service in Ireland; the army also feared that Parliament was too eager to settle with the king.[57] These

---

54. *A Representation of the Army* (14 June 1647), in William Haller and Godfrey Davies, ed., *The Leveller Tracts, 1647–1653* (New York, 1944), 51–63. See also *The Case of the Army* (London, 1647), in *The Leveller Tracts*, 64–87, and Sexby's speech during the Putney Debates, in which he says, "If we had not a right to the kingdom, we were mere mercenary soldiers" (*Clarke Papers*, 1:323).

55. Goodwin, *Right and Might Well Met* (London, 1649), in Woodhouse, *Puritanism and Liberty*, 214. This work has been reprinted more recently in Joyce Lee Malcolm's very helpful two-volume collection, *The Struggle for Sovereignty: Seventeenth-Century Political Tracts* (Indianapolis, 1999), 1:307–59.

56. *Right and Might Well Met*, in Woodhouse, *Puritanism and Liberty*, 215. See also Cromwell's remarks at the Putney debates: "The end [of the Army's actions] is to deliver this nation from oppression and slavery" (*Clarke Papers*, 1:379).

57. The *Clarke Papers* abound with references to the growing mistrust and animosity between the army, Parliament, and the City of London. See, for example, the "Letter from London" (6 May 1647), which refers to the "continued clamors of the city against the Army" (1:26); the account of soldiers' assaulting the House of Commons and the City (June 1647, 1:136, 141); and a report of anti-army sermons by London ministers (July 1647, 1:150). John Milton's *Tenure of Kings and Magistrates* (London, 1648) criticized those, generally Presbyterians, who would settle with Charles: he "exhort[ed] them not to startle from the just and pious resolution of adhering with all their strength and assistance to the present Parliament and Army, in the glorious way wherein justice and victory hath set them" (in *Areopagitica and Other Political Writings*, 56).

disputes had less material aspects as well, however, in the strong support for religious toleration among rank-and-file soldiers and the heavy representation of sectarians in the army.[58] Tolerationist sentiments were reflected in the prevalence of preaching, the eagerness with which soldiers and officers participated in theological debate, and well-documented cases of iconoclasm committed by soldiers.[59] Although officers tended to be more conservative, seeking to preserve more authority over religious affairs for the magistrate,[60] the army's active attention to the politics of religion represented a major obstacle to a negotiated Parliamentary settlement with the king and the enactment of the Presbyterian church system.

Allied with elements of the army during these years, or at least working for many of the same ends, was the Leveller movement in and around London. By 1647, Leveller influence in the army was significant: the Putney debates show that Leveller ideas had made inroads among the rank-and-file, to the consternation of many officers. The Leveller commitment to toleration was one plank of a platform equally concerned with extending the franchise, freeing shopowners and artisans from monopolies, and reforming Parliamen-

58. In this regard, it seems clear that many within the New Model Army saw it as a charismatic community of saints on a divine mission. For more on the revolutionary implications of this sort of self-image, see Walzer, *Revolution of the Saints*.

59. For just one example of such iconoclasm, see the account in Clement Walker, *Anarchia Anglicana; or, the History of Independency* (London, 1649), pt. 2, pp. 152–53, which reports soldiers invading the church at Walton-on-Thames, announcing the abolition of the Sabbath, tithes, ministers, and the Bible itself.

I leave aside the scholarly debate over the specific timing of the army's radicalism. Richard Baxter certainly saw the army as sectarian from the start: see *Reliquiae Baxterianae* (London, 1696), 47–48, 50, 53–54. Mark Kishlansky has argued forcefully that radicalism and religious activism occurred no earlier than 1647, and that before this time the army's concerns were strictly military (honor) and material (pay). Ian Gentles advances a persuasive argument that religion played a central role in the army from its inception, examining the prevalence of piety, lay preaching, and iconoclasm. C. H. Firth attributes the religious radicalism of the army to zealous chaplains, but points out that the army made no attempt to influence Parliament before 1647. For my purposes, these questions are less important than the assertion that by 1647, when conflict with Parliament was becoming increasingly likely, the New Model Army was taking an active stance in favor of a measure of liberty of conscience, and that such a development represented a real source of tension between the army and Parliament.

See Kishlansky, *The Rise of the New Model Army* (Cambridge, 1979); idem, "The Army and the Levellers: The Roads to Putney," *Historical Journal* 22 (1979): 798–824; Ian Gentles, *The New Model Army in England, Ireland and Scotland 1645–1653* (Oxford, 1992), chap. 4; Firth, *Cromwell's Army* (London, 1902), 346–48; and Ashton, *Counter-Revolution*, 163–64.

60. This conservatism on the part of officers extended to both civil and religious affairs, illustrated respectively in the Putney and Whitehall Debates (*Clarke Papers*, 1:226–40, 2:71–132).

tary representation and the legal system.[61] Of course, Leveller propagandists saw these various aims as closely interrelated, seeking to preserve popular liberties against the threat of tyranny from either king or Parliament. Their ability to amass large number of signatures on petitions, along with their leaders' indefatigable energy for publication, made them instrumental in keeping Parliament's feet to the fire of reform and toleration. During 1647 and 1648, Leveller agitation and army support for toleration tended to work toward similar political purposes, to undermine those in Parliament seeking implementation of the Presbyterian system. Indeed, the Leveller/army alliance would later haunt Cromwell and his generals: as they sought to secure order in the wake of Pride's Purge and the execution of the king, some of the most vigorous and persistent calls for liberty would come from their erstwhile Leveller allies.[62]

Finally, the sects which proliferated during the 1640s complete this picture of broader social and political forces pushing for toleration during the later parts of the decade.[63] Sects multiplied as church courts and censor-

61. For a sampling of Leveller writings, see Woodhouse, *Puritanism and Liberty*, 317–78, 426–49, and *The Leveller Tracts*, passim. The best recent discussion of the Levellers and toleration is Alan Craig Houston, "Monopolizing Faith: The Levellers, Rights, and Religious Toleration," in Levine, *Early Modern Skepticism*, 147–61. Houston ties together Leveller antimonopolism and tolerationism, sketching the broad contours of Leveller thought and activism. See also David Wootton, "Leveller Democracy and the Puritan Revolution," in Burns and Goldie, *Cambridge History of Political Thought*, 412–42.

D. B. Robertson claims that "the Levellers were first and foremost religious sectaries" (*The Religious Foundations of Leveller Democracy* [New York, 1951], 121). This seems problematic, since Robertson admits that "Lilburne's religious experience was not essentially different from that which Puritans had come to know through the past two generations and more" (18). He describes Levellers as adhering to an apocalyptic, natural law, Calvinistic, providential view of history and politics. None of these are unique, and their Anglican/royalist opponents, as well as Independents and many Presbyterians, would likely agree on most points. Harold Shaw (*The Levellers* [London, 1968], chap. 1) also sees the Levellers as a spiritual movement, citing Puritanism and Anabaptism as main sources of their ideas, though he incorrectly claims that they sought the separation of church and state (Levellers allowed the civil magistrate to promote preaching and general religiosity). More appropriate, in my view (though perhaps overly Whiggish), is Joseph Frank's view of the Levellers as Calvinist constitutional democrats: although "Calvinist" tells us little that is distinctive about the Levellers, "constitutional democrat" does point us toward something that sets the group apart from their contemporaries. See Frank, *The Levellers*.

62. See *L. Colonel John Lilburne Revived* (London, 27 March 1653), which called Cromwell "the grandest tyrant and traitor that ever England bred." Cited in Pauline Gregg, *Free-Born John: A Biography of John Lilburne* (1961; London, 1986); also in Woolrych, *Commonwealth to Protectorate*, 250.

63. "Proliferate" here is a relative term: although the sects never attracted a numerically significant amount of adherents, hundreds of independent congregations sprang up in London

ship collapsed. Such groups, not satisfied with Westminster Assembly debates over congregational autonomy, demanded a far broader liberty than either Parliament or the Assembly was prepared to grant, and the Assembly's proceedings struck them as replacing one coercive, false church with another.[64] Sectarians often stressed the inward nature of salvation as opposed to outward forms of worship, noting that true religion flows from "an inward principle of faith and love."[65] Politically, in a view inherited from the Separatist tradition, sects tended to differentiate church and state sharply, drastically restricting civil authority over religious affairs. Ecclesiastical forms and compulsory church attendance were at best unnecessary, at worst positively harmful because they imposed a human power between the individual believer and the working of God's grace. Gerrard Winstanley claimed that anyone "strict in a formal customary way of worship, knows not what it is to worship in spirit and truth."[66] John Saltmarsh identified the religious strife of the 1640s as largely due to the fact that "many look too much upon the natural interest of the Reformation, not upon the supernatural," while for William Dell, a fundamental misunderstanding caused people to interpret spiritual things (Reformation) carnally.[67]

Just as Parliament prepared to bring the Presbyterian system into existence, then, its control over the rebellion was slipping away. Elections for church officers did go forward in some places, but the *de facto* lines of power were becoming increasingly clear. In 1647, Baillie referred (in a telling reversal of the nominal authority relationship) to "the army's parliament."[68] After describing the increasing boldness of the army in petitioning and marching on London, Bulstrode Whitelock identifies 1647 as a turning point when

during the 1640s, significantly altering the religious landscape of the city. See J. F. McGregor and B. Reay, eds., *Radical Religion in the English Revolution* (Oxford, 1984), chap. 1, and Christopher Hill, *Some Intellectual Consequences of the English Revolution* (Madison, Wis., 1989), 8–9. The definitive work on the sects remains Hill's *World Turned Upside Down*.

64. See, for example, Roger Williams's *Queries of Highest Consideration* (London, 1644), and William Walwyn, *The Compassionate Samaritane* (London, 1644), 1–5. Walwyn's tract is reprinted in Haller, *Tracts on Liberty*, 3:61–104.

65. Samuel Richardson, *The Necessity of Toleration in Matters of Religion* (London, 1647), 4.

66. *The New Law of Righteousness* (London, 1649), in *The Works of Gerrard Winstanley*, ed. George Sabine (New York, 1965), 209.

67. Saltmarsh, *Dawnings of Light* (London, 1646), 22; Dell, *Right Reformation* (London, 1646), 20–24.

68. *Letters and Journals*, 3:21.

"the parliament began to surrender themselves and their power into the hands of their own army."[69] The culmination of this gradually increasing tension came in the following year with Pride's Purge, in which a company of soldiers blocked moderate members of the Commons from attending Parliament, leaving behind a "Rump" Parliament made up of those sympathetic to the army's cause and opposed to any further negotiations with the king. Besides displaying where real power in England lay, the Purge foreclosed any possibility of a negotiated settlement or the reinstatement of a balanced monarchy. More specifically for the purposes of this study, the purge ended Parliamentary schemes on a number of fronts, including the Presbyterian church system.[70] Pride's Purge marked the death knell of Parliament as an independent political actor through the 1650s, foreshadowed the execution of the king six weeks later, and set the stage for the Commonwealth and Protectorate and Cromwell's rise to power.

TOLERATION DEBATES DURING THE ENGLISH CIVIL WAR: THEOLOGICAL, PHILOSOPHICAL, POLITICAL

Those instigating the rebellion against Charles I, then, sought neither toleration nor liberty of conscience, but rather a reformed Protestant establishment. Of course, events did not proceed precisely as they would have liked. Parliamentarians and Presbyterians were forced to enter into protracted debates with external forces (the army, sects) whose views of the rebellion, its meaning and aims, differed radically from their more modest reforming goals.[71]

---

69. *Memorials of the English Affairs*, 2:151.

70. Ashton notes that defenses of Pride's Purge also involved defenses of toleration, citing *A Declaration of the Parliament of England in Answer to . . . the Commissioners of Scotland* as connecting the two. See his *Counter-Revolution*, 337.

71. Although I speak broadly of toleration and antitoleration in this section, readers will note that gradations occur within each camp. Thus, for example, Independents were more tolerationist than Anglicans and Presbyterians, in that they supported congregational autonomy. Independents were less tolerationist than Separatists and sectarians, in that they insisted that such congregations espouse Protestant orthodoxy. Shifting political developments and diminishing prospects for congregational autonomy within the proposed Presbyterian system pushed Independents toward toleration, though figures such as John Owen and even Jeremy Taylor evidence a great deal of theological conservatism and Protestant orthodoxy in their approach to religious dissent.

The Argument from Scripture and the Civil Versus the Spiritual

Since the debate about toleration in England was a Christian argument carried on in a Christian society—to be more accurate, a *Protestant* argument carried on in a *Protestant* society[72]—appeals to Scripture constituted a powerful rhetorical and polemical tool. Both tolerationists and antitolerationists amassed impressive scriptural cases. Just as Christ had called for the apostles to love each other and to "be one; as thou, Father, art in me, and I in thee" (John 17:21), so had Paul and other early church leaders enjoined Christians to unity. Such injunctions appear throughout the epistles, and opponents of toleration relentlessly pointed out that claims for the toleration of heterodox opinions, and the schism to which such claims would lead, contradicted biblical teachings. Matthew Newcomen took Philippians 1:27, in which Paul calls for the church to "stand fast in one spirit, with one mind striving together for the faith of the gospel," as a sermon text. Bewailing the divisions in the church as contrary to Christian principles, he claimed that church unity was not "a mere *Idea Platonica*" but had existed in the church's past.[73] George Gillespie brought a host of scriptural texts to bear against claims for toleration, seeking, in his terms, a middle ground between Catholic persecution and the sectarian position, which removed all religious functions from the civil magistrate.[74] Adam Steuart adduced twenty-one reasons for opposing toleration, nine of which drew upon scriptural citations, the example of the early church, or apostolic calls for unity.[75] Thomas Edwards went even further, providing twenty scriptural arguments against toleration.[76] Proclaiming that "justice is not contrary to meekness," Samuel Rutherford argued that Pauline calls for humility do not rule out the suppression of heresy.[77] Rutherford also

72. The nexus of Protestantism, "Englishness," and toleration depended heavily, as I have suggested, on long-standing English anti-Catholicism. Although such anti-Catholicism animated opposition to Charles and Laud, it became even more overt and revolutionary during the reign of James II, a professed Catholic. I discuss the importance of Protestantism to nascent English nationalism in the next chapter.

73. *The Duty of Such as Would Walk Worthy of the Gospel: To Endeavour Union, Not Division Nor Toleration* (London, 1646), 8ff. See also the Pauline calls for unity in 1 Corinthians 1:10, 3:3, 12:25; 2 Corinthians 13:11; Philippians 2:2, 3:15–16; Ephesians 4:3; and Galatians 5:20.

74. *Wholesome Severity*, 1–18.

75. *Some Observations*, 61ff.

76. *The Casting Down of the Last and Strongest Hold of Satan; or, A Treatise Against Toleration and Pretended Liberty of Conscience* (London, 1647). See also Edwards's *Antapologia*, 237–40, and *Reasons Against the Independent Government of Churches* (London, 1641), reason 1.

77. *A Free Disputation*, 61.

proceeded through tolerationists' scriptural arguments one by one, refuting them (to his satisfaction) and adding copious scriptural citations of his own.[78] Tolerationists, however, marshaled an equally impressive scriptural arsenal of their own. Roger Williams, in his disputations with John Cotton, made much use of the parable of wheat and tares. When weeds grew up in the wheatfield, Jesus had said, the sower told his servants to let them be, "lest while ye gather up the tares, ye root up also the wheat with them" (Matthew 13:29).[79] Advocates of toleration also pointed to Jesus' noncoercive example, as well as his assertion that his kingdom was not of this world, as arguments against compulsive religion.[80] In response to their opponents' exhortations to Christian unity, those seeking liberty of conscience argued that unity was compatible with diverse forms of worship, and reminded their adversaries of Paul's simultaneous exhortation for Christians to proceed with one another in a spirit of meekness and charity.[81] Paul had indeed called for unity, they conceded; but Paul had also said, "Let every man be fully persuaded in his own mind . . . whatsoever is not of faith is sin" (Romans 14:5, 23). Tolerationists cited other passages from Paul's epistles to emphasize the dichotomy between carnal and spiritual realms (2 Corinthians 10:4, Ephesians 6:11–12); the necessity for personal conviction in religious belief (2 Corinthians 1:24, Galatians 6:3–5, 1 Thessalonians 5:21); and the necessity that the godly be persecuted (2 Timothy 3:12, 2 Peter 2:2). The author of *The Ancient Bounds* drew upon Ephesians 4:1–7 and Philippians 3:16: there is one God, one faith,

---

78. Ibid., chaps. 7–10, 12–21, 23–25. See also *A Letter of the Ministers of London* (London, 1645), sec. 3; *Certain Additional Reasons to Those Presented [by the London Ministers] Against the Toleration of Independency* (London, 1645), sec. 3.

79. The parable of tares and wheat was also used in [Henry Robinson], *Liberty of Conscience* (London, 1644), 55 (also in Haller, *Tracts on Liberty*, 3:107–78), and in [Richard Overton], *The Arraignment of Mr. Persecution* (London, 1645), 24 (reprinted in Haller, *Tracts on Liberty*, 3:205–56).

80. For the renunciation of force, see Matthew 26:52 and Luke 9:54–55. For the otherworldliness of Christ's kingdom, see John 6:15 and 18:36 and, more generally, the injunction to preach and convert (not coerce) in Matthew 28:19–20 and Mark 16:15–20. These passages are cited repeatedly in the tolerationist literature: see, for just several examples, Saltmarsh, *Dawnings of Light*, chap. 2; *John the Baptist, Forerunner of Christ Jesus; or, A Necessity for Liberty of Conscience* (London, 1644), chaps. 1–5, 7, 8, 13–15; and [Robinson], *Liberty of Conscience*, passim.

81. See Romans 15:1–2, 2 Timothy 2:24–26, 1 Corinthians 1:10, and Ephesians 4. These passages are cited in *Bloudy Tenent*, pt. 1; Saltmarsh, *A New Quaere* (London, 1646), 1–2; idem, *Dawnings of Light*, 40ff.; [Robinson], *Liberty of Conscience*; and John Vernon, *The Swords Abuse Asserted* (London, 1648), 10.

and one baptism, yet "unto every one of us is given grace according to the measure of the gift of Christ"; to which the author added, "I know there is but one truth, but this truth can not be so easily brought forth without [liberty of conscience]."[82] Therefore, Christians must bear with each other in humility, since Christ came to save sinners, not to destroy them (1 Timothy 1:13, 15).[83] Tolerationists repeatedly implied a question: would Jesus approve of persecution?[84]

But it was not merely the Christian gospel that the various parties to these debates employed. In an attempt to construct a seamless biblical case supporting the magistrate's duty to promote true religion and restrain heretics and blasphemers, advocates of uniformity evoked the broad powers over religion exercised by kings of Israel. After all, did not Jesus himself say that he had "come not to destroy [the Law], but to fulfill [it]. . . . Till heaven and earth pass away, one jot or tittle shall in no wise pass from the law, till all be fulfilled" (Matthew 5:17–18)? This appeal to the example of ancient Israel formed a central part of antitolerationists' scriptural argument.[85] Use of Old Testament citations, however, did not necessarily signal an opposition to toleration *per se*. Although the army officers at the Whitehall debates supported toleration, they cited the Old Testament as granting a restrictive power (to restrain dangerous vice) to magistrates (*Clarke Papers*, 2:98–101, 109–17). After Goodwin and Clarke opposed granting the civil magistrate any religious authority, Ireton pointed to the kings of Israel as an example of the responsibility of godly magistrates. Jesus himself had not addressed this issue of magisterial responsibility, Ireton claimed, because he was a private individual (2:74, 95, 99–101). Independent divine John Owen agreed. Although admitting that the Old Testament allowed for punishment of idolaters, he added that this was a far different issue than the toleration or suppression of Dissenting Christians. "The[se] penal constitutions of the Judaical polity . . . must be

82. [Francis Rous], *The Ancient Bounds, or Liberty of Conscience*, "A Light to the Work," also 30–31.

83. Busher, *Religion's Peace*, 8; [Rous], *The Ancient Bounds*, 15; *Twelve Weighty Queries of Great Concernment* (London, 1646), no. 7.

84. "Suppose Jesus Christ himself should come again personally, and live amongst us upon earth, I would very fain be assured, how he might be free of being persecuted, and crucified again, according to the principles of such government, if he should either work miracles, or teach, or speak anything besides the rule of man's inventions" ([Robinson], *Liberty of Conscience*, 43).

85. Gillespie, *Wholesome Severity*, 5–10; *A Late Dialogue Betwixt a Civilian and a Divine* (London, 1644), 32–33; Edwards, *Antapologia*, 57ff., 237–39; idem, *The Casting Down*, theses 2, 3; Church of Scotland, *A Solemn Testimony Against Toleration* (Edinburgh, 1649), 4–6.

stretched beyond their limits, if you intend to inwrap heretics within their verge."[86]

The Hebrew Scriptures occupy an ambiguous place in the Christian tradition, and the political use to which various groups put Old Testament citations raised another debate, surrounding the status of Mosaic law and its implications for civil and spiritual affairs in a Christian society.[87] Many tolerationists held the general Christian position (taken from, among others, Luther's *Commentary on Galatians*)[88] that the Gospel had superseded the Law. Roger Williams and other sectarians went further, viewing the Old Testament as purely typological: in other words, events in the kingdom of Israel were important, not for their own sake, but for their foreshadowing of Christ's spiritual kingdom.[89] (Even Williams, however, used Old Testament citations when such would help his case, as did a number of other advocates of toleration.)[90]

A rejection of Mosaic Law tended to go hand in hand with a general rejection of civil power in ecclesiastical affairs, a legacy from English Separatists. Roger Williams illustrates this sectarian approach well. Churches and states are both formed voluntarily and with divine sanction, he explained, but are charged with fundamentally different missions. Posing a sharp dichotomy between the nature of spiritual as opposed to political power, Williams argued that coercion was proper in civil affairs, whereas religious issues could be settled only by persuasion and reminded his readers that "according to John 18:36, my kingdom is not of this world . . . although . . . the church and the civil kingdom or government be not inconsistent . . . yet they are

---

86. *Of Toleration: And the Duty of the Magistrate about Religion*, in *The Works of John Owen*, ed. Rev. William Gould (London and Edinburgh, 1851), 8:166.

87. Here I refer to the *judicial* aspect of the Mosaic law, not the moral law (Ten Commandments).

88. Luther had put it quite baldly: "Because they mingle the Law with the Gospel they must needs be perverters of the Gospel" (*Commentary on Galatians* [1575], sec. 1). See also [Rous], *The Ancient Bounds*, chap. 10; Williams, *Queries of Highest Consideration*, 5; and Walwyn, *The Power of Love*, 27.

89. See Miller, "Roger Williams: An Essay in Interpretation." In his comments at the Whitehall Debates, John Goodwin also expressed support for a typological reading of the Old Testament (*Clarke Papers*, 2:116); as did John Vernon, in *The Swords Abuse Asserted*, 12.

90. Williams cites the swords to plowshares metaphors from Isaiah 2:4 and Micah 4:3–4 in *Bloudy Tenent*, "Scriptures and Reasons . . . Sent to Mr. Cotton," sec. 1. Other tolerationists using Old Testament citations in support of religious liberty include Busher, *Religion's Peace*, 26–27, on the necessity of voluntary sacrifices and offerings (Exodus 25:2, 35:5), and [Rous], *The Ancient Bounds*, chap. 7.

independent according to that Scripture" (*Bloudy Tenent*, 224–25). For Williams, limitation of government was a means of preserving churches' purity, since political power would inevitably corrupt ("Christianity fell asleep in Constantine's bosom" [184]). This separation of spheres tied into a more general argument about the autonomy of congregations, a view that had brought Williams into conflict with Massachusetts divines during the 1630s. Not only should churches be free from government, he claimed, they should be free from each other. Winthrop noted that Williams objected to biweekly ministerial meetings of Massachusetts Bay preachers, claiming that this could be a prelude to "a presbytery or superintendency."[91]

For Williams, as we saw in Chapter 2, the most appropriate way to conceptualize political and spiritual entities was to view the church as "like unto a corporation, society, or company of East India or Turkey merchants" (*Bloudy Tenent*, 73). "All civil states," maintained Williams, "are . . . essentially civil, and therefore not judges, governors, or defenders of the spiritual or Christian state and worship" (3). This view of civil and ecclesiastical affairs represents a dramatic restriction of the civil magistrate's powers over religious affairs. It is not, however, a complete denial of any authority for the magistrate to deal with those who, claiming conscience, violate civil laws. Although consistently denying the civil magistrate's authority to govern church affairs, sectarians agreed with their opponents that civil rulers did have a duty to restrain blatant and persistent vice. (They defined blatant vice far more narrowly and politically than did their adversaries, however, and insisted that such a duty was purely civil.)[92] Although opposing tithes and compulsory church attendance, Gerrard Winstanley admitted that "if any man walk unrighteously toward his fellow creatures in civil matters, the power of the land must punish him."[93]

Opponents of toleration blanched at repudiating Mosaic law, insofar as doing so would seem to loose a whole litany of moral transgressions on society. If magistrates could not prosecute transgressions of the First Table, representatives of the Church of Scotland asked, on what basis could they prosecute

91. *Winthrop's Journal*, 1:113. Williams's congregationalism, though extreme, was not different in kind from prevailing notions in Massachusetts: the ministers responded by assuring Williams that "no church or person can have power over another church" (113).

92. Dell, in *Right Reformation*, admits that the magistrate must restrain the wicked "for the quiet of the state" (27), but he notes that this is not a *spiritual* power.

93. *Truth Lifting Up Its Head Above Scandals* (London, 1648), in Works, 130.

violations of the Second Table such as murder or theft?[94] The erratic and provocative behavior of many sectarians only strengthened the rhetorical power of this evocation of anarchy and licentiousness. Indeed, one of antitolerationists' most consistent (and polemically effective) strategies lay in linking congregationalists and the Dissenting Brethren with radical sects. As we have seen, the authors of *An Apologeticall Narration* had attempted to strike a middle ground that affirmed a national church structure so long as ecclesiastical decisions and discipline were left largely in the hands of individual congregations. In a flurry of activity following its publication, Scots attacked the *Narration* and the Independents' congregational program as schismatic and barely disguised sectarianism.[95] Presbyterians saw *themselves* as occupying the middle ground: in the words of Alexander Henderson, Presbyterian church government occupied a moderate position "betwixt popish and prelatical tyranny, and Brownistical and popular anarchy."[96] This Presbyterian attack, once Anglicanism was no longer a potent political force in England, aimed to deny the distinction between Independents, Separatists, and sects. Thomas Edwards wrote to the authors of the *Narration* that although they publicly disavowed Separatism, "Master Browne and your principles are too nigh a kin."[97] Presbyterians branded Independents as fomenters of "rents and schisms, strife and debate," undermining the office of the minister, and causing general religious and social havoc.[98]

94. Church of Scotland, *Solemn Testimony*, 6–7. See also Edwards, *Antapologia*, theses 13, 14, 17–19, and idem, *The Casting Down*, 23.

95. This debate between Presbyterians and Independents often hinged upon very intricate discussions of the primitive church in Jerusalem, debates not germane to this project. If the church in Jerusalem had been so large that all believers could not have met at once, but instead had had to gather in a number of congregations, then Presbyterians could argue that the subordination of one congregation to the whole was scripturally approved. Independents argued that the church in Jerusalem was one large congregation which could and did gather together, and thus the Presbyterian argument was invalid. See *The Reasons of the Dissenting Brethren Against the Third Proposition, Concerning Presbyterial Government* (London, 1645); *The Answer of the Assembly of Divines unto the Reasons of the Seven Dissenting Brethren* (London, 1644); and *Papers Given in to the [Committee for Accommodation]* (London, 1644).

96. *Reformation of Church-Government in Scotland*, 17. "Brownistical" refers to Robert Browne, one of the original English separatists. See also Samuel Rutherford, *A Peaceful and Temperate Plea* (London, 1642), chap. 18.

97. *Antapologia*, 31.

98. [Forbes], *An Anatomy of Independency*, 5–6. London ministers, heavily influenced by Presbyterianism, concurred: see *A Letter of the Ministers of the City of London*, sec. 3; *Certain Additional Reasons*, sec. 3; Thomas Edwards, *Gangraena* (London, 1646), 156; William Prynne, *Independency Examined* (London, 1644), 6; and *Anti-toleration, or a Modest Defense of the Letter of the London Ministers* (London, 1646), 7–8.

The Presbyterian critique of congregationalist (Independent) church government, and of gathered congregations and sects more generally, linked their Independent opponents with sectarians who rejected Mosaic law and comprehended them all under the heading of dangerous libertines. Antitolerationists repeatedly asserted that toleration would sanction schism within the church, and that this rupture of Christian unity would in turn lead to an onslaught of heresy and irreligion (followed inevitably by licentiousness and anarchy).[99]

We should also keep in mind that these scriptural arguments took place in a society permeated with providentialist assumptions about the course of human events.[100] Such providentialist arguments tended to be either retrospective ones, centering on the military success of the New Model Army as evidence of God's favor for the tolerationist policies it represented; or prospective ones about the eventual triumph of truth over falsehood. An anonymous author cited the fortunes of Cromwell's troops as evidence of God's favor for a policy of toleration, and Thomas Coleman attributed the triumph of the

-----

The connection between undermining the office of minister and rebelling against the civil magistrate is made by Robert Hitchcock, *The Thankful Leper, or Samaritan* (HL Manuscript EL 8178 [35/B/29]), who laments the prevailing condition that "some such apple-squire that in terms of his art can read a lecture upon a hawk or hound holds more familiarity, and is better respected than a poor minister of the gospel that brings unto them the glad tidings of salvation" (27). The freedom from popery that English Protestantism has secured does not satisfy many, Hitchcock complains, "as if this great blessing were not worth thanks . . . there be in this kingdom such unthankful wretches as stick not to cry out, no church, no sacraments, no ministers, no discipline at all . . . O monstrous ingratitude" (36).

99. At some point in nearly every antitolerationist tract, claims of this sort appear. See the following: *Liberty of Conscience Confuted* (London, 1648), 3; [Steuart], *Some Observations*, 61ff.; Rutherford, *A Free Disputation*, chaps. 7–10, 26; Gillespie, *Wholesome Severity*; 17–23; *A Letter of the Ministers of the City of London*, sec. 4; *Certain Additional Reasons*, sec. 4; *The Humble Petition of the Ministers of the Counties of Suffolk and Essex* (London, 1646), 1; *A Late Dialogue*, 31; *The Harmonious Consent of the Ministers . . . of Lancaster* (London, 1648), 16–17; and *A Serious and Faithfull Representation* (London, 1649), 7–8.

100. The best overview of providentialism in seventeenth-century England is Blair Worden, "Providence and Politics in Cromwellian England," *Past and Present* 109 (1985): 55–99; see also, more generally, the introduction to Hill, *English Bible*, and Keith Thomas, *Religion and the Decline of Magic* (New York, 1971), chap. 4.

Providentialism reaches well back in English history. For primary sources, see Foxe's *Acts and Monuments of the English Martyrs* (London, 1583) and *The Lawes of England* (HL Manuscript EL 1182a, n.d., 1620s or 1630s), which places England alongside Israel in providential history: its author cites his real aim as "to prove the sweet harmony and agreement between the Kingdom of England and the Kingdom of Israel [in government and laws]. . . . That though the Jews be dispersed, yet there is still an Israel of God reigning upon Earth" (35).

Parliamentary cause to "a praying army."[101] In addition, army officers and soldiers clearly saw themselves as participating in a defining struggle for popular and religious liberty: references to the providential role of the army in fulfilling God's plan for England recur throughout the *Clarke Papers*.[102]

Providentialist arguments also pointed to the future: many involved the account of Gamaliel in Acts 5:34–39. "[Gamaliel said to the leaders of the synagogue who were incensed at the Apostles' teaching:] Ye men of Israel, take heed to yourselves what ye intend to do as touching these men. . . . Refrain from these men, and let them alone: for if this counsel for this work be of men, it will come to nought: But if it be of God, ye cannot overthrow it; lest haply ye be found even to fight against God." This account gave rise to the title of John Goodwin's *Theomachia*.[103] In addition, a more general defense of toleration as productive of truth (through the clash of ideas) was made, famously, by John Milton in *Areopagitica*.[104] Other tolerationists held a related notion of the robust nature of truth and its ability to prevail without the coercive power of the magistrate.[105] Of course, providentialist arguments cut both ways, and the Restoration of Charles II in 1660, for many opponents of religious dissent and toleration, justified the reimposition of penal laws and persecution of Dissenters.

Skepticism and Toleration: Christian Skepticism and the Search for a (Religiously) Minimal State

In many ways, toleration debates raise questions about the validity and consequences of the increasing skepticism that characterized seventeenth-century England.[106] Skepticism is a notoriously difficult term to define: my

---

101. *A Letter from an Independent to His Honoured Friend, a Presbyterian in London* (London, 1645); Thomas Coleman, *Hopes Deferred and Dashed* (London, 1645), 19.

102. See, for example, *Clarke Papers*, 1:227, 255, 281, 295, 379.

103. Goodwin, *Theomachia; or, The Grand Imprudence of Men Running the Hazard of Fighting Against God* (London, 1644); also in Haller, *Tracts on Liberty*, 3:3–58. Taylor also alludes to the account of Gamaliel (*Theologike Eklektike*, 192).

104. *Areopagitica* (London, 1644); reprinted in *Areopagitica and Other Political Writings*.

105. Owen, *Of Toleration*, 183–84; Busher, *Religion's Peace*, 23; Richardson, *The Necessity of Toleration*, 17–18.

106. English skepticism was influenced by European thinkers, of course, and the essays in Levine, *Early Modern Skepticism*, flesh out some of these broader contexts; see also Richard H. Popkin, *The History of Scepticism from Erasmus to Descartes* (New York, 1964). I am less interested in what one might call radical skepticism, which characterized the beliefs of some sectarians. Such

attention in this section is directed at a widespread school of thought that was compatible with a commitment to Christian doctrine (as had been the earlier humanism of individuals like More and Erasmus), and which stressed the variety of human understandings and the mysteries inherent in biblical texts. Admitting the limits of human knowledge and declining to insist upon specific theological or ecclesiastical dogmas, such skeptics noted, need not undermine Christian unity. Rather, as John Saltmarsh put it, "The common ignorance and infirmity amongst us, may be a rise for a common unity amongst us," while one of William Walwyn's arguments for toleration rested on "the uncertainty of knowledge in this life."[107] In another work, Saltmarsh admitted that he had not presented his defense of liberty of conscience in definitive terms: "I have writ little conclusive or positive: Determination being not the proper work of us, that stand below."[108] Jeremy Taylor held that "because there is a variety of human understandings, and uncertainty in things, no man should be too forward in determining all questions, nor so forward in prescribing to others, that liberty which God hath left us entire by propounding many things obscurely."[109] The repeated use of Jesus' parable of the wheat and tares by tolerationists also suggested that human knowledge and ability to determine spiritual things with certainty were sharply limited.[110]

Skepticism often went hand in hand with a mistrust of claims of infallibility, and was thus a powerful weapon against the Catholic Church. Perhaps the most notable criticism of infallibility claims is Lord Brooke's *Discourse*, which attacked papal pretensions and accused bishops of arrogating to

---

skepticism, as has been well documented by Christopher Hill in *The World Turned Upside Down*, went so far as to question the existence of God, human sin, and a number of other basic Protestant and Christian beliefs, as well as to cast doubt on the grounds of magistracy and civil government. Radical skepticism never obtained except in the minds of a very small number, however, and may have actually backfired politically, driving more moderate skeptics back to Christian orthodoxy in alarm. In fact, some scholars question whether some of the most radical and skeptical sectarians mentioned in seventeenth-century polemics even existed at all. See J. F. McGregor, "Seekers and Ranters," in McGregor and Reay, *Radical Religion in the English Revolution*, 121–39.

107. Saltmarsh, *The Smoke in the Temple* (London, 1646), epistle dedicatory; Walwyn, *The Compassionate Samaritane*, reason 2, p. 10.

108. *Dawnings of Light*, preparatory.

109. *Theologike Eklektike*, epistle dedicatory, 13; chap. 31. See also Goodwin, *Theomachia*, 12, 21.

110. See [Robinson], *Liberty of Conscience*, 55; [Overton], *The Arraignment of Mr. Persecution*, 24; and Williams, *Bloudy Tenent*, chaps. 18–27.

themselves the powers of the whole church.[111] Persecution came into the church with popery, and the structure of bishops merely replicated these claims to infallibility and the coercion they necessarily brought with them, argued such thinkers as Milton and Chillingworth.[112] If we could know God's mind perfectly and infallibly, Henry Robinson suggested, persecution might be justified. However, he added, we do not, and what we do know is revealed to us only gradually.[113]

Sectarians, for their part, often saw little practical difference between Catholic bishops and Anglican ones, or between Anglican bishops and the national Presbyterian structure proposed by Parliament and the Westminster Assembly. True religion, wrote Leonard Busher, comes from "new birth," not birth into one or another national church; and laws requiring individuals to profess the religion of their magistrates are "antichristian, Romish, and cruel."[114] In Milton's famous words, "New Presbyter is but old Priest writ large."[115] Henry Robinson equated prelacy, episcopacy, popery, and Presbyterianism, while at the conclusion of Overton's *Arraignment of Mr. Persecution*, the reader discovers that "Mr. Persecution" is really "Presbyterian Government."[116] John

111. Lord Brooke (Robert Greville), *Discourse Opening the Nature of That Episcopacy, Which Is Exercised in England* (London, 1642), also in Haller, *Tracts on Liberty*, 2:37–163; and William Chillingworth, *The Religion of Protestants a Safe Way to Salvation* (London, 1638). Such political and ecclesiastical uses of skepticism, however, were a two-edged sword, and many of the same arguments used by English Reformers against the Roman church were in turn used against them by Separatists (Christianson, *Reformers and Babylon*).

112. See John Milton, *Of Reformation, and the Causes Which Have Hindered It* (London, 1641); also in *Complete Prose Works*, ed. Don M. Wolfe (New Haven, Conn., 1953), 1:514–617; and idem, *Treatise of Civil Power in Ecclesiastical Causes*. Chillingworth's *Mr. Chillingworth's Letter Touching Infallibility* (London, 1662) and Lord Falkland's *Discourse of Infallibility* (London, 1660) were published posthumously, but give a further sense of their thinking about infallibility. On Chillingworth's endorsement of probabilism as a weapon against infallibility arguments, see Remer, *Humanism*, 146–62.

113. *Liberty of Conscience*, 55. See also the Large Petition of the Levellers, which argues that none should be molested on account of conscience "by judges that are not infallible but may be mistaken as well as other men in their judgments" (in Woodhouse, *Puritanism and Liberty*, 321), and Taylor, *Theologike Eklektike*, epistle dedicatory, 18; chaps. 3–9.

114. *Religion's Peace*, 1. Busher's original essay was addressed to King James: it was reprinted in 1646.

115. See Milton's sonnet "On the forcers of conscience" (1647), in *The Complete Poetry of John Milton*, ed. John T. Shawcross (Garden City, N.Y., 1971), 212. See also Saltmarsh, *A New Quaere*, 2, and *Divine Observations upon the London Ministers Letter Against Toleration* (London, 1645), 5.

116. [Robinson], *Liberty of Conscience*, "To every Christian reader"; [Overton], *The Arraignment of Mr. Persecution*, 34. For essentially the same points, see *Toleration Justified* (London, 1645), 2, and John Goodwin, *Independency Gods verity* (London, 1647), 7–8.

Saltmarsh equated *any* national church system with claims of infallibility.[117] Thus a skeptical philosophical and epistemological stance, consistent with a basic Christian theology, often undermined claims of infallibility and hierarchy and argued in favor of tolerating religious dissenters.

Conversely, *attacks* on toleration often took the form of attacks on skepticism. A fine case in point is Samuel Rutherford's *Free Disputation Against Pretended Liberty of Conscience*. Rutherford argued that skepticism inevitably leads to licentiousness, resulting in a situation in which "conscience is hereby made every man's rule, umpire, judge, Bible, and his God."[118] By removing the authority of tradition, Scripture, councils, and other forms of authority, Rutherford argued, even "moderate" skeptics like Jeremy Taylor eliminated any standard by which one might judge and condemn the behavior of others both in religious and civil affairs. If human fallibility makes moral or religious distinctions unknowable, then certainly "adulterers must be tolerated. . . . Yea, no minister of the gospel should preach to his flock fundamental gospel truths, because he is not infallible."[119] For Rutherford, skepticism exercises a corrosive influence on the unity of Christian doctrine and the ethical foundations of society and will never stay within the bounds set even by well-intentioned tolerationist advocates.

Of course, as with all general statements, we must also consider the important exceptions, among them Thomas Hobbes. Skepticism notwithstanding, Hobbes witnessed a destructive civil war charged by religious differences. His comments on "things tend[ing] to the dissolution of commonwealths" bear all the marks of such religiously driven conflict: want of absolute power, private judgment of good and evil, and "the opinion that there be more . . . sovereigns than one in the commonwealth" (*L*, 215). One set of beliefs might be no truer than the other, Hobbes argued, but one must be chosen and imposed in the name of peace. Hobbes, for example, shared many skeptics' views about the inherent ambiguity of scriptural examples and the uncertainty of human knowledge in supernatural affairs. Regardless of his views on the status of Anglicanism as "true faith" (he was very skeptical, to say the

---

117. Saltmarsh, *The Smoke in the Temple*, "A Way of Peace," no. 12; see also [Rous], *The Ancient Bounds*, 27; William Walwyn, *A Help to the Right Understanding of a Discourse Concerning Independency* (London, 1645), 4–5 (reprinted in Haller, *Tracts on Liberty*, 3:191–201).

118. *A Free Disputation*, "To the . . . reader."

119. Ibid., 45, 195.

least),[120] however, civil peace was always uppermost in Hobbes's mind. His concerns about the social consequences of independent, dogmatic beliefs, especially among elites, has been noted by Deborah Baumgold, who points out that "divided sovereignty . . . institutionalizes elite conflict."[121] Thus he sought to eliminate independent claims of religious authority. Johann Sommerville has accurately captured both Hobbes's skeptical tolerance and his concern with order: "Hobbes argued for a minimalist religion (that is to say, one which consisted of a very small number of fundamental beliefs), and for freedom of enquiry in all areas where reason was capable of adding to human knowledge. At the same time he wished to prevent the spread of ideas which threatened to undermine state security."[122] Hobbes's position was shared by theorists who linked sovereignty with protection: this *de facto* school effectively bolstered Cromwell's claim to rule by claiming that allegiance was due to the sovereign who could preserve order and protect the subject's person.[123]

120. Of Hobbes's religious views, there is no end of controversy. Those making him out either as devout believer or atheist tend to be least convincing. For Hobbes as Calvinist, see A. P. Martinich, *The Two Gods of Leviathan: Thomas Hobbes on Religion and Politics* (Cambridge, 1992); as Socinian, Peter Geach, "The Religion of Thomas Hobbes," *Religious Studies* 17 (1981): 549–58; as atheist, Leo Strauss, *The Political Philosophy of Hobbes: Its Basis and Genesis* (Oxford, 1936); as Anglican, Paul J. Johnson, "Hobbes's Anglican Doctrine of Salvation," in *Thomas Hobbes in His Time*, ed. Ralph Ross, Herbert W. Schneider, and Theodore Waldman (Minneapolis, 1974), 102–25.

The broad range of influences on Hobbes's religious views is explored in Richard Tuck, "The Civil Religion of Thomas Hobbes," in Phillipson and Skinner, *Political Discourse in Early Modern Britain*, 120–38; while Shirley Letwin's warmly appreciative account of Hobbes's Christian skepticism provides an intriguing view: see "Skepticism and Toleration in Hobbes' Political Thought," in Levine, *Early Modern Skepticism*, 165–78. Joshua Mitchell, I think, puts it well, seeing Hobbes as not anti-Christian but rather a highly unorthodox one, in "Hobbes and the Equality of All Under the One," *Political Theory* 21 (1993): 78–100.

121. "Hobbes' Political Sensibility: The Menace of Political Ambition," in Mary G. Dietz, ed., *Thomas Hobbes and Political Theory* (Lawrence, Kans., 1990), 85.

122. *Thomas Hobbes*, 136; see also Dana Chabot, "Thomas Hobbes: Skeptical Moralist," *APSR* 89 (1995): 401–10.

123. Quentin Skinner links Hobbes with such *de facto* theorists as Marchamont Nedham and Anthony Ascham in "Conquest and Consent: Thomas Hobbes and the Engagement Controversy," in *The Interregnum: The Quest for Settlement*, ed. G. E. Aylmer (Hamden, Conn., 1972), 79–98, and "Thomas Hobbes et la defense du pouvoir 'de facto,'" *Revue philosophique* 99 (1973): 131–54. Although Skinner has since altered his view to take into account Hobbes's evolving relationship with the rhetorical tradition (see "Thomas Hobbes on the Proper Signification of Liberty," *Transactions of the Royal Historical Society*, 5th ser, 40 [1990]: 121–51, and *Reason and Rhetoric in the Philosophy of Hobbes* [Cambridge, 1996]), I hesitate to abandon the valuable insights of Skinner's two earlier essays.

Hobbes and other *de facto* theorists notwithstanding, it remains the case that the preponderance of skeptical arguments in the 1640s and 1650s pointed in the direction of toleration. Skepticism possessed an established philosophical pedigree stretching back to ancient times, and its revival during the Renaissance made it a familiar doctrine to seventeenth-century English elites. In its moderate form, skepticism was fully compatible with basic Christian tenets and ethics and allowed the coexistence of a wide latitude of belief regarding rites, ceremonies, and dogmas (assuming, of course, that one's peers were also skeptical). The philosophical spirit behind such moderate skepticism often led to an attempt to define a basic, minimal Christian creed on which all English Protestants could agree. Such Christian minimalists sought to locate a (small) number of fundamental Christian doctrines while simultaneously deemphasizing the elaborate theological and liturgical accretions that had ossified into various orthodoxies over the years. Clearly this type of thinking threw great doubt on Roman Catholic claims of infallibility, but it also undermined the Laudian program of divine-right episcopacy within the Anglican Church *and* the *jure divino* systems of Scottish Presbyterians and the Dissenting Brethren. Christian minimalists sought to mitigate the dogmatism they saw on all sides, pursuing (civil and religious) peace through a religious common ground and a recognition of human fallibility.

The most notable source for this minimal Christian ethics arose in the circle of thinkers who gathered with Lord Falkland at the Great Tew during the late 1630s.[124] The ideal of the Tew thinkers was that of a broad national church that did not exclude or persecute members for objecting in indifferent matters.[125] Had such an effort been successful in the realm of practice, it might have removed many of the religious disputes central to the outbreak of the English Civil War. Unfortunately, such a project was doomed by the aggressive Laudian program of the 1630s as well as by the divine right pretensions of Scottish Presbyterians in the 1640s.

The more general search for a minimally agreeable theology went on throughout the 1640s. Leonard Busher asserted that "all those that confess,

---

124. The definitive reference on the Tew circle, though somewhat dated, remains John Tulloch, *Rational Theology and Christian Philosophy in England in the Seventeenth Century* (Edinburgh and London, 1874), vol. 1. For a more recent commentary, see Barbara J. Shapiro, *Probability and Certainty in Seventeenth-Century England: A Study of the Relationships Between Natural Science, Religion, History, Law, and Literature* (Princeton, 1983), 78–82, and Remer, *Humanism*, 144–45.

125. See Chapter 2, note 69.

freely, without compulsion, that Jesus is the Messiah, the Lord, and that he came in the flesh, are to be esteemed the children of God and true Christians," while William Walwyn stressed helping the poor and feeding the hungry.[126] Thomas Coleman, in a minimalist vein, counseled the Commons to "establish as few things *jure divino*, as can well be."[127]

Jeremy Taylor's *Theologike Eklektike* brings together these two modes of thought, Christian skepticism and Christian minimalism. The basic article of Christian faith, Taylor asserts, is Christ crucified, and the Apostles' Creed represents a reasonable starting point for attempts at unifying disparate Christian perspectives.[128] Assuming that an individual professes such basic beliefs and lives in peace with his neighbors, we should leave him be. Although Scripture sets down basic tenets of faith in plain language, we must concede (given the variety of human understandings and the uncertainty of knowledge) that it also contains many mysteries. Throughout time, churches have sought to resolve such mysteries by relying on traditions, new translations of the Bible, ecclesiastical councils, papal authority, or the writings of church fathers: *all* of these, Taylor points out, are fallible, as is human reason.[129] Somehow we have moved from the simple teachings of Jesus to the arcane complexity of Aquinas's *Summae*.[130] When deciding whether to persecute someone for their religious views, we face two possibilities: either that person is right, in which case we effectively persecute God;[131] or the person is wrong, in which case "why give to error the glory of martyrdom?"[132] Building upon the humility of human understanding and a minimalist interpretation of the requirements of Christian morality, Taylor arrives at religious liberty. Still, he asserts that individuals must obey the magistrate in things indifferent: the difficulty was, and would remain, how to determine which things were indeed indifferent, and which necessary to salvation.

Again, however, Hobbes provides us with a counterweight to this equation of religious minimalism with toleration. Hobbes was personally familiar with

126. *Religion's Peace*, 4; Walwyn, *A Still and Soft Voice from the Scriptures*, 10; see also Walwyn, *The Power of Love*, "To Every Reader."

127. *Hopes Deferred and Dashed*, 24.

128. *Theologike Eklektike*, chaps. 1, 15.

129. Ibid., chaps. 3–9.

130. Ibid., 191.

131. This sentiment, as mentioned above, is reinforced by the account of Gamaliel in Acts 5:34–40, and is also used in Goodwin's *Theomachia*.

132. Taylor, *Theologike Eklektike*, 197.

many in the Tew Circle, and their project was congenial to him, since it offered to remove much of the religious problem without drastic action by sovereign fiat.[133] His skepticism and distrust of the divine right pretensions of Stuart kings and Anglican bishops, papal claims to universal jurisdiction, and fissiparous sectarian enthusiasm manifested themselves in just such a minimal theory of religion and morality. After elaborating nineteen laws and derivations from laws of nature, Hobbes offers "a rule, by which the laws of nature may easily be examined. . . . Do not that to another, which thou wouldest not have done to thyself" (*L*, 144). Religiously, this minimalism is stated most succinctly as "Jesus is the Christ," which Hobbes identifies as the heart of Christian doctrine and "the, *unum necessarium*, only article of faith, which the Scripture maketh simply necessary to salvation" (590). Yet for Hobbes, the political corollary to this religious minimalism, because of the problem of order and the religious issues that fired the Civil War, was not toleration but an absolutist civil religion. This strong defense of sovereign power *might* lead to toleration (circumstances and the sovereign permitting), but did not articulate toleration as a significant part of Hobbes's theoretical edifice.[134] Hobbes sought a theory of sovereignty that would ensure civil order, and was not nearly so concerned about the substantive political commitments that any given sovereign might choose to undertake.

Psychology and Epistemology: "Understanding" Versus "Will," the Inefficacy of Persecution, and the Subjective Element of Conscience

Alongside the scriptural and skeptical arguments just outlined, English tolerationists also stressed an important *epistemological* argument around the nature of belief. According to this view, belief could not be forced because it

133. On the similarities and differences between Hobbes and the Tew thinkers, see Sommerville, *Thomas Hobbes*, 136–37, 166–67, and Noel Malcolm, "Hobbes and Spinoza," in Burns and Goldie, *Cambridge History of Political Thought*, 544–45.

134. Nothing in Hobbes's theory rules out toleration, of course. For more charitable interpretations of the possibility of Hobbesian toleration, see Gary Remer, "Hobbes, the Rhetorical Tradition, and Toleration," *Review of Politics* 54 (1992): 5–33, and Eldon J. Eisenach, *Two Worlds of Liberalism: Religion and Politics in Hobbes, Locke, and Mill* (Chicago, 1981), 70. A similar, though less convincing, case is made in series of essays by Alan Ryan: "A More Tolerant Hobbes?" in Mendus, *Justifying Toleration*; "Hobbes, Toleration, and the Inner Life," in *The Nature of Political Theory*, ed. David Miller and Larry Siedentop (New York, 1983); and "Hobbes and Individualism," in *Perspectives on Thomas Hobbes*, ed. G.A.J. Rogers and Alan Ryan (Oxford, 1988).

was a faculty of the understanding, not of the will. Persecution was not only wrong on scriptural or skeptical grounds, tolerationists claimed, it was ineffective and doomed to fail. Persuasion, not coercion, was the way to deal with spiritual errors. John Musgrave suggested that "in that which consisteth in the persuasion of the heart, corporal violence prevaileth no more than the vapor of wind that blows, to hinder the heat of the fire."[135] Similar sentiments were expressed by Jeremy Taylor, William Walwyn, Leonard Busher, and Richard Overton, all of whom separated the understanding from the will, placed matters of religion and belief in the former, and therefore ruled out attempts at compulsion in matters of conscience.[136] Worse than being ineffectual, persecution was also the sign of a false church and the murderous spirit of Cain. In Winstanley's language, persecution urged by the clergy was a sign of the "first Adam," one in bondage to the flesh and covetous pride.[137]

Along with this expansion of the independent status of belief (independent, that is, of will and volition) went a transformation in the nature of conscience. According to the orthodox view, conscience represented the voice of God within an individual, and it was considered possible to sin against one's conscience by transgressing the law of God.[138] Advocates of toleration

135. *The Conscience Pleading for Its Own Liberty* (London, 1647), 4.

136. Taylor, *Theologike Eklektike*, chap. 13; Walwyn, *The Compassionate Samaritane*, reason 1; idem, *A Prediction of Mr. Edwards His Conversion and Recantation* (London, 1646), 3–4 (reprinted in Haller, *Tracts on Liberty*, 3:339–48); idem, *A Whisper in the Ear of Mr. Thomas Edwards, Minister* (London, 1646), 5 (reprinted in Haller, *Tracts on Liberty*, 3:321–35); Busher, *Religion's Peace*, 2, 5; [Overton], *A Remonstrance of Many Thousand Citizens* (London, 1646), 12ff. (reprinted in Haller, *Tracts on Liberty*, 3:351–70). See also *Twelve Weighty Queries*, nos. 1–2; *Toleration Justified*, 5; *Divine Observations*, 5; and [Rous], *The Ancient Bounds*, chap. 6.

137. See Winstanley, *The New Law of Righteousness* (London, 1649), for the theology of the two men; *The True Levellers Standard Advanced* (London, 1649) and *A New-Yeers Gift for the Parliament and the Armie* (London, 1650), which add the Norman Yoke political argument; and *Fire in the Bush* (London, 1650). (All can be found in Winstanley's *Works*.) See also *Twelve Weighty Queries*, no. 8.

138. However, and here is where the issue gets even more involved, one is bound to follow the dictate's of one's conscience, so one also sins (though not, apparently, so severely) by going against even an erroneous conscience. Thus to avoid sin one has to do the right thing (have a rightly informed conscience) for the right reason (because it is the dictate of conscience, not because one has been compelled by a magistrate). The definitive reference on these issues is D. Odon Lottin, *Psychologie et Morale aux XIIe et XIIe Siècles*, 6 vols. (Louvain, 1942–49); see also Kevin T. Kelly, *Conscience: Dictator or Guide? A Study in Seventeenth-Century English Protestant Moral Thought* (London, 1967). For a more concise overview, in English, see Timothy C. Potts, "Conscience," in *The Cambridge History of Later Medieval Philosophy*, ed. Norman Kretzmann, Anthony Kenny, and Jan Pinborg (Cambridge, 1982), 687–704.

did not reject this formulation, although they did begin stressing the subjective aspect of conscience, in which one sinned by going against the conscience even if one's substantive beliefs are mistaken. When John Cotton referred sardonically to "some point of doctrine which you believe in conscience to be the truth, or . . . practicing some work which in conscience you believe to be a religious duty," Roger Williams replied that one may be persecuted even if one's beliefs are false (*Bloudy Tenent*, 41, 63). These claims also informed many other advocates of toleration. Walwyn declared bluntly that "though the thing may be in itself good, yet if it do not appear to be so to my conscience, the practice thereof in me is sinful."[139] In *A New Quaere*, Saltmarsh cited Paul's epistle: "Let every man be fully persuaded in his own mind," wrote Paul (Romans 14:5, 23), and Saltmarsh warned of the danger of hastily settling Presbyterian church government and "bringing people under a popish implicit obedience."[140]

Still, this argument for toleration did not entirely address the political question at hand and was unlikely to sway those opposing toleration, since antitolerationists rarely argued that one could coerce an individual into holding a given belief.[141] Although George Gillespie did argue that, as a result of punishment, a heretic may "be at least reduced to external order and obedience, being persuaded by the terror of civil power, which may and doth . . . prove a preparation to free obedience," this was not a widespread claim.[142] Rutherford, for example, admitted that conscience is a faculty of the understanding, not the will, and that debates over liberty of conscience were about

---

For a historical source, see HL Manuscript EL 34/B/62, a sermon on Acts 24:16, which notes these two ways to sin, following an erroneous conscience and not following the dictates of conscience. What is necessary for right conduct, the author states, is both the knowledge of God's will and the zeal to do it voluntarily (18).

139. *The Compassionate Samaritane*, 43; see also [Overton], *A Remonstrance of Many Thousand Citizens*, 11. This emphasis on inner convincement is drawn, as noted above, from Romans 14:23. See also *Twelve Weighty Queries*, 3.

140. *A New Quaere*, 1. See also Richardson, *The Necessity of Toleration*, 5, and Saltmarsh, *The Smoke in the Temple*.

141. Not even St. Augustine, who articulated a powerful and coherent theory of persecution and who in many ways laid the foundation for English antitolerationists of the seventeenth century, asserted that force could change belief. See Augustine, Letters 93, 133, and *On the Correction of the Donatists*; more generally on the parallels between Augustinian and later English Protestant views on coercion, see my "Augustine and English Protestants: Authority and Order, Coercion and Dissent in the Earthly City," in *Augustine and Liberal Education: Critical and Prospective Essays*, ed. Kevin Hughes and Kim Paffenroth (Aldershot, 2000), 163–76.

142. *Wholesome Severity*, 32.

actions, not mere beliefs.[143] In toleration debates, the question at hand was often a far more subtle one: whether the magistrate possessed a *restraining* power, an authority to prevent individuals from spreading overt heresies and disruptive religious (by definition, of course, social) messages. This restraining power was the issue, for example, in the Whitehall Debates.[144] There, both Rich and Ireton agreed that conscience itself could not be forced, and that their discussions were meant to decide which sorts of *actions* magistrates were justified in suppressing (*Clarke Papers*, 2:78–81). However, many tolerationists saw beliefs and actions as closely linked. One author argued that liberty of belief implied liberty of action, since faith without works is dead.[145]

If tolerationist arguments stressed an increasingly subjective notion of the conscience (still, of course, firmly within a Christian context), opponents reasserted the traditional understanding, presenting conscience as "God's deputy within us," a "lump of divinity" in the human soul.[146] Thus it was considered possible for an individual to believe something objectively mistaken and against the will of God, and to have an erring conscience. Out of "some tenderness of conscience," then, Rutherford saw toleration as threatening to bring in a "liberty of sinning."[147] Elsewhere Rutherford stated flatly that "all that conscience saith is not Scripture."[148] To the argument that conscience, *in se*, binds an individual to perform the dictate of that conscience, Rutherford responded by again raising concerns about the potential for anarchy and disorder. "This poor argument will conclude against all laws of magistrates, against murderers, bloody traitors . . . the King forbids the English Jesuit to stab the prince . . . doth the supreme magistrate compel this

143. *A Free Disputation*, 3–4, 46.

144. Carolyn Polizzotto, "Liberty of Conscience and the Whitehall Debates of 1648–9," *JEH* 26 (1975): 69–82.

145. *Divine Observations*, 5. William Penn would later develop this claim in greater detail (see Chapter 5).

146. *Anti-toleration*, 5; Rutherford, *A Free Disputation*, 15.

147. *A Free Disputation*, 20. This notion of "erring conscience" was often associated with the idea that "natural" conscience may carry the seed of morality (as, in Christian views, the Old Testament Law and the Commandments), but was also prone to error due to fallen human nature and needed the "enlightening" of Christian revelation. See *A Free Disputation*, 6–7, and Robert Hitchcock, *A Sermon on Law, Nature, and Conscience* (HL Manuscript EL 8389, n.d.). Hitchcock argues that even Gentiles, "though they had not the law written in tablets of stone as had the Jews, yet they had as law which was the ground of that, the Law of Nature written in their hearts . . . for there being but two guides to direct us how to frame our lives, the Law of God, and the Light of Nature" (8, 35).

148. *Joshua Redivivus; or, Mr. Rutherford's Letters* (Rotterdam, 1664), 511.

Jesuit to sin?"[149] For opponents of toleration, if conscience was to mean anything, it had to denote something more than personal whim or fancy: otherwise it is indeed (as a satirical observer put it) simply "a theological scarecrow" designed to shield an individual from the ethical constraints of living in human society.[150]

Behind opposition to the subjectification of conscience lay, again, concerns about anarchy and licentiousness. These purported social consequences were closely related to arguments about theology and church government, since William Prynne saw Independent church government as "a seminary of schisms . . . [and] a floodgate to let in an inundation of all manner of heresies, errors, sects, religions, destructive opinions, libertinism and lawlessness among us."[151] The link between heresy and social chaos, for Prynne, was direct and causal. If compulsion in matters of religion was not acceptable to tolerationists, it was difficult to see how it could be acceptable in any other area of human endeavor: "If liberty be granted in these [e.g., heresy, tolerating false prophets], we know no cause why men that can in such a handsome way pretend conscience for it, should be denied liberty to run into excess and riot."[152] As Gillespie put it, "the very nature of the argument [that compelling against one's conscience compels one to sin] driveth universally against the compelling of any man to do anything which is against his own conscience."[153]

Contemporary Examples: New England and Holland, Toleration and Prosperity

In an argument with special resonance for this comparative study of toleration, advocates of uniformity often cited the lack of toleration for Presbyterians or other religious groups in Massachusetts Bay. Since Massachusetts Puritans shared congregationalist commitments with English Independents, such an argument was a potent polemical weapon.[154] Adam Steuart noted the lack

149. *A Free Disputation*, 140. Of course, both tolerationists and antitolerationists agreed that persecuting someone for a *correctly* informed conscience was indeed sinful, as, for example, Paul's persecution of Christians before his conversion (Acts 9:4).
150. "New Interpreter," HL Manuscript EL 7801.
151. *Twelve Considerable and Serious Considerations*, 7.
152. Church of Scotland, *Solemn Testimony*, 7.
153. Gillespie, *Wholesome Severity*, 23.
154. It is debatable, of course, whether by the late 1640s there was anything more than a bare resemblance between English and American congregationalists. Certainly the 1648 Cambridge Platform in Massachusetts differs markedly from the defenses of toleration that came from within the New Model Army or even, though more limited in scope, from those of the Independents

of toleration for Presbyterians in New England, while another author pointed to the case of Anne Hutchinson to counter Independent arguments for toleration.[155] Gillespie pointed out that although English Independents demanded toleration, they seemed unwilling to grant it whenever they came to power. He noted that Independents and others opposed Presbyterianism because of its purported use of the magistrate's coercive power, yet "this objection doth as much strike against the New England government [as against the Presbyterians]. . . . For in New England there hath been severity enough (to say no worse) used against heretics and schismatics."[156] What those who oppose the magistrate's coercive power in religion must mean, he assumed, was that "they intend only liberty for themselves, not to others that are opposite to them . . . what a grand imposture is this? what a deceiving of the world?"[157] Parliament's introduction of the Directory for Public Worship during the late 1640s—and the simultaneous banning of the Book of Common Prayer— seemed only further evidence of this hostility to toleration on the part of congregationalists and Independents.[158]

Tolerationists, for their part, had long pointed to the Netherlands as a single state in which adherents of many faiths coexisted. Furthermore, they claimed, the analogy to Holland suggested that not only could such a state survive, but it could prosper and thrive. Contrary to antitolerationist claims, John Vernon claimed, religious diversity need not undermine the civil state.[159] Holland contains a variety of churches, John Goodwin pointed out, and yet "how placate, flourishing, and free from disturbance this state hath been."[160] At the Whitehall Debates, Hugh Peter urged his adversaries to "witness the country next from us that hath all the marks of a flourishing state . . . I mean

---

The divergent pathways of English and American Puritanisms are cogently traced in Webster, *Godly Clergy*, chap. 17 and conclusion.

155. [Steuart], *Some Observations*, 18, 64; *Anti-toleration*, 10–11; 18.

156. *Wholesome Severity*, 18.

157. Ibid., 19. See also Edwards, *Reasons Against the Independent Government of Churches*, 32.

158. The *Directory for the Publique Worship of God Throughout the Three Kingdomes* (London, 1646) was approved by the Presbyterian-influenced Long Parliament after it banned the Book of Common Prayer in 1645. A selection from the *Directory* is reprinted in David Cressy and Lori Anne Ferrell, eds., *Religion and Society in Early Modern England: A Sourcebook* (London, 1996), 186–92.

159. *The Swords Abuse Asserted*, 14.

160. *Truth and Innocency Triumphing Together* (London, 1648), 40, 54. See also *Toleration Justified*, 6.

the Low Countries" (*Clarke Papers*, 2:90). John Musgrave evoked the general argument about prosperity by noting that persecution hurts trade.[161] Of course, antitolerationists had a quite different view of Holland, viewing it as factious, licentious, and anarchic, and did not hesitate to say so.[162]

CONCLUSION: OLIVER CROMWELL AND "A NEW WAY OF SETTLING THIS NATION"

The agitation over civil and religious liberty, the tension between army and Parliament, the increasing political presence of sects and religious radicalism, all came to fruition in the Commonwealth (1649–53) and Protectorate (1653–58) periods. This section proceeds largely by way of an examination of the unparalleled role played by Oliver Cromwell in the government of the English commonwealth in the decade before his death in 1658.[163]

Much to the chagrin of more radical rank-and-file soldiers, Cromwell and his fellow army officers, though supportive of religious liberty and opposed to the reimposition of kingly power, were social conservatives, or at least moderates (if such a word can be used to characterize those who over-saw the execution of a king). This moderation and conservatism showed clearly in the Whitehall Debates of 1648 and 1649. There Cromwell's allies, Ireton and Nye, argued for the magistrates' restrictive power (the authority,

161. *The Conscience Pleading for Its Own Liberty*, 13–14.
162. See, e.g., Richard Holdsworth, *An Answer Without a Question* (London, 1649), 6, and [Forbes], *An Anatomy of Independency*, 19.
163. Much of Cromwell's time during the early 1650s was spent subjugating Scotland and Ireland. During that time, Parliament was slow to act on a number of fronts—new elections and a church settlement, to name just two—and with the army's help, Cromwell dissolved it in 1653. His solution was to call the Nominated Parliament, an assembly recruited by army officers. Religious radicals were heavily represented in this assembly, and Cromwell noted that "I never looked to see such a day as this . . . when Jesus Christ should be so owned as He is, at this day, and in this work" (*The Writings and Speeches of Oliver Cromwell*, ed. W. C. Abbott [Cambridge, Mass., 1937–47], 3:63). Still, although religious radicals were well represented in the Nominated (Barebones') Parliament, Whitelock noted that "many [were] persons of fortune and knowledge" (*Memorials of the English affairs*, 4:21). Woolrych (*Commonwealth to Protectorate*, chap. 6) agrees.
But as the Rump Parliament had proven too conservative, the Nominated Parliament threatened to be too radical. A sustained attack on tithes (and, by implication, the role of the civil magistrate in encouraging godly behavior) and the specter of even further radical measures led a group of moderates, alarmed at the radical attack on tithes, to surrender authority to Cromwell. Whether or not he orchestrated this surrender, Cromwell clearly benefited. See Woolrych, *Commonwealth to Protectorate*, chap. 7 (esp. pp. 336–46), on the Barebones' Parliament's final days.

not to compel people to attend church, but to restrain blatant heresy), powers largely derived from the Old Testament example of the kings of Israel. In utilizing these Old Testament citations, they employed common antitolerationist arguments. Sectarians and Levellers opposed the restraining power, arguing for a dramatic restriction of the magistrate's control over religion and denying the relevance of the Hebrew Scriptures in a Christian society.[164]

Cromwell is best described religiously as a congregationalist or an Independent, and bears a theological and ecclesiastical resemblance to many of the New England divines examined in Chapter 2.[165] Although he left no systematic writings on his own religious experience, we do know that Cromwell's position on church issues was equally displeasing to conservatives and radicals. He allowed gathered congregations outside the established church structure, a move that displeased Anglicans and Presbyterians concerned about unity and orthodoxy. At the same time, his relatively narrow definition of Protestant orthodoxy (for the allowance of such congregations) and support for the continuance of tithes and an established church displeased many radicals who saw the execution of the king as ushering in a period of godly reform.[166] Cromwell saw himself as seeking to preserve the moral, religious, and ethical advantages of an established church, while allowing liberty to those Christians who could not, in good faith, affirm its tenets. He repeatedly reiterated that religious differences ought not affect individuals' civil rights, urging in 1647 that "every man that walks peacefully in a blameless conversation, and is beneficial to the commonwealth, may have liberty and encouragement."[167]

Nonetheless, many saw Cromwell as closely aligned with religious radicals. Before the formation of the New Model Army, Cromwell had engaged in a bitter public feud with Essex and Manchester, leaders of the Parliamentary war effort more amenable to negotiating a settlement with the king. His opponents repeatedly pointed to the radicalism of Cromwell's men in their

164. See Polizzotto, "Liberty of Conscience and the Whitehall Debates."
165. For a good overview, see Sarah Gibbard Cook, "The Congregational Independents and the Cromwellian Constitutions," *Church History* 46 (1977): 335–57. The dissension between soldiers and officers mirrors the tensions between sectarians and Independents more generally. All had opposed Laud, and Independents were concerned about congregational autonomy within a Presbyterian system, but important differences, namely the extent of religious liberty each was prepared to grant, remained between Independents and sectarians.
166. For an examination of one such group, see Bernard S. Capp, *The Fifth Monarchy Men: A Study in Seventeenth-century English Millenarianism* (London, 1972).
167. *Writings and Speeches*, 1:460; see also 1:638.

attempts to discredit him.[168] In 1645, Cromwell defended a religious radical among his troops. "Admit he be [an Anabaptist], shall that render him incapable to serve the public. . . . The State, in choosing men to serve them, takes no notice of their opinions, if they be willing faithfully to serve them, that satisfies. . . . Take heed of being sharp, or too easily sharpened by others, against those to whom you can object little but that they square not with you in every opinion concerning matters of religion."[169]

Still, for Cromwell as for his Independent allies, support for toleration was not unlimited, and the limits were not solely the "civil behavior" hinted at in this letter. Certain religious perspectives were to be forbidden. Although Cromwell announced that "as for the people [of Ireland], what thoughts they have in matters of religion in their own breasts I cannot reach; but think it my duty, if they walk honestly and peaceably, not to cause them in the least to suffer for the same," he told the governor at Ross, "if by liberty of conscience you mean liberty to exercise the Mass, I judge it best to use plain dealing, and to let you know, where the Parliament of England have power, that it will not be allowed of."[170] Here Cromwell clearly distinguished between beliefs (the "thoughts . . . in their own breasts") and actions ("exercis[ing] the Mass"), and saw the restriction of certain practices as compatible with liberty of conscience. Prelacy, on the other hand, was too closely implicated with the overthrown regime to be considered safe to permit.[171] In addition, though far more ambiguously, Cromwell was deeply concerned about Scottish Presbyterianism, although not merely because the Scots had invaded England on behalf of Charles in 1648, but because he saw Scottish Presbyterianism as corrosive to civil authority by virtue of its claim to *jure divino* authority. He told the governor of Edinburgh castle that "the ministers of England are supported, and have liberty to preach the Gospel, though not

168. See A.N.B. Cotton, "Cromwell and the Self-Denying Ordinance," *History* 62 (1977): 211–31.

169. "To Major-General Crawford," in Cromwell, *Writings and Speeches*, 1:278. Although Cromwell consistently supported liberty of conscience, this much-quoted letter does not constitute an argument for toleration, but rather a statement of military necessity and perhaps a developing English nationalism. Abbott comments nicely on the letter to Crawford: "Cromwell's position . . . was clear. It had little to do with those abstract principles of toleration and democracy urged by political theorists. It was preeminently practical. There was a war to be won; a king to be defeated; a bench of bishops to be overthrown; and any instrument which would assist in the accomplishment of this great task was to be seized and used" (in Cromwell, *Writings and Speeches*, 1:278).

170. Ibid., 2:202, 2:146.

171. Instrument of Government, in Gardiner, *Constitutional Documents*, 324.

to rail, nor, under the pretence thereof to overtop the civil power, or debase it as they please."[172] More broadly, Cromwell's opposition to these several religious perspectives lay in his conviction that true religion is one of spirit, flourishing in a variety of forms. As J. C. Davis has paraphrased him, Cromwell was an antiformalist, seeking "a religion of conscience, rather than ritual."[173]

Cromwell's first constitution was the Instrument of Government (1653), which instituted the Protectorate. Proclaiming that the "Christian religion, as contained in the Scriptures," was the "public profession of these nations," nevertheless the Instrument did not compel worship in an official church:

That such as profess faith in God by Jesus Christ (though differing in judgment from the doctrine, worship or discipline publicly held forth) shall not be restrained from, but shall be protected in, the profession of the faith and exercise of their religion; so as they abuse not this liberty to the civil injury of others and to the actual disturbance of the public peace on their parts: provided this liberty be not extended to Popery or Prelacy, nor to such as, under the profession of Christ, hold forth and practice licentiousness.[174]

The Instrument shows again Cromwell's attempt to find a *via media* in matters of religious polity: it both expands the theological parameters of the established church and extends protections to congregations gathering outside that establishment. In fact, Blair Worden argues persuasively that Puritan theological conservatism provides the relevant context for Cromwell's religious policy.[175] *Within* the established religious structure, Cromwell would have the state church administered by "triers" and "ejectors," committees charged with improving the quality of the ministry (a standard Puritan complaint

172. *Writings and Speeches,* 2:335–36.
173. J. C. Davis, "Cromwell's religion," in *Oliver Cromwell and the English Revolution,* ed. John Morrill (London, 1990), 191; for his similarly antiformalist politics, see Johann P. Sommerville, "Oliver Cromwell and English Political Thought," in the same volume, 234–58.
174. Instrument of Government, in Gardiner, *Constitutional Documents,* 324.
175. "The lessons of Puritan theology did not all point in one direction" (Blair Worden, "Toleration and the Cromwellian Protectorate," in *Persecution and Toleration,* ed. W. J. Sheils [Oxford, 1984], 207). I disagree, however, with Worden's claim that Cromwell wanted Protestant union and not toleration. The two seem not mutually exclusive, and toleration was not, as Worden claims, an exclusively negative term during the seventeenth century. In fact, toleration was often discussed in the context of a search for Protestant unity against the international Catholic threat: see Hill, *English Bible,* pt. 3.

against Anglican clergy since Jacobean times). *Outside* the official church, within the confines of fairly basic Protestantism, Cromwell protected the rights to free exercise of religion by independent congregations, assuming basic standards of civil behavior and lawfulness.

Cromwell's views on church government and toleration closely followed those of the Independent divine John Owen. Owen proclaimed the magistrate's duty to declare, protect, and support the preaching of the Gospel (with public space and funds), but to allow peaceable dissenters to live unmolested.[176] This position had an element of theological conservatism to it, in that Owen used Old Testament texts to argue for the magistrate's duty to restrain blatant heresy. Owen also considered the failure to act against false religion a potential threat to a people's salvation and a sure way to bring God's disfavor, a position he shared with, among others, many New England magistrates and divines. At the same time, Owen asserted that magisterial opposition to false religion need not replicate Anglican persecution, but instead serve to bolster orthodox, independent Protestant congregations wherever they might spring up.[177]

This Cromwellian system of religious toleration provided a far greater degree of religious freedom than had ever existed previously in England. It was also extremely fragile, resting as it did on Cromwell's personal prestige and skill in balancing army, Parliament, and the varied religious groups in the country. Though religious liberty would be scaled back somewhat under a new constitution in 1658 (which granted Cromwell increased powers as head of state), and radically reversed under early Restoration Parliaments, the Commonwealth and Protectorate periods would provide a touchstone for political and religious debate for years to come. F. D. Dow claims that the "existence of dissent, and with it the *de facto* case for toleration, was to be an ineradicable legacy of the Interregnum."[178] If English religious dissent proved ever more difficult to suppress (as Parliaments under Charles II and James II were to find out), many of the reasons for this resilience—communi-

---

176. See Owen, *Of Toleration*.

177. See Owen, *Righteous Zeal Encouraged by Divine Protection*, in *Works*, 8:127–62. Owen was also instrumental in proposing basic principles of church government and Protestant orthodoxy out of which the Cromwellian church eventually emerged: see "Propositions humbly tendered to the committee for propagating the gospel" (*Perfect Diurnall*, 25 March 1652, 1776–77).

178. *Radicalism in the English Revolution*, 73. Harrington incorporated liberty of conscience into his republic: see "The Model of the Commonwealth of Oceana," nineteenth order, and "A System of Politics." Both are contained in *The Commonwealth of Oceana and A System of Politics*, ed. J. G. A. Pocock (Cambridge, 1992), 127, 282–83.

cation, organization, and the experience of freedom—were due to the "brief summer of religious liberty"[179] under Cromwell.

All in all, though, political and religious affairs had moved a long way from the (by comparison) modest reforming goals of 1642. One historian of the English Civil War has referred to the period as "a story of unforeseen consequences."[180] This characterization does not reflect merely post-hoc twentieth-century observations: Bulstrode Whitelock surveyed the past decade in the wake of the army's dissolution of Parliament in 1653.

> Thus it pleased God, that this assembly, famous through the world for its undertakings, actions, and successes, having subdued all their enemies, were themselves overthrown and ruined by their servants, and those whom they had raised, now pulled down their masters. An example never to be forgotten, and scarce to be paralleled in any story, by which all persons may be instructed how uncertain and subject to change all worldly affairs are, how apt to fall when we think them highest.[181]

Surveying these toleration debates, one is struck by Cromwell's moderation. Rejecting the theological and political extremism that claimed the magistrate had no religious authority, as well as divine right claims of Presbyterianism and episcopacy, he sought a public church that would eschew excessive doctrinal arguments and appeal to a broad segment of the populace. At the same time, within Protestant parameters, the Cromwellian regime tolerated an extraordinarily wide range of religious activity. Ultimately, the experiment proved too short-lived to assess whether it might have engendered popular loyalty. The production of such loyalty seems unlikely, though, given the association of Cromwellian religious liberty with a widely unpopular military regime. Cromwell's system pleased neither sectarians (who wanted more liberty) nor Presbyterians, Anglicans, or Catholics (who wanted more for themselves, less for sectarians).

I have argued in this chapter that religious liberty as the outcome of the English Civil War does not imply that religious liberty was a goal of those

179. Barker, "Achievement of Oliver Cromwell," 13.
180. Woolrych, *Commonwealth to Protectorate*, 1.
181. *Memorials of the English Affairs*, 4:6–7.

initiating the conflict. Indeed, the relatively broad toleration of the Cromwellian regime did not resemble the intentions of any significant segment of English society on the eve of the Civil War in 1642. The overthrow of Parliament in Pride's Purge made clear that it was the army, not Parliament, that possessed *de facto* power and, with it, the ability to bring an ordered resolution to years of instability. Antitolerationists continually voiced concerns about order, yet it was the tolerationist army that proved able, at least in the short term, to bring about such stability.

4

THE GLORIOUS REVOLUTION

The 1640s All Over Again?

I was forced to conclude an opinion . . . that nothing can be more anti-Christian, nor more contrary to sense and reason, than to trouble and molest our fellow-Christians, because they cannot be exactly of our minds, in all the things relating to the worship of God.

—Duke of Buckingham, *A Short Discourse*

A toleration, when it is granted, implies only a removal of such penalties as the law would otherwise inflict upon those who disobey it . . . it does not either abrogate, or suspend, or dispense with the law, but only bridles and reins up the execution of it.

—[John Norris], *The Charge of Schism Continued*

Of late bold priests swarmed with popish zeal warmed,
And all godly Protestants sorely alarmed,
With damned Latin tongue, and puffed up lung,
They roared out their matins and vespers so long.
   Nay so bold were they
   As to preach and to pray
In our learned city, the old silly way,
But now neither Papists, nor foreigners tarry
Here, under the reign of William and Mary.

—*England's Congratulation*

In the previous two chapters, I have attempted to show that debates over religious dissent and toleration represent concrete historical and political issues as much as purely philosophical or theological ones. In Massachusetts, the religious dissent of Roger Williams, Anne Hutchinson, and others arose against the backdrop of internal and external threats to the colony's existence. Civil magistrates suppressed those Dissenters to preserve civil peace and the social order as well as to defend theological orthodoxy. During the 1640s and 1650s in England, toleration was imposed on a perhaps-unwilling populace, not through the victory of tolerationist ideas, but through the victories of Cromwell's New Model Army. In Chapter 5, we shall see that the Keithian schism in Philadelphia threatened the political, social, and ecclesiastical supremacy of leading Pennsylvania Quakers precisely when other domestic troubles loomed in the colony and Penn himself was under suspicion (or arrest) in England.

England's 1688 Revolution does not differ from the foregoing examples in this regard. During the 1680s, arguments about toleration and liberty of conscience raised, not just theological and ecclesiastical issues, but important political and constitutional ones as well. Toleration during the Restoration and Revolutionary periods in English history was inseparable from concerns about the implications of a Catholic monarch for English Protestantism, as well as broader debates over sovereign power and royal prerogative. Both of these concerns evince a growing English nationalism that came to see James II as a threat to English liberties. For the purposes of this study, of course, the great achievement of the decade lies in the Toleration Act of 1689, which exempted Protestant Dissenters from penalties for not attending Anglican services, guaranteed the right of Dissenting congregations to gather publicly, and opened the doors of Parliament to most Protestant Dissenters. If viewing toleration as a purely philosophical or theological phenomenon overlooks vital political and social context, however, then examining only the Toleration Act itself ignores the many developments that led up to it, and only in whose context the legislation becomes intelligible. In the words of Richard Ashcraft, "Against the grandiose claims advanced by intellectual historians on behalf of an enlightened cultural consciousness of seventeenth-century Englishmen . . . must be set the fears, prejudices, miscalculations, political exigencies, and unintended consequences on the part of historical actors who actually secured the political enactment of religious toleration."[1]

---

1. "Latitudinarianism and Toleration: Historical Myth vs. Political History," in *Philosophy, Science, and Religion in England, 1640–1700*, ed. Richard Kroll, Richard Ashcraft, and Perez Zagorin (Cambridge, 1992), 152.

In this chapter, I emphasize three main points, each of which illustrates the important role played by the 1680s in the ongoing development of toleration as a philosophical and political phenomenon. First, I stress that one of the chief reasons for James II's overthrow in 1688 was the almost-unanimous *opposition* among the English political nation to his dogged pursuit of toleration. In this pursuit, James's penchant for strategies of, at best, dubious legality earned him little more than disapproval and mistrust; such mistrust only compounded the willingness of his fervently anti-Catholic opponents to ascribe the basest motives to a king so openly Catholic. This ubiquitous English anti-Catholicism should also remind us of how many seventeenth-century English thinkers viewed *Protestant* toleration as part and parcel of a developing English nationalism that traced back at least as far as Henry VIII's break with Rome.[2] James's means of procuring religious liberty, relying upon a contested area of the royal prerogative that involved suspending and dispensing with Parliamentary legislation, was seen by many as an ominous precedent threatening the role of Parliament and the balance of the "ancient constitution."[3] Of course, James clashed with Parliamentarians and other opponents on many issues, and a host of disputes led to the events of 1688. But toleration provides a specific example of the general and highly contested issue of the dispensing and suspending powers.

This first claim, that opposition to toleration somehow set the stage for the Toleration Act, is perhaps ironic from a view that sees 1688 as a watershed for religious freedom.[4] James's Declaration of Indulgence (1687, reissued in 1688) alienated his oldest allies, Anglican royalists who opposed any grants of leniency to religious dissenters. As we shall see, these Tory allies had remained faithful to James (then duke of York) during the Exclusion Crisis

---

2. See, for example, the Act in Restraint of Appeals (1533), with its proclamation that "this realm of England is an empire." As Colin Haydon puts it, "Anti-catholicism . . . was an ideology which promoted national cohesion, countering, though not submerging, the kingdom's political divisions and tensions. It showed what it was—despite these—to be English by emphasizing what it was to be unEnglish" ("'I Love My King and My Country, But a Roman Catholic I Hate': Anti-catholicism, Xenophobia, and National Identity in 18th Century England," in *Protestantism and National Identity: Britain and Ireland, c.1650-c.1850*, ed. Tony Claydon and Ian McBride [Cambridge, 1998], 49).

3. The dispensing and suspending powers were elements of the royal prerogative. Dispensing involved the king's remitting of penalties for violation of laws in individual cases, when (presumably) a national emergency or other pressing need made such a step necessary. Suspending powers were much broader, and much more highly contested: the purported right of the monarch to suspend the enforcement of laws for whole groups, rather than in discrete individual cases.

4. See, e.g., George Sabine, *A History of Political Theory*, revised ed. (New York, 1950), chap. 26, and Jordan, *Development of Religious Toleration in England*, vol. 4.

(1679–81), when Whigs proposed barring him from the succession. Yet James's open and vocal Catholicism solidified Parliamentary and popular mistrust of his motivations, preventing him from forging alliances with Protestant Dissenters who would have benefited most from his support for liberty of conscience. The prominent exception of William Penn, whom we shall meet in Chapter 5 and who tirelessly supported James's tolerationist cause, only highlights the fact that most Protestant Dissenters were as virulently anti-Catholic as their Anglican counterparts, and were wary of accepting a toleration without any foundation in law.

Second, this chapter addresses an important aspect of the intellectual history of toleration debates in late-seventeenth-century England. Despite the fact that the 1688 Revolution and the Toleration Act, which followed a year later, provide one of the most celebrated examples of seventeenth-century tolerationist successes, advocates of toleration did not advance a single new argument for liberty of conscience during those years. Each justification put forward by tolerationists had been introduced during the English Civil War, Commonwealth, and Protectorate. (To be fair, no new antitolerationist arguments were put forward either.) In examining toleration debates during the 1680s, we see the enduring importance of the English Civil War in questions of religious politics. But we do not find a new approach to toleration: we find the old approach, with new political and social dynamics.

I do not mean to deny the importance of, for example, Locke's *Letter Concerning Toleration*, probably the single best-known plea for toleration in the Western political tradition.[5] Locke's work on toleration is significant, not because it advances new or previously unheard-of arguments for toleration, but because it so concisely synthesizes nearly a century of ongoing debate on this vexing political problem. The period under consideration in this chapter produced a great deal of debate over toleration and liberty of conscience, as had the 1640s and 1650s. As with his *Second Treatise*, Locke occupies an important role in the debates over toleration far beyond the simple question of whether or not he advanced a "unique" perspective. In the toleration debates of the 1680s, there simply was no unique perspective.

---

5. Locke's influence on the American constitutional tradition, through Jefferson, is explored in Sanford Kessler, "Locke's Influence on Jefferson's 'Bill for Establishing Religious Freedom,'" *Journal of Church and State* 25 (1983): 231–52, which expands upon an earlier piece by S. Gerald Sandler, "Lockean Ideas in Thomas Jefferson's Bill for Establishing Religious Freedom," *Journal of the History of Ideas* 21 (1961): 110–16.

If no new arguments were presented in support of toleration, to what should we ascribe the passage of the Toleration Act? The claim that "nothing new" appeared during the 1680s calls for a closer examination of the political context that enabled those favoring a limited, Protestant toleration successfully to oppose James's use of the suspending power; and later, to use William's expressed desire for easing penalties on Protestant Dissenters to ensure passage of the Toleration Act. I argued in Chapter 3 that Cromwell's tolerationist Protectorate resulted largely from the army's support for religious liberty. The Toleration Act of 1689, similarly, resulted not from the victory of tolerationist ideas but from a confluence of political factors that made Protestant unity against suspicion of Catholicism override the liberty James offered to Dissenters. Most Anglicans, as we shall see, sought not to overthrow the king but to impress upon him the seriousness of the tolerationist course on which he was embarking and to urge him to rebuild the traditional Anglican/Tory political alliance (which had nothing to do with seeking toleration). As in the 1640s, however, events overtook the intentions of those who initiated them.

Third, in this chapter I emphasize that the legislation passed by Parliament was as important as a *rejection* of James's broad toleration proposals (as well as a rejection of calls for comprehending dissent *within* the Church of England) as it was for the dissent that it did protect. Despite the fact that the Act represented a huge advance for Dissenting Protestants and discreet Catholics, the religious liberty granted by the Toleration Act was far less extensive than that which Cromwell's Protectorate, not to mention James's Declarations of Indulgence, had guaranteed. The Test Act, for example, remained in effect into the nineteenth century, barring Catholics and non-Trinitarian Protestants from serving in public office.[6] The Toleration Act required Dissenting congregations to apply to Anglican bishops for licenses, and to leave their doors unlocked during worship services. Penalties for nonattendance of Anglican services, though suspended, remained enshrined in law. As with my earlier point about a lack of originality in toleration debates during the 1680s, this observation about the important limits of the

6. Passed by Parliament in 1673, the Test Act required abjurations of Catholic doctrine and oaths of allegiance to the English monarch as a condition of holding public office. The Test Act is reprinted in J. P. Kenyon, ed., *The Stuart Constitution: Documents and Commentary*, 2d ed. (Cambridge, 1986), 461–62; see also the "Act for the more effectual preserving of the King's person and government by disabling Papists from sitting in either House of Parliament" (*Stuart Constitution*, 465–66), which concludes with the crucial clause that "nothing in this Act contained shall extend to his royal Highness the duke of York" (466).

Toleration Act's protections is not intended to minimize the enormous historical milestone the Act represents, but to suggest that although years of struggle were required to achieve the protections of the Act, this legislation represents the *beginning* and not the end of a long process by which religious minorities would become incorporated into full membership in the English polity.[7]

BACKGROUND AND CONTEXT: RESTORATION AND EXCLUSION CRISIS

Stuart kings after the Restoration (1660) were decidedly more receptive to the idea of toleration (or indulgence)[8] than were Restoration Parliaments. Charles II had signaled a willingness to "indulge tender consciences" in his Declaration of Breda, just prior to the Restoration, and issued Declarations of Indulgence in 1662 and 1672.[9] He was forced to withdraw both, however, because of Parliamentary resistance. Parliamentary opponents asserted that such royal actions ignored *their* role in governing the commonwealth under the traditional understanding of the English ancient constitution, in which

---

7. Again, as with any statement of this kind, we must specify more carefully the point being made. Of course the Toleration Act *was* the end of *something*, namely the political effort to achieve Anglican uniformity through the persecution of religious dissent. My aim in making this statement is to dissuade scholars from focusing too closely on the "snapshot" and thus losing the broad sweep of events into which the Toleration Act entered, and which it was instrumental in shaping. That broad sweep displays both the Act's inherent limitations and the great advance it represented over previous practice, and we should do full justice to both. I elaborate on these points later in the chapter.

8. "Toleration," "comprehension," and "indulgence" were the three major terms used in this debate. "Toleration" and "indulgence" were often used interchangeably, though there is a slight difference. "Toleration" referred to liberty of worship outside the Anglican Church, whereas "indulgence" denoted, more specifically, how such liberty would likely come about: through a royal grant (rather than Parliamentary legislation) "indulging" Dissenters, remitting penalties for nonattendance at Anglican services. Comprehension denoted the movement to enlarge the parameters of acceptable Anglican belief and practice to encompass orthodox Protestants. Support for comprehension, for example, did not necessitate support for toleration, and in fact many Presbyterians saw comprehension as making toleration unnecessary, since only heretics or factious sectarians could balk at subscribing to a relaxed Anglican establishment. Presbyterians often opposed toleration, which would likely encompass even radical sectarians, in favor of comprehension, in which they could be incorporated into an expanded Anglicanism. For a fuller discussion, see Roger Thomas, "Comprehension and Indulgence," in *From Uniformity to Unity, 1662–1962*, ed. Geoffrey F. Nuttall and Owen Chadwick (London, 1962), 191–253, and Charles F. Mullett, "Toleration and Persecution in England, 1660–1689," *Church History* 18 (1949): 18–21.

9. The texts of these declarations are contained in Kenyon, *Stuart Constitution*, 379–84.

monarch and Parliament shared power in a balanced arrangement.[10] Parliament reestablished the Church of England during the early 1660s, upon a narrow doctrinal basis that resulted in many ministers resigning or being ejected from their positions.[11] Restoration Parliaments were hostile to religious dissent, associating it with the regicide of 1649, recalling the legacy of Cromwell's Protectorate,[12] and becoming increasingly concerned about the possibility of toleration serving as a cover for reintroducing Catholicism into England.[13] Formally reestablishing the Anglican supremacy, Parliament passed the Clarendon Code, a series of measures aimed at suppressing religious dissent, between 1661 and 1665. These acts further restricted the rights of independent congregations to assemble, reinstated the Book of Common Prayer, and required assent to its liturgy by all clergy.[14]

Restoration England, then, repeatedly witnessed not merely a clash of *substantive* positions on the issue of toleration (royal support, Parliamentary opposition), but also increasing suspicion on the part of Parliament regarding

10. The definitive reference on the ancient constitution remains J.G.A. Pocock, *The Ancient Constitution and the Feudal Law: A Study of English Historical Thought in the Seventeenth Century* (Cambridge, 1957). See also Glenn Burgess, *The Politics of the Ancient Constitution: An Introduction to English Political Thought, 1603–1642* (University Park, Pa., 1992).

11. In other words, the Act of Uniformity required sworn clerical assent to the Book of Common Prayer and Anglican articles of faith. Many Presbyterians and other ministers objected to certain doctrinal or liturgical elements in the Prayer Book or the Thirty-Nine articles. Others objected to the insistence upon them as a condition of ministry.

12. See Barry Reay, "The Quakers, 1659, and the Restoration of the Monarchy," *History* 63 (1978): 193–213.

13. Recall that Catholicism was not seen as simply a false religion, but as a seditious political doctrine that implied allegiance to a foreign power, the pope, instead of the English monarch. Thus Locke (and most other tolerationists) excluded Catholics from any proposed toleration scheme.

14. The best overviews of Restoration religio-political debate are Paul Seaward, *The Cavalier Parliament and the Reconstruction of the Old Regime, 1661–1667* (New York, 1988), 162–95; J.A.I. Champion, *The Pillars of Priestcraft Shaken: The Church of England and Its Enemies, 1660–1730* (New York, 1992); John Spurr, *The Restoration Church of England, 1646–1689* (New Haven, Conn., 1991); and Tim Harris, Paul Seaward, and Mark Goldie, eds., *The Politics of Religion in Restoration England* (Cambridge, Mass., 1990). More generally on the Restoration, see John Miller, *Restoration England: The Reign of Charles II* (New York, 1985), and Paul Seaward, *The Restoration, 1660–1688* (New York, 1991).

Paul Seaward claims that viewing Parliament as hostile to toleration and the Crown as in favor of it oversimplifies a complex set of political positions, theories, and negotiations. His elaboration of the course by which the Restoration settlement came into existence (*Cavalier Parliament*, chap. 7) illuminates the maneuvering engaged in by both sides. Still, as a general statement, presenting Parliament as attempting to restrict religious liberty and the Crown as seeking toleration does capture the overall contours of early Restoration religious politics for the purposes at hand.

the powers claimed by the king in implementing such toleration. Questions of toleration during the Restoration were always twofold: (1) did one support or oppose toleration, and for which groups; and (2) did one support or oppose how Charles II (and later James II) sought to achieve such toleration? Both Charles and James issued Declarations of Indulgences, attempting to institute toleration without Parliamentary assent. Even many who favored liberty of conscience were deeply disturbed by the precedent they saw in this extralegal pursuit of toleration by royal decree, involving as it did the claim to an extensive royal prerogative just decades after Parliament and king had taken up arms against each other. James made extensive use of dispensing and suspending powers as well, claiming the authority to halt enforcement of certain ecclesiastical laws not only in individual cases but as they related to entire groups of people (namely, his fellow Roman Catholics). To Parliamentary advocates, Stuart claims to such dispensing and suspending powers struck at the heart of their idea of England as a law-governed society, in which the monarch and Parliament *shared* in the task of legislation.

Ubiquitous anti-Catholicism, as well as Parliamentary suspicion of royal motives and commitment to Protestantism,[15] received additional force in the 1670s, as Charles entered into an alliance with France and Louis XIV (and at the same time, war with England's sometime Protestant ally, the Dutch). Charles's 1672 Declaration of Indulgence appeared in the context of hostilities with the Dutch and plans for a standing army, both of which were associated with his pro-French policy and instantly aroused anti-Catholic sentiments.[16] As I have stated before, the chronology of specific events is not my main focus here: more important for the purposes at hand is the fact that Locke, the first earl of Shaftesbury, and their Whig allies eventually came to see, in the 1660s and 1670s, signs of a growing conspiracy to assert divine right theory, achieve absolute monarchy, and overthrow Parliament.[17] The "popish plot" of the

15. There were good reasons for this suspicion. This increasingly close alliance between Charles II and Louis XIV included secret clauses in the Treaty of Dover (1670), in which Charles agreed to convert to Catholicism in return for French aid. See Ashcraft, *Revolutionary Politics*, chap. 1, for a helpful discussion. Charles professed Catholicism on his deathbed.

16. Fears of a standing army as threatening to popular liberties were deep-seated in English thought. For an overview, see Lois G. Schwoerer, *"No Standing Armies!" The Antiarmy Ideology in Seventeenth-Century England* (Baltimore, 1974).

17. [Locke], *A Letter from a Person of Quality to His Friend in the Country* (London, 1675); also in *State Tracts: Being a Collection of Several Treatises Relating to the Government* (London, 1693), 41–56. Whether such a conspiracy had any chance of success is another matter, and John Miller has argued that it did not. Still, this would hardly have been apparent (nor,

later 1670s, with its tales of a conspiracy to bring Catholicism into England under the cover of religious toleration, fueled the Whig effort to exclude James from the succession, even though it seems unlikely that such a plot was ever seriously planned.[18] Nevertheless, *rumors* of the plot provided a polemical bonanza for Whigs, bolstering their claims that England required a Protestant king to secure its liberties, and that toleration under a Catholic king would be the first step to bring England under papal control.[19]

The more immediate background to the Revolution of 1688, and the one more relevant to the concerns of this chapter, lies earlier in the same decade in the politics of the Exclusion Crisis. Although the Exclusion Crisis was not a toleration debate *per se*, it did raise a number of political questions that were animated by religious differences. The crisis originated in concerns about the duke of York (later King James II), who was next in the line of succession after his brother, Charles II, and openly Roman Catholic. During the Exclusion Crisis, Whigs (led by the first earl of Shaftesbury, Locke's patron) played on traditional English anti-Catholicism, seeking to raise concerns about the safety of English liberties, both political and religious, under a Catholic monarch.[20]

---

perhaps, would it have mattered) to Locke and his contemporaries. See John Miller, "The Potential for 'Absolutism' in Later Stuart England," *History* 69 (1984): 187–207. Steven Pincus sees the nascent English nationalism that eventually led to the 1688 Revolution as grounded in an opposition to the importation of French-style government to England: see "'To Protect English Liberties': The English Nationalist Revolution of 1688–1689," in *Protestantism and National Identity*, 75–104.

18. David Allen has argued that threats to order in London came as much from antipapal agitation than from any actual Catholic plotters. See "The Role of the London Trained Bands in the Exclusion Crisis, 1678–1681," *English Historical Review* 87 (1972): 287–303.

19. The definitive work on the plot itself is J. P. Kenyon, *The Popish Plot* (London, 1972); see also John Miller, *Popery and Politics in England, 1660–1688* (Cambridge, 1973).

The contemporary accounts are myriad: *The Popish Plot, Taken out of Several Depositions* (London, c. 1680), also in *Somers Tracts*, 8:54–60; Charles Blount, *An Appeal from the Country to the City* (London, 1679), in *Somers Tracts*, 8:401ff; *The Case of Protestants in England Under a Popish Prince* (London, 1681), in *Somers Tracts*, 8:147–66; John Phillips, *The Character of a Popish Successor* (London, 1681), in *State Tracts*, 148–64. Shaftesbury had earlier spoken of Ireland and Scotland as the "doors" to England ("Speech to Parliament, November 1678," in Scott, *Somer Tracts*, 8:48–50), through which slavery and popery might come, and the plot did nothing to allay these fears. See also *The Lord Shaftesbury His Speech to the House of Lords* (24 March 1679), HL Manuscript EL 8422.

20. For an overview of the early Whig movement, see J. R. Jones, *The First Whigs: The Politics of the Exclusion Crisis* (London, 1961); Melinda S. Zook, *Radical Whigs and Conspiratorial Politics in Late Stuart England* (University Park, Pa., 1999); and Richard L. Greaves, *Secrets of the Kingdom: British Radicals from the Popish Plot to the Revolution of 1688–1689* (Stanford, Calif., 1992). For an overview of Whig literature, see O. W. Furley, "The Whig Exclusionists: Pamphlet Literature in the Exclusion Campaign, 1679–1681," *Cambridge Historical Journal* 13 (1957): 19–36.

Whigs claimed that a Catholic monarch would bring in persecution of English Protestants and a more general abrogation of English laws and the subjugation of the realm to papal authority.[21] As one contemporary put it, "As soon as ever the papal authority is admitted among us, all the Protestants in these nations are dead men in law. . . . Our estates, lives, and souls are in extreme hazard."[22] Whigs asserted the supremacy of Parliament and its role as guarantor of the people's interest, and thus its right to alter the royal succession and exclude James.[23] By now scholars generally agree that Locke's *Second Treatise* was written during or shortly after the Exclusion Crisis, *calling for* resistance to James rather than justifying William's recent invasion, and that its calls for legislative supremacy represent an endorsement of the Whig/Parliamentarian cause of exclusion.[24] Several scholars have gone so far as to call the Exclusion Crisis an "attempted Whig revolution."[25]

Tories, however, skillfully raised the specter of political and religious radicalism, linking Whigs and "excluders" to the radicalism of the 1640s and 1650s and insisting that anarchy would follow the implied popular sovereignty of Whiggism. The lessons of history, for Tories, were clear: to allow dissidents and dissenters to challenge royal power, especially given fallen human nature, the likelihood of human error, and English history, would result in chaos, civil war, and irreligion.[26] In other words, they claimed, Whigs

---

21. Samuel Johnson, *Julian the Apostate* (London, 1682); Henry Care, *English Liberties* (London, 1682). On Johnson and Care more specifically, see Zook, *Radical Whigs*, chaps. 2–3.

22. *The Case of Protestants*, in *Somers Tracts*, 8:153, 164.

23. Algernon Sidney, *Discourses Concerning Government* (London, 1698), ed. Thomas G. West (Indianapolis, 1990), passim; Thomas Hunt, *Mr. Hunts Argument for the Bishops Right* (London, 1682). See also B. Behrens, "The Whig Theory of the Constitution in the Reign of Charles II," *Cambridge Historical Journal* 7 (1941): 42–71.

24. The extensive scholarly debate over the specific timing of Locke's authorship of the *Second Treatise* is beyond the scope of this chapter. Peter Laslett placed its composition during the Exclusion Crisis, not the Revolution, and that general specification is sufficient for the purposes at hand. See Laslett, "The English Revolution and Locke's 'Two Treatises of Government,'" *Cambridge Historical Journal* 22 (1956): 40–55: More generally, see Laslett's introduction to his edition of Locke's *Two Treatises of Government* (Cambridge, 1963).

25. Francis Spring Ronalds, *The Attempted Whig Revolution of 1678–1681* (1937; Totowa, N.J., 1974); Mark Knights, *Politics and Opinion in Crisis, 1678–1681* (Cambridge, 1994), 4–5; Zook, *Radical Whigs*, xiii.

26. Again, the literature is extensive, and not the focus of this chapter. For the connection to Parliamentary radicalism of the Civil War era, see Samuel Parker, *Religion and Loyalty* (London, 1684); Roger L'Estrange, *The Case Put, Concerning the Succession of His Royal Highness the Duke of York*, 2d ed. (London, 1679); and John Nalson, *The Complaint of Liberty and Property, Against Arbitrary Government* (Edinburgh, 1681). For claims about anarchy and irreligion, see

were using fears of a Catholic monarch to mask the same aim that they shared with their Parliamentary predecessors of 1642: political rebellion. George Burhope accused "fanatics" of "intend[ing] under pretense of opposition to popery [to] set up the good old cause [of 1642] again." Popery, Presbyterianism, and sectarianism, he claimed, "never set foot in any nation, but it brought with it animosities . . . divisions, wars, rebellions, and at last ruins."[27] One scholar has argued that "no doubt there might have been a revolution in 1681 if the memories of 1642 had been less vivid. The lesson of 1642, however, had been very thoroughly learned."[28] After Charles's dissolution of Parliament in 1681, the Exclusion Crisis was effectively over and a Tory reaction set in at the local level, supplanting Whigs from many of their positions in local government. In 1683 the Rye House Plot, a purported scheme to seize or assassinate Charles II and secure a Protestant successor, was foiled, resulting in the execution of several prominent Whigs and the flight of many others.[29] Shaftesbury died shortly thereafter in Holland, and James's decisive crushing of the ill-fated Monmouth's Rebellion in 1685 solidified his grasp on the throne.[30]

Although not couched in the form of a classic toleration question ("Shall group x be permitted to worship?"), the Exclusion Crisis nevertheless displayed the deep divisions among English elites on the subject of religion and monarchy.[31] Was Catholicism compatible with "Englishness," let along English

---

William Falkner, *Christian Loyalty* (London, 1684), bk. 2; Edmund Bohun's preface to Filmer's *Patriarcha* (London, 1685); and Parker, *Religion and Loyalty*.

27. *A Seasonable Discourse to the Clergy and Laity in a Visitation Sermon* (1680), HL Manuscript EL 8388 (35/B/38), 9. See also *The Western Rebel* (London, 1685), which refers to "Religion, that old stale pretense / For traitors to mount on the neck of their prince" (1).

28. Behrens, "Whig Theory of the Constitution," 44. Jonathan Scott concurs: "Public memory of the popery and arbitrary government of 1628–41 was overridden by that of 1642–59" ("England's Troubles: Exhuming the Popish Plot," in Harris, Seaward, and Goldie, *Politics of Religion*, 127).

29. As with the original popish plot, it remains unclear how real this plot was as well. Nonetheless, also like the popish plot, its polemical importance was huge.

30. The duke of Monmouth was Charles II's illegitimate son, and the hopes of many English Protestants lay with him as fears of James's Catholicism arose in the Exclusion Crisis. Monmouth led a short-lived and ill-fated attempt to take the throne in 1685. It was suppressed easily and ruthlessly, and he was executed. For accounts of this "Western rising," see Robin Clifton, *The Last Popular Rebellion: The Western Rising of 1685* (London, 1984), and Peter Earle, *Monmouth's Rebels: The Road to Sedgmoor, 1685* (London, 1977).

31. The more straightforward pleas for toleration were never absent during these years, of course. See, for example, Thomas Delaune, *Compulsion of Conscience Condemned* (London, 1683); William Penn, *Some Sober and Weighty Reasons Against Punishing Protestant Dissenters* (London, 1682); John Owen, *Indulgence and Toleration Considered: In a Letter unto a Person of Honour* (London, 1667), in *The Works of John Owen*, ed. Rev. William Gould (London and

magistracy? Would Catholics necessarily subvert political allegiance to England to the dictates of the pope? Does the ascendancy of one group, Catholics, threaten the existence of all others? All of these questions would be revisited at the end of the decade. What was fairly clear, though, was that (as Craig Rose puts it), "The Restoration had been a disaster for Protestant union."[32]

THE POLITICS OF TOLERATION: SUBSTANCE, PROCEDURE, AND JAMES'S CAMPAIGN FOR LIBERTY OF CONSCIENCE

In many ways, the short reign (1685–88) of James II confirmed the worst Whig fears about a Catholic king, the Stuart propensity for extralegal political activities, and the perceived Stuart desire for absolute rule.[33] James maintained a standing army after the successful suppression of Monmouth's Rebellion, further alienating English already fearful of absolute monarchy and distrustful of James's intentions. Louis XIV's revocation of the Edict of Nantes in 1685 and the ensuing persecution of French Protestants (along with James's refusal to engage Louis in defense of Protestantism, as many urged)[34] ignited already-heated English anti-Catholicism and reinforced suspicion of James's pro-French politics. Later, it would also bolster the case of William of Orange, who—although "lack[ing] the traditional sanction of hereditary succession"— held a long-standing place of prominence among European defenders of Protestantism as an implacable foe of the French.[35] (Indeed, William would lead England into war with France shortly after his accession.)

Edinburgh, 1851), vol. 13; J[ohn] H[umfrey], *The Authority of the Magistrate, About Religion, Discussed* (London, 1672); and Slingsby Bethel, *The Present Interest of England Stated* (London, 1671). Gary S. DeKrey surveys the various sorts of conscience arguments advanced during the Restoration in "Rethinking the Restoration: Dissenting Cases for Conscience, 1667–1672," *Historical Journal* 38 (1995): 53–83.

32. *England in the 1690s: Revolution, Religion, and War* (Oxford, 1999), 161.

33. Robert Beddard goes so far as to call the Revolution of 1688 a "Whig revolution." See his "Unexpected Whig Revolution of 1688," in *The Revolutions of 1688: The Andrew Browning Lectures 1988*, ed. Beddard (Oxford, 1991), chap. 1. For general overviews of the events of James's reign, see Maurice Ashley, *The Glorious Revolution of 1688* (London, 1966), and Stuart E. Prall, *The Bloodless Revolution: England 1688* (Madison, Wis., 1972).

34. Pincus emphasizes this popular anti-French rhetoric, noting its religious as well as pragmatic elements: see "To Protect English Liberties," esp. pp. 81–89.

35. Rose, *England in the 1690s*, 20. See also Tony Claydon, *William III and the Godly Revolution* (Cambridge, 1996), chaps. 1–3. The European perspective is also addressed by the

James reigned, then, against a European background. He practiced a policy of exempting Roman Catholics from the requirements of the Test Act, received papal emissaries, and reinstituted celebration of the mass in the royal household. In April 1687, James issued a Declaration of Indulgence, granting liberty of conscience and worship to Roman Catholics and Protestant Dissenters, and exempting public officials from compliance with the Test Act. Legally speaking, the Declaration was based upon the king's suspending power. James's support for toleration came from a number of conventional sources, including the idea that persecution "destroys [the interest of government] by spoiling trade, depopulating countries, and discouraging strangers"; that it was ineffectual and "never obtained the end for which it was employed." "And in this we are the more confirmed by the reflections we have made upon the conduct of the four last reigns. For after all the frequent and pressing endeavours that were used in each of them to reduce this kingdom to an exact conformity in religion, it is visible the success has not answered the design, and that the difficulty is invincible."[36] James hoped to receive Parliamentary approval for this step, and began an unsuccessful campaign to pack the next Parliament with members willing to codify his Declaration into law. These actions progressively alienated his staunchest allies, Anglican royalists opposed to the toleration of religious dissent (whether Catholic or Protestant), who had supported James's cause during the Exclusion Crisis and had trusted his promises to maintain the Church of England in its privileged social position.[37]

Shrewdly, James reissued his Declaration in the spring of 1688, commanding that it be read from all Anglican pulpits. He was clearly attempting to drive apart Anglicans and Dissenters, the nation's two major Protestant groups. James's reasoning was clear: if Anglicans refused to read the Declaration, Dissenters would (continue to) view them as persecutors hostile to religious liberty. Furthermore, the long-held Anglican doctrine of passive obedience to the monarch would be exposed as hollow. If, on the other hand, Anglicans complied and read the Declaration, James's tolerationist policy would receive

---

essays in Jonathan I. Israel, ed., *The Anglo-Dutch Moment: Essays on the Glorious Revolution and Its World Impact* (Cambridge, 1991).

36. The text of the Declaration is found in Kenyon, *Stuart Constitution*, 389–91, quotation at 389.

37. This gradual process by which James alienated his most loyal allies is well traced in G. V. Bennett, "The Seven Bishops: A Reconsideration," in *Religious Motivation: Biographical and Sociological Problems for the Church Historian*, ed. Derek Baker (Oxford, 1978), 267–87, and John Miller, "James II and Toleration," in *By Force or By Default? The Revolution of 1688–1689*, ed. Eveline Cruickshanks (Edinburgh, 1992), 8–27.

the church's imprimatur, in appearance if not in reality.[38] However, James had miscalculated. Anglican bishops, after lengthy discussions, convinced Dissenters of the danger of accepting toleration on the king's terms. In these discussions, Anglican bishops promised to explore the possibility of comprehending Presbyterians and other moderate Dissenters into the Anglican establishment.

The unanimity within the Anglican community against reading James's Declaration, as well as the tacit agreement reached with Dissenters, emboldened the bishops to petition the king, begging him to withdraw his command that it be read from the pulpits.[39] This petition was as shrewd as James's original command, for in it the bishops focused solely on procedural issues. They objected to the dispensing and suspending powers ("which hath often been declared illegal in Parliament") that James claimed as the legal basis for the Declaration, specifically denying "any want of duty and obedience to your Majesty [or] any want of due tenderness to Dissenters," with whom they pronounced themselves willing to discuss arrangements for comprehension.[40] Furthermore (largely because of the successful Anglican campaign), Dissenters did not flock to James with the expected expressions of gratitude for his extension of liberty of conscience, and those who did (e.g., Penn) were generally seen as royal apologists without significant public support.[41] James's attempts to prosecute the bishops for sedition showed how far he had traveled from his former alliance with Anglican royalists, and the bishops' acquittal illustrated how opposed influential public opinion was to James's toleration.[42]

38. Given the intense commitment of the Restored Anglican hierarchy to the doctrine of passive obedience, James probably had good reason to expect that the clergy would read the proclamation, if grudgingly. The fear of giving the appearance of Anglican approval to James's toleration is voiced by the author of *Three Queries, and Answers to Them* (London, 1688), 2.

39. The painstaking process of achieving this unanimity among influential Anglican bishops is related in great detail in Roger Thomas, "The Seven Bishops and their Petition, 18 May 1688," *JEH* 12 (1961): 56–70.

40. Kenyon, *Stuart Constitution*, 407.

41. Halifax characterized the declarations of thanks that James was able to come by as a "little less improper than love letters that were solicited by the lady to whom they are to be directed." See his *Letter to a Dissenter*, reprinted in Prall, *Bloodless Revolution*, 306.

42. The bishops' acquittal represented, to many of James's supporters, a capitulation to anti-Catholic popular opinion. One contemporary satirist referred to "our sovereign Lord the rabble" ("An Epitaph on Passive Obedience," HL Manuscript EL 8780, 23). W. A. Speck comments cogently on the bishop's refusal and subsequent acquittal: The refusal "gave a moral lead to Englishmen reluctant to resist the King, and a signal to him that he could no longer rely on the passive obedience of his subjects. . . . By acquitting the seven bishops, the jury in effect found James guilty" (*Reluctant Revolutionaries: Englishmen and the Revolution of 1688* [Oxford, 1988], 221, 223).

John Miller rightly notes that James "seemed to go out of his way to give credibility to . . . fears of popery and arbitrary government."[43] He had not only lost his old allies, but also failed to win new ones.

An intense debate, then, over the limits (if any) of royal prerogative lay at the root of James's troubles with Parliament and animated the opposition he encountered from various corners. Did the king possess authority not only to dispense with laws in specific instances but to suspend them wholesale?[44] James's use of Catholic officers to oppose Monmouth's Rebellion in 1685, an apparent violation of the Test Act, was upheld by the judiciary in the controversial case of *Godden v. Hales* (1686), but in that instance (and others like it) James had merely dispensed with the requirements of the Test Act in individual cases. The broader suspending powers associated with the Declarations of Indulgence of 1687 and 1688, to many, went far beyond what had been practiced up to that point, suspending the enforcement of Parliamentary legislation wholesale with no clear limitations. Furthermore, in James's case, given his overt Catholicism, claims to extensive prerogative were intertwined with the fear for English liberties under a Catholic monarch that had fired political debates since the Exclusion Crisis (indeed, since the reigns of Mary Tudor and Elizabeth). Thus on both procedural (his claims to the suspending power) and substantive grounds (his commitment to toleration), James came into conflict with Parliamentarian understandings of the traditional balance of power and mixed monarchy.[45] As we have seen, then, since the Restoration impulse for toleration often came from the monarch and was resisted by Parliament, toleration arose in a context in which both substance and procedure were vitally important.

43. "Crown, Parliament, and People," in J. R. Jones, ed., *Liberty Secured? Britain Before and After 1688* (Stanford, Calif., 1992), 69. Elsewhere, Miller has written that "James had, it seemed, far from dividing his Protestant subjects, united them in support of a comprehension and toleration in which only his fellow-Catholics were to find no place" ("James II and Toleration," 22).

44. For a fuller treatment, see Howard Nenner, *By Colour of Law: Legal Culture and Constitutional Politics in England, 1660–1689* (Chicago, 1977), and idem, "Liberty, Law, and Property: The Constitution in Retrospect from 1689," in Jones, *Liberty Secured?* 88–121. Constitutional issues also receive a great deal of attention in Speck's *Reluctant Revolutionaries*, chap. 2.

45. Speck claims that James never actually broke the law. "James might have strained his prerogative to the limit, but he never went beyond it. That he acted impolitically, even rashly, cannot be denied, that he acted unconstitutionally can" (*Reluctant Revolutionaries*, 153). Speck may be right, in a technical sense. What is ultimately at issue, however, is the *impression* given to Parliamentarians or the country at large. On this count, because of the mistrust that had accumulated over the years of James's reign, the king blundered badly.

Not surprisingly, some voiced support for James on *both* substance (toleration) and procedure (securing it by a royal declaration). According to this view, toleration was the important and overriding goal, and to be distracted by arguments over means was to squander an ideal political opportunity to ensure religious liberty. Proponents of such a position tended to highlight the magistrate's right and duty to do whatever was required to secure the people's welfare (*salus populi suprema lex est*), one of the strongest arguments in favor of the extensive royal prerogative claimed by James in suspending penal laws.[46] James expressed his hope that his Declaration of Indulgence would "unite [his subjects] to us by inclination as well as duty" and enable the English people "to live at ease and quiet."[47] Most seventeenth-century thinkers, as we saw in Chapter 3, affirmed the magistrates' right to uphold basic religious principles. Given a basic, minimally Christian understanding of these principles, rather than the fine distinctions of Anglican theology, such an understanding might justify extending toleration even to politically loyal Roman Catholics.[48] For example, the author of *The Great Case of Toleration* argued that the magistrate's duty concerned, not the extirpation of heresy, but the promotion of such basic Christian principles as were found in the Apostles' Creed.[49] To allay suspicions of James's motivations, some proposed a "new Magna Carta" to secure the civil rights of all regardless of their religious beliefs.[50]

Such proposals for a new Magna Carta, however, did not reassure those who had witnessed James and his brother dispensing with inconvenient laws

46. James Paston, *A Discourse of Penal Laws in Matters of Religion* (London, 1688), 32–34; Henry Care, *Liberty of Conscience, Asserted* (London, 1687), preface; and *An Expedient for Peace* (London, 1688), 1. Such justifications for James's actions often bordered on Erastianism.

A similar view from our own time is Richard E. Boyer's highly sympathetic portrayal of James's actions, in his *English Declarations of Indulgence, 1687 and 1688* (The Hague, 1968).

47. Declaration of Indulgence, in Kenyon, *Stuart Constitution*, 410, 411.

48. *A Letter in Answer to a City Friend* (London, 1687), 5–7. As we shall see in Chapter 5, William Penn also suggested that "civil interest" rather than religious uniformity was the glue of society, and that given certain guarantees against treasonous or seditious behavior, Catholics might be tolerated.

49. *The Great Case of Toleration Stated* (London, 1688), 8–9.

50. For the "new Magna Carta" proposals, see *An Expedient for Peace*, 32–33. Penn supported the anonymous publication of *The Excellent Privilege of Liberty and Property* (Philadelphia, 1687), which included the text of Magna Carta and related documents. It was at this publication that Comber's criticisms ([Thomas Comber], *Three Considerations Proposed to Mr. William Penn, Concerning . . . His New Magna Charta for Liberty of Conscience* [London, 1688]) were directed.

in the past.[51] What guarantees would anyone have that James would not set aside this new Magna Carta in order to impose Roman Catholicism? Who, or which institution, could limit the designs of an absolute monarch? One author suggested that those concerned about James's behavior should "endeavor to secure our substantial liberties, our English liberties we have, and ought to have, rather than to get the name of new ones, which may fatally bring us into greater bondage in the end": another held that "as the wisdom of our ancestors established all these laws for the support of our Church, and so eminent a part of them have stood whole ages; is it not impudence in us to pretend to be wiser than all our forefathers?"[52] Given the presence of ecclesiastical courts that imposed civil penalties for religious offenses, as well as James's maintenance of a standing army, the potential for *enforcing* any restrictions on royal power seemed bleak. For these writers, the desirability of toleration was less important than the threat that dispensing and suspending powers posed to the balanced constitution and the legislative role of Parliament.

Others opposed to James's actions omitted any mention of the specific issue of toleration, focusing solely on the dangerous *procedural* precedent set by royal suspensions of Parliamentary law. Gilbert Burnet, for example, left aside the question of liberty of conscience entirely, pointing instead to "the King's suspending of the laws [which] strikes at the root of this whole government."[53] For those attempting to convince Dissenters to reject James's proposed toleration, this meant convincing the Dissenters to value procedure over substance. It was natural for Dissenters to want liberty, but "the most pernicious designs have been carried on, under the most plausible pretenses."[54] The Test Act, according to this view, was not persecution on religious grounds, not simply the exclusion of an unpopular religious minority, but a means to safeguard the commonwealth against foreign influences and

---

51. *Some Queries Concerning Liberty of Conscience, Directed to William Penn and Henry Care* (London, 1688), 1, 3. Shaftesbury had claimed that "popery and slavery like two sisters go hand in hand," and wondered, "Can we expect to enjoy our Magna Charta long under the same persons and administration of affairs if the Council table there can imprison any nobleman without bringing him to trial, or giving the least reason for what they do ?" (*Speech to the House of Lords*, 24 March 1679, 1).

52. [Comber], *Three Considerations*, 4; *A Friendly Debate upon the Next Elections of Parliament, and the Settlement of Liberty of Conscience* (London, 1688), 3.

53. *A Letter, Containing Some Reflections on His Majesties Declaration for Liberty of Conscience* (London, 1689), 4.

54. Daniel Defoe, *A Letter to a Dissenter from His Friend at the Hague* (London, 1688), 1.

domination.[55] Another author suggested that once Parliament confirmed James's Declarations with tolerationist legislation, he would immediately dissolve it and return to personal rule.[56] A group of French ministers who had fled French persecution into Germany weighed in on the Declaration:

> The Declaration of which we speak is designed for two purposes: the one, the re-establishment of popery; the other, the extinction of the reformed religion in England. The former of these designs appears openly in it. The second is more concealed. . . . We will say nothing of a third design, which is, the oppression of the liberties of England for the establishment of an absolute authority, but will leave it to the politicians to make their reflections upon it.[57]

In two important works, the marquis of Halifax united the substantive and procedural objections to James's Declarations by noting that the king's actions proposed *unlimited* toleration, a danger to the English constitution: taking away the penal laws and Test Act "is but one step from the introducing of popery . . . [the Declaration proposes] an unlimited and universal toleration, which the Parliament in 1672 declared illegal and which has been condemned by the Christian church in all ages . . . [and which alters the constitution]."[58] Substantively, Halifax sought to remind Dissenters of the deep distrust and hatred Protestants had always received from Catholics. Dissenters should "suspect your new friends": it is quite likely, he argued, that Dissenters "are therefore to be hugged now, only that you may be better squeezed later." Procedurally, of course, the precedent of James's toleration threatened English law itself.

> If the case then should be, that the price expected of you for this liberty, is giving up your right in the laws, sure you will think twice,

55. "Is not this oath a civil test, though it may seem in some sort religious? Since it is only a renouncing of a foreign usurped power" (*Some Queries*, 2). Burhope claimed in 1680 that the popish plot had shown that "it is hardly possible for a vassal to the court of Rome to be a good subject to the King of England" (*A Seasonable Discourse*, 1). Again, we find English nationalism directly alongside English anti-Catholicism.

56. *Some Queries*, 3.

57. *A Letter of Several French Ministers Fled into Germany upon the Account of the Persecution in France* (London, 1688), 3. The tract is generally attributed to Pierre Jurieu.

58. *A letter from a Clergy-Man in the City, to His Friend* (London, 1688), 1, 5.

before you go any further in such a losing bargain. After giving thanks for the breach of one law, you lose the right of complaining of the breach of all the rest; you will not very well know how to defend yourselves, when you are pressed; and having given up the question, when it was for your advantage, you cannot recall it, when it shall be to your prejudice.[59]

Robert Ferguson also brought together the substantive and procedural critiques, and illuminated Parliamentary concerns for the rule of law and England's Protestant heritage, citing the receipt of a papal nuncio, the threat to English liberties, and James's claim to dispensing power as reasons for viewing James as having forfeited his crown.[60]

This project is not concerned with the details of the ensuing invasion by William of Orange, the desertion of James's supporters, James's flight to France, and William's move to the throne.[61] We should realize, however, not only that the bishops who declined to read James's Declaration did not see *themselves* as seditious, but that in fact they set out to reinvigorate the Anglican-Tory alliance with the Crown after their acquittal.[62] They retreated almost immediately from the vague promises regarding comprehension that they had made to Dissenters during the controversy over James's Declaration and called on James to summon a free (i.e., not packed) Parliament to secure the church's position. James, however, vacillated as the news of Williams's impending invasion trickled in, eventually fleeing and setting at naught these conciliatory efforts. Anglicans had never wanted toleration and had considered comprehension only when they deemed it necessary to preserve the broad front of English anti-Catholicism and the consequent preservation of the church's privileged (social, political, and economic) status. The Anglican position of passive obedience involved a great deal of subtlety, and their broader position regarding toleration encompassed far more than a simple opposition to the suspending and dispensing powers. Thus it is not entirely accurate to suggest, as one contemporary satirist did, that the church supported

---

59. *Letter to a Dissenter*, in Prall, *Bloodless Revolution*, 302, 306.

60. *A Brief Justification of the Prince of Orange's Descent into England* (London, 1689), 19.

61. These developments are well elaborated in Speck, *Reluctant Revolutionaries*, chap. 10, and Rose, *England in the 1690s*, chap. 1.

62. The bishops had never wanted revolution, but wanted James "to come to his senses and realize the error of his ways" (Speck, *Reluctant Revolutionaries*, 224).

passive obedience "as long as for it they were preferred."[63] Although they had claimed to represent passive obedience to the monarch, Anglicans had always asserted that such obedience was not unlimited. The Anglican hierarchy opposed toleration as antiscriptural and contrary to calls for Christian unity, claiming that it would lead to lawlessness, irreligion, and anarchy. Thus it represented a substantive evil (*malum in se*), a transgression of God's law which no Christian could safely countenance, as opposed to a necessary evil (*malum prohibitum*), which a sovereign might have no choice but to exercise in certain limited circumstances. Furthermore, Jesus had entrusted the clergy (and especially the bishops, as successors of the apostles) to guard the church against such dangers, and therefore they were bound in conscience to refuse. As Mark Goldie puts it, the bishops' Tory ideology held that "no earthly power could legitimately coerce God's anointed prince, but no anointed prince could violate a Christian's hope of salvation."[64] The bishops certainly had not wanted James overthrown, and neither did they want William as king: five of the seven bishops who had petitioned James refused to take oaths of loyalty to the new monarchs.

"THIS OBSERVATION IS NOT NEW": TOLERATION DEBATES DURING THE 1680S

Tolerationist arguments during the 1680s, like those of earlier years, were based upon scriptural, epistemological, and practical foundations. Antitolerationists, like their predecessors during the 1640s and 1650s, stressed the dangers toleration posed to social order and civil peace.

---

63. "An Epitaph on Passive Obedience," 23.

64. "The Political Thought of the Anglican Revolution," in *The Revolutions of 1688*, 135. Goldie presents Anglican "church absolutism" as seeking a middle ground between (Lockean) popular resistance theories and (Hobbesian) legal positivism or Erastianism. He suggests the term "non-assistance" as more accurate than the conventional "non-resistance," since Anglicans did not equate disobedience (e.g., the refusal to read James's declaration) with rebellion (116–17).

For a seventeenth-century discussion of this issue, see Richard Langhorne, *Considerations Touching the Great Question of the King's Right in Dispensing with the Penal Laws* (London, 1687). Langhorne used the vocabulary of *malum in se* and *malum prohibitum*, although unlike many others he saw James's actions as acceptable. Regarding the clergy as having a special responsibility to protect the church, see Halifax's *Letter from a Clergy-Man*, 2–3.

Toleration: Theology, Epistemology, and Prosperity

As in previous years, proponents of toleration drew upon the examples of Jesus, the apostles, and the early church. As had Roger Williams before him, George Care cited the parable of the wheat and tares, noting that nowhere did Jesus give believers permission to persecute.[65] Other tolerationists echoed these claims. The duke of Buckingham, for example, referred to persecution as "contrary to the doctrine and practice of Jesus Christ."[66] Accusations of faction and sedition often hurled at religious dissenters were nothing new, Henry Care pointed out. In fact, such charges had been made about Jesus himself.[67]

Often this attention to the early Christians led to a more general argument about the basic features of Christianity, which in some ways resembled earlier attempts of the Tew Circle to identify a minimal Protestant creed and eschew intricate doctrinal arguments.[68] Gilbert Burnet emphasized Christ's call to love our enemies, pointing out how the early church disapproved of persecution for conscience's sake.[69] One author asserted that the real Christian is the individual with "holiness, purity, piety, charity, belief in God, and faith in our Lord Jesus Christ."[70] Pointing to the underlying message of meekness and humility that lay at the heart of the Christian message, William Shewen asserted that "there is no ground nor foundation for sanguinary laws, nor for any sort of persecution, violence, or cruelty about religion, in the lovely, meek, quiet and innocent spirit of Christianity."[71] Where persecution has

65. *Liberty of Conscience Asserted and Vindicated* (London, 1689), 4–7. The author of *The Plea of the Harmless Oppressed* (London 1688), a Dissenter, concurred (9). The parable of wheat and tares is found in Matthew 13:24–43.

66. *A Short Discourse*, 19.

67. *Liberty of Conscience Asserted, or a Looking-Glass for Persecutors* (London, 1687), 3–7. The fear of Christians withdrawing their allegiance to government, he went on to say, was entirely without foundation (21).

68. See the discussion of the Tew Circle in Chapter 3. These efforts to minimize the necessary elements of Christianity often suggested a broadened base of acceptable Anglican doctrine, and thus pointed toward comprehension. Such efforts did not, however, necessarily lead in a tolerationist direction.

69. *The Case of Compulsion in Matters of Religion, Stated* (London, 1688), 6–11. See also *An Expedient for Peace*, 12.

70. *An Expedient for Peace*, 4. See, for comparison, the works of William Walwyn: *A Still and Soft Voice from the Scriptures; The Power of Love* (London, 1643); and *The Compassionate Samaritane*.

71. *A Brief Testimony for Religion* (London, 1688), 8. See also *A Discourse of Toleration* (London, 1691), 4.

come in, Shewen continued, it has been of human origin. Those who called themselves Christians and persecute were in fact "wolves in sheep's clothing."[72] Another author offered the Golden Rule, "that golden and everlasting rule of God and nature, to do as we would be done unto," as an argument for repealing the Test Act and penal laws.[73]

As in previous years, those supporting religious liberty were forced to address the historical issue of the kingdom of Israel and the related theological issue of the status of Mosaic (judicial) law in a Christian society. Recall that during the 1640s, claims that suppression of religious dissent lay within the civil magistrate's purview were bolstered by citations from the Hebrew Scriptures. The general tolerationist, and mainstream Christian, view that Jesus had fulfilled the Law and given a new message of love and mercy went a long way toward addressing their opponents' objections on this score. James Paston devoted a sermon to Luke 9:55, in which several of the disciples wanted Jesus to call down fire on the Samaritan town. Paston used Jesus' refusal to do so, not only illustrate the differences between Gospel meekness and the Law's "eye for an eye" approach, but to articulate a much broader claim about the Law's intermingling of civil and ecclesiastical power, and its Gospel antithesis.[74] In a novel twist on this familiar theological dispute, an anonymous author noted that ancient Israel was not so hostile to liberty of conscience as many assumed: Israelites, he claimed, always made allowance for *proselyti domicili* (strangers within their borders), from whom was required only obedience to minimal basics of ethical conduct.[75]

Another aspect of the theological and scriptural argument that survived well into the 1680s was the radical dichotomization between the civil and spiritual realms, an attempt to define religious functions out of the purview of the magistracy. The proponents of this approach, which was part of the

72. *A Brief Testimony*, 13. See also [William Penn], *Considerations Moving to a Toleration, and Liberty of Conscience* (London, 1685), 1. The author of *The Great Case of Toleration Stated* argued that, with the exception of basic fundamentals of Christianity (the Apostles' Creed, for example), the civil magistrate is not charged with suppressing heresy (8–9).

73. *A Few Short Arguments Proving That Tis Every Englishman's Interest as Well as Duty . . . to Endeavor the . . . Repeal of All the Religious Penal Laws and Tests* (London, 1687), 1. The title page of Penn's *Letter from a Gentleman . . . upon the Penal Law and Test* (London, 1687), renders the Golden Rule into Latin: "Quod tibi non vis fieri, alteri non feceris."

74. *A Discourse of Penal Laws*, 5–16; see also Care, *Liberty of Conscience Asserted and Vindicated*, 3.

75. *A Letter to a Member of Parliament, for Liberty of Conscience* (London, 1689), 1–2.

legacy of English Separatism, derived it from the example of Jesus himself.[76] Jesus had, after all, stated that his kingdom was not of this world.[77] To Richard Burthogge, civil government and the Christian religion had fundamentally different ends, and no necessary relationship existed between the two.[78] "The principle of religion is inward, spiritual, divine," wrote another proponent of the civil/spiritual dichotomy, "the chief end of magistracy, laws and government among men, is to preserve and defend their properties, liberties, and lives, from such as would spoil and rob them of either."[79] According to Burnet, Christianity simply contains no temporal dimension. "Actions which concern human society belong indeed to the authority of the magistrate . . . but our thoughts, with relation to God, and such actions as arise of those thoughts, and in which others have no interest, are God's immediate province." The magistrate usurps God's sovereignty by interfering with matters of conscience, violating the essential pre-political right "of worshipping God according to our conviction."[80]

In addition to scriptural and theological arguments, tolerationists reiterated conventional epistemological ones as well. Belief is a faculty and function of the understanding, not of the will, they argued, and therefore it is not within an individual's power to change his or her religious views. Since God is "to be glorified in a free and voluntary obedience of his rational creatures,"[81] force is to be abjured, since it cannot bring about the true and voluntary belief demanded by God. "It is not in our power to believe as we please," one author wrote, and since "our errors are not voluntary, we ought not to be punished for them."[82] Not only does persecution violate Christian charity, Buckingham argued, but it is "contrary to sense and reason . . . [and] absurd to attempt to convince a man's judgment by anything, but reason."[83] A further

76. The most familiar example of this argument from the 1640s is Williams, *Bloudy Tenent.*
77. The reference is to John 18:36. See *An Expedient for Peace,* 17, and *Bloudy Tenent,* 249; 224–25.
78. *Prudential Reasons for Repealing the Penal Laws Against All Recusants, and for a General Toleration* (London, 1688), 1–2.
79. Shewen, *A Brief Testimony,* 5; 20. While not agreeing with this argument entirely, the author of *Liberty of Conscience Explicated and Vindicated* (London, 1689) notes the magistrate's responsibility regarding life, liberty, and property (17).
80. *The Case of Compulsion,* 4–5.
81. *The Great Case of Toleration Stated,* 4.
82. *A Discourse of Toleration,* 6. See also Penn's *Reasonableness of Toleration* (London, 1687), 9–11.
83. *A Short Discourse,* preface, 20.

corollary to this argument about belief, understanding, and will claimed that force can succeed only in making hypocrites and dissemblers. "To force men to the service of God," wrote one author, "makes often but hypocrites, whose presence there should be voluntary, or else it is neither acceptable to God . . . nor to good men."[84]

Tolerationists also argued from skepticism. All human beings are susceptible to error, wrote Burnet, even those in power, and we should not underestimate the influence of custom, tradition, and even "fancy" in the formation of an individual's beliefs.[85] This skeptical argument proved useful, as had its corollary during the 1640s, in evoking Protestant unity against Roman Catholic claims to (papal or conciliar) infallibility.[86] Of course, Burnet argued, a moderate acknowledgment of human fallibility need not lead to radical skepticism or nihilism. But Christians must realize that neither magistrates nor priests can serve as infallible interpretive guides.[87] Indeed, St. Paul himself persecuted Christians before his conversion.[88] Another author noted the variety of human understandings, that "it is as impossible to make all men's consciences of the same extent and latitude, as to make all men's shoes of the same size."[89] Tolerationists reminded their audiences that the unity called for by Paul was possible without imposed religious uniformity. Universal agreement was highly unlikely, "though . . . not united in opinion, yet . . . in love, that very love would compose our differences, and settle a firm and undisturbed peace among us."[90]

If there is a difference between toleration debates during the 1640s and those of the 1680s, it seems to be one of emphasis. Authors gave far more attention to prudential and straightforwardly political arguments for toleration in the latter half of the seventeenth century than during the Civil War years. Many writers pointed toward tolerationist solutions out of prudence,

---

84. [George Care], *Liberty of Conscience Asserted and Vindicated*, 15. See also Paston, *A Discourse of Penal Laws*, 32–33; *Plea of Harmless Oppressed*, 9; and *Liberty of Conscience Explicated*, 9, 16.

85. *The Case of Compulsion*, 3. See also *An Expedient for Peace*, 15.

86. See, e.g., the Anglican disclaiming of popish "slavish obedience" by the author of *A Letter in Answer to a City Friend*, 3–4, and Richard Kidder, *The Judgment of Private Discretion in Matters of Religion, Defended* (London, 1687).

87. For magistrates, see Burnet, *The Case of Compulsion*, 3–4; for priests, Kidder, *The Judgment of Private Discretion*, 19–20.

88. *A Discourse of Toleration*, 9–10. For Paul's role in persecuting early Christians, see Acts 6–9.

89. *A Letter to a Member of Parliament*, 4.

90. *A Discourse of Toleration*, 7.

noting that persecution simply had not worked, that religious dissent remained an apparently ineradicable feature of the English politico-religious landscape.[91] Not only had repression not converted or cowed Dissenters, it had set the nation against itself, dividing neighbor against neighbor. Fine distinctions of theology might animate divines, but an average person understood compulsion quite well and knew that it bred hatred between individuals and religious parties.[92] Threats to political and social stability, according to this argument, lay not in the existence of dissent, but in the relentless and cruel campaigns to suppress it.[93] In this sense, ironically to many seventeenth-century minds, it was not toleration that produced civil strife but rather the repression of liberty to worship. Shewen saw the zeal to "hate or hurt" one's neighbors over religious differences as a sign of the "religiously mad or mistaken."[94]

This "battle fatigue" and increased attention to prudence is, on a pragmatic level, understandable. During the Civil War years, the victory of the New Model Army fired the providentialist sense that toleration was a policy blessed by God. Such assumptions, however, were sorely tested by the collapse of the Protectorate after Cromwell's death and the ensuing Restoration of Charles II. By the 1680s, fifty years of political struggle, civil war, regicide, army rule, the Restoration, the repression of dissent, the popish plot, and the Exclusion Crisis seem to have taken their toll socially.[95] Perhaps this argument, prudential as it was, began to be heard more charitably by a nation (or at least the influential segments of a nation) increasingly weary of such deep-seated religious strife, and the recurrent political and constitutional crises it engendered.

In addition to arguments about the ineffectiveness of persecution in obliterating dissent (and the unfortunate *effectiveness* of it in alienating one English subject from another), tolerationists revived arguments about trade and prosperity. Cornelius de Witt noted the industry of Dissenters and the

---

91. [Burthogge], *Prudential Reasons*, 3; Paston, *A Discourse of Penal Laws*, 34; *An Expedient for Peace*, 28.

92. See Burnet, *The Case of Compulsion*, 14.

93. *A Discourse of Toleration*, 7.

94. *A Brief Testimony*, 10.

95. Stephen Macedo writes that "battle fatigue presented the state with an opportunity to rise above divisive conflict and focus on the pursuit of shared interests and aims" ("Toleration and Fundamentalism," in *A Companion to Contemporary Political Philosophy*, ed. Robert E. Goodin and Philip Pettit [Cambridge, Mass., 1993], 622).

tendency of persecution to depopulate countries. Those who benefited from liberty of conscience, he wrote, "are not idle drones or spendthrifts, but generally the most sober and industrious of any country."[96] Burthogge stated simply, "Trade is the interest of England, and liberty of conscience is the interest of trade."[97] The prominence of these economic arguments was partially due to the presence of many Whig exiles in Holland during the 1680s (Locke, Shaftesbury, and others), and the observations they made there. Holland also occupied an important symbolic role for many English, since it was (in English eyes) the other pillar of European Protestantism and a potential ally against the encroachments of expansionist Catholic sovereigns in France and Spain.[98] At the same time, some who opposed James's means of pursuing liberty of conscience, or who supported a more limited toleration on different grounds, objected to the reduction of such an important philosophical or theological issue to mere economics. Burnet lamented the low public standing of the Church of England, "and now the encouragement of trade, the quiet of the nation, and the freedom of conscience are again in vogue."[99] In the future, he asked, under different circumstances, might a criterion of national prosperity support taking actions against Protestants?

Prosperity and trade encouraged *civil* interest, which reinforced the Separatist view of government as solely concerned with the "externals" of human life: "Nothing binds more firmly than interest . . . [this freedom] ties all the inhabitants where they have it, into a strict fidelity to that power which grants it."[100] Such arguments about civil interest, theoretically at least, could include Catholics who professed purely spiritual allegiance to the pope,

---

96. *A Letter from Holland, Touching Liberty of Conscience* (London, 1688), 2. See also Care, *Liberty of Conscience Asserted and Vindicated*, 17. For an overview of these sorts of arguments, see Richard B. Schlatter, *The Social Ideas of Religious Leaders, 1660–1688* (New York, 1940), 165–73. J. R. Jones claims that James and his apologists "avoided intellectual arguments in favor of toleration, preferring to emphasize political and economic advantages that they claimed would accrue to all subjects" ("The Revolution in Context," in Jones, *Liberty Secured?* 18; a similar claim is made by Miller, "James II and Toleration," 10–11). These claims, while certainly overstated, do point to the increasing prominence of prudence and prosperity as themes in English political debate later in the seventeenth century.

97. *Prudential Reasons*, 9. See also *Liberty of Conscience Explicated*, 17–18.

98. Of course, England and Holland had fought each other over trade-related matters, but recall the rhetorical appeal to Holland discussed in Chapter 3. For tolerationists, Holland provided an example of the peaceful coexistence of many faiths. (For antitolerationists, of course, it symbolized chaos and licentiousness.)

99. *A Letter*, 3.

100. De Witt, *A Letter*, 3. See also [Penn], *Considerations*, 4–5.

although such claims had a great deal of popular prejudice to overcome.[101] Given that one lived in peace with one's neighbors, this argument suggested, he should not be molested on account of his religious beliefs.[102]

Even given the civil emphasis of such arguments, tolerationists tended to delimit the liberty they sought a bit further, hastening to assure their audience that "toleration is not a toleration to do mischief."[103] It did not mean the sanction of atheism, blasphemy, or other beliefs contrary to natural law, noted one author, since these contravene the "natural" conscience that even non-Christians possess.[104] George Care denied defending blasphemy or disruptive behavior, but instead pleaded for "a just liberty in such controversial things of religion, as they who have forsaken the Church of Rome do differ in . . . supposing that in the meantime they behave themselves peaceably, and live without any civil injury."[105] Most tolerationists, like Care, explicitly denied that they would grant liberty to Catholics, given concerns about the security of the commonwealth from external enemies. Still, this was as much a political as a religious category for suppression, and Care specified that "papists are not to be punished as heretics."[106]

Although, as I pointed out, Locke does not offer new or unprecedented arguments for toleration, his *Letter Concerning Toleration* does provide a synthesis of existing arguments in a highly effective polemical form. Locke evokes the Christian minimalism of an earlier time by claiming that "if the Gospel and the Apostles may be credited, no man can be a Christian without charity and without that faith which works, not by force, but by love."[107] He elaborates on the distinction between civil and spiritual realms, asserting the dichotomy between church and commonwealth by identifying their different organizing principles, ends, and means:

---

101. See G. T., *A Letter in Answer to Two Main Questions* (London, 1687), which asserts Catholics' loyalty while pointing out that Protestants have plotted far more recently against the monarchy: "the West [Monmouth's Rebellion], the Rye, and forty-eight" (7).

102. *An Expedient for Peace*, 1.

103. Ibid.

104. *Liberty of Conscience Explicated*, 8. See also Care, *Liberty of Conscience Asserted and Vindicated*, 3.

105. Care, *Liberty of Conscience Asserted and Vindicated*, i.

106. Ibid., 24.

107. *Letter*, 23. Locke also rejects the example of the ancient kings of Israel (44–45), along with the possibility of locating infallible guides in either the magistrate (37–38) or the church (49).

The commonwealth seems to me to be a society of men constituted only for the procuring, preserving, and advancing of their own civil interests. Civil interests I call life, liberty, health, and indolency of body; and the possession of outward things, such as money, lands, houses, furniture, and the like. . . .

A church then I take to be a voluntary society of men, joining themselves together of their own accord, in order to the public worshipping of God, in such a manner as they judge acceptable to him, and effectual to the salvation of their souls. (*Letter*, 26, 28)

Thus Locke removed nonseditious religious belief from the provenance of politics. Jesus' example was crucial here, as he had "sent out his soldiers to the subduing of nations . . . not armed with the sword, or other instruments of force, but prepared with the Gospel of peace, and with the exemplary holiness of their conversation" (*Letter*, 25). Adding the epistemological argument, Locke reiterates that belief is independent of the will, located instead in the understanding. "True religion consists in the inward and full persuasion of the mind. . . . [S]uch is the nature of the understanding, that it cannot be compelled to the belief of any thing by outward force" (*Letter*, 27).

Belief and politics thus operate on two fundamentally different levels, and political means are ineffective to secure religious belief. Even if the magistrate is an enlightened one, forced religion lacks the necessary element of voluntary individual assent. Combining the epistemological argument with the fact that Jesus persecuted no one, Locke finds toleration consistent with human reason and Christian doctrine. Nor does he omit prudential and economic arguments. Quite simply, civil society is grounded upon civil interest, and civil interest is aided by toleration *and* by the exclusion of potentially seditious groups from the scope of toleration.[108] Strife is caused, not by toleration, but by the thirst for liberty brought forward by a persecuting magistrate (*Letter*, 47, 55). Thus Locke highlights the most salient and commonly employed arguments of his contemporaries in favor of toleration; indeed, the implications of Locke's sharp delineation between church and commonwealth

---

108. The civil emphasis of civil society is evoked by the Lockean distinction between church and commonwealth, and more generally in Locke's *Second Treatise*, chap. 9.

have led some to assert that Locke advocated full disestablishment of the Anglican Church.[109]

Antitoleration: Reviving the 1640s, Ecclesiology, and the Utility of "a Little Smart"

Opponents of toleration also reiterated the conventional arguments that had been employed by their predecessors during the 1640s and 1650s. In fact, they had one great advantage over earlier generations of antitolerationists: they could draw upon the events of the 1640s and 1650s as examples of the mischief that religious dissent can visit on a society. The Civil War years proved enormously effective rhetorically: advocates of uniformity branded tolerationist religious dissidents as the political and religious heirs of the rebellious spirit that had borne fruit in the English Civil War and execution of Charles I. They sometimes suggested that much of the unrest of the past fifty years could be traced back to Puritan restless rebelliousness from the earliest days of the Elizabethan church settlement. "Those that strained at the cap and surplice, could well enough digest rapine, sacrilege, and regicide," argued one.[110]

Linking claims for toleration to advocacy of popular sovereignty and other extreme political positions, Henry Maurice pointedly stated the threat such views presented. The danger to the state had already been displayed, he asserted,

> by an unnatural and unfortunate rebellion, by the deliberate and solemn murder of a most excellent and merciful prince, by a heavy and tedious tyranny of many years, by several conspiracies since the Restoration, by association against the succession of His Majesty, and a formed project of rebellion . . . in short, by the incessant working of a turbulent spirit. . . . Experience has found [faction and conscience] to be inseparable companions in the bodies of our Dissenters.[111]

109. See Schochet, "John Locke and Religious Toleration." As I noted in the preface, I disagree with this interpretation. The "snapshot" of Locke's *Letter* I have provided does not address the important development of his thought between 1660 and 1689: I deal with this issue in much more depth in Chapter 6, as an example of the importance of political context in toleration debates. Locke's development is traced most fully in John Marshall, *John Locke: Resistance, Religion and Responsibility* (Cambridge, 1994).

110. *The Danger and Unreasonableness of a Toleration* (London, 1685), 3, 4.

111. *The Antithelemite* (London, 1685), 3, 4.

William Falkner linked tolerationists with the murder of Charles I, while Edmund Bohun, in his preface to Filmer's *Patriarcha*, recalled the Exclusion Crisis as animated by those with "extravagant hopes that the Commonwealth of England might take another turn upon the stage."[112] The continued clamor for liberty of conscience must surprise anyone "but merely versed in the transactions of these 40 last years," noted one author; while another pointed to "the fresh bleeding wounds of these three nations" as an argument for unity in church and state.[113]

More generally, this evocation of the 1640s and 1650s equated toleration and religious dissent with social anarchy, licentiousness, and chaos. The public allowance of diverse religious practices "doth naturally improve into contentious disputes, and those disputes (if not restrained) break out into civil wars."[114] Contempt for magistracy soon follows contempt for ministry, and were the magistrate to grant toleration, individuals would soon claim conscience for "anything concerning God and man, how holy or just so ever it were, that did dislike him."[115] The specifically religious implications of this argument lay in the claim that the anarchy toleration brought in would lead to the collapse of morality and the triumph of irreligion and license: "When men may do anything they think right, they will go near to think any thing right," wrote Thomas Ashenden during the Exclusion Crisis.[116] Connecting toleration with popular sovereignty, Falkner linked both with "anarchy" and "irreligion," claiming that if this view of conscience and its prerogatives were to triumph, it would destroy civil government, and "we should live as among wolves."[117]

---

112. Falkner, *Christian Loyalty*, 357–58; Bohun, "Preface," in Filmer, *Patriarcha*, A3. The finest example of this genre, though beyond the scope of this chapter, is probably Samuel Parker, *A Discourse of Ecclesiastical Polity* (London, 1669). The revival of interest in Filmer, evinced by the number of new editions of *Patriarcha* during the late 1670s and early 1680s, provided Locke, Algernon Sidney, and James Tyrrell with the opportunity to articulate their Whig political theories. See, especially, Locke, *Two Treatises* (London, 1690); Sidney, *Discourses Concerning Government*; and Tyrrell, *Patriarcha non Monarcha* (London, 1681). Also see Mark Goldie, "John Locke and Anglican Royalism," *Political Studies* 31 (1983): 61–85, for the broader context of the revival of Filmer; and for Filmer more specifically, the introductory and bibliographic materials in *Patriarcha and Other Writings*, ed. Johann Sommerville (Cambridge, 1991), ix–xxxvii.

113. *The Danger and Unreasonableness*, 1; Edward Wetenhall, *The Protestant Peace-Maker* (London, 1682), 40. See also Thomas Ashenden's *No Penalty, No Peace* (London, 1682), 1–2.

114. William Assheton, *A Seasonable Discourse Against Toleration* (London, 1685), 17.

115. *The Danger and Unreasonableness*, 3.

116. *No Penalty, No Peace*, 13; also 232ff. See also Wetenhall, *Protestant Peace-Maker*, 40–50.

117. *Christian Loyalty*, 292, 364.

Like their opponents, antitolerationists also supplied extensive scriptural justifications for their position. Many of their arguments reiterated long-running calls for uniformity as the Christian ideal of unity and church harmony. This ideal of unity, with its criticism of separating sects, had animated English religious politics for much of the Restoration period.[118] The antitolerationist argument from Christian unity sought to shift the blame for religious dissension from "persecuting" Anglicans to fissiparous sects. The underlying basis for many of these discussions of unity lay in the contested notion of *adiaphora*, or "indifferent" things in religious worship.

Tolerationists often argued that ecclesiastical authorities and civil magistrates should insist on only those ceremonies or practices with specific biblical sanction for their performance. Their opponents, noting that Dissenters often acknowledged the Anglican Church's status as a true church, argued that schism on the basis of admittedly indifferent matters was unjustified and contrary to Pauline injunctions to Christian unity.[119] The debate over *adiaphora* quickly reached a standstill. One side claimed that the church could not require a practice not specifically outlined in the Bible; the other pointed out that with no biblical injunction *against* a given practice, the call for obedience of Romans 13 and the Pauline commitment to unity required Dissenters to set aside their schismatic behavior. If separation for the sake of "greater purity" is sanctioned, where will such schism end? asked Stillingfleet.[120] If the differences between Anglicans and Dissenters were only over indifferent things, "why should they be so unreasonable as to separate from us, and to make or continue a perpetual breach for things of little moment?"[121] Why

---

118. The great examples of this position are Edward Stillingfleet's *Mischief of Separation* (London, 1680) and *The Unreasonableness of Separation* (London, 1682). Stillingfleet supported comprehension on some points, as a necessary step to secure Protestant unity. At the same time, he harshly condemned the sects as lacking charity and a commitment to Christian unity.

119. See Philippians 1: 27; 1 Corinthians 1:10, 3:3, 12:25; 2 Corinthians 13:11; Philippians 2:2, 3:15–16; Ephesians 4:3; and Galatians 5:20. These calls for unity make up the bulk of Stillingfleet's *Mischief* and *Unreasonableness*.

A related argument about the *adiaphora* involved a unique twist on the nature of scriptural justification. Henry Maurice pointed out that Jesus had nowhere *ruled out* compulsion in matters of conscience. "As for using force in matters of religion," he wrote, "I do not know any passage in all the gospels, that absolutely and expressly forbids it." True, Christ had used no force, but he was a private person and not a civil magistrate (see *The Antithelemite*, 10–11). Although the *adiaphora* occasioned extensive debate, it seems doubtful that Maurice's particular take on this argument was either widespread or very persuasive.

120. Stillingfleet, *Mischief*, passim; *Unreasonableness*, 112–13.

121. [Maurice], *The Antithelemite*, 46–47.

could Dissenters' "tender consciences . . . not dispense with a few innocent and harmless ceremonies of the Church of England, from which they differ in things not necessary to salvation?"[122] Misguided insistence upon church purity, they asserted, had led sectarians to destroy church unity. Even after the passage of the Toleration Act, Anglicans did not relent in their accusations of schism: John Norris reminded his readers that Dissenters were still schismatics, though tolerated, and that the legal penalties had only been suspended, not repealed.[123]

Other opponents of toleration employed traditional arguments about the example of ancient Israel and its implied corollary in the English royal supremacy. They asserted that the king should be supreme over both church and state, as the kings of Israel had been.[124] Arguments placing such emphasis on royal supremacy, of course, risked being branded "Hobbist," especially when Assheton stated that "the supreme magistrate must determine what circumstances shall be used in the worship and service of God."[125] Seeking to avoid such a label, such authors quickly asserted that the royal supremacy was to be used for the promotion and preservation of the true Christian religion. "Magistracy," wrote one, "under the Gospel, is for the good of the church."[126] If Hobbes and the Anglican royalists of the 1680s shared a general Erastian position, the latter group stressed the "Anglican" as much as the royalist.[127] In this Anglican emphasis we see the roots of their bitter disappointment with James's tolerationist policies as his reign progressed.

122. *The Danger and Unreasonableness*, 1.
123. *The Charge of Schism Continued* (London, 1691), 7–15.
124. See Falkner, *Christian Loyalty*, bk. 1; Ashenden, *No Penalty, No Peace*, 14–15. Recall that William Prynne had expressed similar Erastian sentiments during the 1640s, against the divine right proposals of both Independents and Presbyterians. See Chapter 3.
125. *A Seasonable Discourse Against Toleration*, 13.
126. *Four Grand Questions Proposed* (London, 1689), 7, also 8–9.
127. Of course, for Hobbes royal supremacy did not involve two separate spheres over which the king had final authority. Hobbes's system abolished the separation between spiritual and temporal authority altogether. "There is . . . no other government in this life, neither of state, nor religion, but temporal; nor teaching of any doctrine, lawful to any subject, which the governor both of the state, and the religion forbiddeth to be taught. And that governor must be one; or else there must needs follow faction and civil war in the commonwealth, between the Church and the State" (*L*, 316). My point is that both Hobbes and Anglican royalists reinforced absolutist political theory, and the charges of Hobbism leveled at Anglican royalists were not entirely fallacious. Stillingfleet was forced to refute charges of Hobbism (*Unreasonableness*, 132). See John Marshall, "The Ecclesiology of the Latitude-men, 1660–1689: Stillingfleet, Tillotson, and 'Hobbism,'" *JEH* 36 (1985): 407–27. The best overview of Anglican royalism during this time period is Goldie, "John Locke and Anglican Royalism."

In addition, opponents of toleration advanced philosophical arguments, continuing to assert the traditional understanding of conscience against the more subjective aspect advanced by tolerationists (with its increasing emphasis on voluntarism). The notion of erroneous conscience stressed the fallenness of human nature and drew strength from the empirical, historical arguments about the past consequences of religious division and dissent. In this view, what was often passed off as "conscience" was in reality little more than opinion, whim, fancy, or desire, the tendency of people "to follow after novelty and new-fangledness."[128] Persecution was not simply forcing an individual to do something he preferred not to do with regard to religion, argued Maurice, but "an inflicting, of outward temporal evils, for the exercise of true religion." On this understanding, French Protestants, and not English Dissenters, were persecuted, for they suffered for "a religion, which we verily believe to be true."[129] Assheton defined persecution similarly, as "an inflicting, of outward temporal evils, for the exercise of true religion."[130] Since Anglicans required nothing that was contrary to Scripture (indifferent matters being just that, indifferent, and binding once commanded by the sovereign), there could be no persecution in suppressing Dissenters. Claims of conscience, therefore, simply did not apply.[131]

One of the great obstacles to overcoming religious divisions, antitolerationists suggested, was human ignorance and weakness, their tendency to be drawn into what Ashenden called "novelty and new-fangledness." Most people, he suggested, would never have separated from the Anglican Church if they had known the real issues of dispute between the church and Separatists. Unfortunately, they did not know them any more than they knew "Arabic."[132] In fact, Maurice suggested a distinction between belief and action similar to that made by Hobbes: any Englishman may follow his "conscience," worshiping God as he sees fit, "provided always, that he keep his opinion to himself, or to his family, and make them a rule only for his family. But if such a man will go publish his opinions, and entangle the consciences of others, and seek to draw disciples after him, and make a party, and cause

---

128. Ashenden, *No Penalty, No Peace,* 9. Such claims to conscience, according to Ashenden, "[set] up a tribunal in every man's factious fancy" (*No Penalty, No Peace,* 19).
129. *The Antithelemite,* 9–10, 51.
130. *A Seasonable Discourse Against Toleration,* 8.
131. Ibid., 9–10.
132. *No Penalty, No Peace,* 22.

divisions amongst His Majesty's subjects, he is to be restrained, he is not to be tolerated."[133] This claim lay at the heart of Stillingfleet's earlier attack on Separatism and sectarianism: claims to "conscience" do not change the objective nature of right and wrong, nor do they absolve one of sin if what one is doing is wrong. Indeed, we have no proof that things are actually as we think they are, and we must allow the possibility that we are mistaken.[134] Not all opinion is conscience, argued Falkner. People examine their "consciences" far less than they ought, and many claims to conscience are simply disguised willfulness.[135]

These examples suggest a novel political corollary to the skepticism that often lay behind claims for toleration, a rival politics of skepticism far more in line with that of Hobbes's Erastianism. If one cannot prove that a particular church practice is required or forbidden by God, then one certainly cannot argue that its performance has any effect on one's salvation one way or the other. Thus, because fallen humanity is, not merely prone to error, but also likely to persist in selfish and prideful attachments to those errors, resistance is illegitimate. One author admitted that unnecessary impositions were undesirable, but a universal toleration was worse, in that it subverted Christian faith and church government.[136]

Finally, on the epistemological level, antitolerationists, as they always had, agreed with their opponents that force could not alter belief. This admission did not weaken their arguments for uniformity, however. While no one argued that force could change one's understanding, antitolerationists altered the purported goal of compulsion in matters of religion. In their view, "a little smart" might lead to a reexamination of false beliefs and an increased receptivity to the truth.[137] Force may only make hypocrites, as tolerationists claimed, but this in itself was not an argument for liberty of conscience, since over the long run "[those holding erroneous beliefs] may profit so much by what they hear and see, as to be convinced of the folly of their former way."[138] In addition, antitolerationists reminded audiences that forcing belief

---

133. *The Antithelemite*, 20. Falkner also argued for a distinction between belief and action, noting that "a capacity of discerning . . . [one's] duty in matters of religion" is not the same as liberty to practice whatever one becomes convinced that duty is (*Christian Loyalty*, 275).

134. Stillingfleet, *Mischief*, 42; *Unreasonableness*, 344–50.

135. *Christian Loyalty*, 280ff.

136. *Four Grand Questions*, 17–23.

137. Ashenden, *No Penalty, No Peace*, 22.

138. *The Antithelemite*, 18.

was not the same as the more straightforward power of restraining blatant error and heresy, which mainstream opinion had always granted, and continued to grant, to the civil magistrate.[139] Although the magistrate "cannot [force belief in Christ], because faith is an act of the understanding and [not] the will," he can require church attendance and punish grievous offenses in the interest of fostering general religiosity, social peace and civil behavior.[140] This argument evoked the earlier words of John Cotton, in his disputations with Roger Williams. "Better hypocrites than profane persons. Hypocrites give God his due in an outward form at least."[141]

Finally, since tolerationists during the 1640s had pointed to the example of Holland, and continued to do so in their arguments about prosperity, trade, and toleration, antitolerationists responded in kind. Maurice echoed earlier views of Holland as factious and anarchic.[142] In addition, opponents of liberty of conscience again brought up the example of New England, as evidence that those claiming toleration actually seek "a total extirpation of whatever is contrary to their humors and designs."[143]

THE TOLERATION ACT: A GLASS HALF EMPTY? A GLASS HALF FULL?

Since William had expressed his willingness to ease penalties on Protestant Dissenters by repealing penal laws,[144] the political choice facing English political and religious elites upon William's accession to the throne lay between toleration and comprehension.[145] Protestant unity was a long-held ideal in

---

139. The army officers had supported such a position at the Whitehall Debates. See also Ashenden, *No Penalty, No Peace*, 15–17.

140. *Four Grand Questions*, 12.

141. In Hutchinson, *The History*, 2:132.

142. *The Antithelemite*, 56ff.

143. Assheton, *A Seasonable Discourse Against Toleration*, 82.

144. Gasper Fagel, *A Letter, Writ by Mijn Heer Fagel, Pensioner of Holland . . .* (Amsterdam, 1688), 1–2.

145. I mean this statement about the choice facing William and others solely in a political sense. It is not helpful, in my view, to claim that "historically, the battle for toleration was already almost won when [Locke's] *Letter* was published, for it was impossible that the old uniformity should be maintained after the Revolution." See Gough, *John Locke's Political Philosophy*, 219. W. K. Jordan makes a similarly unhelpful assertion and dates the "triumph" of toleration even earlier, claiming that "the case for religious toleration had been won by 1660; there remained only the difficult process of accommodating institutions to the fact of historical change" (*Development of Religious Toleration in England*, 4:469).

English thought, and at least a degree of theological compatibility existed between moderate Presbyterians and the Anglican hierarchy, as evidenced by ongoing Presbyterian efforts at comprehension since the 1660s. Virtually no influential Anglicans, however, supported either comprehension or toleration. Forced to choose, Anglicans generally considered toleration the lesser of two evils: they opposed it, but comprehension would infect the church itself, whereas toleration at least maintained the parameters of orthodox Anglican belief intact.[146] John Spurr has argued that "indulgence was established in default of comprehension and . . . the church's obduracy lies close to the heart of any explanation of the failure of comprehension."[147]

The Act that eventually emerged from Parliament represented well the "moderation" of King William III, both as a stated position and as a concession to the realities of English politics. As laid out in Gasper Fagel's noted letter, William and Mary positioned themselves as opposed to James's "extreme" embrace of universal toleration, which included Catholics and involved plans for repealing penal laws and the Test Act. Instead, they supported a restrained Protestant toleration in the interest of anti-Catholic unity. Such a grant of liberty, in their view, could be helpful in securing English and (since they viewed political developments from a Dutch perspective as well) European

---

Claims like Gough's and Jordan's rely upon a notion of "historical inevitability" that may be only dimly visible to the actors under consideration, and cannot withstand serious historical examination. For example, Gough refers to religious liberty as "logically the outcome of the protestant belief that each individual (with God's assistance) could interpret Scripture for himself" (*John Locke's Political Philosophy*, 194). I have suggested, in Chapters 2 and 3, that there is nothing logical about the purported connection between Protestantism and toleration. See also Isaiah Berlin, "Historical Inevitability," in *Four Essays on Liberty*.

146. Rose, *England in the 1690s*, chap. 5. Comprehension was supported by many, as it represented a way to simultaneously preserve England's understanding of itself as a Protestant nation and eschew persecution. Comprehension remained a long-standing ideal in the Anglican tradition—attracting such important figures as Coleridge, Thomas Arnold, and Benjamin Jowett in the Broad Church movement—involving a move away from the notion of an established church as guardian of a particular creed or dogma, toward viewing the church as the institutionalization of a generic English Protestantism. For an overview of the Broad Church movement, see Josef L. Altholz, *Anatomy of a Controversy: The Debate over "Essays and Reviews" 1860–1864* (Aldershot, 1994).

147. "The Church of England, Comprehension, and the Toleration Act of 1689," *English Historical Review* 104 (1989): 946. Schochet also traces out the events leading up to the passage of the Toleration Act in "The Act of Toleration and the Failure of Comprehension: Persecution, Nonconformity, and Religious Indifference," in Dale Hoak and Mordechai Feingold, eds., *The World of William and Mary: Anglo-Dutch Perspectives on the Revolution of 1688–89* (Stanford, Calif., 1996), 165–87.

Protestantism.[148] Initially, William had preferred that Catholics, though excluded from holding public office, be granted the right to worship. He considered their exclusion from public office a necessary requirement for the political security of the kingdom, and such an exclusion had similarly obtained in Holland under William. The inability of Catholics to participate in government was inconvenient, William admitted, but it did not constitute persecution *per se*, since "their persons, their estates, and even the exercise of their religion [is] assured them."[149] William and Mary were essentially *politiques*, less concerned with theology than with civil peace. When unable to secure private Catholic worship in the Toleration Act, they accepted the limitations of prevailing English anti-Catholicism and did not push beyond liberty for Protestant Dissenters.[150]

The Toleration Act represented the "first statutory grant of toleration in English history."[151] It also presents a dilemma for scholars attempting to assess its place in the history of religious freedom, since "almost without exception those who acted in the defense of constitutional liberties and the rule of law also showed themselves to be oppressors of the Catholic minority."[152] The Act ensured a narrower religious liberty than had James's Declarations, and hemmed in Protestant Dissenters with a number of restrictive provisions. The Test Act remained in force, so that Protestants who refused to swear oaths remained barred from officeholding, and the Toleration Act did not extend to "any person who shall deny in preaching or writing the doctrine of the Blessed Trinity."[153] In addition to the customary oaths professing

148. For more on this Dutch perspective, see the essays collected in Hoak and Feingold, *The World of William and Mary*. Opposition to Louis XIV formed the cornerstone of William's early Protestant foreign policy: "Since King Louis was the champion of persecuting popery, his defeat would constitute a great triumph for the Protestants of Europe" (Rose, *England in the 1690s*, 112). This is not to say that William viewed foreign policy as a religious crusade, only that piety and policy went hand in hand. See Israel, "William III and Toleration," and Pincus, "To Protect English Liberties," 94–102.

149. Fagel, *Letter*, 4.

150. See the introduction to Grell, Israel, and Tyacke, *From Persecution to Toleration*, as well as Israel's "William III and Toleration," in the same volume, for a portrait of William as *politique*.

151. Miller, "James II and Toleration," 23. The text of the Act is reprinted in *English Historical Documents*, vol. 8, 1660–1714, ed. Andrew Browning (New York, 1953), 400–403.

152. J. R. Jones, "The Revolution in Context," in Jones, *Liberty Secured?* 17. This is, of course, another way of saying that Parliamentary opposition to James's extralegal activities involved opposition to his attempts at toleration.

153. *English Historical Documents*, 8:403. Six years later, affirmations were permitted in lieu of oaths for those who scrupled at swearing. See Ethyn Williams Kirby, "The Quakers' Efforts to Secure Civil and Religious Liberty, 1660–1696," *Journal of Modern History* 7 (1935): 401–21.

allegiance to William and Mary, as well as rejecting the temporal jurisdiction of the pope and abjuring Roman Catholicism, the Act required Dissenters to obtain a license for their congregations from an Anglican bishop. They were required to leave their doors unlocked during worship. Tithes remained in force. All preachers had to subscribe to the Anglican Articles of Religion, with exceptions made for several contested doctrinal areas. Although the freedom granted by the Toleration Act would eventually lead to broader understandings of liberty of conscience and the institutional requirements of such liberty, that broad historical importance lay years in the future and could not have been apparent to Dissenters in 1689. What was apparent in 1689 was a limited freedom of worship coinciding with "the continuing second-class status of Protestant Nonconformists . . . [based on] expediency and calculation."[154]

The legislation's official title illustrates this minimal nature of the liberty granted by the Toleration Act. It omits the words "toleration" and "indulgence" altogether. Instead, Parliament passed "An Act for Exempting Their Majesties' Protestant Subjects Dissenting From the Church of England From the Penalties of Certain Laws."[155] The Act's preamble mentions none of the elaborately articulated theological, philosophical, or epistemological justifications for toleration, but rather states baldly that "some ease to scrupulous consciences may be an effectual means to unite Their Majesties' Protestant subjects in interest and affection."[156] William's propagandists also stated largely prudential reasons for the Act, focusing on trade and prosperity. The advance of the nation "lie[s] in the freedom and flourishing of trade . . . while people are in danger of suffering about religion," wrote one, "they dare not launch into trade, but keep their money."[157] (To be sure, James had referred to the effect of toleration on subjects' affection toward the monarch, but he had gone on to note that persecution was illegitimate and ineffectual.) As John Marshall observes, "The toleration established in 1689 in England was not established on the principles of [Locke's] *Letter Concerning Toleration*

---

154. Gordon J. Schochet, "From Persecution to 'Toleration,'" in Jones, *Liberty Secured?* 155–56. For the broader evolution of religious liberty after 1689, see R. K. Webb, "From Toleration to Religious Liberty," in Jones, *Liberty Secured?* 158–98.

155. *English Historical Documents*, 8:400.

156. Ibid.

157. James Fraser, *King William's Toleration, Being an Explanation of That Liberty of Religion Which May Be Expected from His Majesty's Declaration* (London, 1689), 3–4.

but only by limited exemptions from the penalties of the law and then only for orthodox Protestants and not for antitrinitarians."[158] The legislation presented a cramped set of grudging political compromises, historic in their implications but (intentionally) limited in their formulation.

Still, if we refrain from measuring the toleration of 1689 with a twenty-first-century yardstick, the Toleration Act did represent a major step forward in the history of religious freedom in England. Protestant Dissenters received liberty to worship publicly on a statutory, rather than royally granted, basis. Although penal laws were not repealed and Dissenters merely exempted from their penalties, this exemption had the force of both Parliament and monarch behind it, and was not subject to the procedural wrangling over royal prerogative that had doomed many earlier efforts to secure toleration. In a sense, the Toleration Act evokes a grand solution to the debates of the 1640s and 1650s, the victory of the Independent over the Presbyterian ideal.[159] The idea of a uniform, unified national church, even if this involved a relaxation of the parameters of official doctrine and compliance, gave way to the coexistence of established ecclesiastical order with Dissenting groups of various kinds. The legal guarantees extended to Dissenting sects represented a real departure from previous practice. The ideal of Anglican unity, achieved through uniformity and ecclesiastical discipline, was jettisoned from English religious politics. The Act maintained the restrictive parameters of Restored Anglicanism and the exclusion of Catholics and non-Trinitarian Protestants from public office (and thus the Anglican monopoly on positions of influence),[160] while exempting Dissenters from the fines for nonattendance of Anglican services inflicted upon them by penal laws.

CONCLUSION

From modest beginnings, the Toleration Act laid a foundation for the gradual acceptance of religious minorities into English public life, a process that would unfold with varying degrees of success over the next two centuries. It granted

158. *John Locke*, 454.
159. Peter White, "The Twilight of Puritanism in the Years Before and After 1688," in Grell, Israel, and Tyacke, *From Persecution to Toleration.*
160. Including, for example, the profession of teaching, which remained under Anglican control. See David L. Wykes, "Quaker Schoolmasters, Toleration, and the Law, 1689–1714," *Journal of Religious History* 21 (1997): 178–92.

less extensive liberty than many Dissenters would have liked, and certainly far more than many Anglicans preferred. Though a limited and purely prudential measure, eschewing any mention of the long-standing theological, philosophical, or epistemological arguments in favor of toleration, the Act rightly occupies a crucial place in the history of religious liberty as the first legislative grant of toleration to English Dissenters. At the same time, we should remember that the Anglican monopoly on officeholding and positions of public trust was maintained through the retention of the Test Act.

We have seen in this chapter how James's quest for toleration aroused and united opposition to him. On both procedural and substantive grounds, James quickly came to be seen as the enemy of English liberties. The presence of a united opposition to this policy—an opposition that included Anglicans as well as Protestant Dissenters—began the chain of events that eventually led to James's flight and William and Mary's assumption of the throne. Few who began the opposition to James desired to depose him or saw their actions as revolutionary; they were, as Speck calls them, "reluctant revolutionaries." In this history of unintended consequences, we find echoes of another not-so-distant episode in English history: as had been the case fifty years previous, opponents of Stuart kings saw themselves as the guardians of the balanced constitution, the role of Parliament in the commonwealth's governance, and the orthodox Protestantism that the Anglican Church represented. In those days, as well, events outstripped the intentions of those who had set them in motion.

Advocates of toleration advanced a plethora of arguments during the 1680s, none of which represented a new perspective or approach to justifying liberty of conscience. Their opponents showed a similar reliance on familiar and often very effective justifications for uniformity and ecclesiastical discipline. As (again) had been the case during the Civil War years, persuasive philosophical or theological treatises did not win the battle for toleration. Instead, a combination of inept royal statesmanship (James's progressive alienation of his Anglican royalist allies), ubiquitous English anti-Catholicism, and a prosaic concern for stability and prosperity led William and Mary to exempt Protestant Dissenters from penalties for not attending Anglican services. From its evocation of Cromwell's Protectorate, regicide, civil war, and anarchy during the early Restoration, the idea of toleration had become something much different by 1689: within modest limits, the prerequisite for an ordered, workable political settlement that would unite English Protestants under the new regime. This new regime, this developing English nationalism, relied heavily on a general notion of Protestantism in both religious faith and foreign policy. Persecution would only hinder England's important business, be it commercial or religio-political. We should remember, however, that during services Dissenters still could not lock their doors.

5

PROSECUTION OR PERSECUTION?

Quakers, Toleration, and Schism in Early Pennsylvania

This much can I say, that I had an opening of joy as to these parts in the year 1661 at Oxford, twenty years since; and as my understanding and inclinations have been much directed to observe and reprove mischiefs in government, so it is now put into my power to settle one.

—William Penn, "To Robert Turner . . ." (April 12, 1681)

Oh! whither do you think these things will run? Will it not give people just cause to say, the Quakers are turned persecutors?

—Thomas Budd, *A True Copy of Three Judgments*

Now . . . these complainers of persecution, had egregiously transgressed [the law to secure the magistrates' reputation from slander], and . . . they did endeavour to raise sedition and subvert the government, and for that cause only, and not upon any religious account they were prosecuted.

—Samuel Jennings, *The State of the Case*

William Penn's endeavor in Pennsylvania has, for good reason, long been considered one of the most important episodes in the history and development of American religious liberty. Penn consistently sought to protect citizenship and officeholding rights for adherents of the broad spectrum of religious groups who resided in his colony, and a remarkable religious diversity characterized the colony from its earliest years. Pennsylvania, historians often assert, is also important in terms much broader than those of the seventeenth century, as a foundation of the American constitutional commitment to the separation of church and state.[1] The colony's reputation for religious liberty is justified—although it is true that Penn and his colony have suffered almost as much as Massachusetts Puritans from sentimentalized hagiography[2]—but below I shall explore how the difficult task of securing social order in the face of strident dissent bedeviled Pennsylvania magistrates, just as it had Massachusetts governors and the English Parliament during their own episodes of religio-political agitation.

During 1692 and 1693, the Keithian schism in the Philadelphia Meeting divided the colony's Quaker community and resulted in civil prosecutions of religious dissidents. The schism, which raised important issues in terms of the colony's internal political dynamics as well as its wider relationship with English authorities, illuminates the difficulty that Quaker authorities faced in attempting to realize, in practical terms, the theoretical principles of liberty of conscience that they had articulated so powerfully as Dissenters in England.

This Keith affair turned out to be, not merely a minor religious quarrel, but part of a broader set of attacks on the colony's government and Penn's proprietorship. How Keithians and mainstream Quakers justified themselves in terms of Christian orthodoxy, liberty of conscience, and the requirements of ordered society throughout the course of the schism provides insight into the translation of religious differences into civil ones. Keith's theological

---

1. See, e.g., Edwin Scott Gaustad, *A Religious History of America*, new revised edition (San Francisco, 1990), 97–98; Arthur M. Schlesinger, *The Birth of the Nation: A Portrait of the American People on the Eve of Independence* (New York, 1968), 94–95; Joseph E. Illick, *Colonial Pennsylvania: A History* (New York, 1976), chap. 11; Winthrop S. Hudson, *Religion in America*, 4th ed. (New York, 1987), 96–97; Curry, *First Freedoms*, 144, 147, 156, 171, 182, 196–97; Patricia U. Bonomi, *Under the Cope of Heaven: Religion, Society, and Politics in Colonial America* (New York, 1986), 33–37, 81; and Sally Schwartz, *"A Mixed Multitude": The Struggle for Toleration in Colonial Pennsylvania* (New York, 1987), chap. 1 and epilogue.

2. See, e.g., Henry J. Cadbury, "Persecution and Religious Liberty, Then and Now," *PMHB* 68 (1944): 359–71, which, after describing that Jews and Catholics could neither vote nor hold office in early Pennsylvania, notes their "full political and economic equality with entire freedom to worship God according to the dictates of their own consciences" (366); William Wistar Comfort, *William Penn: A Tercentenary Estimate* (Philadelphia, 1944); Robert L.D. Davidson, *War Comes to Quaker Pennsylvania, 1682–1756* (New York, 1957), esp. chap. 1; William Hepworth Dixon, *William Penn: An Historical Biography* (Philadelphia, 1851); Robert Proud, *The History of Pennsylvania . . . 1681–1742*, 2 vols. (Philadelphia, 1797); Samuel M. Janney, *The Life of William Penn* (Philadelphia, 1852); and Hugh Barbour, "William Penn, Model of Protestant Liberalism," *Church History* 48 (1979): 156–73.

orthodoxy and his unwillingness to compromise the purity of the church—his strenuous objections to moral laxity and theological "error" among Friends— set him on a collision course with more "worldly" and pragmatic Quaker ministers.[3]

The Keith affair, then, shows us how a theological dispute within a colony's dominant religious group—especially in a colony founded with explicitly religious purposes, like Pennsylvania (and indeed, Massachusetts fifty years earlier)—leads inevitably to wider social and political unrest. In this sense, Keith holds a place equal to Williams and Hutchinson, whose clashes with authority challenged the parameters of acceptable public belief and behavior in their colony.[4] Furthermore, Keith's arguments are preserved for us in ways that Williams's and Hutchinson's were not—that is, in the voice of the accused at the time of the disputes—through Keith's alliance with printer William Bradford. The presence of this written record makes the Keith affair uniquely profitable for scholars, a fact that has not often been appreciated by scholars of early Pennsylvania history. Its outcome was no different than that of Hutchinson or Williams, but unlike those other episodes, in the Keithian controversy scholars have a clear picture of the dissent, in the dissenter's own words.[5] Examining both the (comparatively) broad religious liberty that obtained in early Pennsylvania as well as the dynamics of the Keithian schism and prosecutions will illuminate the threats that Keithians posed to the public role of Pennsylvania Quakers, calling into question *both* hagiographic claims

3. Of course it is not entirely accurate to refer to "Quaker ministers," since the group rejected the conventional idea of a clergy. I use the term "minister" as a synonym for "Public Friend," denoting those Friends who played a regular and prominent role in Meetings, and often traveled to other colonies to defend Quaker principles. I use the terms "Quaker" and "Friend" interchangeably in this chapter.

4. I intend the comparative statements about Keith, Williams, and Hutchinson only to refer to the dynamics between dissenters and a dominant colonial group. I do not claim that Keith achieved prominence comparable to the other two dissenters in any kind of enduring sense, or that he influenced the development of American colonial politics, but only that a parallel dynamic seems to be at work in the lives of young colonies whereby theological differences within a dominant group give rise to social and political dissension.

5. For Hutchinson, we have Winthrop's *Short Story*, with the vitriolic preface by Thomas Weld, along with the account of her examination in Thomas Hutchinson's *History*. Although the "Examination" is a transcript of the trial, or close to it, from it we learn little about the relationship between Hutchinson's specific dissent and her broader theological or political views. For Williams, only scattered correspondence survives from before 1640. He and Cotton rehearsed their interpretations of Williams's expulsion a decade later. For much of this time Williams was in England campaigning for religious toleration, a struggle that undoubtedly colored his (as well as Cotton's) memories.

about a Pennsylvania based upon an "absolute claim for men's relative coscience"[6] and the claims by Keith and his followers that they had been persecuted solely on account of religious belief.

BACKGROUND TO COLONIZATION: PENN'S POLITICAL THOUGHT AND ARGUMENTS FOR LIBERTY OF CONSCIENCE IN ENGLAND

Even considering Penn's extended absence from his colony from 1684 to 1699, the politics of religion in colonial Pennsylvania are closely intertwined with its founder's political career. With an improved understanding of Penn's intentions in Pennsylvania, we may appreciate more fully the magnitude of his achievement as well as its shortcomings.[7] The translation from Penn's political thought as dissident in England to governor in America is not automatic, but the former provides the backdrop, context, and motivating impulse for the latter.

William Penn converted to Quakerism in early 1667, and religious concerns informed his political thought throughout the rest of his life.[8] The Quakers were just one of many sects to emerge from the strife of the 1640s in England: their denial of the Trinity, doctrine of inner light, and refusal to swear oaths and show social deference instantly drew critical attention.[9] The Quaker doctrine of the "inner light" brought accusations of anarchic tendencies from

6. Barbour, "William Penn," 167.

7. I do not propose a direct correspondence between Penn's writings on liberty of conscience and the views of all Pennsylvania settlers. As with Massachusetts, individuals came to Pennsylvania for a number of reasons, and it is highly unlikely that settlers uniformly affirmed Penn's aggressive advocacy of religious liberty. My focus, however, is not on whether or not all Pennsylvanians agreed with Penn on given issues, but on how Penn, through his influential role in the structuring of colonial institutions, sought to secure religious toleration as a fundamental right of all settlers.

8. The best account of Penn's religion is Melvin B. Endy, Jr., *William Penn and Early Quakerism* (Princeton, 1973). See also Endy, "Theology in a Religiously Plural World: Some Contributions of William Penn," *PMHB* 105 (1981): 453–68; William Wistar Comfort, "William Penn's Religious Background," *PMHB* 68 (1944): 341–58; and Richard T. Vann, *The Social Development of English Quakerism, 1655–1755* (Cambridge, Mass., 1969).

9. In the final preparation of this chapter, I was fortunate to have the opportunity to consult an advance copy of Rosemary Moore's *The Light in Their Consciences: The Early Quakers in Britain 1646–1666* (University Park, Pa., 2000). Drawing on published and unpublished sources, including the work of both Quaker apologists and their harshest critics, Moore's study improves immeasurably our understanding of the thought, practices, and institutional development of early Quakerism. Other important sources on early Quakerism include Vann's *Social Development of English Quakerism*, Barry Reay's *Quakers and the English Revolution* (New York, 1985), and W. C. Braithwaite's classic study, *The Beginnings of Quakerism* (London, 1912).

English critics just as Hutchinson's covenant of grace had from New England Puritans.[10] Quakers were sometimes associated with the rationalistic Socinians because they denied the Trinity.[11] The matter of oaths raised several questions, chiefly the meaning and source of their refusal. Were Quakers refusing to swear because of an (atheistic) absence of belief, or did they owe allegiance to a (Catholic) foreign power? Either way, their loyalty was suspect. Finally, the refusal to show social deference through such actions as removing hats brought accusations of leveling tendencies. Thus Quakers were accused of either having no religion or a dangerous one, of holding dangerous political or economic and social principles, or no principles at all.[12] William Penn had ample opportunity to respond to these accusations, putting his several imprisonments to use writing tracts defending both his particular religion and the principle of liberty of conscience.[13]

For primary historical sources, see George Fox's *Journal or Historical Account of the Life, Travels, Sufferings, Christian Experiences and Labor of Love in the . . . Ministry of . . . George Fox* (London, 1694). See also Penn, *A Brief Account of the Rise and Progress of the People, Called Quakers* (1694), in *Works*, 1:858–92; idem, *No Cross, No Crown* (1668), in *Works*, 1:272–440; Robert Barclay, *Theologiae vere Christianae apologia* (Amsterdam, 1675), later translated as *An Apology for the True Christian Divinity* (London, 1678); George Keith, *The True Christ Owned* (London, 1679); and idem, *The Fundamental Truths of Christianity* (London, 1688). On oaths, see Penn, *A Treatise of Oaths* (London, 1675), in *Works*, 1:612–72.

Melvin B. Endy, Jr., convincingly argues against the common tendency to see Quakers as Puritans *in extremis*: see his "Puritanism, Spiritualism, and Quakerism."

10. Critics traced Quakerism to Winstanley's mystical Digging, and hurled at Quakers the familiar litany of epithets: Antinomian, Familist, Anabaptist, and Ranter. See, for just one example, [Thomas Comber], *Christianity No Enthusiasm* (London, 1678). Both Anne Hutchinson and Roger Williams were accused of Quakerism by some of their critics: see Vann, *Social Development of English Quakerism*, 30–31; Lovejoy, "Roger Williams and George Fox"; and Moore, *Light in Their Consciences*, chap. 9.

11. Penn's *Sandy Foundation Shaken* (London, 1670), in *Works*, 1:248–66, was widely viewed as influenced by Socinianism. Indeed, one of the elements of the "sandy foundation" that Penn sought to shake was the doctrine of the Trinity. Vincent Buranelli points out, though, that Quakers denied the Trinity to equate Christ with God, whereas the Socinians denied the Trinity to deny the divinity of Christ. In time, the difference became apparent, and Penn soon repudiated Socinian ideas. See Buranelli, "William Penn and the Socinians," *PMHB* 82 (1959): 369–81.

12. This very cursory summation of the charges against Quakers is meant only to give a general sense. There are literally hundreds of published attacks on the group. For just two examples, see [Comber], *Christianity No Enthusiasm*, and Robert Fleming, *A Survey of Quakerism* (London, 1677).

13. Penn usually employed the term "liberty of conscience," and I follow his usage. It is important to keep in mind, though, that by this he generally meant the easing of penalties on religious dissenters, and not disestablishment of the Anglican Church. As I elaborated in the preface, few during the seventeenth century systematically distinguished between the terms "liberty of conscience" and "toleration." For how Penn saw religious liberty as potentially compatible with a religious establishment, see J. William Frost's careful discussion of Penn's "non-coercive Quaker establishment"

As we saw in Chapter 4, Restoration England was not a hospitable place for Quakers and other sectarians, given the hard line against religious dissent taken by the Anglican hierarchy and the gradually deteriorating relationship between Parliament and king. In the elections of 1679 Penn, a moderate Whig, supported Algernon Sidney for Parliament, suggesting that liberty of conscience would proceed from the election of a more enlightened Parliament. With Sidney's defeat (twice), and the continuing mistrust between king and Parliament, Penn began to seek land in America to enact the "holy experiment" that England seemed incapable of supporting. He received the colonial charter in 1681: his personal friendship with James, duke of York (later King James II), as well as debts owed him by the crown, helped secure his case at a time when Charles II was increasingly occupied by conflicts with Parliament.[14] In 1682 Penn crossed the Atlantic, and in the following spring the first Pennsylvania General Assembly adopted the *Frame of Government* by which the colony would be ruled for the next ten years.

Given Penn's early Whig sympathies, it is not surprising that he placed a great deal of emphasis in his political thought on the ancient constitution, the traditional understanding of English politics (epitomized by Magna Carta and its elaboration of English native rights) in which Parliament and monarch shared in the government of the realm. Though notoriously difficult to articulate and frequently employed for polemical purposes, the ancient constitution symbolized, for Penn and other Whigs, English liberties and a balanced governing relationship between king and Parliament, established from antiquity and offering a standard against which to judge the particular actions of particular Parliaments. "We are English men," Penn wrote in 1680,

> a title full of liberty and property, the foundation of the government
> of this kingdom to claim which, is not only our interest but our duty.
> . . . We have a right to our lives, liberties, and estates, and that none

---

("Religious Liberty in Early Pennsylvania," *PMHB* 105 [1981]: 449), and idem, *A Perfect Freedom: Religious Liberty in Pennsylvania* (Cambridge, 1990), 18ff.

14. Joseph E. Illick suggests that getting English agitators out of the realm, as well as easing the financial expense of maintaining New York, may have appealed to the Stuarts. See "The Pennsylvania Grant: A Re-evaluation," *PMHB* 86 (1962): 375–96. A similar interpretation was advanced earlier in Fulmer Mood, "William Penn and English Politics 1680–81: New Light on the Granting of the Pennsylvania Charter," *Journal of the Friends Historical Society* 32 (1935): 3–19.

of these are to be taken from us but by the judgment of twelve of our peers . . . this has for ages been the common and fundamental law. . . . We take further leave to remind you that the civil society or government of this country is antecedent either to protestancy or popery.[15]

The ancient constitution was a lifelong political commitment for Penn. In 1687, he based his case for repeal of penal laws and the Test Act on "native rights, the Great Charter, what we all of us call, our birthright."[16] If English subjects do not hold their property by virtue of church membership or attendance, but rather by established custom and usage, how can they be deprived of such property (in the form of forfeitures and fines) for religious nonconformity?[17] For Penn, the ancient constitution said nothing about a coercive national religion: the civil allegiance of English subjects had nothing to do with adherence to a specific religious dogma.

The Whig version of the ancient constitution presented Parliament as the representative of the English people, with a share of the commonwealth's governance. Penn's views on consent as the foundation of political legitimacy, then, derive from the particularities of English birthright, rather than Old Testament exegesis or theories about what individuals would do in a natural state. This reliance on the ancient constitution was uniquely suited to Penn's purpose, which was to convince an English audience that a policy of religious toleration was in perfect keeping with its own customs. His contractarianism was more historicized and specifically English than, for example, Puritan covenant theology. In *The Great Case of Liberty of Conscience*, Penn obliquely referred to liberty of conscience as one of "those freedoms, to which we are entitled by English birthright."[18] (Although his writings contain copious biblical references, Penn never suggested that existing societies reenacted covenants between God and Abraham or Israel.) Writing in support of Sidney

---

15. "Petition to Parliament," c. November 1680, in *PWP*, 2:52.

16. [Penn], *A Letter from a Gentleman . . . upon the Penal Law and Test*, 8.

17. "To J. H. and his companions, Justices in Middlesex," 31 March 1674, in *Works*, 1:168–69 (also *PWP*, 1:277–82); *England's Present Interest Considered* (1675), in *Works*, 1:690–91; "Narrative of the Sufferings of Quakers in the Isle of Ely," c. November 1671, in *PWP*, 1:223–24. Penn also asserted this claim that penal laws violated the ancient constitution in his proposed toleration bill of 1678; see *PWP*, 1:537.

18. *The Great Case of Liberty of Conscience* (1670), in *Works*, 1:445.

later in the same decade, he specified what the birthright entailed and connected it to contractarian politics.

> We, the Commons of England, are a great part of the fundamental government of it; and three rights are so peculiar and inherent to us, that if we will not throw them away . . . they cannot be altered or abrogated. . . .
> The first of these fundamentals is property, that is, right and title to your own lives, liberties, and estates. . . .
> The second . . . is legislation, or the power of making laws; No law can be made or abrogated without you. . . . *No law can be made, no money levied, nor a penny legally demanded (even to defray the charges of the government) without your own consent.*: Than which, tell me, what can be freer, or what more secure to any people?
> [The third is] . . . your share in the judicatory power, in the execution and application of those laws, that you agree to be made.[19]

As late as 1687, when shifting political alliances had transformed his earlier Whiggism into a search for liberty of conscience through royal indulgence, Penn evoked the language of consent: "You claim the character of Englishmen. Now, to be an Englishman, in the sense of the government, is to be a freeman, whether Lord or Commoner, to hold his liberty and possessions by laws of his own consenting unto."[20]

Despite the democratic, individualistic potential of such contractarian political rhetoric (methodologically, *a la* Hobbes, or politically, *a la* Locke), Penn was in many respects a typical English gentleman, "plac[ing] a higher value on social order than most Quakers."[21] His contractarianism was more parliamentarian than leveling. He saw no contradiction between political contract theory and its implicit egalitarianism on the one hand and hierarchical social or political forms on the other. He always saw Parliament as subject to a more fundamental law (the ancient constitution, not to mention natural

---

19. *England's Great Interest, in the Choice of This New Parliament* (1679), in *Works*, 2:679.

20. *Good Advice to the Church of England* (1687), in *Works*, 2:771.

21. Endy, *William Penn and Early Quakerism*, 326; also 350. Even a highly sympathetic scholar admits that Penn was "a culture snob" (Barbour, "William Penn," 160).

law), and "at all times used a wide repertoire of approaches to toleration, tailored to the immediate audience."[22]

The Quaker political program during the Restoration generally involved calling for, not the disestablishment of the Anglican Church, but rather the easing of penalties on Dissenters, the mitigation of imprisonment and seizures of property, and the securing of the right to forgo oaths in favor of affirmations in legal settings.[23] A national church per se was not, for Penn, illegitimate, although coercion and persecution by such a church was. "I am for a national church as well as [the Church of England] is, so it be by consent, and not constraint," he asserted.[24] "That the Church of England is preferred . . . must not be repined at: Let her have it, and keep it all. . . . But to ruin dissenters to complete her happiness . . . is Calvinism in the worst sense."[25]

Penn's arguments for liberty of conscience and toleration for Quakers followed all of the conventional routes rehearsed in Chapters 3 and 4: belief as a purely intellectual phenomenon, which force (even if used for Truth's sake) was simply unable to effect; the necessity of positive conviction for salvation (the subjective element of conscience); the example of Jesus and the primitive church; the division of spheres into civil and spiritual, with the civil magistrate having firm control over the former but not the latter; and pragmatism, prudence, and prosperity, which appealed to more prosaic, but no less important, earthly concerns.

---

22. Barbour, "William Penn," 163. See also Edward C.O. Beatty, *William Penn as Social Philosopher* (New York, 1939), 65ff.

23. See Kirby, "The Quakers' Efforts," and Craig W. Horle, *The Quakers and the English Legal System, 1660–1688* (Philadelphia, 1988). All of these goals were political or legal: in this respect I disagree with Sally Schwartz, who states in *"A Mixed Multitude"* that "Pennsylvania was not founded on the principle of toleration, but of tolerance. Tolerance describes liberal attitudes toward members of other religious, national, or cultural groups, or acceptance of the right not to conform and to hold different beliefs" (8–9). Whatever "liberal" attitudes may denote (or may have denoted three hundred years ago), at the end of her account of Pennsylvania's early days Schwartz writes of the "commitment to toleration" in "Penn's colony . . . devoted to religious liberty" (298). I discuss this terminological issue, and my reasons for focusing on political, legal, and institutional issues than attitudinal ones, briefly in the preface, and in more detail in my "Tolerance, Toleration, and the Liberal Tradition."

24. *Good Advice to the Church of England* (1687), in *Works*, 2:754.

25. *Persuasive to Moderation* (1686), in *Works*, 2:745. As we saw in Chapter 3, when examining the disagreements between Presbyterians and Independents (Dissenting Brethren) in the Westminster Assembly, Penn's critics would likely have viewed the type of national church he supported as a hollow shell without any power to impose discipline upon its members.

Most basically, Penn asserted, coercion in matters of religion *does not work*. Echoing earlier arguments, he held that belief was a function of the understanding and not of the will, that judgments could not be brought into being by force. Force can make hypocrites, but "never did it convert or preserve one soul to God."[26] Coercion operates on the outer man, while true religion resides within.[27] Persecution, if by that term we mean attempting to change belief by coercion, was a category mistake, since "the understanding can never be convinced by other arguments than what are adequate to her nature."[28] In the preface to his *Great Case of Liberty of Conscience*, Penn wrote of "faults purely intellectual" which external penalties were unable to alter.[29] During the 1680s, Penn maintained this line of argument, rejecting Cotton's earlier position regarding the punishment of erroneous conscience. "I do not intend," he wrote, "that any person or persons should be in the least harmed for the external exercise of their dissenting conscience in worship to God, though erroneous: for though their consciences be blind, yet they are not to be forced; such compulsion gives no sight, neither do corporal punishments produce conviction."[30] For Penn toleration was, in the truest sense of the word, *reasonable*: it accorded with the nature of human understanding and the exercise of human intellect.[31]

While attempting to remove religious belief from the sphere of civil power, Penn consistently sought to enlarge liberty of conscience to include religiously inspired *conduct*. In this regard, he rejected standard antitolerationist arguments postulating a dichotomy between belief and action in which the civil magistrate was justified in restricting the latter though not the former. "Liberty of conscience . . . is this; namely, the free and uninterrupted *exercise* of our consciences, in that way of worship, we are most clearly persuaded,

---

26. "To the council and senate of the city of Embden" (1674), in *Works*, 1:610.

27. For the inner nature of religion, see *No Cross, No Crown* (1668), in *Works*, 1:272–440, esp. chap. 6.

28. "To Lord Arlington," 1669, in *Works*, 1:153 (also *PWP*, 1:89–97). See also "Narrative of the Sufferings of Quakers in the Isle of Ely," in *PWP*, 1:225; *A Persuasive to Moderation* (1686), in *Works*, 2:744–45; and *An Address to Protestants*, pt. 2, sec. 5 (1679), in *Works*, 1:778.

29. *The Great Case of Liberty of Conscience* (1670), in *Works*, 1:444, 452.

30. *A Brief Examination and State of Liberty Spiritual* (1681), in *Works*, 2:697. See also Penn's letter to William, Prince of Orange, 26 February 1680, in *PWP*, 2:27.

31. See, finally, Penn's appropriately titled *The Reasonableness of Toleration* (London, 1687), 9–11, for a concise synthesis of this "reasonability" and its relation to the points made in this paragraph.

God requires us to serve him in . . . which being, a matter of faith, we sin if we omit."[32] As late as 1686, Penn defined liberty of conscience as the "free and open profession of the duty to God, as man perceives it,"[33] always with the understanding that such profession was not itself incompatible to human society or social order.

Not only was the use of force inappropriate from a psychological point of view, and not only did belief imply action, but the fallibility of human knowledge argued against persecution as well. This point contained both epistemological and ecclesiastical connotations, since the assumption of infallibility (be it papal or conciliar) was seen by many Protestants as the great error of the Roman Catholic church. "We must never reproach the papists with persecuting Protestants, if Protestants themselves will persecute Protestants because of some different apprehensions about religion," Penn wrote to the Prince of Orange.[34] Epistemologically, Penn stressed the inherent partiality of understandings of Truth and the humility called for by such an admission.[35] Protesting that coercion for conscience's sake violates "the meekness of the Christian religion," Penn pointed out that "such magisterial determinations carry an evident claim of infallibility, which Protestants have been hitherto so jealous of owning."[36] In one of his earliest battles with the English legal system, Penn had accused the judge of forgetting his English Protestant

> forefathers[' respect] for liberty of conscience. . . . Twas then plea good enough, my conscience won't let me go to Mass, and my conscience wills that I should have an English testament. But that simple plea for separation then reasonable is now by you that pretend to succeed them, ajudged unreasonable and factious. I say, since the only just cause of the first revolt from Rome was a

---

32. *The Great Case of Liberty of Conscience* (1670), in *Works*, 1:445 (emphasis added); also 447. For the belief/action dichotomy, and its use in both seventeenth-century and twentieth-century political philosophy, see Chapter 7.

33. *A Persuasive to Moderation* (1686), in *Works*, 2:729.

34. "To William, Prince of Orange," 26 February 1680, in *PWP*, 2:26.

35. *England's Present Interest Considered* (1675), in *Works*, 1:672–705, chap. 2; in *An Address to Protestants of All Persuasions* (1679), Penn cautions Protestants to "flee Rome at home!" (*Works*, 1:750).

36. *The Great Case of Liberty of Conscience* (1670), in *Works*, 1:447–48. As we shall see, George Keith would raise this issue of infallibility in his criticisms of Quaker ministers.

dissatisfaction in point of conscience, you cannot reasonably persecute others, who have right to the same plea.[37]

For Penn, however, saying that one must be convinced in one's own mind regarding the truth of religion was not an invitation to anarchy and license. Since the sects that had emerged from the English Civil War were often accused of just such anarchic tendencies (and since, as an English gentleman, he valued social order), Penn hastened throughout his writings to clarify the magistrate's role in suppressing vice and dangerous behavior. Penn affirmed the duty and right of civil magistrates to punish evildoers in *The Great Case* and in petitions to Parliament in April 1671.[38] Although he opposed the use of force to impose religious practice on individuals, Penn did assert that certain moral and ethical positions simply could not be held conscientiously, since they violated fundamental dictates of Nature or widely accepted standards of behavior. This assertion echoed traditional claims about the "natural" conscience, which, although in need of the "enlightening" of Christian revelation, was still capable of understanding basic morality. "There can be no pretense of conscience to be drunk, to whore, to be voluptuous, to game, swear, curse, blaspheme, and profane. . . . These are sins against nature; and against government, as well as against the written word of God. They lay the ax to the root of human society."[39] Years later Penn reiterated these points, writing that "I always premise this conscience to keep within the bounds of morality, and that it be neither frantic nor mischievous, but a good subject, a good child, a good servant, in all the affairs of life."[40] Those who threaten human society are not those holding "erroneous" religious views, but "those who maintain principles destructive of industry, fidelity, justice, and obedience."[41] Toleration properly conceived was not a cover for sedition

37. "Injustice Detected," February 1671, in *PWP*, 1:200. See also "Narrative of Sufferings," in *PWP*, 1:222–30, sec. 5; *The Great Case of Liberty of Conscience* (1670), in *Works*, 1:444–46, 448, 454–57; *Good Advice to the Church of England* (1687), in *Works*, 2:752–54; and [Penn], *A Letter from a Gentleman . . . upon the Penal Law and Test*, 5–7.

38. *The Great Case of Liberty of Conscience* (1670), in *Works*, 1:447, 457–58, postscript (465–67); "Petition to Parliament," April 1671, in *PWP*, 1:205–8.

39. *An Address to Protestants of All Persuasions* (1679), in *Works*, 1:733. Part 1 of *An Address* is taken up entirely with condemnations of drunkenness, fornication, gambling, and the like. For the natural and enlightened (Christian) conscience, see Rutherford, *A Free Disputation*, 6–7.

40. *A Persuasive to Moderation* (1686), in *Works*, 2:729.

41. "To Lord Arlington," 19 June 1669, in *Works*, 1:153 (also *PWP*, 1:92).

or irreligion, but the setting free of pious dissenting consciences to discharge their obligations to God as best they saw fit.

Certainly the magistrate could and should punish those who violated standards of civil behavior. Such a grant of authority, however, did not extend to the maintenance of a persecuting religion. This redefinition and restriction of the magistrate's role was, for Penn, largely derived from the example of Jesus in the gospels, and the early history of the Christian church. He often attributed persecution to mistaken notions about the nature of Jesus' ministry and kingdom. Coercion is unchristian, says Penn, because Jesus "defined to us the nature of his religion in this one great saying of his, My kingdom is not of this world."[42] Jesus never used the sword to set up his church, Penn noted in a letter to the king of Poland.[43] He attributed the rise of persecution in the Christian church to earthly designs of power-seeking clergy, giving voice once again to the long tradition of English anticlericalism.[44] Penn unified the arguments from reason and those from Scripture in his letter to the prince elector of Heidelberg: religious toleration is both "natural, because it preserves nature from being made a sacrifice to the savage fury of fallible, yet proud opinions . . . [and] Christian, since the contrary expressly contradicteth both the precept and example of Christ."[45]

The summation toward which all of Penn's arguments for liberty of conscience point is the notion of England as a civil commonwealth, characterized by a reverence for traditional standards of political legitimacy (the ancient constitution) and united in a general Protestantism and basic Christian moral code. This commitment to civil unity, for Penn, contained within it the standard dichotomization proposed by many tolerationists, most notably Roger Williams, between the carnal (i.e., civil or political) and spiritual realms. In Penn's words, the failure to understand Christ's "unworldly way of speaking" of his kingdom lay at the root of all persecuting policies: "This gross apprehension of the nature of Christ's kingdom may well be an occasion of their mistake about the means of promoting it, else it were not credible,

---

42. *The Great Case of Liberty of Conscience* (1670), in *Works*, 1:448–49. The reference is to John 18:36.

43. "To the King of Poland," 4 August 1677, in *PWP*, 1:437.

44. See especially *An Address to Protestants* (1679), in *Works*, 1:774–77.

45. "To the Prince Elector Palatinate of Heidelberg," 25 June 1677, in *Works*, 1:75 (also *PWP*, 1:451–54). See also *Good advice to the Church of England* (1687), in *Works*, 2:750–51, and *An address to Protestants* (1679), in *Works*, 1:752–56; 766–73; 800–803.

that men should think, clubs, prisons, and banishments the proper mediums of enlightening the understanding."[46] Jesus' kingdom was not of this world: "What use can there be of worldly weapons to erect or maintain it?"[47]

This notion of *civil interest* as the cement of civil society appears throughout Penn's works. "Certainly there is such a thing as civil uniformity, where a religious one may be inobtainable, and methinks there can be nothing more irrational, than to sacrifice the serenity of the one, to an adventurous (if not impossible) procurement of the other," he wrote in 1673.[48] Years earlier, he had asked rhetorically, "What if I differ from some religious apprehensions? Am I therefore incompatible with the being of human societies?"[49] Penn asserted, in his *One Project for the Good of England*, that "civil interest is the foundation and end of civil government."[50] He invoked the ship of state metaphor on a number of occasions, arguing that "men embarked in the same vessel, seek the safety of the whole in their own, whatever other differences they may have."[51] In other words, "as Englishmen, we are . . . mutually interested in the inviolable conservation of each other's civil rights."[52] Assuming that English citizens lived peaceably with their neighbors, Penn wondered "whether going to parish churches, hearing of common prayer, and receiving confirmation by the hands of a bishop are such absolute and necessary qualifications to being good shipwrights, clothiers, masons, husbandmen, etc."[53] He compiled extensive lists of tolerationist rulers and regimes, pointing out how civil interest could coincide with religious diversity.[54]

46. "To William, Prince of Orange," 26 February 1680, in *PWP*, 2:27.

47. "Petition to Parliament," c. November 1680, in *PWP*, 2:54. See also "To the Earl of Arran," 9 January 1684, in which Penn calls on the earl not to "vex men for their beliefs and modest practice of that faith with respect to the other world, into which providence and sovereignty, temporal power reaches not, from its very nature and end" (*PWP*, 2:511).

48. "To Justice Fleming," 1673, in *Works*, 1:157 (also *PWP*, 1:268–69).

49. "To Lord Arlington," 19 June 1669, in *Works*, 1:153 (also *PWP*, 1:92). See also "To the Earl of Orrery," 4 November 1667, in *Works*, 1:3 (also *PWP*, 1:51–52), and *England's Present Interest Considered* (1675), in *Works*, 1:696–97.

50. *One Project* (1679), in *Works*, 2:682 and passim.

51. *A Persuasive to Moderation* (1686), in *Works*, 2:727, 729, 737.

52. *Good Advice to the Church of England* (1687), in *Works*, 2:772.

53. "Petition to Parliament," c. November 1680, in *PWP*, 2:53. See also *An Address to Protestants* (1679), in *Works*, 1:797–98, and *England's Great Interest* (1679), in *Works*, 2:68.

54. *The Great Case of Liberty of Conscience* (1670), in *Works*, 1:459–62; *Persuasive to Moderation* (1686), in *Works*, 2:730–37, 747–48; *Good Advice to the Church of England* (1687), in *Works*, 2:757–63.

Civil interest, of course, required a common political allegiance, and in seeking toleration for Quakers Penn was not above raising suspicions about English Catholics.[55] He stressed Quakers' Protestantism, distinguishing them from those who "own another temporal power superior to the government they belong to."[56] "All English Protestants, whether conformists or nonconformists agree in this, that they only owe allegiance and subjection unto the civil government of England . . . [and] they do not only consequentially disclaim the pope's supremacy, and all adhesion to foreign authority under any pretence, but therewith deny and oppose the Romish religion, as it stands degenerated from Scripture."[57] Even so, Penn never suggested persecuting Catholics. He concluded a letter to an imprisoned Roman Catholic by saying that, although he disagreed on many points of theology, "I am, by my principle, to write as well for toleration for the Romanists."[58] Penn would not persecute law-abiding Catholics who affirmed civil allegiance.[59] "For though I give the true liberty of soul and conscience to those only that are set free by the power of Christ . . . yet I do not intend, that any person or persons should be in the least harmed for the external exercise of their dissenting consciences in worship to God, though erroneous."[60]

Finally, Penn did not neglect concerns of prudence and prosperity. On a purely prudential level, Penn counseled the Church of England to consider the consequences of a future magistrate adopting persecuting principles: their own children would suffer, as had Protestants in the days of Queen Mary.[61] Similarly, in the context of James II's attempts to extend toleration during the late 1680s, Penn noted to Anglicans that persecution threatened to drive Dissenting Protestants into a political alliance with English Catholics.[62] But if invocations of prudence were not enough, Penn asserted that prosperity would follow a relaxation of the enforcement of penal laws. "The kingdom is under a great decay both of people and trade," he wrote in 1680, "does

55. As I pointed out in Chapter 3, and as became increasingly clear in Chapter 4, this English anti-Catholicism forms a constant backdrop to any study of English toleration debates.

56. *One Project for the Good of England* (1679), in *Works*, 2:683.

57. Ibid., 2:683–84.

58. "To Richard Langhorne," 1671, in *Works*, 1:43 (also *PWP*, 1:209–11).

59. After 1692, Pennsylvania was the only American colony to allow public celebration of the mass. See Joseph J. Casino, "Anti-popery in Colonial Pennsylvania," *PMHB* 105 (1981): 279–309.

60. *A Brief Examination* (1681), in *Works*, 2:696–97.

61. *England's Present Interest Considered* (1675), in *Works*, 1:693–94.

62. *Good Advice to the Church of England* (1687), in *Works*, 2:767.

not [persecution] lessen the imperial crown and dignity of this realm, if it ruins trade, lessens and impoverishes the people, and increases beggery?"[63] He concluded *One Project* with an appeal to the prosperity of the kingdom. "I ask, if more custom comes not to the king, and more trade to the kingdom, by encouraging the labour and traffic of an Episcopalian, Presbyterian, Independent, Quaker, and Anabaptist, than by an Episcopalian only? . . . What schism or heresy is there in the labour and commerce of the Anabaptist, Quaker, Independent, and Presbyterian, more than in the labour and traffic of the Episcopalian?"[64] Although religious dissent had been associated for many years with Cromwell's republicanism and antimonarchical politics, Penn argued that this need not be the case. Not only does toleration not threaten monarchy, but "experience tells us, where [toleration] is in any degree admitted, the King's affairs prosper most; people, wealth, and strength being sure to follow such indulgence."[65]

PENNSYLVANIA

Foundations of Pennsylvania's Religious Liberty: Government and Society

> I have so obtained [land in America] and desire that I may not be unworthy of [God's] love, but do that which may answer his kind providence and serve his truth and people; that an example may be set up to the nations. There may be room there, though not here, for such an holy experiment.[66]

Penn's attempts to win toleration for Dissenters (specifically, Quakers) were, as I have noted, notoriously ineffective. Given the widespread fears of sectarian-inspired chaos and anarchy (in the 1660s),[67] along with fears of popish plots and seditious Catholics (in the 1670s) discussed in Chapter 4, prospects for

63. "Petition to Parliament," c. November 1680, in *PWP*, 2:51–52.
64. *One Project* (1679), in *Works*, 2:685.
65. *Persuasive to Moderation* (1686), in *Works*, 2:734. See also *Good Advice to the Church of England* (1687), pt. 3, in *Works*, 2:764ff.; *The Great Case of Liberty of Conscience* (1670), in *Works*, 1:455; *One Project* (1679), in *Works*, 2:685–86; and *An Address to Protestants* (1679), in *Works*, 1:798.
66. "To James Harrison," 25 August 1681, in *PWP*, 2:108.
67. See Reay, "The Quakers, 1659."

liberty of conscience grew increasingly bleak. If toleration in England was not to be forthcoming, perhaps the creation of a new society could do better. Penn used all means at his disposal to maximize the religious liberty that would obtain in his colony. The first draft of his *Fundamental Constitutions of Pennsylvania* rehearsed several standard arguments for toleration—Christ did not persecute, a successful colony would need to attract "sober people of all sorts"—and listed liberty of conscience as the first such fundamental constitution.[68] Asserting that government is "by the consent of all" established to prevent corruption, in his early drafts of colonial government Penn provided for an extensive popular role in the colony, including legislative initiative in the Assembly and the instruction of delegates, that representatives "may always remember that they are but deputies and men intrusted to the good of others and responsible for that trust."[69]

The mechanics of Pennsylvania government would undergo steady revision and retreat from these earlier, more ambitious republican plans.[70] This perceived retreat provided the occasion for Penn's falling-out with his former ally Algernon Sidney, who reportedly claimed that Penn "had a good country, but the basest laws in the world, not to be endured or lived under . . . [and] the Turk was not more absolute than [Penn]."[71] Nevertheless, Penn's Whig emphasis on the ancient constitution continued in his new endeavor. In his colonizing activities in West Jersey, Penn sought to replicate the ancient constitution "as near[ly] as may be conveniently agreeable," and in both colonies he guaranteed jury trials.[72] He explicitly linked the safeguarding of English liberties with religious liberty by affirming the Petition of Right and the Magna Carta. Penn wrote in the *Frame of Government and Laws Agreed upon in England* that "any government is free to the people under it (whatever be the frame) where the laws rule, and the people are a party to those

68. "The Fundamental Constitutions," c. summer 1681, in *PWP*, 2:143.

69. Jean R. Soderlund, ed., *William Penn and the Founding of Pennsylvania, 1680–1684: A Documentary History* (Philadelphia, 1983), 98, 100.

70. There are reasons to see this "retreat" as related to Penn's need for investors and capital: see Gary B. Nash, "The Framing of Government in Pennsylvania: Ideas in Contact with Reality," *WMQ* 23 (1966): 183–209. For the discussion in more depth, see Nash's *Quakers and Politics: Pennsylvania, 1681–1726* (Princeton, 1968), chaps. 1–2, esp. p. 53.

71. "To Algernon Sidney," 13 October 1681, in *PWP*, 2:124. Sidney's republicanism is presented in his *Discourses Concerning Government*. On Sidney's political thought, see Alan Houston, *Algernon Sidney and the Republican Heritage in England and America* (Princeton, 1991).

72. Trial by "Juries of peers" or "the law of the land" were guaranteed by chapter 39 of the Magna Carta. See also chapter 19 of the *West New Jersey Concessions* (*PWP*, 1:398).

laws, and more than this is tyranny, oligarchy, and confusion."[73] In both his English and American activities, Penn based legitimate government upon the consent of the governed and saw liberty of conscience as a central ingredient of legitimate government.

How did Penn seek to implement these theoretical commitments, the legacy of his English campaigns for toleration, in America? In a sense, it was the absence of certain elements of English politics that would ensure religious liberty in Pennsylvania society. Pennsylvania as the founder envisioned it would have no established church, no doctrinal tests for officeholding, no system of tithes to support the ministry, and no requirements for the swearing of oaths in legal settings. Although Penn's republican plans for participatory politics were gradually jettisoned as preparations for America proceeded, the founder never retreated from his search for the widest possible religious liberty, and all limitations on religious practice were forced upon an unwilling Penn by royal officials.

The absence of an established church in the colony represents one of the most important deviations from English practice. As I noted previously, Penn's practical goal was never the disestablishment of the Anglican Church, but an easing of the penalties on Dissenters.[74] In his colonizing ventures, Penn retained somewhat more flexibility than had been available to him in the context of Restoration English politics. Although he did not establish any church in his colony, he did appreciate the moral and civil influence that religious bodies had on their members.[75]

73. *William Penn and the Founding of Pennsylvania*, 122.

74. Indeed, I have argued (in the preface, and throughout Chapters 2–4) that very few religious dissenters in seventeenth-century England proposed disestablishing the Anglican Church, or advanced anything other than political arguments for toleration alongside the established church.

75. J. William Frost's characterization that Penn wanted "the Society of Friends [to] occupy a position comparable to that of the Church of England" with major exceptions (e.g., no legal establishment, no tithes) strikes me as quite defensible, although Frost would likely emphasize the similarities—a broad social influence wielded by members of one faith—while I would stress the "major modifications." See Frost, *A Perfect Freedom*, 18.

Similarly, I find Frost's point about the possible compatibility of a "non-coercive Quaker establishment" with religious liberty ("Religious Liberty in Early Pennsylvania," 449) persuasive. We should not assume, in my view (and, I think, in Frost's), that the existence of an established church *ipso facto* rules out the possibility of religious freedom in a given community; nor, for that matter, that the absence of an established church *assures* the presence of religious liberty. Certainly the "major modifications" Frost mentions between the Anglican and intended Quaker model are highly significant, and for many would signify the lack of a true establishment. For others, however, the modifications from English practice would be essential steps to secure religious liberty for non-Quakers.

In effect, then, Penn separated the moral and ecclesiastical functions of civil magistracy, and affirmed the right, even the *duty*, of political leaders to uphold the former. The distinction, for Penn, echoed his clarification that Christian liberty was not to be equated with license. In early Pennsylvania, as the founder envisioned it, civil magistrates were to be empowered to enforce observance of the Sabbath, to regulate, if not outlaw, taverns, and to restrain vice more generally. Penn did not view public enforcement of the Sabbath as equivalent to the imposition of a religious worship on his colony: in his words, refraining from labor on the Sabbath "may the better dispose [citizens] to worship God according to their own understandings."[76] The first draft of the *Fundamental Constitutions* declared that "there shall be no taverns, nor alehouses, endured in the [province], nor any playhouses, nor morris dances, nor games as dice, cards, board tables, lotteries, bowling greens, horse races, bear baitings, bull baitings, and such like sports, which tend only to idleness and looseness."[77] Since "the wildness and looseness of the people provoke[s] the indignation of God against a country," Penn restated these prohibitions in his final version of the *Frame of Government and Laws Agreed upon in England* (in *PWP*, 2:225). When Penn did draw up a tavern law, he included a number of very detailed regulations regarding the rates that innkeepers could charge and the personal conduct that was to be required of the guests at such establishments.[78]

Penn's original plans called for the extension of a broad liberty of conscience to all professing theistic beliefs. Basic civil rights were not to depend on religious profession. Through the absence of a legally established church and system of compulsory tithes, he attempted to provide the colony's inhabitants, particularly Quakers, with a significantly wider latitude in matters of faith and practice than existed in England. The dominance of Quakers in society and politics would, in his mind, provide general religious and ethical

76. *Frame of Government and Laws Agreed Upon in England*, in *PWP*, 2:225. Benjamin Furly, a fellow Quaker, disagreed strongly with Penn on the issue of the Sabbath, seeing the Sabbath law as "a vile snare to the conscience of many, who do not look upon that day as of any other than human institution." See "Benjamin Furly's Criticism of *The Frame of Government*," post May 1682, in *PWP*, 2:234.

77. "Fundamental Constitutions of Pennsylvania," in *PWP*, 2:151. In Penn's draft of the *Laws Agreed Upon in England* (c. April 1682), he restates his opposition to "all prizes, plays, may games, gamesters, masques, revels, bullbaitings, cockfightings, bear baitings, and the like, which excite the people to rudeness, looseness, and irreligion," accounting them petty treason (*PWP*, 2:209).

78. "Tavern Regulations," c. 23 March 1683, in *PWP*, 2:367–68.

advantages, while avoiding the problems associated with the Anglican establishment, namely its propensity to persecute Dissenters. As he put it in the first *Fundamental Constitution*, "every person that does or shall reside therein shall have and enjoy the free possession of his or her faith and exercise of worship toward God, in such a way and manner as every person shall in conscience believe is most acceptable to God."[79] The final version of Penn's *Frame of Government and Laws Agreed upon in England* echoed these sentiments:

> All persons living in this province who confess, and acknowledge the one almighty and eternal God, to be the creator, upholder, and ruler of the world, and that hold themselves obliged in conscience to live peaceably and justly in civil society, shall in no ways be molested or prejudiced for their religious persuasion or practice in matters of faith or worship, nor shall they be compelled to frequent or maintain any religious worship, place, or ministry whatever. (*PWP*, 2:225)

Officeholding represented another area in which Penn attempted to loosen stringent English regulations. Initially (in the sixth draft of the *Frame of Government*, c. January 1682; in *PWP*, 2:192), Penn had tentatively suggested that officeholders be required simply to profess a belief in god, but in the final *Frame and Laws Agreed upon in England* he replaced this clause with the more stringent requirement that they profess Christianity. Compared to prevailing practice in England under the Test Act, of course, such a requirement represented a significantly more relaxed standard. Penn's ambitious plans for doing away with religious tests altogether, however, were overruled by English authorities under section 7 of the colonial charter, which provided for review of Pennsylvania legislation by royal officials. After the Glorious Revolution, Pennsylvania officeholders were required to subscribe to the Toleration Act, although Governor Benjamin Fletcher (ruling while Penn's charter was temporarily revoked) allowed Quakers to affirm rather than swear the attestations of allegiance and abjurations of Catholic doctrine. Upon his return to the colony in 1700, Penn removed all religious qualifications for officeholding, only to have the Crown reinstate the terms of the Toleration Act four years later.[80]

---

79. *Fundamental Constitutions of Pennsylvania* (c. 1681), in *PWP*, 2:143.

80. The development of officeholding requirements is traced by Charles J. Stille, "Religious Tests in Colonial Pennsylvania," *PMHB* 9 (1885): 365–406, and Frost, "Religious Liberty in Early Pennsylvania."

The refusal to mandate oaths in legal proceedings provided one further area of departure from English practice. From the earliest drafts of his fundamental constitutions to the final *Frame of Government*, this commitment of Penn's remained firm. The nineteenth fundamental constitution provided that "all evidence shall be by subscription after this form, I A.B. do from the very bottom of my heart hereby engage and promise in the presence of God and this court to declare the whole truth."[81] Further drafts of Pennsylvania's laws called for witnesses to "solemnly promise" to tell the truth in legal settings, and the issue was finalized as the thirty-sixth "Law Agreed Upon in England."[82]

Penn saw religious freedom as possible within the context of a socially dominant faith, and always thought of his "holy experiment" as a Quaker colony. Indeed, Edwin Bronner refers to Penn as expecting "the Light . . . to permeate every facet of life in the plantation, and particularly the government."[83] Penn boasted about the spirit of "unanimity" that prevailed in the colony's early government: although such claims were somewhat far-fetched and the colony was far less unified than Penn indicated, the claims illustrate the degree to which Penn judged his "holy experiment" on the degree to which it could evoke the singleness of purpose he associated with the Quaker Meeting.[84] Even if the members of such a faith monopolized positions of political and economic influence, religious liberty would thrive if all were granted freedom of worship and an equal set of political liberties.[85] As in England, Penn sought to cement the bonds of Pennsylvania society through civil interest, not a uniform faith.

81. "Fundamental Constitutions of Pennsylvania," in *PWP*, 2:150–51.

82. "Draft of Laws Agreed Upon in England," c. April 1682, in *PWP*, 2:208; Final version of Laws, in *PWP*, 2:223.

83. "The Failure of the 'Holy Experiment' in Pennsylvania, 1684–1699," *Pennsylvania History* 21 (1954): 95. See also J. William Frost, "Pennsylvania Institutes Religious Liberty," *PMHB* 113 (1988): 323–48.

84. "The general assembly about a month since passed 83 laws, and all but 3 and those trivial without any nay" ("To John Blaykling and Others," 16 April 1683, in *PWP*, 2:377). "I have held two General Assemblies with precious harmony, scarce one law that did not pass with a nemine contradicente" ("To John Alloway," 29 November 1683, in *PWP*, 2:504). The editors of the *Penn Papers* note, in footnotes to each of these passages, that Penn paints a rather rosy picture of actual events.

85. In his examination of early Pennsylvania, Frost defines religious freedom as "the equality of all men and all churches before the law" ("Pennsylvania Institutes Religious Liberty," 328). If Penn had forgone legal establishment but allowed social predominance of Friends in the public life of the colony, such freedom could have been achieved.

In the early years of the colony, Pennsylvania was populated by a socially and politically predominant Quaker majority as well as a wide variety of other religious groups.[86] Although Friends occupied most influential positions in society, government, and the economy, a variety of ethnic—Germans, Dutch, French, Swedes, Scots, and Irish—and religious—Anglican, Presbyterian, Baptist, Lutheran, to name just a few—groups contributed to a vibrant colonial religious life.[87] A bit optimistically, Penn described these various groups as "of one kind, and in one place and under one allegiance, so they live like people of one country," while later in the 1690s Gabriel Thomas similarly claimed that "[Anglicans and Quakers] live friendly and well together."[88] Daniel Francis Pastorius noted in 1691 that "we [in the German settlement at Germantown] live peaceably and contentedly": he attributed this partly to Penn's benevolence in allowing Germantown special permission to order its own internal affairs.[89]

Of course, such diversity did not always function smoothly and harmoniously, and Pennsylvania was not immune to intergroup strife. Part of the political struggle between the "upper" and "lower" counties (i.e., those areas over which Penn and Lord Baltimore disputed) lay in a rough distinction between Quaker and non-Quaker.[90] In fact, the Keithian schism and the social and political turmoil that it spawned may have contributed to the growth of the Quakers' most severe critics, as Anglicans petitioned successfully in 1695 for the establishment of an Anglican congregation in the colony.[91] The presence of a variety of religious groups directly reflected Penn's intentions in founding his colony, although in hindsight his confidence in the ability of individuals of various religious persuasions to work together for the common good may have been excessive. Numerous descriptive accounts of early Penn-

---

86. See, for example, the accounts collected in Albert Cook Myers, ed., *Narratives of Early Pennsylvania, West New Jersey, and Delaware*, Original Narratives of Early American History (New York, 1912).

87. See, e.g., Albert Cook Myers, *Immigration of the Irish Quakers into Pennsylvania, 1682–1750* (Swarthmore, 1902; reprint, Baltimore, 1985).

88. Penn, *A Further Account of the Province of Pennsylvania*, in Myers, *Narratives*, 260; 329. See also Pastorius's "Circumstantial Geographical Description of Pennsylvania" (1700), chap. 13, in Myers, *Narratives*, 387–88.

89. Pastorius, "Letter from Pennsylvania," October 10, 1691, in Myers, *Narratives*, 415; "From Philadelphia," May 30, 1698, also in Myers, *Narratives*, 436.

90. See Edwin B. Bronner, *William Penn's "Holy Experiment": The Founding of Pennsylvania, 1681–1701* (New York, 1962), 55–59.

91. See ibid., 200–201, and Schwartz, *"A Mixed Multitude,"* 57–59.

sylvania life testify to the variety of religious experience in the colony, as well as the frequent contention brought about by such variety.

The Keithian Schism: Overview and a Brief Chronology

Pennsylvania's early years, on the whole, provide a remarkable testimony to the success of Penn's tolerationist ideal: indeed, how Penn saw Pennsylvania *failing* to live up to his expectations illustrates the inherent difficulty of the endeavor as well as the high standards that the founder set for himself and his colony. The universal recognition of Penn's success in carving out a colony that protected liberty of conscience has historically led scholars to overlook the issues surrounding the prosecution of George Keith. Those who have attended to the Keithian schism have generally not seen the affair as a genuine locus of debate regarding the toleration of religious dissent. For example, Edwin Bronner dryly notes that the trials "were a credit to no one," repeatedly referring to the controversy as a "quarrel."[92] As politics, the Keithian controversy is sometimes cited in the history of colonial printing,[93] but hardly ever in studies of colonial religious politics. Thomas J. Curry's fine study of church and state in the colonies, for example, does not mention Keith or the schism at all.[94]

Only a few scholars of early Pennsylvania have explored the theological, social, and political dimensions of this divisive and highly charged series of events. Those who have have proposed several explanations. Gary Nash saw the schism as replicating a political and economic struggle for power, with Keith's theological dissent appealing to those opposed to "the alliance of merchants and prosperous landowners."[95] Jon Butler has portrayed the schism as animated by a sharp Keithian dissent regarding the nature and extent of

---

92. *William Penn's "Holy Experiment,"* 152. The two best recent treatments of the history of Pennsylvania religious liberty treat the schism almost exclusively as an internal Quaker matter, downplaying the legal and political aspects of the case. See Frost, *A Perfect Freedom*, and Schwartz, *"A Mixed Multitude,"* 55–57.

93. See James N. Green, "The Book Trades in the Middle Colonies, 1680–1720," in *A History of the Book in America*, vol. 1, *The Colonial Book in the Transatlantic World*, ed. Hugh Amory and David D. Hall (New York and Worcester, Mass., 1998); see also David L. Johns, "Convincement and Disillusionment: Printer William Bradford and the Keithian Controversy in Colonial Philadelphia," *Journal of the Friends Historical Society* 57 (1994): 21–32.

94. *First Freedoms*, 73–77. Keith and the schism are not mentioned in Gaustad, *Religious History* or Hudson, *Religion in America* either.

95. *Quakers and Politics*, 109.

ministerial authority within the Quaker community, while J. William Frost locates the root of the controversy in the theological disputes regarding the bodily resurrection of Christ.[96] Still others attribute the strife to Keith's contentious personality, perfectionism, disputatiousness, and unwillingness to compromise.[97]

My interpretation of the crisis as a potential locus of debate over toleration and liberty of conscience does not rule out any of the foregoing interpretations. Indeed, each of these scholars has put a finger on a crucial aspect of the schism. Nash, for example, rightly points to the more worldly tensions that beset the young colony, illustrating how economic and political coalitions formed to oppose the influence of prominent Friends. Many of Keith's supporters were indeed of more "common" status, as Butler has pointed out.[98] Butler's account of ministerial authority, on the other hand, rightly highlights the disputes that erupted between Keith and the Public Friends over his proposed church reforms, proposals that would have restricted the ministers' influence in Pennsylvania society. But as Frost points out, the great majority of strife between Keith and the Public Friends took place after he had been disowned, and thus does not necessarily tell us anything about the roots of the controversy.[99]

The reasons for the more general lack of attention to the Keithian schism are, I think, several and insufficient. Keith himself was almost universally reputed to be a highly contentious individual.[100] Subsequent scholars have

96. See Butler, "'Gospel Order Improved': The Keithian Schism and the Exercise of Quaker Ministerial Authority in Pennsylvania," *WMQ* 31 (1974): 431–52; J. William Frost, introduction to *The Keithian Schism in Early Pennsylvania* (Norwood, Pa., 1980), x–xi; and "Unlikely Controversialists: Caleb Pusey and George Keith," *Quaker History* 64 (1975): 16–36.

97. Edward J. Cody, "The Price of Perfection: The Irony of George Keith," *Pennsylvania History* 39 (1972): 1–19; Bronner, William Penn's *"Holy Experiment,"* chap. 8.

98. "Into Pennsylvania's Spiritual Abyss: The Rise and Fall of the Later Keithians," *PMHB* 101 (1977): 151–70.

99. Introduction to *The Keithian Schism*.

100. The classic histories of Pennsylvania are harshly critical of Keith. Consider the following:

[Keith] possessed considerable literary attainments, and being quick of apprehension and logical in argument, he had been regarded as an able champion for the faith he professed, but unhappily he was too fond of disputation, and finding his brethren in religious profession could not unite in all his theological views and nice distinctions, he became sour and censorious. (Janney, *Life of William Penn*, 363)

[Keith was] a man of quick natural parts, and considerable literary abilities, acute in argument, and very ready and able in logical disputations, on theological subjects, but said to be, of a brittle temper, and overbearing disposition of mind, not sufficiently

thus not found in Keith the kind of noble fighter for religious liberty *a la* the later Williams (for, indeed, he was not), nor the oppressed martyr *a la* Hutchinson or the Quaker missionaries in Massachusetts during the 1650s.[101] Keith's personal religious history, and the confusion sown by his shifting affiliations, provide a second reason why the schism has received less attention than it might otherwise have. After his unsuccessful attempts to reform Pennsylvania Quakerism, Keith returned to England to seek redress from Friends there, only to be disowned at the 1695 Yearly Meeting in London.[102] He later became a member of the Church of England, taking holy orders in 1699 and returning to America. There Keith engaged in protracted debates both with Massachusetts divines (whom he had earlier debated as a Quaker) and with Quakers in the middle colonies. Through all of his shifting denominational affiliations, Keith claimed, he never changed his fundamental beliefs, a statement that led one satirical observer to dub him "the eighth wonder of the world."[103] Third, the Keith affair had an ambiguous outcome. No one was sentenced to prison, nor were the fines apparently ever collected. In this sense, it is difficult to argue, as one can clearly do for the expulsions of Williams and Hutchinson or the gruesome punishments inflicted upon Quakers in

tempered and qualified with that Christian moderation and charity, which give command over the human passions. (Proud, *History of Pennsylvania*, 1:363)

[Keith] is said to have been a man of quick natural parts and considerable literary attainments, fond of disputation, acute in argument, and confident and overbearing in the same. . . . He ridiculed some of [the Society of Friends'] customs, and certain also of its religious tenets, though he had once written in their defense. He passed contempt on the decisions of some of the Meetings. (Thomas Clarkson, *Memoirs of the Private and Public Life of William Penn* [Philadelphia, 1814], 63)

Even one commentator who admits that previous authors "have told little except the bad temper, violent language, and self-will of Keith," admits that "he certainly had the natural indignation of a zealot, he was habituated to the bitterness of expression of that age, in which the Quakers had been about as bitter as others" (Charles Keith, *Chronicles of Pennsylvania* [Philadelphia, 1917], 1:213).

101. Only one biography—over fifty years dated by now—exists: Ethyn Williams Kirby, *George Keith* (New York, 1942).

102. Keith's running debate with English Quakers is beyond the scope of this chapter. See Keith, *Gross Error and Hypocrisy Detected* (London, 1695) and *Bristol Quakerism Exposed* (London, 1700); John F[i]eld, *The Weakness of George Keith's Reasons for Renouncing Quakerism* (London, 1700); and idem, *Light and Truth Discovering Sophistry and Deceit* (London, 1701).

103. The full title of this work illustrates the ridicule that his opponents heaped upon him: *One Wonder More, Added to the Seven Wonders of the World. Verified in the Person of Mr. George Keith, Once a Presbyterian, Afterwards About Thirty Years a Quaker, Then a Noun Substantive at Turners-Hall, and Now an Itinerant Preacher (upon His Good Behavior) in the Church of England: and All Without Variation (as Himself Says) in Fundamentals* (London, c. 1701).

Massachusetts or by Laud on Prynne, Burton, and Bastwick in England, that Keith was persecuted *per se*. Nonetheless, I shall consider the possibility that, as one historian has put it, the Keithian controversy represents "religious persecution by indirection . . . [in which] both liberty and property [were] taken away judicially by the opposing party in a religious dispute."[104]

George Keith arrived in Philadelphia in 1689, after having played an important role in spreading and defending Quakerism throughout England, Scotland, and the colonies. Keith's educational background and willingness to enter into debate served him well in his repeated defense of Quakers and his disputations with Massachusetts divines.[105] But Keith was troubled at the theological laxity he found among Friends in the middle colonies, not only in "lay" Quakers but also among some of the most prominent Public Friends. Like the Puritans of Massachusetts, Keith saw a religious body's refusal to affirm orthodox Christian doctrine as a threat to both the salvation of its members (who could thus be seduced by false beliefs) and the social standing of the entire group. Throughout 1690 and 1691, the main body of Pennsylvania Quakers continued to rebuff Keith's attempts to have more clearly Christian statements of belief—including a type of Christian catechism and a plan to incorporate elders into a more formalized Meeting structure—adopted by the Meetings.[106] William Stockdale, a prominent minister and member of the Provincial Council, accused Keith of heresy because of his insistent stress on "the man Christ Jesus." At the January 1692 Monthly

104. Keith, *Chronicles of Pennsylvania*, 1:224; 235–36.

105. Keith was unsuccessful in arranging an actual debate with Cotton Mather. The result was a series of protracted written refutations: Keith, *The Presbyterian and Independent Visible Churches in New-England* (Philadelphia, 1689); James Allen, Joshua Moody, Samuel Willard, and Cotton Mather, *The Principles of the Protestant Religion Maintained* (Boston, 1690); Keith, *The Pretended Antidote Proved Poyson* (Philadelphia, 1690); and Keith, *A Serious Appeal to All the More Sober, Impartial, and Judicious People in New-England* (Philadelphia, 1692).

106. Keith, *A Plain Short Catechism for Children and Youth* (Philadelphia, 1690); "George Keith's articles of Church Fellowship, or Gospel Order and Discipline Improved," SW Proud MSS, Folder C. (This second document is a transcript by Robert Proud.) Later, Public Friends referred to Keith's proposals as an "[attempt] to new model us into a church discipline and order . . . wherein divers things [were] new and strange to us" (Public Friends to Friends in England, 4 mo 1692, HV Reel 2, p. 23).

Ethyn Williams Kirby refers to Keith's stress on sound Christian doctrine as his "increasing conservatism" (*George Keith*, 53), but in fact these doctrinal concerns formed a central part of Keith's career as Quaker apologist dating back to the 1670s. For Keith, as for most early Quakers, Quakers were orthodox Christians, and the "Inner Light" was not an invitation to license but a sign of Christ's indwelling within the believer. See, on early Quakers and Christianity, Moore, *Light in Their Consciences*.

Meeting another minister, Thomas Fitzwater, accused Keith of "denying the sufficiency of the Light within"; in other words, asserting that something in addition to the Light was necessary to salvation. A further theological dispute, which Keith's ally Thomas Budd claimed as the heart of the schism, arose surrounding the bodily resurrection of Christ.[107] The Public Friends' meeting records document Keith's increasing agitation over the lack of Christian orthodoxy among Pennsylvania Quakers. As they put it, Keith claimed that "there were not more damnable errors and doctrines of devils amongst any of the Protestant professions than was amongst the Quakers."[108] Tensions continued to rise. When a delegation of Public Friends asked Keith to retract his criticisms, he replied defiantly that "he denied [their] authority . . . he denied [their] judgment, he did not value it a pin, he would trample it as dirt under his feet." Keith further claimed that not one Quaker minister preached true Christian doctrine.[109] On another visit, he called the Meeting of the Public Friends "rank popery."[110]

Early in spring 1692, Keith and his adherents began meeting separately from the main body of Philadelphia Quakers; in June of that year, Keith was disowned by the ministers' Meeting. At this point, the Keithian schism was just that: a division within the Philadelphia Meeting and the Meeting of Public Friends. Members of each Meeting continued to frequent the other, promoting their version of the separation and defending themselves against each other's accusations. The Keithians offered propositions for reunification as well as other suggestions for healing the schism.[111] During the summer of that year,

107. The theological roots of the schism are recounted in [Keith], *Some Reasons and Causes of the Late Separation That Hath Come to Pass at Philadelphia* (Philadelphia, 1692), 8–9, and [Thomas Budd], *A True Copy of Three Judgments . . . Against George Keith and His Friends* (Philadelphia, 1692), 1. Budd locates the issue of bodily resurrection as the nub of these differences in *A Just Rebuke to Several Calumnies, Lies, and Slanders* (Philadelphia, 1692), 3.

J. William Frost also cites the resurrection of the body as the central theological issue in the schism. See his introduction" to *The Keithian Schism*, x–xi, and "Unlikely Controversialists."

108. Minutes, Meeting of Public Friends, 1 mo 5 1691/2, HV Reel 2, p. 14.

109. Ibid., 4 mo 5 1692, HV Reel 2, p. 15.

110. Ibid., 4 mo 17, 1692, HV Reel 2, p. 16.

111. "Some of our principles to which if you agree we are the more like to agree with you in other things" (SW Keithian Controversy MSS, n.d.), deals primarily with the theological and ecclesiastical aspects of the schism; "Some propositions in order to heale the breach that is amongst us" (SW Keithian Controversy MSS, 1692 2 mo 18) is more personality-related. These propositions, however, met with no success, in large part because the Keithians insisted upon an almost complete capitulation by their opponents. See also the letter from Keithians to the Philadelphia Monthly Meeting, May 15, 1692, reprinted in *Some Reasons and Causes*, 26–27.

Keith forged an alliance with William Bradford, the colony's printer, and published his side of the controversy. This step forced the quarrel squarely into the social and political realm. In his *Appeal,* published late in the summer of 1692, Keith reiterated his charges of theological error and laxity among Pennsylvania Quakers, called for the Yearly Meeting to address the issues of Quaker church discipline and government, and questioned the appropriateness of Quakers exercising magistracy.[112]

Thus in the summer of 1692, the Keithian schism expanded its scope and intensity in two ways: through the medium of the press in the alliance between Keith and Bradford, and by raising the explicitly political question of whether Quakerism was consistent with the exercise of magistracy. Thomas Budd, one of Keith's closest allies, accused the Quaker ministers of behaving like persecuting magistrates.[113] Keith himself responded to the judgment of Public Friends, reiterating his criticism of the theological laxity and error among Pennsylvania Quakers. Keith asserted that "men may believe anything, and yet be owned, if they come to Meetings, and use plain language, and plain habit, and be not grossly scandalous."[114] He also claimed public support and fidelity to the true principles of Quakerism. "Hundreds here-away of the more sincere sort of Friends, do object . . . against the too-great laxness of

112. *An Appeal from the Twenty-Eight Judges to the Spirit of Truth and True Judgment* (Philadelphia, 1692). The *Appeal* is important in colonial history for a number of reasons. Not only is it an expression of the religious issues that animated the Keithian disputes, but it also occupies an important role in the history of a free press in the colonies, since it was for this publication that Bradford was arrested and his type confiscated. Also, the trial that was occasioned by the *Appeal* figures importantly in the history of American law; Bradford raised an important question in his defense, whether the jury was to rule strictly on fact (i.e., did Bradford or did he not print the *Appeal*), or on the *law* as well (i.e., was the *Appeal* actually, as the justices claimed, a seditious libel). Bradford claimed the latter, and his account of the trial, hardly coincidentally, evokes Penn's own famous dramatization of his trial with William Mead. See Penn, *The People's Ancient and Just Liberties Asserted* (London, 1670), which is also reprinted in "The Author's Life," in *Works,* 1:12ff.

The issue of Quakerism and magistracy was given added urgency in 1691, when some individuals stole a ship from Philadelphia. The Quaker magistrates had to decide upon a course of action. To act forcefully against the crew would involve coercion and thus violate their principles of pacifism, while to do nothing would signal (to their critics, at the very least) an unwillingness by the government to protect private property. Eventually Peter Boss, who later became a Keithian sympathizer, stormed the boat (without weapons), causing the thieves to flee. Keith criticized the magistrates for hiring armed men, even though it is unclear how much actual violence took place. See Bronner, *William Penn's "Holy Experiment,"* 149–50.

113. *A True Copy.*

114. *An Account of the Great Divisions Amongst the Quakers in Pennsylvania* (London, 1692), 14–15.

discipline among us," he wrote, echoing John Wheelwright's appearance before the Massachusetts General Court by asserting that "it is no reviling to speak the Truth."[115]

What happened next is not entirely clear.[116] In October, a grand jury presented indictments of four Keithians, including Keith himself, on a variety of charges, many of which derived from the *Appeal*'s final four points (which criticized magistrates for actions incompatible with Quaker principles). Other charges were based upon Keithians' strident and often personal denunciations of the colony's magistrates, particularly Thomas Lloyd and Samuel Jennings. Keith and Budd defended themselves by claiming that their harsh words were directed against the magistrates as fellow church members and not in their public capacities, and that thus they were being prosecuted civilly for a religious

---

115. Ibid., 14, 22. Recall that Wheelwright was forthright about the possibility that his fast day sermon might "cause a combustion in the church and commonwealth" ("Sermon," 169).

116. Opposing parties offer conflicting accounts. The year 1692 apparently saw two parallel Yearly Meetings in Pennsylvania. Francis Makemie, a prominent Presbyterian minister, asserted that Keith "came through with flying colors," that the Yearly Meeting vindicated Keith and condemned Thomas Lloyd, perhaps the most influential politician in the colony, a Quaker minister, and one of Keith's most vigorous critics (Francis Makemie, *An Answer to George Keith's Libel* [Boston, 1694], 101–2. This is also the version presented in Keith, *Chronicles of Pennsylvania*, 1:227–29). Samuel Jennings, another Quaker minister and colonial magistrate, echoed the Pennsylvania Quaker view that after attempts at reconciliation with the Keithians, which were met with evasion and obstruction, Keith was disowned (*The State of the Case* [London, 1694], 21–25). In addition, the Yearly Meeting witnessed several testimonies against the schismatics.

In addition to affirming the Public Friends' rebuke of Keith, the Meeting received condemnations of the separatists from the Bucks County and Philadelphia Quarterly Meetings (1692 Yearly Meeting Minutes, HV Reel 7X, pp. 28, 31, 32; the Bucks County Meeting condemnation is housed at the Historical Society of Pennsylvania, Etting Collection [Early Quakers], p. 79). The Yearly Meeting also approved a letter to local Meetings justifying its disowning of Keith, noting that his actions had brought scorn and derision on Quakers and that "he and they still persisting [after admonition] and like evil men and seducers wax[ed] worse and worse in the aforesaid wicked practices" (Yearly Meeting to Monthly and Quarterly Meetings in Pennsylvania and New Jersey, HV Reel 7X, 34). The Meeting drafted a letter to Friends in England, noting the Keithians' separate Yearly Meeting and continuing divisiveness (To the Yearly Meeting in London from the Yearly Meeting at Burlington, September 7, 1692, HV Reel 7X, 35–36). Without naming names, the Yearly Women's Meeting noted "a spirit of prejudice which hath prevailed with some," asserting the Christian orthodoxy of Pennsylvania Quakers (Yearly Meeting of Women Friends at Burlington to the Yearly Meeting of Women Friends in London, September 7, 1692, HV Reel 136A, 8). Over the course of the next several months, condemnations of Keith and his followers also came in from Barbados and Maryland ("To George Keith and the rest of the separate company in Pennsylvania," from Six Weeks Meeting at Bridgetown, Barbados, September 12, 1692 [SW Keithian Controversy MSS, 1692 7 mo 12]; "To George Keith" from Yearly Meeting, Treadhaven, Maryland, October 4, 1692 (SW Keithian Controversy MSS, 1692 8 mo 4).

disagreement.[117] In the end, the results of the trial were ambiguous: Keith and Boss were convicted of "speaking slightingly" of the magistrates and fined (though the fine was apparently never collected). The jury was unable to reach a verdict on Bradford, although it was six months before his press and type were returned.

In 1693, Keith received a certificate of good standing from the newly appointed Governor Fletcher, and Bradford's equipment was returned.[118] Pennsylvania Quakers apparently prepared a defense of their actions, but published nothing until 1694, when the controversy had largely died down.[119] In 1693, Keith published several further tracts driving home the social and political differences that had compounded the theological debate, one an antislavery tract and the other a "testimony and caution . . . that [Quakers, especially ministers] should not be concerned in worldly government."[120] A conference between the two sides in June 1693 apparently degenerated into name-calling and recrimination, and the ever dimmer prospects for recon-

117. Keith presented the trials in dramatic form, not unlike Penn's earlier portrayal of his trial with Mead. See [Keith], *New England's Spirit of Persecution Transmitted to Pennsylvania* (Philadelphia, 1693); reprinted as *The Trials of Peter Boss, George Keith, Thomas Budd, and William Bradford, Quakers* (London, 1693).

118. Keith claimed that this inability to reach a verdict on Bradford resulted in the jury's being ordered to reconvene and held without food, in the manner of the Penn-Mead jury in 1669 (*New England's Spirit of Persecution*, 36). There is no evidence to support this claim.

On April 27, 1693, Bradford petitioned Governor Fletcher for the return of his printing equipment. With the approval of many on the Council, Fletcher ordered Bradford's possessions returned. On June 20 of the same year, Keith petitioned the governor, and Fletcher ordered a certificate of good behavior drawn up. See *Colonial Records* (Philadelphia, 1852), 1:366–67, 378.

119. In the Friends Historical Library at Swarthmore College (Misc. MSS, 1693), there is a document by Thomas Lloyd entitled *Philadelphia's Tears* (c. 1693). It appears to be an introduction to a pamphlet that was never published. In it, Lloyd professes tenderness and exasperation toward Keith, and hopes for reconciliation. Pennsylvania Quakers, he writes, had for years "borne with [Keith] in his . . . unseasonable peevishness, and hitherto undergone his unjust reproach, without the least reply in our vindication . . . [in hopes that] our forbearance towards him would have softened him toward a speedier reconciliation." Unfortunately such hopes proved unfounded, and "in this small treatise, for the sake of many sober inquirers, to gratify the expectation of several of our Friends in these parts and in Europe, [we] give in this following faithful relation according to the best of our observation and remembrance." Such a document, if ever written, would constitute a vital piece of historical evidence.

In their account to Friends in England (1694), Pennsylvania Quakers noted that although they had refrained from publishing it, "we have something by us in manuscript to be made public in its season" (postscript). This might refer to *Philadelphia's Tears*. Frost claims that Philadelphia Quakers waited to respond until Keith was no longer a Quaker (*The Keithian Controversy*, xviii).

120. *An Exhortation and Caution to Friends, Concerning the Buying and Keeping of Negroes* (New York, 1693); idem, *A Testimony and Caution* (Philadelphia, 1693).

ciliation seemed finally dashed when Keith claimed that, concerning the theological disputes forming the core of the schism, he would accept the judgment of "no man or communion or number of men on earth."[121] Shortly thereafter, Keith sailed for England to press his case with English Quakers (who themselves disowned him in 1695). Some former Keithians returned to their former Meetings, some moved on to more mystical religious commitments, and some joined Pennsylvania's Anglicans or Baptists.[122]

Beginning with a dispute over the nature of bodily resurrection and the person of Jesus, then, the Keithian schism also involved controversies over the necessity of belief in "the man Christ Jesus." But as with the cases of Roger Williams and Anne Hutchinson, the Keith affair was never solely a dispute about theology. Emanating out of that theological critique were substantive disagreements with prevailing colonial practice concerning the relationship between church and state that threatened the young colony and its Quaker magistrates internally and externally. Internally, as the schism increased in bitterness, Keith increasingly raised questions about the close interconnection of ministry and magistracy in Pennsylvania. Given that his chief targets and most vigorous opponents were Thomas Lloyd, William Stockdale, and Samuel Jennings, all prominent magistrates as well as Quaker ministers, such criticisms must be granted at least a measure of plausibility. Externally, the Keithian schism became part of an ongoing debate during the 1690s concerning whether Quakers were fit to govern a colony. This debate animated critics in both England and America, and was given added urgency when the Crown revoked Penn's charter during 1693 and 1694. Whether threatening the dominant role of Public Friends within colonial society and government or providing ammunition to English and American critics, Keithians soon came to be seen as a threat to the colony's very foundations as Penn had envisioned them.

Internal Critique: Ministry and Magistracy

To begin to understand the Keithian controversy, we must explore how these theological arguments radiated outward, raising broader social and political

121. Public Friends to Friends in London, June 9, 1693, SW Keithian controversy MSS, 1693 4 mo 9.

122. See William Davis, *Jesus, the Crucified Man* (Philadelphia, 1700), for one who continued his spiritual odyssey after Keith departed, and James and Esther Cooper, "Acknowledgment of having followed George Keith" (SW Misc. MSS 1695 11 mo 9), for repentant Quakers. More generally, see Butler, "Into Pennsylvania's Spiritual Abyss."

issues. In addition to its origins in the theological disputes over the nature of bodily resurrection and necessity for belief in "the man Christ Jesus," the Keith affair contained an important ecclesiastical dimension. His failure to force the Pennsylvania Quakers to adopt a formal creed and church government frustrated Keith deeply. The coalescence of Public Friends against him, and their success in exacting condemnations of his sympathizers from a number of Meetings, infuriated Keith, who saw in such activities, not only the domineering, overbearing nature of "popish" priests, but also the implicit threat of prosecution (since many Public Friends were also public magistrates) through the fateful intertwining of ministry and magistracy. Public Friends were not satisfied, Budd claimed, with the publication of their condemnations against Keith, but

> where they think their said judgment will not readily be swallowed down, they will follow it from meeting to meeting, clothed with their magistratical robes, and if any Friends show their dislike of having it imposed on them without their own consent, and consideration of the matter, presently threaten to bind them . . . and call out for a constable, thereby endeavoring to trample us down by their magistratical power and authority.[123]

Keith's theological critique and religious dissent, in many ways, raised issues similar to those raised by Roger Williams's Separatism. As with Williams, Keith's experiences during the schism and trials clearly sensitized him to the dynamics of ministry and magistracy, and the dangers of vesting such extreme power in a small group of individuals. Recall that Williams had denied the magistrate the authority to enforce the First Table or to interfere in any way with church doctrine and discipline. Keith, however, far surpassed Williams in his separation of nature and grace, arguing in his *Testimony and Caution* that *no* Christian, and certainly no minister, should hold the office of magistrate. He was not arguing for lawlessness and took great pains to acknowledge magistracy to be an ordinance of God and the duty of all Christians to obey. Keith's complaint was not with magistracy or political obedience, but with Christians exercising such authority. He argued forcefully that Christ had forbidden his followers to use the carnal sword, practices universally agreed

123. *A True Copy*, 12.

upon as constitutive of civil magistracy. For Keith, this restriction ruled out Christians' exercise of corporal punishment or any other type of coercion required by the office of magistrate. He presented the argument from Scripture and the early church as definitive, stressing that "just men may be found, and have been found amongst those called heathens or Gentiles."[124] Of course, having recently been prosecuted by a civil court composed largely of Quaker ministers, one cannot ignore the personal impetus Keith had for making this argument. But he first raised the question well before his trial, in the *Appeal* to the 1692 Yearly Meeting, and the peace testimony was an established and recognized element of Quaker doctrine.[125]

Along with the general concern about the overlap of ministry and magistracy in Pennsylvania, many of Keith's complaints rehearsed standard anti-Catholic and anticlerical views about priestly imposition, excessive hierarchy, and the stifling of individual conscience. These criticisms also fit in well with traditional defenses of Quakers as true Protestants. A Quaker meeting could not decide matters of conscience, Keith claimed, and he became even more vocal after his encounter with the London Yearly Meeting in 1694. "Though men may choose representatives to sit in a national assembly, to judge of worldly matters, and to make laws for the outward man, yet I deny that they can choose representatives to judge of matters of faith and salvation, that bind the conscience singly as such, for this were downright popery."[126] "To require an absolute submission to any man or men was antiprotestant and antiquaker," Keith claimed, presenting an aggressive Protestant face, "and was rank popery. . . . [u]pon the whole, he [would] give no absolute but conditional submission, which condition is to leave it to the judgment of spirit of truth and he himself to judge what is according to the spirit of truth."[127] After being disowned by the 1695 Yearly Meeting in London, Keith claimed that the Second Day Meeting, which oversaw the publication of Quaker works, "may be fairly compared to the conclave of cardinals in Rome."[128]

124. *A Testimony and Caution*, 8.

125. *An Appeal*, 7; The peace testimony ("A declaration from the people of God, called Quakers . . .") is reprinted in *New England's Spirit of Persecution*, 37–38. For an overview of the tension between the peace testimony and governing a colony, see Herman Wellenreuther, *Glaube und Politik in Pennsylvania 1681–1776: Die Wandlungen der Obrigkeitsdoktrin und des Peace Testimony der Quaker* (Cologne, 1972), esp. chaps. 2–3.

126. *A Seasonable Information and Caveat Against . . . Thomas Ellwood* (London, 1694), 27.

127. Public Friends to Friends in London, June 9, 1693, SW Keithian controversy MSS, 1693 4 mo 9. See also SW Keithian controversy MSS, 1693 4 mo 8.

128. *The Anti-Christs and Sadducees Detected* (London, 1696), 3.

Time after time, Keithians referred to their condemnation by Pennsylvania Friends as "rank popery."[129] Keith viewed Public Friends as arrogating to themselves the disciplinary responsibilities of the entire church, a sure sign of Catholic impulses:

> To lodge the judgment wholly in Friends of the ministry, and to deny all other Friends to have a share in the judgment, even when the difference is in a matter of doctrine, we judge is an encroachment upon our Christian liberty, and savors too much of the church of Rome . . . to give an absolute submission implieth absolute infallibility, that no society of men pretendeth unto, but the church of Rome.[130]

"Upon the pretense of their being ministers," Keith wrote to Pennsylvania Friends in the *Appeal*, "[Public Friends] claim a superiority over you . . . (too like the Roman-hierarchy)."[131]

In their assessments of the schism, several prominent Quakers and Public Friends claimed that Keith merely objected to Quaker principles when his proposals failed to gain the Meeting's support.[132] We should not assume that Keith's criticism of the close association between Meeting and state was simply a case of "sour grapes," however. Complaints about the overbearing nature of Quaker ministers was not unique to Keith: no less a Friend than George Fox had earlier cautioned Friends about this very issue.[133] Indeed, Penn himself initially seemed sympathetic to Keith's position, counseling forbearance and criticizing the personality clashes that seemed to be driving the schism, "not considering how much and how far they should have born for [Keith's] sake that has born so much for us all." While criticizing Keith's separation, Penn reported that "I am ready to believe [Thomas Lloyd's] height,

---

129. [Budd], *A True Copy*, 12.

130. *Some Reasons and Causes*, 12. Keith expresses similar sentiments in *A Further Discovery of the Spirit of Falsehood and Persecution in Samuel Jennings* (London, 1694), 33.

131. *An Appeal*, 1. See also *The Heresy and Hatred That Was Falsely Charged upon the Innocent, Justly Returned upon the Guilty* (Philadelphia, 1693), 6–7.

132. The 1693 Yearly Meeting Minutes, HV Reel 7X, p. 38a. See also the Public Friends condemnation of Keith reprinted in Budd, *A True Copy*, 4: "He hath long objected against our discipline, even soon after his coming among us, and having prepared a draft of his own, and the same not finding the expected reception, he seemed disgusted since."

133. Keith cites Fox in *A Further Discovery*; see also Butler, "Gospel Order Improved," 440–43.

has administered occasion for a difference in spirit."[134] This apparent temporizing greatly dismayed Pennsylvania Quakers, and Hugh Roberts wrote Penn that "thee canst hardly believe that [Keith] is gone as bad as he is . . . I never saw a man (under any profession) in more passion and bitterness of spirit and more ready to catch and to discover the weakness of Friends, than he is."[135] In fact, a group of prominent Quakers related the 1694 Yearly Meeting's "dislike" of the Keithian prosecutions to Pennsylvania Friends, although their concern was primarily religious in nature (and they may have reconsidered once they had to deal with Keith firsthand upon his return to England).[136]

Keith and his ally Peter Boss defended themselves at their civil trial by claiming that their actions were of a religious nature and thus fell under the realm of conscience. Furthermore, they claimed, the entire dispute was an internal Quaker church matter and not of a civil nature. For example, "as to calling [Samuel Jennings] . . . ignorant and presumptuous, was not said of him, as he was a magistrate, but as he professed himself to be a Christian and minister of Christ."[137] The reviling of a magistrate was quite different than what they had in fact done, they claimed, which was the chastisement of a fellow member of the Society of Friends, in either private correspondence (Boss's letter to Jennings) or in a Meeting (Keith's critical remarks about Lloyd). Certainly the mutual admonition of church members, Keith argued, did not fall within the purview of the civil magistrates: if it did, he implied, he found it difficult to see what had been gained by journeying to America and guaranteeing liberty of conscience in Pennsylvania.

The magistrates' response to this Keithian claim evoked that of the Massachusetts governors years earlier in the Hutchinson and Wheelwright cases. The Pennsylvania court distinguished between cases of conscience and civil crimes; allowing actions undermining respect for civil magistrates to pass unpunished would throw society's very foundations into jeopardy.[138] Colonial

134. "To Robert Turner," 29 November 1692, in *PWP*, 3:354.
135. "From Hugh Roberts," c. early 1693, in *PWP*, 3:359.
136. Penn later wrote of Keith's disownment by the 1695 Yearly Meeting that Keith "is, as before, most passionate, rude, and outrageous." See "To Robert Turner and Thomas Holme," in *PWP*, 3:409.
137. *New England's Spirit of Persecution*, 28.
138. Bradford himself seems to have at least partially accepted this distinction—though clearly not the category into which the Court placed his own actions—when he told the court that the *Appeal* was "not seditious, but wholly relating to a religious difference" (*New England's Spirit of Persecution*, 34).

settlements, as young and fragile societies, had a responsibility to protect the reputation of their magistrates from slander and subversion, and claims of conscience could not excuse socially disruptive or politically seditious conduct. Keith had slandered the civil magistrates, Caleb Pusey later asserted, "pretending it was for matters purely religious."[139] "All men that are brought before magistrates and courts, are not sufferers for religion," Pusey wrote elsewhere. "Men may be abusers of Christian liberty, by doing things under pretense of conscience and religion, for which magistrates may be justifiable to call them to account, and (if occasion be) to punish them for it."[140] Jennings articulated the magistrates' defense against charges of persecution, echoing the notion that persecution involved punishment for godly behavior (and, drawing on the orthodox notion of conscience as obedience to God, that objective standards existed for determining what constituted persecution) and reiterating the conscience/civil offense dichotomy. In other words, "Persecution is a suffering inflicted upon the sufferers, for the discharge of their duty to God. Prosecution is a justice done on transgressors of the law, for their injuries done to men, or blasphemies to God. . . . [Keith and his followers] did endeavour to raise sedition and subvert the government, and for that cause only, and not upon any religious account, they were prosecuted."[141] Taking great pains to distinguish between the first eight points of Keith's *Appeal*, which touched strictly on theological disputes with other Quakers, Jennings pointed to the final four which formed the basis of the prosecution. These charges departed from purely church-related business and raised harsh criticisms of Pennsylvania magistrates, questioning the suitability of Friends to govern.

Keith, however, drawing upon the more subjective understanding of conscience, echoed Roger Williams in insisting that Jenning's definition of persecution was too narrow, "not including such suffering as is inflicted upon men, that may be in error, and hold erroneous doctrines and principles. . . . The true definition of persecution is a suffering inflicted upon the sufferers, not only for the discharge of their duty to God, but for all that a man thinks to be his duty to God."[142] Keith (rightly, in a sense) pointed out that this was more in keeping with traditional Quaker formulations of liberty of conscience such as those found in many works by Penn.

139. *Satan's Harbinger Encountered* (Philadelphia, 1697), 58.
140. *A Modest Account from Pennsylvania* (London, 1696), 39.
141. *The State of the Case*, 45–46.
142. *A Further Discovery*, 40–41. Compare Williams, *Bloudy Tenent*, 41, 63.

Theologically, then, the Keithian controversy in early Pennsylvania originated in George Keith's dissatisfaction with the lack of Christian orthodoxy among Pennsylvania Quakers. This concern for the church's purity led to debates over the Inner Light and its relationship to the Christian faith more generally, and raised disputes over the bodily resurrection of Christ and Christian believers. These debates in turn led to broader complaints about overbearing ministers, and finally to civil prosecutions and Keithian claims of persecution. As the conflict widened in scope, the perceived threat to Pennsylvania practice moved from the Meeting to civil institutions. Magistrates saw the Keithian party as potentially undermining the basis of Pennsylvania society, which had always been predicated upon the maintenance of Quakers in positions of power, and Quaker ministers as prominent and influential public voices.

External Context: The Administration of Justice in Pennsylvania and the Suitability of Quaker Magistrates

Of course, the internal dynamics of colonial life represent only part of the overall picture when looking at forces that impinge on religious dissent. No colony existed in a vacuum, and we must also consider external threats to complete a portrait of the context within which such dissent arose. By doing this, we gain a richer understanding of the difficulties colonial magistrates faced in creating and sustaining political societies. Recall the tensions with English authorities that formed the backdrop for Williams's expulsion; recall also that Hutchinson's trial took place against the backdrop of the Pequot War of 1636–38. The Keithian schism occurred in the aftermath of the English Revolution and Penn's ongoing struggle to retain control of his colony. In the wake of James II's overthrow, his ally Penn was viewed with great suspicion in England. Accused of treason and placed under house arrest, Penn was forced to name a non-Quaker governor to rule in his place during 1689 and early 1690, and temporarily lost control of his colony entirely. His unpopularity and legal troubles armed critics of his colonizing venture, who tended to focus on the administration of justice and the issue of the colony's defense.

If Keith's claims that Quakerism ruled out magistracy were damaging to Friends eager to prove their fitness for rule, and corrosive to the internal status of Quaker ministers, the prosecutions themselves merely fueled critics outside the colony. Quakers had made much of their opposition to persecution in England, such critics claimed, yet the case of Keith pointed out that they were in fact no different than their former Anglican adversaries, indeed no different than New England persecutors. "The Quakers in England used to plead with the rulers, against the King's laws, for liberty of conscience," Daniel Leeds wrote. "But now, being got in the saddle of government, and being rulers themselves, they deny liberty of conscience to others," and use their authority to harass one who had fallen out of fellowship with them.[143] Thomas Holme wrote to Penn from Pennsylvania, "there are grudges in some, that none are put in places of power but Friends."[144] Keith himself raised this issue, asking rhetorically, "What will the people in New England say, who have formerly persecuted our Friends there; and what will others say, that have fresh in memory the frequent outcries and complaints of Friends against persecution in former days?"[145]

Quaker magistrates not only persecuted Keith against all of their purported principles, but they also (claimed opponents) denied Anglicans in Pennsylvania the free exercise of their religion. A petition from the colony's Anglican community begged William and Mary to "rescue them from the many hardships and pressures which overrideth them under the present administration of Quakers."[146] This complaint referred to political affairs in Pennsylvania as well as religious ones, since the refusal of Quakers to swear oaths, and the institutionalization of that refusal in the prohibition on oaths in the colony's legal proceedings, jeopardized the entire system of justice in the eyes of many non-Quakers. Anglicans objected to being tried by juries who were not forced to swear. To them, this practice violated English law and their rights as English subjects.[147] I have not addressed the issue of oaths *per se* in this account of the Keithian controversy, primarily because it was

143. Daniel Leeds, *News of a Trumpet Sounding in the Wilderness* (New York, 1697), 93 (also 86–87); Francis Bugg, *News from Pennsylvania* (London, 1703), 26. See also HL Manuscript EL 9598, a letter of Robert Snead, 6 May 1698: "Here is no living for any that are not Quakers, without it be altered, we had better live under the French king" (1).

144. "From Thomas Holme," 25 November 1686, in *PWP*, 3:131.

145. *The Causeless Ground of Surmises, Jealousies and Unjust Offenses Removed* (London, 1694), 13.

The condition of Anglicans in *Massachusetts* is addressed in "The humble answer of Edward Randolph to His Majesties question in Council; viz, what disadvantage doth arise to persons inhabiting the Massachusetts colony who are conformable to the Church of England?" (HL Manuscript EL 9605). Randolph reported that "they have not the free exercise of their religion. . . . They are not admitted to be freemen nor capable of being elected into the magistracy" (1).

146. *The Humble Remonstrance of His Majesty's Most Loyal Subjects of His Majesty's Province of Pennsylvania*, May 26, 1694 (HL Manuscript EL 9596), 1.

147. See "The Anglican Petition," c. 1695–96, in *PWP*, 3:444.

not an issue in the schism or prosecutions. Considering religious division in early Pennsylvania more broadly, though, oaths and affirmations were clearly an issue between Quakers and non-Quakers.[148]

Besides prosecuting Keith and denying religious liberty to others, the critique continued, Quakers *refused* to prosecute members of their own faith when evidence was presented against them.[149] Penn admitted hearing "vile and repeated slanders cast on the province, or you rather and the rest of the magistracy, whom they represent . . . as ambitious . . . as partial, to offenders that profess truth, not the same punishments to others."[150] The culmination of this particular critique came in Daniel Leeds's vicious (and memorably named) polemic *News of a Strumpet Co-habiting in the Wilderness*, which detailed a host of accusations, many sexual in nature, against prominent Quaker magistrates, and the failure of Pennsylvania courts to prosecute or punish the offenders.[151] Virtually all of these critics cited the Keith affair at some point, as an example of the untrustworthiness of Quaker magistrates in civil affairs.[152]

English and American critics also assailed Pennsylvania Quakers for their refusal to participate in colonial defense measures against the French and Indians. Defense of the colonists' lives and properties was considered the most fundamental responsibility of civil government, and here again critics found Pennsylvania Quakers sorely lacking. One of the many conflicts between Governor Blackwell and the colony's Quaker legislators lay in the Assembly's reluctance to provide support for defensive preparations.[153] The Quaker peace

148. See J. William Frost, "The Affirmation Controversy and Religious Liberty," in *The World of William Penn*, 303–22. One Anglican critic claimed that because of the inability to swear oaths in Pennsylvania, "[we] are consequently deprived of the most eminent privilege enjoyed now by the English nation" (*The Humble Remonstrance*, 1–2).

149. See *The Humble Remonstrance*, complaining of unequal justice; as well as a letter from Robert Snead, HL Manuscript EL 9588.

150. "To the Commissioners of State," 21 December 1687, in *PWP*, 3:168. See also "An abstract of several informations relating to irregular proceedings and other undue practices in Pennsylvania," in *Correspondence Between William Penn and James Logan, 1700–1750*, ed. Edward Armstrong and Deborah Logan (Philadelphia, 1870), 24–26. This report by Colonel Quary set off an extended round of denials by Penn and repeated charges by his critics. See also "To William Markham and the Council," 5 September 1697, in which Penn pleads that "you take care that justice be impartially done upon transgressors" (*PWP*, 3:518).

151. *News of a Strumpet Co-Habiting in the Wilderness* (New York, 1701); see also Bugg, *News from Pennsylvania*, 21–25.

152. *News of a Strumpet*, chap. 9.

153. On Blackwell, see Bronner, *William Penn's "Holy Experiment*," 130–31, and "From the Provincial Council and Assembly," 18 May 1691, in *PWP*, 3:318.

testimony proved the main obstacle here, and as we have seen in his prohibition on Friends exercising magistracy, Keith took that peace testimony to an extreme that those seeking to downplay the tension between Quakerism and magistracy found disturbing.[154] In a sense, Pennsylvania Quakers were caught on the horns of a dilemma: Keith and his followers accused them of engaging in coercion for several (in their view) isolated incidents required to maintain civil order, while other critics accused them of not using *enough* coercion, failing to support the force necessary to defend their colony. Regardless of their differences with Keith about theology or the incompatibility of Quakerism with magistracy, however, the Quaker-dominated Assembly proved stubbornly resistant, not only to organizing a militia, but also to supporting any private or intercolonial defense endeavor with public funds. In this they went beyond the witness of Penn himself, who had promised compliance with defense plans as a condition of receiving back his charter in 1694 and who advised Quakers in Pennsylvania to support plans for a militia as a necessary evil.[155]

Critics did not miss their chance to draw attention to the issue of colonial defense: Bugg noted that "they count it unlawful, under the Gospel, for the civil magistrate to punish heinous offenses and capital crimes with death, or go to war, either offensive or defensive (if the occasion be never so just and honorable) or to swear in any cause."[156] Anglicans in Pennsylvania petitioned the king that "the whole government is put into the hands of the Quakers who not only refuse to settle the militia but give all discouragement they can to so good a work whereby the province and his Majesty's subjects are extremely exposed to ruin both by French and Indians."[157] Because of this state of affairs, another Anglican complained, "the country lies naked, and defenseless, and exposed to be ruined and made a prey of by any enemy that shall first invade it."[158]

In these attacks on Pennsylvania Friends, the trials of Keith and his followers were often cited as evidence of Quaker unsuitability for magistracy. Penn wrote that "the trial of G.K. has been industriously spread all about the nation . . . the advantage the disaffected among us make by it against unity,

154. For the peace testimony see *New England's Spirit of Persecution*, 37–38, and Wellenreuther, *Glaube und Politik*, esp. chaps. 2–3.
155. "Report of the Lords of Trade," 3 August 1694, in *PWP*, 3:397; "To Arthur Cook and others," 5–9 November 1695, in *PWP*, 3:416.
156. *News from Pennsylvania*, 7.
157. "The Anglican Petition," c. 1695–96, in *PWP*, 3:443–45.
158. *The Humble Remonstrance*, 3.

against Friends having power, against me, and you in particular are great and lamentable."[159] Later in the 1690s, Pennsylvania's government and institutions were defended vigorously by Caleb Pusey, who reiterated the strictly civil nature of the charges against Keith and his supporters. Pusey's defense was a rearguard action, though, and almost purely defensive in nature.[160]

CONCLUSION

Nothing in this chapter's discussion of Keith and the Quaker response to him should be read to understate the remarkable success that Pennsylvania represented in the early colonial world. Although Penn saw his colony as falling woefully short of his high ideals, Pennsylvania was probably the colony most hospitable to religious dissenters. Even in the wake of royal intervention and the overruling of Penn's original intentions, the colony sought to guarantee civil and political rights to adherents of a broad variety of religious faiths, and to protect the religious practices of its citizens to as great a degree as possible.

The Keithian schism suggests, however, that even the most propitious circumstances do not assure a smooth transition from tolerationist theory to practice. As with the earlier cases of Williams and Hutchinson in Massachusetts, the larger context of relations with, and political developments in, England set the backdrop for a rigorous defense of authority and the political suppression of religious dissent. A pitched pamphlet battle erupted later in the 1690s, and the Keith affair was often cited by those unhappy with the administration of justice in Quaker Pennsylvania. Since these complaints were directed as much at English audiences as American ones, and since Penn fought an almost constant battle to retain control of his colony after 1688, the Keith affair represents far more than a single Quaker schism, but instead evokes the complex interplay of internal and external factors that influenced the colony's development.

The Keithian schism, in many ways, resembles the earlier controversies over Williams and Hutchinson in Massachusetts: it began as an internal theological debate within the colony's dominant religious group. Since both colonies

159. "To Friends in Pennsylvania," 11 December 1693, in *PWP*, 3:383.
160. *A Modest Account*; idem, *Satan's Harbinger Encountered*.

were founded with explicitly religious objectives, such a controversy necessarily entailed public consequences. Of course, the two colonies were founded with very different religious objectives, and Puritanism and Quakerism offer drastically different approaches to toleration and religious diversity. All three examples of religious dissent, however, represent qualitatively different phenomena than either religious dissident *qua* invading outsider, whether that "outside" be geographical (e.g., Quaker missionaries in 1650s Massachusetts)[161] or socioeconomic (i.e., challenge from outside a society's ruling elites, such as New Model Army religious radicalism and other lower-class sectarian agitation in England). Williams and Hutchinson, we must remember, were Puritans, albeit unorthodox ones. Keith was a Quaker. In fact, it was the intra-elite nature of the disputes that gave them much of their bitterness.

Recall that Williams's Separatism and Hutchinson's Antinomianism reared their heads at precisely the wrong time for Massachusetts Puritans: prospects for leniency, always dubious because of the difficulty of creating and maintaining social order, were diminished by threats to the colony's charter in England and increased tensions with the Indians. The situation of Pennsylvania Quakers was not entirely different. The implications of Keith's teaching regarding the incompatibility of Quakerism with the exercise of magistracy would have been enormous in internal terms (by weakening the authority of Public Friends and Quakers more generally), representing the rejection of Penn's intentions in colonizing and a retreat from the prominent social and political role the founder had envisioned for Friends. Its publication was also poorly timed for Penn's attempt to regain control over the colony. As with Williams's Separatism, Keith's vocal insistence that Quakerism was incompatible with force (and thus with the performance of magistracy) was bound to give aid to those in England who attacked the administration of Pennsylvania under Quaker magistrates. Again, religious dissent (in the eyes of Pennsylvania magistrates) threatened the bases of civil order.

As noted above, Bradford's press was returned to him in 1693 by Governor Fletcher, who also provided a certificate of good standing to Keith. These actions effectively ended the Keithian controversy as a "live" issue in Pennsylvania politics, though it reverberated in polemics for years. What differentiates the two episodes, of course (Williams and Hutchinson on the one hand, Keith

---

161. What I mean here is that, unlike Williams and Hutchinson, the Quaker missionaries were not members of the Massachusetts Bay community prior to their religious dissent, but were seen as "invaders."

on the other), is the severity of the punishment visited upon dissidents in Massachusetts. Still, the Keithian experience suggests that differences in theologies and attitudes toward liberty of conscience between Massachusetts Puritans and Pennsylvania Quakers may have proven less important, when an actual case of virulent dissent arose, than the common task they both faced of building a new community.

6

REVISITING EARLY MODERN TOLERATION
AND RELIGIOUS DISSENT

By examining toleration debates in a variety of contexts (temporal, geographical, political), I have attempted to evoke the many different issues and meanings toleration raised for different audiences. I turn now to exploring some ways in which revisiting these debates can enrich conventional understandings (or conversely, correct conventional misunderstandings) of the roots of liberal toleration in Anglo-American political thought. These correctives are not merely historical curiosities: as I have maintained throughout this study (and will explore in more depth in Chapters 7 and 8), early modern toleration forms the basis for many scholars' *continuing* understanding of the nature, promise, and limitations of liberalism more generally.

In this chapter, I focus on three general areas, which roughly parallel the three "myths" about religious toleration outlined in Chapter 1. First, I explore how the question of social order and stability framed toleration debates, how the threat (indeed, the outbreak) of civil strife loomed large in the reactions of antitolerationists to the arguments of their interlocutors. Far from being debated as an abstract principle of justice or philosophy, religious toleration evoked years of ongoing political, often armed, discord. For tolerationists to prove successful, they had to overcome the powerful and compelling claims that religious and political subversion were intimately linked. Along these lines, I examine the evolution of Locke's view on toleration as emblematic of the importance of political context and questions of order in tolerationist arguments. Second, I highlight the intensely Christian (indeed, Protestant) nature of early modern toleration debates, and how *both* sides in disputes over toleration attempted to articulate the meaning and salient elements of an identifiably *Christian* (again, generally *Protestant*) ethos. *Both* sides in seventeenth-century toleration debates saw themselves as Christians, and scriptural "bombs" were dropped equally vigorously by both sides. This stress on Christianity also relates, more broadly, to common assumptions about "necessary" relationships between skepticism and toleration: devout believers often supported religious liberty, and skepticism lends itself to a variety of political platforms. In my brief consideration of the work of Thomas Hobbes, I point out that this purported relationship is neither close nor necessary. Third, I consider the implications as well as the limitations of the commonly described "negative" nature of liberal freedom, of which religious toleration forms a central part. This discussion leads into a broader consideration, in Part II, of the important role played by conscience and toleration in contemporary liberal theory. I argue—initially in this chapter, but more fully in Chapters 7 and 8—that the aim of early modern tolerationists was not a state based upon broad notions of social egalitarianism or equal respect, but a *modus vivendi* system that protected rights of Dissenting congregations to gather and worship. This minimalism, I suggest, represents the enduring legacy of early modern religious toleration.

TOLERATION AND SOCIAL ORDER: POLITICAL CONTEXT AND THE FEAR OF ANARCHY

Religious liberty is a political luxury, a derivative value that can be meaningfully pursued only after a whole host of other social and political questions are at least provisionally settled. Contemporary arguments that religious liberty is a natural right, in my view, achieve a morally resounding rhetorical appeal while sacrificing an appreciation and acknowledgment of the context in which religious liberty came to be perceived as any sort of right.[1] In other words, one must address, in Judith Shklar's words, "the political conditions that are necessary for the exercise of personal freedom."[2] The desirability of

---

1. For a treatment of "primacy-of-right theories" that "take as the fundamental, or at least a fundamental, principle of their political theory the ascription of certain rights to individuals," see Charles Taylor, "Atomism," in *Powers, Possessions, and Freedom*, ed. Alkis Kontos (Toronto, 1979), 40.
2. "The Liberalism of Fear," in *Liberalism and the Moral Life*, ed. Nancy Rosenblum (Cambridge, Mass., 1989), 21.

toleration, in a philosophical or theological sense, does not even become an issue if such liberty is widely viewed as threatening violent civil conflict or the breakdown of social institutions.

Such a claim (that freedom and toleration are empirically derivative rather than philosophically paramount) takes issue with strong natural-rights arguments that privilege such rights claims over more minimal notions of toleration.[3] More accurately, perhaps, I might instead say that regardless of their philosophical priority, natural-rights arguments remain *politically irrelevant* before the question of order is settled. The degree to which grants of political or religious freedom *actually do* threaten the social order, of course, is itself a political question, subject to a variety of interpretations, as we have seen throughout this project. Samuel Rutherford and the Massachusetts Puritans saw religious dissent and toleration as undermining the beliefs and practices necessary to a godly society, while John Locke attributed the social strife that religion had undeniably produced not to religious liberty but to the alienation and resentment that followed the *suppression* of rights to worship. In other words, for Locke religious liberty was a necessary (though clearly not, in its own right, sufficient) prerequisite for an ordered civil society, and the *absence* of toleration constantly threatened to bottle up resentments that would eventually spill over into civil strife.

Antitolerationists, as we have seen, mercilessly attacked their opponents as either covertly or overtly fostering a climate of anarchy and lawlessness. These claims linking toleration and licentiousness were not merely polemical ploys (though they certainly were also that for some), but often evidence of genuine concern for social solidarity exhibited by individuals across the religio-political spectrum in times of great upheaval.[4] Since religious uniformity historically had underlain social stability and political allegiance, antitolerationists viewed dissent in religion as tantamount to treason. Roman Catholics, for

3. For seventeenth-century natural-rights arguments, see Williams, *Bloudy Tenent*; for twentieth-century thinkers, see Robert Nozick, *Anarchy, State, and Utopia* (New York, 1974), and Milton Friedman, *Capitalism and Freedom* (Chicago, 1962). Gordon Schochet has recently revived this distinction in his study of Locke's theory of toleration (see my comments in the preface).

4. In our time, such a sentiment has been expressed by Justice Scalia in the *Smith* case (1990). "Any society [that required religious exemptions from facially neutral criminal laws] would be courting anarchy," he argues, noting that the inconvenient impositions on conscience in a democracy are preferable to the alternative in which "each conscience is a law unto itself." This selection from Scalia's *Smith* opinion is reproduced in William B. Lockhart, Yale Kamisar, Jesse H. Choper, and Steven H. Shiffrin, *Constitutional Law: Cases—Comments—Questions*, 7th ed. (St. Paul, Minn., 1991), 1174–75.

example, were suspected of disloyalty almost by definition, while the Protestant Dissenter Cromwell served as orthodoxy's *bete noire* for years to come. As we saw in Chapter 4, even many who *supported* toleration shied away from James II's extralegal means of pursuing it, fearing the establishment of an absolutist precedent.

Any historical study worth the name, then, must appreciate the gravity with which antitolerationists approached the claims of their opponents. One way of doing so, I have suggested, is to appreciate how antitolerationists saw the calls for religious liberty as a radical threat to society itself. When Roger Williams attacked the foundations of the Massachusetts Bay Colony by denying the legitimacy of the colonial charter and the magistrate's role in religious affairs, he was assaulting a centuries-old understanding of the responsibilities and powers of magistrates, as well as the more specifically Puritan notion of the godly and their role in reforming the world. Anne Hutchinson, John Wheelwright, and their followers, in disrupting church services, refusing to participate in colonial defense, and calling for "spiritual warfare" against those preaching a false gospel, fulfilled all of the magistrates' worst fears about the social consequences of strident religious dissent. Both Williams and the Hutchinsonians asked Massachusetts Puritans, in a sense, to trust them, that the consequences of their dissent would not be the example of Muenster but rather a pacific civil order.[5] Hobbes's attention to the precarious nature of social order and the recurrent threat of its breakdown were not merely abstract philosophizing: although the English Civil War was not initiated by tolerationists, the prevalence of such sentiment within the New Model Army and the example of Cromwell's Protectorate, to many observers, linked rebelliousness, regicide, and religious freedom.[6] Presbyterians and Anglicans, united on few issues of church government or political philosophy, nevertheless found

---

5. In Chapter 2, I quoted Theodore Dwight Bozeman on this point. To reiterate, Bozeman argues that "the task of Rhode Island was the almost impossible one of eclipsing the ready memory of Munster by providing a . . . demonstration that violent chaos was not the necessary result of a departure from the established model of religious uniformity" ("Religious Liberty and the Problem of Order in Early Rhode Island," 57).

6. See Hobbes's *Behemoth, or the Long Parliament* (1682), ed. Ferdinand Tonnies, 2d ed. (London, 1969), for these explicit historical connections. A young John Locke drew similar conclusions, advising his readers to "look some years back: he will find that a liberty for tender consciences was the first inlet to all those confusions and unheard of and destructive opinions that overspread this nation" (selection from the *First Tract of Government* [1660], in Locke, *PW*, 144).

common ground in opposing the provocative and erratic tendencies of sectarians, and in blaming religious dissidents for the execution of the king.[7]

The concern for social order runs like a red thread throughout seventeenth-century toleration debates. Many influential political and religious actors in late Stuart England (for good reason) associated the pursuit of a broad toleration with a subversion of lawful government and an assault on the ancient constitution. The consequences of such royal conduct threatened to once again put the nation under the personal rule of a monarch bent on establishing an absolute regime. Such a danger, for many, was so serious as to lead them to *oppose* toleration from James although they supported it in principle. In Pennsylvania, George Keith's religious dissent took aim at the established centers of power in Pennsylvania society, the Philadelphia Meeting and the colonial government. As he soon found out, theological dissent raised in the meeting led to broader social dissension, which in turn was suppressed by the government.

It is important to reiterate that antitolerationists often had good reasons for being concerned about the social and political consequences of toleration. These concerns might be based upon the past actions of those preaching toleration (rebellion and regicide), the examples of others in similar situations (the lack of reciprocal toleration for Anglicans, Quakers, or Presbyterians in New England or Pennsylvania), or the potential for religious dissent to begin a slide into anarchy or chaos (Muenster or, to some, the Interregnum). We should not lose sight of the radical nature of the measures tolerationists proposed. Proponents of religious liberty sought to dissociate two phenomena (civil and ecclesiastical power) that had been closely affiliated for centuries.[8] Religious functions had long been assigned, without a great deal of controversy, to the civil magistrate, and antitolerationists found it difficult to comprehend how, if one might legitimately beg indulgence in religious matters, individuals would not claim conscientious objection to any laws they found inconvenient or simply unpleasant.

---

7. Note, for example, the defensive tone of *The Dissenting Ministers Vindication of Themselves from the . . . Murder of King Charles I . . . ,* in *Somers Tracts,* 5:258–62, which reiterates the Protestant orthodoxy that animated the initial resistance to Charles and Laud and disclaims any responsibility for the King's execution or toleration. A regicide, the authors proclaim, is "not agreeable to any word of God, the principles of the Protestant religion . . . or the fundamental constitution and government of this kingdom" (261).

8. On this close interconnection between Christianity and politics in the broader context of Western thought and history, see Peter Iver Kaufman, *Redeeming Politics* (Princeton, 1990).

In response to claims for toleration, some theorists—Hobbes being the most sweeping and vigorous—proposed bringing civil and ecclesiastical power back together entirely. A devotion to social peace and security animates all of Hobbes's writings, which he hoped would find their way to a sympathetic sovereign who would put them to use to bring about social peace. In addition, Hobbes saw no conflict between natural reason and revelation. Through the extensive—if highly unorthodox—scriptural exegesis and extrapolation of "the principles of Christian politics" in part 3 of *Leviathan*, Hobbes argued that both reason and revelation pointed to absolute sovereignty as "the high way to peace."[9] At times, Hobbes was

> at the point of believing my labor as useless as the commonwealth of Plato. For he also is of opinion that it is impossible for the disorders of state, and change of governments by civil war, ever to be taken away, till sovereigns be philosophers. But when I consider again . . . I recover some hope that . . . this writing of mine shall fall into the hands of a sovereign who will consider it himself . . . and by the exercise of entire sovereignty in protecting the public teaching of it, convert this truth of speculation into the utility of practice.[10]

Hobbes surveyed the political and religious landscape of the mid-seventeenth century, noting the centrifugal tendencies of various sects, and saw toleration as an issue of divided sovereignty destructive of civil peace. Massachusetts Puritans saw similar proclivities in Antinomianism and Roger Williams. To Hobbes, toleration in light of recent English history would have been disastrous, inviting further social disintegration and religio-political chaos. Psychological or epistemological reasons for distrusting overarching truth claims and dogmatic appeals to authority gave way, in the wake of civil war, to a realization of how violent religious differences, and how fragile civil peace, could be.

Hobbes's solution to the problem of religious dissent, though drastic, addressed a basic concern of those living in times of religiously inspired strife:

9. *L*, chap. 32; Thomas Hobbes, *De Cive [Philosophical Rudiments Concerning Government and Society]* (1651), ed. Howard Warrender (Oxford, 1983), 32.

10. *L*, 243–44. See also Hobbes's praise of Thucydides, who (he claims) did not write history "to win present applause, as was the use of that age; but for a monument to instruct the ages to come . . . a possession for everlasting." See Hobbes's 1628 translation of Thucydides' *Peloponnesian War* (Chicago, 1989), 576.

the fear that, in supporting political freedom for certain conscientious dissenters, or in opposing (perceived or real) ecclesiastical abuses, tolerationists would rend the fabric of society itself, perhaps irreparably. To many English observers, just such a series of events had come to pass during the 1640s. Such an experience only strengthened the resolve of those already skeptical (on theological or philosophical grounds) of extensive claims of conscience, to prevent the recurrence of such catastrophic events. Early reports out of Rhode Island did not appear to justify overly optimistic conclusions about the potential for peaceful coexistence between adherents of divergent religious commitments. If one feels that one's community is threatened with destruction, questions of substantive politics take on a distinctly secondary importance.[11] Only *after* the question of order is settled can one begin to discuss the details of social and political organization, of which religious freedom and its boundaries form a key element.

However, Hobbesian absolutism and a strict Separatist dichotomy between the civil and the spiritual hardly exhaust the options available to early modern thinkers. A variety of political proposals sought, more modestly, to establish the conditions of basic social order, while ensuring some latitude for loyal, pious (generally, Protestant) dissenters to practice according to the dictates of their consciences. Such proposals often remained firmly within long-established political channels. During the 1640s, for example, the Westminster Assembly and Parliament (though quarreling over the location of ecclesiastical sovereignty), attempted to settle the religious differences within the nation and to allow for some degree of autonomy to individual congregations, while firmly controlling the established church and avoiding the descent into chaos they feared from the Civil War. The New Model Army, it turned out, and not the

11. I emphasize the "If one feels that . . ." element of this sentence. I do not claim that tolerationists *actually did* represent a threat of anarchy. Some probably did, some clearly did not. My point is that to many skeptical observers such claims were entirely plausible.

One's view of the likelihood of toleration leading to social chaos and destruction, of course, is itself a reflection of one's view of human nature. Those who see humans as primarily driven by passions or indelibly marked by original sin (e.g., respectively, Hobbes and Augustinian Puritans) will be highly suspicious of certain types of conscience claims. If, on the other hand, one sees humans as possessing the (at least latent) capacity for self-control, discipline, and probabilistic rationality (e.g., Locke), one's view of toleration will likely be much more charitable. (I thank Richard Ashcraft for encouraging my thoughts along these lines [personal communication, June 22, 1994].) James Tully sees the "disciplinary" elements of Lockean toleration as fundamental and troubling: see his "Governing Conduct," in *Conscience and Casuistry in Early Modern Europe*, ed. Edmund Leites (New York, 1988), 12–71; for a more sympathetic portrait, see chapter 9 of Taylor's *Sources of the Self.*

Parliament or the Assembly, could *in fact* guarantee order, and thus was able to influence the terms of the religious settlement in a much different direction. The Pennsylvania Quaker Meeting, in its constituent Monthly and Quarterly Meetings, did allow a variety of competing theological perspectives to coexist (this latitude was, in fact, largely responsible for Keith's dissent, a point to which I return below). It was only when Keith began to take his dissent *outside* the Meeting, to draw social and political battle lines, that civil action ensued. Again, order and sovereignty were seen as the precursor to *any* particular politics.

Of course, there are two sides to this question of order. As the seventeenth century went on, and the existence of religious dissent became more firmly established in English national life, one could argue more persuasively that the threat to order and stability came not from religious dissent *in se*, but rather its persecution and suppression, and the disenchantment with civil magistracy that such suppression engendered. As Locke put it, "If men enter into seditious conspiracies, tis not religion that inspires them to it in their meetings; but their sufferings and oppressions that make them willing to ease themselves. Just and moderate governments are every where quiet, every where safe. But oppression raises ferments, and makes men struggle to cast off an uneasy and tyrannical yoke" (*Letter*, 52). In other words, tolerationists claimed that people do not dissent in religious matters in order to cloak rebellion, but instead rebel when they are unable to worship as they see fit, given the overwhelming importance attached to salvation. Thus persecution, not toleration, threatened the social order. The pursuit of individual salvation, for Locke as well as for many others, was of the utmost importance, although the degree to which religious grounds may be adduced to justify political rebellion remained unclear.[12] Many other advocates of toleration emphasizing the "civil interest" argument—the emergent English nationalism exemplified by Penn, and discussed in Chapters 4 and 5—stressed that a grant of basic

12. Gordon J. Schochet claims that "the revolution or resistance [Locke] had in view sprang from religious considerations. . . . There is a crucial link between the denial of religious freedom and the right of revolution which can be seen throughout the *Two Treatises*" ("Toleration, Revolution, and Judgment," 85). Such an assertion, in my view, is greatly overstated. For a more accurate view of the role of religion in Locke's *Second Treatise*, see Marshall, *John Locke: Resistance, Religion, Responsibility*, chap. 6, which notes the silence on religion that characterizes that work (see esp. 288–91). Nathan Tarcov also notes that the argument about life, liberty, and property in the *Second Treatise* "is made without reference to specifically religious rights" ("John Locke and the Foundations of Toleration," in Levine, *Early Modern Skepticism*, 180).

toleration, given certain concrete safeguards against sedition, would unite subjects in allegiance to the monarch. Indeed, this "civil unity" argument is the *only* justification for toleration stated in the preamble to the Toleration Act of 1689. Only when they could make this argument convincingly, though, could tolerationists have any hope of political victory. So long as toleration threatened or seemed to threaten civil peace, any grants of religious liberty remained highly unlikely.

I should be clear: no one in the seventeenth century sat down to read Locke's *Letter* and found themselves so taken with Locke's reasoning that he or she changed positions on the issue. In the first place, Locke advanced no new arguments, so anyone even remotely familiar with English toleration debates would have already heard everything that Locke had to say. But my point, more fundamentally, is this: the validity of Locke's arguments about religious individualism, voluntarism, the prosperity and trade benefits of toleration, or even the example of Jesus and the Apostles, would be virtually *irrelevant* if one was convinced that religious freedom threatened to bring in social chaos. In other words, only *after* one became convinced that toleration did not threaten society's basic existence could one attend to Locke's arguments. Many antitolerationists in the 1680s continued to view toleration and disorder as fundamentally related; given the history of these debates, they may have had good reason to think so.

The answer an individual gives to the questions of toleration relies heavily on his or her assessment of the *context* in which arguments for religious freedom are forwarded. The question of order, in other words, is a highly situated one politically. Seventeenth-century tolerationist ideas were never presented in philosophic, ethereal isolation: they appeared in the guise of New Model Army iconoclasts, breaking into churches to destroy icons and deface prayer books; a king (Charles I or James II) who seemed unwilling to take his role as part of a balanced constitution; and threats to such basic social institutions and practices as magistracy and ministry in Massachusetts and Pennsylvania. Religious dissenters appeared to many observers, not as strong and sincere individuals insisting on obedience to the dictates of conscience, but as Hutchinsonians amassing arms and shouting down Boston ministers; Keithians calling leading figures in Pennsylvania society liars, cheats, and gamblers; Quakers throwing blood on Anglican altars; or Whigs attempting (by force, if necessary) to interfere with the lawful succession to the English throne.

Timing, in all of these cases, is revealing. In the minds of antitolerationists, the association of Parliamentary opposition to Charles I (later erupting into armed conflict) with increasingly strenuous Puritan calls for reform of the English church, cemented the link between religious enthusiasm and antiroyal political positions. Similarly, events during the Restoration, Exclusion Crisis, Popish Plot, and Revolution in England highlighted the shifting focus of public concern: although in the early Restoration years Protestant Dissenters evoked the specter of Cromwell's Protectorate, by the mid- to late-1680s James II's toleration and Catholicism represented the most salient and immediate threat to English liberties.

Roger Williams and Anne Hutchinson attacked the structures of authority in Massachusetts society just as other threats to that society's survival reared their heads. Although the likelihood of indulgence toward Williams and his Separatist views was always minimal (given both the difficulty of maintaining social order and the significant substantive differences between Puritans and Separatists), even these chances were radically diminished by forces in England that Williams's critique appeared to abet. Opposing Williams and Hutchinson, then, was not merely opposing Dissenting religious *ideas*, but reasserting and reconstituting the *practical* bases of communal life against those who would undermine its foundations.[13] These enemies of course varied: in the case of Williams, English authorities represented the most immediate political threat, while the Antinomian affair boiled over roughly simultaneously with the Pequot War of 1636–38. The situation of the Pennsylvania magistrates was not entirely different from that of their early Massachusetts counterparts. The Keithian schism occurred in the aftermath of the English Revolution and Penn's ongoing struggle to retain control of his colony. After William's accession, Penn was placed under house arrest several times and had his charter revoked for over a year. One of the chief arguments made by English and American critics of the Quaker regime, as we saw in Chapter 5, was that Quaker principles precluded the maintenance of a militia and thus the most basic function of a civil government, the physical protection of its citizens. As with Williams's Separatism, Keith's insistence that Quakerism rule out force of any kind, including the performance of magisterial duties, inevitably gave support to those attackers of the Pennsylvania colonial government. Keith's

---

13. The great value of Seligman's *Innerworldly Individualism*, on which I relied heavily in Chapter 2, lies in the close attention the author gives to Puritan leaders' reassertion and creative reconstitution of the bases of their communal life.

teaching about the peace testimony and its implications for Quakerism and magistracy would likely never have persuaded any prominent Pennsylvania Quaker. Publishing in 1692 and 1693, however, with the precarious legal foundation of the colony still unresolved, Keith virtually assured himself the unified opposition of influential Pennsylvania Friends.

In all of these cases, political context shapes the contours of political debate by rephrasing general arguments and vocabularies (toleration, liberty, order) into intensely particular and partisan discourse. The example of Jesus and the early church; the extravoluntary nature of the will; the search for prosperity, trade, and civil allegiance: all of these philosophical arguments appear in the heat of political struggle and are received by audiences attuned and sensitive to political developments, both past and current. To illustrate the importance of political context, I examine Locke's transition on the issue of toleration. By examining Locke, who penned perhaps the best-known plea for toleration in the Western tradition, we gain a renewed appreciation for the important contextual elements that affect the work of *all* authors.

Locke's Developing Position on Toleration: Emblematic, If Not New

Saying, as I did in Chapter 4, that Locke's arguments for toleration were not new does not mean that Locke is not important. His work epitomizes developing Whig ideology on a number of fronts, among them toleration and Parliamentary sovereignty.[14] In fact, a consideration of Locke's work illuminates the shifting political contexts of Restoration and Revolutionary England. Locke began his career opposed to extensive religious liberty, given his view of the excesses of Cromwellian politics and the background of civil war and regicide. Over the course of thirty years, however, he came to support a very different understanding of the role of toleration in ensuring authentic religious commitment as well as civil peace.[15]

In 1660, just after the Restoration of Charles II, Locke responded to a tract that advocated a general toleration for all, including Catholics. His response departs sharply from his later views. What remains consistent is

14. See Richard Ashcraft and M. M. Goldsmith, "Locke, Revolution Principles, and the Formation of Whig Ideology," *Historical Journal* 26 (1983): 773–800. More generally, Locke's work on toleration as epitomizing Whig principles is the focus of Ashcraft's *Revolutionary Politics.*

15. The best recent treatment of Locke's evolution on the issue of toleration, indeed the best book on Locke in recent years, is Marshall, *John Locke.* In this brief account, I shall be merely sketching out a picture that Marshall paints in vivid detail.

Locke's admission of the sovereign's right to regulate "indifferent" things. While the Locke of 1685 would exclude from indifferency matters directly related to religious worship, the younger Locke defined things indifferent quite broadly. Essentially, the magistrate must decide indifferency: anything else invited anarchy. "Let the people . . . but once hear that the magistrate hath no authority to injoin things indifferent in matters of religion, they will all at an instant be converts, conscience and religion shall presently mingle it self with all their actions and be spread over all their whole lives to protect them from the reach of the magistrate. . . . Magistracy itself will at last be concluded antichristian."[16] Having viewed the proliferation of radical sects and their frequent "enthusiastic" denials of political authority, Locke welcomed the Restoration of Charles II and hoped for an end to what he considered religious chaos: "I would men would be persuaded to be so kind to their religion their country and themselves as not to hazard again the substantial blessings of peace and settlement in an overzealous contention about things, which they themselves confess to be little and at most are but indifferent."[17] The vivid example of regicide in 1649 and the close association between religious and political dissent led Locke, as well as many of his peers, to mistrust Dissenters and their calls for indulgence; Locke warned of "people who are ready to conclude God dishonoured upon every small deviation from that way of worship which either education or interest hath made sacred to them, and that therefore they ought to vindicate the cause of God with swords in their hands."[18] Locke did voice some favorable sentiments regarding comprehension, and supported including moderate Presbyterians, for example, within the parameters of Anglican belief and practice. But this tells us nothing about his view on the matter of toleration.[19]

16. *Scritti Editi e Ineditti Sulla Tolleranza*, ed. C. A. Viano (Turin, 1961), 43–44.

17. Ibid., 16. For just one example of how fears of religious chaos informed Restoration hostility to toleration, see Reay, "The Quakers, 1659."

18. Selection from *First Tract of Government* (1660), in Locke, *PW*, 145.

19. Richard Tuck has argued that Hobbes's and Locke's positions on toleration were similar in the early 1660s. "*Leviathan* was a book that sought to persuade its readers of two things: First, that there was no source of moral or religious judgment in a commonwealth independent of the sovereign; and second, that the very lack of such a source implied toleration" ("Hobbes and Locke on Toleration," in Dietz, *Thomas Hobbes and Political Theory*, 169). I agree with Tuck's assessment of the first goal of *Leviathan*, but not with the second. It is likely that Hobbes and Locke *were* allies on the question of toleration early in the 1660s, as Tuck argues, but this is because Locke was much closer to Hobbes's absolutism: thus Hobbes and Locke in 1660 *opposed* toleration. Each may have personally favored a more inclusive Anglican creed, and thus *comprehension* (expansion of Anglican doctrine to encompass a broader segment of the English religious public).

Between 1660 and 1667, Locke's views on toleration underwent a significant change. The legitimacy of sovereign control over indifferent things remains in the 1667 *Essay Concerning Toleration*, but John Dunn rightly notes that "attention is shifted from the issue of what subjects are obliged to do (obey) to the question of what obligations of obedience a ruler is justified in exacting."[20] According to Locke in 1667, opinions and actions are divisible into three types: "purely speculative opinions and divine worship," which are irrelevant to government or society; "practical principles or opinions" concerning social relations, which are in their nature neither good nor bad (*PW*, 187); and "duties of the second table," moral virtues and vices that concern social relations but are also, *in se*, good or bad (191). The first "have an absolute and universal right to toleration" (194). Assuming the sincerity of the professor, acknowledging the extravoluntary nature of belief (since "a man cannot command his own understanding" [188]), Locke removes such ideas entirely from the sphere of political power. He admits that the second, practical opinions, have "a title also to toleration" (191), but only insofar as they do not cause civil discord. Locke refuses a purely subjectivist rule of conscience, but counsels prudence to the magistrate and evokes a "separate spheres" argument in which (as for Penn and Williams) politics deals with externals and religion with belief:

> That in any actions flowing from any of these opinions, as also in all other indifferent things, the magistrate has a power to command or forbid so far as they tend to the peace, safety, or security of his people . . . yet he ought still to have a great care that no such laws be made, no such restraints established, for any other reason but because the necessity of the state and the welfare of the people called for them. (193)

The final category of actions and opinions again returns to Locke's minimal definition of politics: if the authority of the magistrate is for civil peace and

---

But a personal view does not necessitate a political commitment; and support for comprehension did not equate to support for toleration.

I find Farr, "Atomes of Scripture: Hobbes and the Politics of Biblical Interpretation" (also in Dietz, *Thomas Hobbes*, 172–96), more convincing than Tuck on this point; see also Glenn Burgess, "Thomas Hobbes: Religious Toleration or Religious Indifference?" in Nederman and Laursen, *Difference and Dissent*, 139–62.

20. *The Political Thought of John Locke: An Historical Account of the Argument of the "Two Treatises of Government"* (London, 1969), 30.

security alone, "he is not bound to punish all [vices] . . . he may tolerate some vices, for I would fain know, what government in the world doth not?" (196).

Locke's most mature work on toleration is the *Letter Concerning Tolera-tion*. I addressed its primary arguments, and how they mirror conventional seventeenth-century tolerationist positions, in Chapter 4.[21] The *Letter* contains a number of similarities with the 1667 *Essay*: absolute toleration in basic articles of faith, toleration of practical beliefs within the limits of community welfare, and the refusal to equate sins or vices with civil crimes (*Letter*, 43–47). Rejoining the recurrent debate over indifferent things, Locke legiti-mizes the magistrate's ability to regulate such things, but denies that the magis-trate may arbitrarily decide indifferency (41). Things indifferent in everyday life (bread, wine, water, and so on) become invested with religious signifi-cance in the context of worship, he maintains, and are thus no longer indif-ferent (40–41). Midway through the *Letter*, Locke encapsulates his entire approach: "The care therefore of every man's soul belongs unto himself, and is to be left unto himself" (35). Religious judgment is not subject to the will— we cannot choose, but are persuaded of one or another route to heaven— indeed, our judgment *determines* our will.[22]

We cannot assess Locke's views on toleration, then, unless we take into account its substantive development.[23] We cannot understand its substantive

---

21. The variety of Locke's arguments is also cogently canvassed in Tarcov, "John Locke."

22. *Letter*, 27; *Essay Concerning Human Understanding*, pt. 2, chap. 21, sec. 48.

23. For a very different view, see Robert P. Kraynak, "John Locke: From Absolutism to Toleration," *APSR* 74 (1980): 53–69. Kraynak equates liberal toleration with the skeptical abso-lutism of Hobbes, claiming that "Locke's argument [in the *Letter*] makes a subtle transition from an honest critique of hypocrisy—that even the truth cannot save without sincere belief—to an assertion of 'subjectivism'—that the truth can not be true if it is not sincerely believed to be true" (65). Despite the brief quotation provided by Kraynak, Locke never claimed that "sincere belief [is] the cause of a doctrine's truth" (65). Kraynak's misreading of Locke on this point results, ironically, from what he accuses others of doing: misunderstanding early liberal thinkers by imposing contemporary categories. His polemic against contemporary liberalism as sanctioning relativist skepticism and thus "an ultimate uniformity of opinion" (68) is at times convincing, but has little to do with Locke, whose attention to the voluntaristic nature of belief and conscience was firmly anchored in his Christian faith. True, Locke's is an "enlightenment account of Christianity" (54), heavily anticlerical, but this is no less Christian than more orthodox Calvinist, Anglican, or Catholic views.

Kraynak consistently implies that Locke's limiting of toleration for the sake of national security does away with any principled commitment to toleration: the *Letter* "assert[s] liberty of conscience as a right . . . [yet note the] absence of an argument from principle for this right. . . . Locke's argument, therefore, is actually a prudential accommodation to the political and psycho-logical consequences of man's pride in his reason. . . . Locke thereby achieves the height of prudence, not by open expediency, but by asserting a general principle with pointed reminders of

development unless we take into account the context in which this development occurred. The Protectorate's tolerationist religious policy had fostered many radical sects hostile to organized religious institutions and political authority, and the two years between Cromwell's death and Charles II's Restoration had reawakened in many minds the dangers of divided or democratic sovereignty.[24] In 1660, English political elites recognized the dangers of tyranny and democracy, and were willing to risk the former to avoid the certain disaster of the latter. Locke was wholly conventional in opposing toleration at that point, while supporting some degree of comprehension for orthodox Protestants (primarily moderate Presbyterians).

Why did Locke's views change so over the years? It is impossible to know with precision the factors working on Locke between 1660 and 1667. The most obvious would be his exit from Oxford and entrance into Shaftesbury's service. Scholars have suggested other possibilities: a 1665 visit to Cleves, where he witnessed adherents of many faiths living peacefully together; a particularly compelling sermon he attended in 1665 or 1666, notes of which survived among his papers; or the example of English Dissenters, whose patient suffering greatly impressed him.[25] Originally Locke trusted Charles to effect a moderate religious settlement: when the king failed to do so and Parliament stepped in with decidedly less sympathy for Dissenters, Locke's confidence in the character of the magistrate as an element of his theory was likely diminished.[26] Events after 1667, in all likelihood, only strengthened Locke's steadily increasing receptiveness to tolerationist ideas. His entrance into Shaftesbury's household and involvement in the Whig cause are clearly central to understanding this ideological evolution.

Early in the 1680s, Locke fled to the Netherlands, where he saw religious toleration in practice and cultivated a friendship with Dutch tolerationist

---

its limits" (66). But if asserting general principles and articulating specific applications with specific limitations may only be accounted "prudential," it is not clear to me that any thinker has ever advanced principled arguments.

24. See Reay, "The Quakers, 1659," and Hill, *World Turned Upside Down*.

25. On the visit to Cleves, see Esmond S. DeBeer, "Locke and English liberalism: The *Second Treatise of Government* in Its Contemporary Setting," in *John Locke: Problems and Perspectives*, ed. John W. Yolton (New York, 1969), 36; on the sermon, see Ashcraft, *Revolutionary Politics*, 92–94; and on the example of the Dissenters, see Tully, "Introduction," in Locke, *Letter*, 5–7.

26. On this point, see James Tully, "Locke," in Burns and Goldie, *Cambridge History of Political Thought*, 645–48.

Philip van Limborch.[27] In 1685 Louis XIV revoked the Edict of Nantes, which had—if sometimes uneasily—guaranteed toleration for French Protestants since 1598. Meanwhile, in England, the locus of concern, for many, was shifting from Protestant Dissenters to Catholics. As the memory of the Civil War and Protectorate years faded, the political issues seemed less a fear of anarchy and lawlessness than a concern about Catholic tyranny and absolutism, and Locke's ideological evolution may have mirrored these broader shifts in public opinion.[28] The context for Locke's *Letter* is multifaceted, then, but clearly a variety of English and European factors combined to push Locke toward toleration as his career progressed. Regardless of the specific timing of his change in views regarding toleration, the essential elements of Locke's mature position were largely in place by 1667, though many of these awaited final elaboration in the *Letter*.

The years 1689–90, then, saw the publication of Locke's three most important writings: *A Letter Concerning Toleration, An Essay Concerning Human Understanding,* and *Two Treatises of Government.* In Locke's mature political and philosophical system, toleration forms an essential part of a broader approach to social and political life, formed from the experiences of the preceding thirty years.[29] The essential elements run something like this. Individuals bear ultimate allegiance to God, as God's property.[30] Political society concerns the "externals" of earthly life: individuals voluntarily agree to establish governments to preserve their lives, liberty, and estates and ensure their common safety. Religion consists of "an inward persuasion of the mind," unalterable by physical force, and salvation is an individual responsibility

27. Jonathan Israel, the leading historian of seventeenth-century Dutch thought (and more specifically, Dutch tolerationist thought), has stressed the important influence of Dutch events and ideas on English theory and practice. See Israel, "Intellectual Debate About Toleration in the Dutch Republic" and "Toleration in Seventeenth-Century Dutch and English Thought."

28. This is of course a relative statement. The literature on toleration is voluminous throughout the seventeenth century, and my point here is that the issues raised by James's open Catholicism and Louis XIV's revocation of the Edict of Nantes pushed fears about Catholicism and absolutism to the forefront. For many, to be sure (as we saw in Chapter 4 when considering Tory polemics during the Exclusion Crisis), the memory of the Civil War and Protectorate years never faded.

Steven C. A. Pincus argues that English public opinion shifted noticeably during the 1670s: see "From Butterboxes to Wooden Shoes: The Shift in English Popular Sentiment from Anti-Dutch to Anti-French in the 1670s," *Historical Journal* 38 (1995): 333–61.

29. The broad scope of the Lockean corpus is brilliantly explicated in Dunn, "Bright Enough for All Our Purposes," 133–53; also in Tarcov, "John Locke."

30. *Second Treatise*, chap. 2, sec. 6.

involving faith, reason, and revelation: part 4 of the *Essay* elaborates Locke's understanding of the fundamental differences between these types of experience, reason based on deductions from natural faculties (sensation and reflection) and faith consisting of propositions supported by the credit of the proposer.[31] Individuals voluntarily construct religious societies to pursue salvation as best they understand its requirements for their lives: assuming that the means employed are peaceful and nonseditious, the magistrate's authority does not extend to them. Thus we find the removal of purely religious beliefs from the sphere of political society. The welfare of the community represents the legitimate province of political magistrates, but that welfare must be defined solely in terms of civil interest.

Locke's Christianity, like that of Hobbes, manifested itself in a minimalism in which reason and revelation, though fundamentally different, were not seen as exclusive. We can know the existence of God from the structure of human self-understanding;[32] we can know elements of natural law by reason;[33] but particular religious doctrines reach beyond the realm of knowledge and into that of faith. Part of Locke's aim in the *Essay* consisted of placing the Christian faith on a firmer footing than tradition and authority. "[Locke] is personally convinced of the absolute truth of Christianity and the simple demands of faith drawn from the Scriptures, but . . . he is equally certain that the supposed defenders of the faith have been derelict in the performance of their duty, in attempting to support religion with arguments from authority rather than with the evidence supplied by reasoning."[34] Locke's theology is sketched out in *The Reasonableness of Christianity*, and is implied by his comments on the un-Christian nature of persecution that open the *Letter*. Like Hobbes, he sees belief in Christ as Messiah as the *unum necessarium* of salvation.[35] At the same time, human knowledge *was* limited, severely limited in supernatural matters, and it would be abusive for a magistrate to impose a doctrine that could not be proven correct. But again, this is the Locke of 1685 and later, not the Locke of 1660. The Locke of 1660 might have admitted, as

31. *Essay Concerning Human Understanding*, pt. 4, chaps. 16, 17, 18.
32. Ibid., pt. 4, chap. 10.
33. *Second Treatise*, chap. 2, sec. 6.
34. Richard Ashcraft, "Faith and Knowledge in Locke's Philosophy," in *John Locke: Problems and Perspectives*, ed. John W. Yolton (New York, 1969), 202. Richard Vernon describes Locke's theory of knowledge as "not skeptical, [but] narrow in scope" (*Career of Toleration*, 53).
35. See Locke's *Reasonableness of Christianity, as Delivered in the Scriptures* (1695), ed. George M. Ewing (Chicago, 1965), esp. secs. 27, 28, 52.

did Hobbes, that the magistrate could not force belief, but only action. The political consequences of such an admission at that time, however, were not toleration, but Hobbesian sovereignty and uniformity.

What made Locke's eventual tolerationist commitment possible was his growing view that the threat to civil peace and order lay not in granting excessive liberty to religious dissenters, but in the threat of absolutism and the subversion of the English constitution posed by James II (and, as previously mentioned, in a broader European perspective, by Louis XIV's revocation of the Edict of Nantes and the influence of his Dutch exile on his thinking).[36] Locke excludes from his toleration groups that, in his view, threaten social order, namely, atheists and Catholics: he does not offer an abstract defense of conscience, but instead seeks to protect pious Protestant dissenters whose religious exercise does not threaten civil peace.[37] He disavows any who would use religion as a cover for political rebellion, since true religion revolves around the search for salvation and not the contestation for political power. Locke's expectation that people could engage in peaceful commerce and the basic requirements of political society while holding divergent religious beliefs was central to his theory in its mature expression. It was also an expectation that Locke could never have held in the context of the 1650s and 1660s.

THE RELIGIOUS IMPULSE BEHIND RELIGIOUS TOLERATION: THE SUBJECTIFICATION OF CONSCIENCE, PERFECTIONISM, AND RELIGIOUS FREEDOM

Richard H. Popkin has noted the "curious fact that the opposing positions of skepticism about religion and religious dogmatism provided two of the major roads to toleration in theory and practice in early modern Europe."[38]

---

36. Of course, in reality things were not so clear cut. Religion was often considered an issue of national security and the only guarantee of "the basics of human society." Nonetheless, unlike the Massachusetts Puritans, Hobbes, or Anglican royalists, Locke considered toleration the rule from which deviations must be justified.

37. Herein lies my difference with such scholars as Gordon Schochet; as I mentioned in the preface, Schochet argues that Locke sought not toleration, not a "granted privilege" from the state, but rather "genuine 'religious liberty' as a matter of right" ("Toleration, Revolution, and Judgment," 85).

38. "Skepticism about Religion and Millenarian Dogmatism: Two Sources of Toleration in the Seventeenth Century," in Laursen and Nederman, *Beyond the Persecuting Society*, 232.

Close and careful examination of the contexts and conditions in which toleration was debated during the seventeenth century leads us to reemphasize as
well the importance of religious radicalism in sparking religious dissent and
(often) religious liberty. As William McLoughlin points out with regard to
the American tradition, we must recognize that religious liberty is a river into
which many streams feed, and tolerationist arguments during the seventeenth
century were advanced as often by religious extremists (concerned to keep
their worship pure and free from the state) as by the sort of secular, Enlightenment rationalists more familiar to the standard treatments of toleration
and liberalism.[39] A study of the Keith affair suggests another name in the
category of such religious radicals: not that Keith had an enduring impact
on American politics (he did not), but that in his critique of church and state
he raised issues similar to those raised by Williams and Hutchinson, and cried
out against the intermingling of ecclesiastical and political power in the name
of orthodoxy and piety.

Conscience: Perfectionism and the Increasing Emphasis on Subjective Assent

Perhaps the most important contribution of early modern tolerationists to
the ongoing history of religious liberty concerns the transformation of the very
idea of conscience itself. Well into the seventeenth century, as we have seen,
conscience represented the voice of God within an individual, and it was
considered possible to sin *against* one's conscience by transgressing God's
law. Seen in this way, conscience implied a degree of *knowledge* (*con-scientia*)
and not simply personal opinion, and it was possible for one to act sincerely
upon mistaken beliefs, and to err in the process. The term "erroneous conscience" formed a familiar part of the theological literature of the period and
animated orthodox antitolerationist literature.[40] By emphasizing persuasion
and the necessity for positive, subjective conviction *alongside* (never in place

---

39. *Soul Liberty*, ix–xii. I do not mean to suggest a firm dichotomy between seventeenth-
century defenses of religious freedom (based upon religious purity) and eighteenth-century ones
(informed by Enlightenment *philosophes*, stressing political values, and often religiously indifferent). I intend this comment only as a general suggestion, a potential future avenue for consideration. If there is anything to be said for such a suggestion, then Locke's synthesis of Christian,
philosophical, psychological, and pragmatic arguments for toleration might represent a bridge
between the two.

40. See Chapter 3, note 138.

of) these traditional understandings of conscience, tolerationists sought nothing less than a complete transformation of the debate over conscience and its implications for politics and society.

In its orthodox formulation, "conscience" represented the faculty that enabled an individual to know what God required, and thus inherently carried with it an objective standard of right and wrong. For Francis Bugg, conscience represented "an ability in the understanding of man, by a reflective act to judge of himself in all he does, as to his acceptance or rejection with God." Through the conscience, "God keeps up his solemn claim of sovereignty over us, in our own breasts."[41] Robert Sanderson located conscience "in the middle, below God, but above man: it is subject to God as His minister, but rules man as his Lord. . . . [T]he immediate norm or law of conscience is Right Reason . . . conscience is therefore said to be right when it is in accord with Right Reason in accord with that law which God, the highest law-giver, has set over it."[42] William Ames referred to "the adequate rule of conscience" as "the revealed will of God by which man's duty is prescribed and made known to him."[43] For John Sharp, the "rule of conscience . . . can be nothing but the law of God. For nothing can be a duty but what God's Law hath made so."[44]

Early modern tolerationists attempted to ease penalties on individuals who could not, in good faith, worship according to a national church. Most seventeenth-century advocates of religious toleration were, as we have seen, committed (even radical) Christians who did not deny the essentially theological nature of conscience. They did, however, stress a subjective element of that faculty. Roger Williams epitomized this tendency toward an increasingly subjective understanding of conscience when he argued that one is persecuted even if one's beliefs or practices, objectively considered, are false.[45] Since conscience was a faculty of the understanding and not the will, it could not be coerced into believing one thing or another. Locke and Penn agreed.[46] The

41. *De Christiana libertate* (London, 1682), 1, 13.
42. Praelictio II, n.1, in *Complete Works*, ed. W. Jacobson (Oxford, 1884), 4:23; Praelictio II, n. 3, in *Complete Works*, 4:24.
43. *De conscientia et eius Iure vel Casibus* (Amsterdam, 1630), 3–4.
44. *A Discourse Concerning Conscience* (London, 1684), 8.
45. *Bloudy Tenent*, 41; 63. For Williams and other tolerationists, this claim was based upon Romans 14:23, in which Paul had written that "whatsoever is not of faith is of sin," and Romans 14:5, which called on each believer to be "fully persuaded in his own mind."
46. Locke, *Letter*, 27; Penn, "To the council and senate of the city of Embden" (1674), in *Works*, 1:610.

increasing insistence on subjective assent in support of religious toleration, and the corresponding psychological or epistemological assertion that conscience could not be forced, represent perhaps the two most important conceptual developments in the early modern emergence of toleration.

Liberty of conscience was thus related to religious voluntarism: voluntarily worshiping a certain way was considered almost as important as the objective correctness (or lack thereof) of the mode of worship itself. Voluntarism is not the same thing, strictly speaking, as *choice*: in other words, tolerationists did not claim that one *chose* one's beliefs, but rather that the understanding was persuaded, inexorably so, of the truth of a given faith.[47] Not only were individuals obligated to do God's will, tolerationists argued, they were obligated to do it voluntarily and without threat of punishment for nonperformance, or else the obedience lacked merit. Although erroneous belief should be vigorously contested with argumentation and exhortation— "The greatest duty of a Christian," Locke wrote in the *Letter*, is to "employ as many exhortations and arguments as possible as he pleases, toward another man's salvation" (*Letter*, 47)—coercion was to be forsworn as both ineffectual and un-Christian. Seventeenth-century toleration debates in England focused largely on the ability of religious dissenters to gain freedom of public worship and assembly, as the necessary institutional and social corollaries to the dictates of free (even if erroneous) conscience.[48]

From more radical religious perspectives, the tolerationist commitment to an increasingly subjective notion of conscience was often part of a more general phenomenon in which the "inner" nature of religion and religious experience was elevated to the forefront at the expense of forms, doctrines, and liturgies. Following McLoughlin's usage, I refer to this tendency as religious perfectionism. McLoughlin characterizes perfectionism by describing the perfectionist's

47. Indeed, one could do the right thing for the wrong reason and still err in the process, for even if the religion that was imposed upon an individual was in fact the true faith, without the individual's assent that worship was invalid (again, see Romans 14:23) (*Letter*, 26–27).

48. I assume a distinction between coercion and persuasion here, and indeed throughout the project. Such a position is questioned by William Walker, who claims bluntly that "persuasion is force" ("Force, Metaphor, and Persuasion in Locke's *Letter Concerning Toleration*," in Nederman and Laursen, *Difference and Dissent*, 210). Such a broad claim, in my view—though conceptually intriguing—does not help us understand the kind of religious violence that early modern tolerationists were trying to avoid and the kinds of restraints they wished to place on actions to suppress unorthodox religious beliefs.

reliance on the Holy Spirit for inner direction, belief in a literal Bible to which the Christian must conform, absolute faith, and the necessity for external conformity to internal convictions of divine duty. . . . In the case of most of the perfectionist . . . groups the individuals concerned have such strong convictions of the necessity of following the divine promptings they feel in their hearts that they refuse to heed any . . . [religious or ecclesiastical] restrictions.[49]

Certainly such a description evokes aspects of the Hutchinsonians and their dissent from Massachusetts orthodoxy, as well as early Quaker incursions into the colony. I wish to use the term "perfectionist" a bit more broadly, however, to encompass both Roger Williams's Separatism and George Keith's complaints about Quaker laxity in Pennsylvania, as well as the English sectarian tradition that sought an ever purer church. The fissiparous tendencies of English sectarianism were in a sense a form of ultra-Puritanism, driven by a similar—even *less* compromising—perfectionist dynamic. In their attempts to rid the church of human accretions, and to return to the simplicity and purity of the early Christians, sectarians continuously railed against Anglican laxity and ceremonialism just as earlier generations of English Puritans had railed against (and, overtly or covertly, separated from) the Anglican Church. Roger Williams knew this dynamic well, and famously turned it back on John Cotton in their correspondence during the 1640s.

Both Williams and Keith, as we have seen, cared passionately about the purity of their churches. Of course, their opponents did also. These two, however, were extremely unwilling to make the compromises with pragmatic reality that institutional forces and the ambiguity of everyday life often seemed to demand, compromises that might include worshiping with the unregenerate (in the interest of general salutary effects achieved by requiring church attendance), having Quaker ministers exercise magistracy, or countenancing questionable theological beliefs in the interest of social or church unity. For both Williams and Keith, purification of the church and its reestablishment

---

49. *Soul Liberty*, 107. McLoughlin also notes that "it takes strong faith to stand up against the established order and declare one's independence from it. . . . But by the same token this reliance on an inward spiritual power that comes directly from God can lead to extremely radical behavior when it is divorced from any other means of authority or control" (107).

For a close look at one perfectionist religious movement, see McLoughlin, *Soul Liberty*, chap. 4. See also Cody, "Price of Perfection."

upon sound Christian doctrine should be one's foremost task, regardless of the cost in social or political disruption. In the case of such disruption, Keith asserted, it is not the separatists who are to be condemned, but those holding false views that make such a separation necessary, "as when the sun shines warm on a dung-hill, the dung-hill is to be blamed for the stink, not the sun."[50]

Recall that for Williams, the problem with Massachusetts Bay churches was that they included individuals who could not provide certain proof of their election, thus raising the possibility of spiritual "pollution" of the elect. The Separatist solution was to recongregate pure churches of true saints. Keith also emphasized the importance of a pure church, railing against the laxity and error that characterized not merely the average Quaker meeting but even the views of their most prominent ministers. Furthermore, Keith argued, the refusal of Friends to correct these erroneous opinions threatened their spiritual and temporal standing. "To uphold [gross errors against the Christian faith]," he wrote, "is to bring reproach to Truth and our holy profession, and to the body of our faithful Friends. . . . [T]hat society is to be turned away from . . . that doth tolerate [erroneous views and individuals] and bring them not to due conviction and condemnation."[51]

Of course one person's "laxity" was another's necessary compromise with the reality of living in an imperfect world. We might view this tension between purity and unity as a general dilemma of dominant social groups and the frequent necessity of pragmatism in the interest of preserving social harmony. Massachusetts Puritans, for example, viewed Williams's Separatism and Hutchinson's Antinomianism much as Anglicans viewed the sects, as dangerous brands of extremism that sacrificed unity for the sake of an elusive and specious perfection, be it a wholly pure church or immediate revelation from God. Forcing the issue of doctrinal orthodoxy was not a high priority for Pennsylvania Quakers either, given the important task of creating an effective colonial government and maintaining the prominent social, economic, and political position they enjoyed. Insisting on perfection would lead only to friction and disunity. The example of Penn, a sectarian in England and later a representative of authority in Pennsylvania, is instructive here. Forced

---

50. Keith and Thomas Budd, *False Judgments Reprehended* (Philadelphia, 1692), 6.

51. *Some Reasons and Causes*, 17. Recall Nathaniel Ward's concern regarding the implications of tolerating religious dissent for the Massachusetts community's spiritual health: he "dare[d] to aver, that God doth no where in his word tolerate Christian states, to give tolerations to such adversaries of his truth, if they have power in their hands to suppress them. . . . Poly-piety is the greatest impiety of all" (*The Simple Cobbler*, 6, 8).

to make a number of painful compromises in order to regain his colonial charter in 1694, he wrote to Pennsylvania Quakers that "we must creep where we cannot go."[52] Compromise and imperfection were inherent in worldly pursuits, he implied, even to the unpalatable extent of agreeing to supply militiamen in violation of the long-standing Quaker peace testimony.[53] Pennsylvania Quakers approached Keith's ambitious religious program and critique similarly, implying that the costs of enforcing such discipline (even had they been convinced that it was a desirable course of action, which they were not) far outweighed any gain in orthodoxy that might result.

This discussion of perfectionism and its propensity to foster separation suggests that we might refer to the sectarian impulse for religious freedom as an *exclusionary* defense of freedom, since so many of the sects rejected the Anglican Church's encompassing of all English within its fold. Williams and other Separatists similarly sought to preserve the purity of their worship by withdrawing from fellowship with the geographically based Massachusetts Bay congregations.

More generally, the religious perfectionist often encountered the epithet "enthusiast," one who views him- or herself as so filled with the Holy Spirit that social conventions are laid aside. Winthrop referred to Anne Hutchinson's religious dissent as "the most dangerous enthusiasm in the world."[54] In England as well, the religious radicalism present in the New Model Army served as a graphic reminder of the connection between "enthusiasm" and religious toleration. The symbolism of army iconoclasm and the fiery sermons of army chaplains seemed to instill in the army the sense that they were fighting as much for reformation as for popular liberty, or rather, that the two were inseparable. The goal of such fighting, then, for Cromwell, was the establishment of freedom to worship in a pure manner, uncontaminated by unbelievers or state interference. (Though Cromwell, as we have seen, *did* retain a state church, he also allowed a variety of congregations to exist outside that church structure.) Enthusiasm itself does not, of course, lead directly to toleration. By chipping away at orthodoxy, however, it often loosens the communal bonds that serve to unify communities, creating an opening for dissent to take hold.

52. "To the Provincial Council," in *PWP*, 3:405.
53. I use the peace testimony here solely as an analogy, since Pennsylvania Quakers were rigid on this point, and obstructed as far as possible efforts to raise troops.
54. "The Examination," in Hutchinson, *The History*, 1:387.

Perfectionist religious dissidents spurred on religious freedom, indirectly in Massachusetts and Pennsylvania, and quite directly in England, in the guise of the New Model Army. However, as I suggested in Chapter 2, the role played by Williams and Hutchinson in the history of religious freedom remains highly ambiguous. We have no evidence to conclude that Williams advanced a theory of religious freedom while he was in Massachusetts. (His actions in the founding and early history of Rhode Island are of course another matter.) Hutchinson, on the other hand, asserted her religious dissent vigorously and disruptively (and was arguably unjustly prosecuted and expelled). The fact of persecution and repression on religious grounds, however, proves only that one has had political forces mobilized against oneself. It tells us nothing about whether the beliefs that bring on such persecution contain an (implicit or explicit) theory of religious freedom. Both Williams and Hutchinson sought to have their theological perspectives (and their ecclesiastical and political implications) *prevail*, not simply coexist with Puritan "error."

The Keithian schism, in many ways, represents a set of disputes that parallel the earlier controversies over Williams and Hutchinson in Massachusetts. Beginning as a theological debate within the colony's dominant religious group, it quickly became an ecclesiastical, social, and political conflict whose consequences were hotly discussed on both sides of the Atlantic. The legal issues raised by Keith, and the responses they evoked in Pennsylvania magistrates, proved remarkably similar to those of the earlier Massachusetts trials. The claim of conscience against a dominant religious body; the spilling over of that claim into personal, social, and political unrest; and the reestablishment of orthodoxy in the form of a legal proceeding against the dissident. Given the substantive contrast between Puritan and Quaker views regarding toleration, one might have expected the course of religious dissent in Pennsylvania to have run more smoothly.

Skepticism and Toleration: The Case of Hobbes

Skepticism of ecclesiastical or political authority claims influenced the increasing assertion of conscience as the seventeenth-century progressed. Some scholars have linked this skepticism with emergent modern science and mechanical philosophy.[55] Many scholars recognize, however, that a basic equation of

55. Cragg, *Freedom and Authority*, chaps. 2, 9; Hill, *World Turned Upside Down*, 89–90, chap. 14; idem, *Century of Revolution*, 79.

skepticism/toleration and antiskepticism/antitoleration is far too simplistic. In this section, I explore the thought of Hobbes as a way of making the tension between skepticism and toleration more explicit. Philosophical and epistemological positions, as I argued in the previous section, are always located in social, political, and historical contexts, and these contexts shape how individuals extract specific political lessons from their general commitments. An epistemological stance does not constitute a political position; and given the enormous upheavals the English Civil War occasioned, we should not be surprised to find skepticism (which is often a basis for tolerant attitudes toward the views of others) amenable to a number of political perspectives. The Stoic elements of skeptical thought often led, not to assertions of individual conscience based on an individual interpretation of Scripture or an opposition to infallibility claims in general, but to the "relativist" view that, in Peter Burke's words, "political arrangements, like other customs, vary from place to place and from time to time, and that there is no reason to argue that one such arrangement is in itself better than another. . . . The wise man, according to the skeptics, will live his life in conformity with the customs of his country, although he will not accept the arguments put forward for the superiority of those customs."[56] Richard Tuck has persuasively traced the complex relationship between skepticism and toleration, pointing out how skeptics were often as concerned about social order and avoiding anarchy as their more "certain" contemporaries.[57]

Tuck's important scholarship on Hobbes more specifically represents a detailed examination of how skepticism need not result in tolerationist politics, since for Hobbes skepticism was not an isolated epistemological commit-

---

56. "Tacitism, Scepticism, and Reason of State," in Burns and Goldie, *Cambridge History of Political Thought*, 494. Skepticism of various kinds appeared in the works of a variety of early modern European thinkers, forming the backdrop as well as the contemporary context for Hobbes's skepticism. See the essays in Levine, *Early Modern Skepticism*, especially the following: Alan Levine, "Skepticism, Self, and Toleration in Montaigne's Political Thought"; Michael Gillespie, "Descartes and the Question of Toleration"; Steven B. Smith, "Toleration and the Skepticism of Religion in Spinoza's *Tractatus Theologico-Politicus*"; and Kenneth R. Weinstein, "Pierre Bayle's Atheist Politics."

57. See Tuck, "Scepticism and Toleration in the Seventeenth Century," in Mendus, *Justifying Toleration*, and more generally Tuck's *Philosophy and Government, 1572–1651* (Cambridge, 1993). Again, as with my treatment of Locke in the previous section, I shall be sketching only the outline of a picture painted in great detail by others. My point is not to capture all the nuance of Hobbes's role in the history of skepticism, but to relate Hobbes's commitments to the broader concerns of this project, and to use him as an illustration of the general phenomenon of skepticism and toleration.

ment, but a starting-point from which he sought to reconstruct an absolutist politics. Tuck views Hobbes as seeking "a philosophically sensitive response to the skepticism of both classical antiquity and modern Europe . . . an answer to both Pyrrho and Descartes."[58] In other words, Hobbes sought a skeptically informed response to skepticism, a skeptical route to certainty.[59]

For Hobbes, overarching substantive truth claims[60] are unjustified on a number of fronts. This skepticism is illustrated graphically in Hobbes's distinction between religion and superstition: the only difference between the two, Hobbes tells us, is that religion is "publicly allowed" while superstition is not (*L*, 31). Ignorance of causes represents one of the primary roots of *both* religion and superstition, and the salient difference between the two lies, not in their substance, but in each's relation to the sovereign's position regarding public theology and religious practice. Regardless of the truth or falsity of various religious beliefs, the need to seek peace (the fundamental dictate of natural law) requires the repositing of sovereign power over church and state in the civil sovereign.[61] The institutional expression of religion is more social and political than theological, and extensive debates over the objective veracity of one or another set of beliefs are misplaced. Hobbes's unique and totalizing brand of Erastianism, in the words of one scholar, consolidates "political and ecclesiastical right . . . into a single sovereign right."[62]

Hobbes's nominalism further illustrates his skepticism regarding the validity of much human knowledge. Tracing human thought to motion and

58. "Optics and Sceptics: The Philosophical Foundations of Hobbes' Political Thought," in *Conscience and Casuistry in Early Modern Europe*, ed. Edmund Leites (New York, 1988), 236, 257.

59. The following account of Hobbes is adapted from my "Tolerance, Toleration, and the Liberal Tradition."

60. As opposed to, of course, overarching *methodological* truth claims: for Hobbes, there is only one method to arrive at sound data about the world around us. This is, of course, dogmatic, in a sense, as pointed out by Robert Kraynak in *History and Modernity in the Thought of Thomas Hobbes* (Ithaca, N.Y., 1992), chap. 8. What I am suggesting here is that for Hobbes, regardless of the truth of the scientific method, the unlikelihood that individuals will actually reason to sound conclusions (and that it is in a way *not natural* for them to do so), combined with the unsatisfactory nature of "conventional wisdom" or common sense (e.g., the political turmoil of England in the 1640s), necessitates the choice and imposition of sovereign power.

61. *L*, 80; see also Thomas Hobbes, *Elements of Law* (1650), ed. Ferdinand Tonnies, 2d ed. (New York, 1969), 74.

62. F. C. Hood, *The Divine Politics of Thomas Hobbes: An Interpretation of Leviathan* (Oxford, 1964), 244.

sense, Hobbes similarly explains the many errors into which individuals fall when attempting to *communicate* their thoughts (*L*, 17). One important way to avoid such error, according to Hobbes, is correct and consistent naming, even though he admits that names as such are strictly of human origin and instrumental: "A name or appellation therefore is the voice of a man, arbitrarily imposed, for a mark to bring to his mind some conception concerning the thing on which it is imposed."[63] Truth, for Hobbes, is nothing more (and nothing less) than "the right ordering of names in our affirmations" (*L*, 19), and we cannot conclude truth or falsity from experience.[64]

Hobbes's skepticism regarding sense perception and speech extends to moral and evaluative notions as well; hence his famous statement that "whatsoever is the object of any man's appetite or desire that is it which he for his part calleth good; and the object of his hate and aversion, evil. . . . For these words of good, evil, and contemptible are ever used with relation to the person that useth them, there being nothing simply and absolutely so."[65] Essentially we can say very little about the ultimate grounds of validity for our own or others' beliefs. Even science is conditional, not absolute, knowledge; in other words, it is knowledge, not of the "x is" sort, but of the "if x, then y" sort (*L*, 36, 47). Of course, acknowledging the conditionality of human knowledge does not prevent Hobbes from passing severe judgment on those whose views he finds dangerous to peace, for example "those that are possessed with an opinion of being inspired," or "one that preached in Cheapside from a cart . . . that he himself was Christ."[66] Here, though, we must be clear that Hobbes objects, not so much to the erroneous view *in se*, but the implications of that view for social peace. The erroneous views of one man may be quite harmless, "yet when many of them conspire together, the rage of the whole multitude is visible enough. . . . they will clamour, fight against, and destroy those by whom all their lifetime before they have been protected and secured from injury" (*L*, 42).

---

63. *Elements of Law*, 18; see also Hobbes, *Elements of Philosophy, the First Section, Concerning Body* (1656), ed. William Molesworth (London, 1839), 16.

64. *Elements of Law*, 16–17. Of course, it may be *prudent* to act on the basis of experience. But "we cannot from experience conclude, that any thing is to be called just or unjust, true or false, nor any proposition universal whatsoever, except it be from remembrance of the use of names imposed arbitrarily by men" (*Elements of Law*, 16–17).

65. *L*, 28–29; *Elements of Law*, 29.

66. *L*, 42; *Elements of Law*, 42.

Unfortunately, given human passion and the egoism that leads each to pursue pleasure, individuals rarely exercise moderation and prudence. Others are opaque to us. We can see universal processes (e.g., passion, appetite/aversion) in them and ourselves, but concerning the specifics of individual views, it is as difficult to proclaim that one with a different view is fundamentally mistaken as it is to be sure that we ourselves have, without error in *ratio* or *oratio*, controlled passion and reasoned from sense to speech. Conflict is bound to arise between different interpretations and objects of human passion, and "when there is a controversy in an account, the parties must by their own accord set up for right reason the reason of some arbitrator or judge . . . for want of a right reason constituted by nature" (*L*, 23). Again, it is important to point out that, for Hobbes, these disputes, and the differences between individuals from which they arise, are grounded in human nature and the human sensory experience of the external world. Passions underlie speech just as they lie at the root of voluntary motions, and "because the constitution of a man's body is in continual mutation, it is impossible that all the same things should always cause in him the same appetites and aversions; much less can all men consent in the desire of almost any one and the same object."[67] Given the way in which the diversity of human experiences and objects of human passion can lead to conflict and war, the need for an arbitrarily imposed sovereign nominalist becomes all the more urgent.

A skeptical understanding of the bases of human experience, then, does not lead Hobbes to support toleration on principle, though of course pragmatic or prudential concerns may make such a policy possible, even advisable.[68] In explicating the rights of civil sovereignty, Hobbes includes "judg[ing] of what doctrines are fit to be taught [the citizens] . . . as a thing necessary to peace" (*L*, 113–14). "We are to remember, that the right of choosing what doctrines are fit for peace, and to be taught the subjects, is in all commonwealths inseparably annexed . . . to the sovereign power civil . . . therefore Christian kings are still the supreme pastors of their people, and have the power to ordain what pastors they please, to teach the church, that is, to teach the people committed to their charge" (366).

---

67. *L*, 28; see also *Elements of Law*, 23.
68. See Remer, *Humanism*, chap. 4; also see Remer, "Hobbes, the Rhetorical Tradition, and Toleration." Eldon Eisenach also notes the prudential nature of Hobbesian toleration, pointing out that, while possible, it "requires one to place heavy burdens on the person of the sovereign" (*Two Worlds of Liberalism*, 70).

Hobbes admits that conscience is beyond the reach of the sovereign, and that "no human law is intended to oblige the conscience of a man, but his actions only."[69] "A private man," he notes, "has always the liberty, because thought is free, to believe or not believe in his heart those acts that have been given out for miracles" (*L*, 300). In matters of public religious profession, though, the sovereign must provide authoritative guidance to avoid the potential anarchy of private interpretation.[70] "We are not every one, to make our own private reason, or conscience, but the public reason, that is, the reason of God's supreme lieutenant, judge; and indeed we have made him judge already, if we have given him a sovereign power, to do all that is necessary for our peace and defense . . . when it comes to confession of that faith, the private reason must submit to the public" (L, 300). Hobbes asserts that men "can never by their own wisdom come into the knowledge of what God hath spoken and commanded to be observed." Instead, they "for the most part, rather draw the Scripture to their own sense, than follow the true sense of Scripture."[71]

In the third part of *Leviathan*, Hobbes moves away from natural principles of reason toward the idea of a Christian commonwealth. He grounds God's sovereignty, not in creation (like Locke) but in God's irresistible power, and presents a more particular analogy of Israel as God's civil sovereignty, founded and based upon the consent of the Israelites to God's government.[72] "I find the kingdom of God to signify . . . a kingdom properly so named, constituted by the votes of the people of Israel in peculiar manner, wherein they chose God for their king, by covenant made with him" (*L*, 272). Analytically, this argument mirrors Hobbes's political model of the contractual basis of legitimate authority and the impossibility of laws binding the sovereign. Moses, by this account, performed the role of sovereign, and Aaron's ecclesiastical authority was subject to Moses' sovereignty.[73] In these latter days, however, we no longer have miracles, prophets, or direct communication with God, and our only guide is Scripture. The same reasoning that led Hobbes

---

69. *Elements of Law*, 114.

70. The best recent treatment of Hobbes on private interpretation is Farr, "Atomes of Scripture." See also Gary L. McDowell, "Private Conscience and Public Order: Hobbes and *The Federalist*," Polity 25 (1993): 421–44.

71. Hobbes, *Behemoth*, 46, 51.

72. *L*, 235–36; 318–22; see also Hobbes, *De Cive*, 204–10. See also *The Lawes of England*, 1–7.

73. *L*, 320, 321; Hobbes, *De Cive*, 204–10.

to absolute civil sovereignty argues for that sovereignty in religious affairs as well, to avoid a spiritual state of nature. The sovereign must decide what constitutes Scripture. Skepticism has little to do with toleration or freedom.

Skepticism, for many seventeenth-century tolerationists, provided a ready source of ammunition in opposition to the claims of divine right made by Anglican royalists and the claims of infallibility made by Roman Catholics, as well as the more general structures of (political, social, ecclesiastical) authority in society. Still, we must remember the importance of political context and the constant concern for social order elaborated in the previous section, the concern voiced by many about the social consequences of such skepticism. Not only did antiskepticism often provide the basis for antitolerationist arguments, but skeptics themselves were far from united as to the political implications of their epistemological claims. For every John Saltmarsh and William Walwyn, raising doubts about orthodox theological positions and arguing from such uncertainty for broadly tolerationist politics, there were antiskeptic, antitolerationists like Samuel Rutherford and Thomas Edwards, as well as skeptical, starkly Erastian advocates of uniformity such as Hobbes, concerned as much with preserving social order as making accurate statements about the nature of truth and human knowledge.

MODUS VIVENDI POLITICS: THE MINIMAL, BUT CRUCIAL, NATURE OF EARLY MODERN TOLERATION

Despite the fact that I used the term "perfectionist" in the previous section to describe a type of religious commitment that often came into conflict with proponents of uniformity or orthodoxy, I hasten to add that the aim of such religious dissidents tended, in the political sphere, to be far more modest than the word "perfectionist" might initially suggest. Religious perfectionists, and tolerationists more generally, sought primarily to be left alone to pursue their own visions of what God required of them. In their view, a great step *forward* in the creation of an authentic religious commitment required a great *constriction* in the role of civil government in the religious realm. Tolerationists ascribed to civil government such basic functions as securing minimal conditions of social peace and order. In their view, such a properly defined government would maintain society's cohesion even if deep divisions on ultimate issues persisted between its citizens, and would not require individuals to sacrifice individual conscience for the sake of communal uniformity.

Roger Williams provides an especially clear example of this political minimalism: in his search for an ever purer church, Williams stripped government of functions long-associated with civil magistracy, namely the enforcement and promulgation of the true religion. The end result sought by Williams was a government that safeguarded the voluntary associations of individuals, whose churches he characterized, as we have seen, as "like unto a corporation, society, or company of East India or Turkey merchants" (*Bloudy Tenent*, 73). Recall Williams's preface to the *Bloudy Tenent*: "All civil states . . . are proved essentially civil, and therefore not judges, governors, or defenders of the spiritual or Christian worship" (3). For Williams (as for most of his fellow tolerationists), what was most important was that people sought salvation, as best they could understand its requirements on their lives: such a position (in their view), far from undermining true religion, was its most effective guarantor.

Tolerationists, then, sought a sort of "negative liberty"—noncoercion and state neutrality in the sectarian strife of the seventeenth century[74]—to allow individuals to live out their varying convictions about salvation. As opposed to many contemporary liberal theorists, early modern tolerationists did not praise autonomy for its own sake, but only in contexts in which it enabled one to act in religiously responsible ways to secure the ultimate good of personal salvation. To their opponents, of course, the definition of "religiously responsible" was highly problematic, and the absence of any social consensus as to what constituted such behavior was generally taken to signal the onset of licentiousness and rebellion.

Tolerationists, then, had a relatively minimal notion of what government should do. They tended to focus their notions of community on *civil* issues or general Christian morality, rather than contested sectarian doctrines. They did not view toleration as a means to effect widespread social agreement on religious issues, nor did they foresee the eradication of widespread hostility to dissenters or, necessarily, broader notions of social equality between dissenters and adherents of dominant faiths. Recall the limitations inherent in

74. I emphasize the neutrality concerning *sectarianism*, as opposed to a more general notion of state neutrality common among twentieth-century liberal theorists. As we have seen, most tolerationists did not object to the state fostering general Christian (or, more accurately, Protestant) values as long as the state did not persecute in the service of sectarian doctrines.

the Toleration Act of 1689, and the social and political monopoly achieved (indeed, foreseen and intended by the founder) in early Pennsylvania. If people were given the freedom to pursue their own conceptions of religious truth without the interference, let alone persecution, of government, tolerationists held, then a great good would have been achieved.

Now this political minimalism that I am identifying as fundamental to the early modern tolerationist program does have a type of dynamic to it, and the power and ongoing consequences of tolerationist victories in the seventeenth century are undeniable. Clearly the achievement of the basic rights of assembly and worship paved the way for more "positive" developments in the history of formerly persecuted groups. Despite the limitations in the Toleration Act, that legislation provided the basis for further attempts to expand the scope of religious freedom. By exempting Protestant Dissenters from English penal laws, under certain conditions, Parliament did not merely end one era (that of persecution and a program of religious uniformity), but it also, probably unintentionally, *set in motion* a movement for broader religious liberty.[75] During the decade following the Act's passage, Quakers were successful, after years of political struggle, in achieving the right to make affirmations, rather than swear oaths, in legal proceedings. Such a struggle was one step removed from persecution, but it involved the ability to exercise one's conscientious beliefs in at least one public setting without penalties.[76]

In the nineteenth century, Parliament finally repealed the Test Act, which had prevented English Catholics and non-Trinitarian Protestants, not to mention Jews, from serving in public office. Individuals had not been, strictly speaking, "persecuted" under the Test Act. They had, however, been denied full participation in public life on account of their religious beliefs. These broader notions of religious liberty began slowly, proceeded haltingly, and remained largely focused on the political, institutional, and legal realms, eschewing more expansive notions of social equality and acceptance. What we in the late twentieth century call liberalism, insofar as it traces some of its key elements to seventeenth-century political debate, remains largely institutional and state-centered in its approach to politics.

75. For the historical development of progressively more expansive notions of liberty, see Schochet, "From Persecution to 'Toleration,'" and Webb, "From Toleration to Religious Liberty," both in *Liberty Secured? Britain Before and After 1688*, ed. J. R. Jones (Stanford, Calif., 1992).
76. See Kirby, "The Quakers' Efforts."

What tolerationists sought, then, was a way of living together—literally, a *modus vivendi*—a way of negotiating differences without resorting to the bloodshed that had littered the European landscape for years. Herein lies one of the great legacies of toleration for the history of liberal thought and practice: the recognition that, as John Rawls would later put it, societies would continue to be characterized, not just by pluralism, but by *reasonable* pluralism (*PL*, xxvi–xxvii). Since the development and use of reason was a responsibility placed upon humans by God himself, tolerationists argued, one should not expect that all would reach the same conclusions about issues of ultimate significance, given the variety of human understandings and the different capacities of various individuals.[77] The variety of ethnic and religious communities that settled in Pennsylvania during the early years of colonization; the early years of Rhode Island and its often-tenuous hold on public order; the proliferation of sects during the 1640s and 1650s in England, illustrate this phenomenon graphically: tolerationist policies there sought not state proselytization, but the creation of a public space in which individuals and groups of differing persuasions could live out their own conceptions of religious truth and the demands it placed on human life.

CONCLUSION

These discussions—the question of social order and the importance of political context, the heavily Christian nature of tolerationist arguments and thus the uneasy relationship between skepticism and toleration, and the political minimalism represented by the "negative" nature of *modus vivendi* arrangements in the early modern world—highlight some of the more overarching lessons that a revisitation of early modern toleration debates teaches. Each represents the broader view afforded us when we draw back from the historical material and look for new insights on, or correctives to conventional understandings of, the history of toleration in the seventeenth century.

Toleration debates, we must remember, took place in highly specific, situated political contexts. In many of these contexts, and for good reason, antitolerationists deemed the social order to be extremely fragile and tolera-

77. As Thomas Paine put it in the following century, "I do not believe that any two men, on what are called doctrinal points, think alike who think at all" (*Rights of Man*, ed. Eric Foner [1792; New York, 1984], 271).

tion as threatening anarchy and chaos. Skepticism and religious perfectionism often contributed to a weakening of religious uniformity and political hierarchy, although generalizations about the link between philosophical or theological perspectives and political positions must be made with great caution. Finally, we should remember that the tolerationist agenda was in a key sense limited to a few basic propositions: salvation was the ultimate good; personal assent was necessary for salvation to be effected; and individuals and groups convinced of one or another route to salvation ought to be permitted to pursue those routes, without fear of persecution or imprisonment.

PART TWO

Toleration Across Time:
Contemporary Issues in
Theory and Practice

7

TOLERATION AND POLITICAL LIBERALISM

John Rawls's Shrinking Liberty of Conscience

The tension between liberalism and religion, whether perceived or real, is age-old. As we have seen throughout this study, the early liberal struggle for religious toleration attacked the close association of civil and ecclesiastical authority. Its opponents viewed this campaign (rightly, in many ways) as destructive of the kind of religious uniformity that underlay social solidarity, communal ties, and basic moral conduct.[1] Years later, Alexis de Tocqueville noted the important role played by religion in restraining individualistic, potentially hedonistic values in the nineteenth-century United States.[2] In recent years, works of religious or communitarian commentary have often criticized liberalism for producing atomistic individuals who lack affective ties, faith commitments, or ethical concerns transcending individual (usually short-term) preference.[3] As the twentieth century drew to a close, renewed interest in the relationship between religion and liberalism raised both practical and

1. Claims of this sort were ubiquitous in antitolerationist campaigns throughout the seventeenth century. If a magistrate could not coerce in matters of religion, the argument went, it was difficult to see how compulsion could be acceptable in any area of human endeavour: "If liberty be granted in [heresy], we know no cause why men that can in such a handsome way pretend conscience for it, should be denied liberty to run into excess and riot" (Church of Scotland, *Solemn testimony*, 7). "When men may do anything they think right, they will go near to think any thing right," wrote Thomas Ashenden during the Exclusion Crisis (*No Penalty, No Peace*, 13, also 232ff.).

2. Alexis de Tocqueville, *Democracy in America*, ed. Phillips Bradley (1848; New York, 1945), vol. 1, chap. 17, pp. 310–25.

3. See, for example, Robert Bellah et al., *Habits of the Heart: Individualism and Commitment in American Life* (New York, 1985); Alasdair MacIntyre, *After Virtue: A Study in Moral Theory* (Notre Dame, 1981); Christopher Lasch, *The Culture of Narcissism: American Life in an Age of Diminishing Expectations* (New York, 1979); and Sandel, *Democracy's Discontent*.

theoretical questions about the potential degrees of accommodation between the two.[4] Issues of accommodation invariably raise issues of conscience, as citizens of liberal democracies seek to live out their faith commitments while retaining the hard-won separation of civil and spiritual power bequeathed to them by earlier generations of theorists and political actors.

John Rawls is the preeminent liberal theorist of our time, locating his "political liberalism" as the culmination of three hundred years of theorizing about the good society, a theorizing that is rooted in the seventeenth-century struggle for religious toleration. More radically, however, Rawls makes the ambitious claim that "were justice as fairness to make an overlapping consensus possible it would *complete* and *extend* the movement of thought that began three centuries ago with the gradual acceptance of the principle of toleration and led to the nonconfessional state and equal liberty of conscience" (*PL*, 154; emphasis added). Such a bold statement of historical and contemporary import demands close scrutiny.

In this chapter, I argue that Rawls's "completion and extension" of liberty of conscience represents, instead, a retreat from the philosophical and political foundations of that movement. My exposition relies heavily on evidence from the toleration debates that have played such an important role in this project, and which occupy a formative historical role for Rawls.[5] Religious toleration, as we have seen, represented one of the most persistently divisive political issues of the seventeenth century. Although tolerationists were arguing against the *legal* prohibition of certain forms of worship

---

4. For the more theoretical aspects of this issue, see Robert Booth Fowler, *Unconventional Partners: Religion and Liberal Culture in the United States* (Grand Rapids, Mich., 1989); Michael J. Perry, *Love and Power: The Role of Religion and Morality in American Politics* (New York, 1991); Kent Greenawalt, *Religious Convictions and Political Choice* (New York, 1988); the essays collected in Patrick Neal, *Liberalism and Its Discontents* (New York, 1997); and the seminal study *Christ and Culture* by H. Richard Niebuhr (New York, 1951). For more straightforwardly political treatments in the accommodationist mode, see Stephen L. Carter, *The Culture of Disbelief: How American Law and Politics Trivialize Religious Devotion* (New York, 1993), and Richard John Neuhaus, *The Naked Public Square: Religion and Democracy in America* (Grand Rapids, Mich., 1984).

5. Clearly Rawls is attempting to *broaden* the notion of conscience in order to secure liberal freedoms, and we should not expect him wholly to echo the commitments of early modern thinkers. If his system requires *repudiating* basic arguments for liberty of conscience, however, his ambitious assertion must certainly be cast into doubt.

As this book went to press, I became aware of a parallel, though somewhat differently focused, argument taking issue with Rawls's claims to having completed and extended the history of liberty of conscience. See Wolfson, "Two Theories of Toleration."

and not the more abstract notions of acceptable political justifications that animate Rawls's attention to public reason and the overlapping consensus, the insights of early modern tolerationists into the nature of belief and the bonds of political society shed light on Rawls's ambitious claims for his political liberalism.

My argument will be fairly straightforward. Rawls's insistence on the use of public reason forces individuals with non-mainstream comprehensive doctrines (Rawls's stand-in term for fundamental religious, philosophical, or moral foundations)[6] to choose between several alternatives: (1) to *change* the comprehensive doctrine to fit the conditions of publicity; (2) to *dissemble*, manufacturing a "public" justification for political stances, thus disguising one's true motives; (3) through civil disobedience or other direct action, to seek to change the parameters of public debate (to the end that a marginal position will eventually become widely accepted); or (4) to temporarily violate the strictures of public reason by advancing comprehensively derived views, so long as he or she follows such a violation with sufficient public reasons in due course. The first two of these solutions, however, run counter to the historical development of liberty of conscience that Rawls seeks to extend—the development of liberty of conscience that I have traced in this book—while the third fails because of Rawls's pervasive emphasis on stability in *Political Liberalism*. The fourth possibility would, if valid, hold out the promise of effectively mediating between comprehensive doctrines and publicly reasonable political justifications. This position, however, misrepresents the nature of moral reasoning and comprehensive doctrines themselves. In conclusion, I argue that underlying Rawls's liberalism is, at best, a split between belief and action that has historically worked against liberty of conscience; and at worst a scheme of repression and self-censorship which renders comprehensive doctrines meaningless.

---

6. This chapter, following the concerns of the larger project, will take issue with the Rawlsian exclusion of religion from politics, but equally cogent critiques could be cited of the more generally exclusive nature of Rawlsian politics and neutralist liberalism more generally. See, for example, Ed Wingenbach, "Unjust Context: The Priority of Stability in Rawls' Contextualized Theory of Justice," *AJPS* 43 (1999): 213–32. See also Stanley Fish, "Mission Impossible: Settling the Just Bounds Between Church and State," *Columbia Law Review* 97 (1997), in which Fish criticizes neutralist liberals for creating "an epistemological criminal class that includes racists, anti-Semites, and uncompromising religionists in an undifferentiated mix joined together by an obdurate refusal to 'listen to reason'" (2283).

RELIGIOUS TOLERATION AND LIBERTY OF CONSCIENCE IN THE RAWLSIAN SYSTEM

Liberty of conscience is, for Rawls, firmly ensconced within the first principle of justice (*TOJ*, 61; *PL*, 5), and he provides two main routes to this liberty. The first utilizes the original position, in which individuals under a "veil of ignorance" choose principles of justice. Since no one knows which religious or moral beliefs he or she might hold in society, Rawls argues, and since all know the importance of such doctrines (through general knowledge about "the laws of human psychology" [*TOJ*, 137]), the participants must provide for liberty of conscience. "They cannot take chances with their liberty by permitting the dominant religious or moral doctrine to persecute or to suppress others if it wishes" (*TOJ*, 207; see also *PL*, 310–11). Rawls, however, admits that a solely analytical or strategic defense of liberty of conscience "is not an argument' (*PL*, 310–11). At a more philosophical level, liberty of conscience serves as a necessary prerequisite for individuals to exercise their moral powers, to develop, revise, and pursue their conceptions of the good over the course of a lifetime (*PL*, 335; also 310–15). Although liberty of conscience may be restricted in the interests of order and security (*TOJ*, 212–14; *PL*, 341), justice as fairness requires a broad tolerationist commitment in order to function meaningfully.[7]

Religious toleration and liberty of conscience also play a crucial historical role in Rawlsian liberalism. At the outset of *Political Liberalism*, Rawls locates early modern toleration debates as singularly formative of contemporary liberal societies. "The historical origin of political liberalism (and of liberalism more generally) is the Reformation and its aftermath, with the long controversies over religious toleration in the sixteenth and seventeenth centuries" (*PL*, xxiv). On this point, Rawls is clearly right. The importance of toleration debates for Rawls is difficult to overstate, since the presence of a variety of competing comprehensive doctrines in society sets the political agenda that his theory seeks to address. According to Rawls, the victory of toleration in the seventeenth century resulted in the acceptance, not only of pluralism, but

7. Toleration as necessary for human development is echoed by David A.J. Richards, who asserts that "conscience and the social contract rest . . . on an underlying political ideal of the moral sovereignty of the people." He also suggests Rawls's reasoning from the original position: "Each person would reasonably demand [the inalienable right to conscience] as a protection of freedom and rationality, the highest-order good." See Richards, *Toleration and the Constitution*, 98, 101.

of *reasonable* pluralism (xxiv–xxv); not simply doctrinal diversity *in se*, but the further claim that such diversity is an inescapable (and not lamentable) fact of human existence springing from the very nature of human reason.[8] Designed for a society founded not upon "agreement on a general and comprehensive religious, philosophical, or moral doctrine" (xxv) but on far more restrained notions such as political allegiance and loyalty, Rawls's political liberalism does not concern itself with "general problems of moral philosophy" (xxviii).

For Rawls, the *overlapping consensus* and *public reason* play key roles in mediating between comprehensive doctrines and day-to-day political arguments. The exercise of political power is acceptable only if undertaken for reasons that all citizens, whatever their comprehensive doctrines, can affirm (*TOJ*, viii, sec. 3; *PL*, 137ff.) Political justice, for Rawls, is "freestanding" and not tied to any comprehensive doctrine; rather, it receives support from a variety of reasonable comprehensive doctrines (the overlapping consensus), each from its own perspective.[9] He makes quite clear that this overlapping consensus grounding the political conception of justice is not merely a *modus vivendi* (*PL*, 146–54; IPE, xliii) but a *moral* concept, a common ground necessary for the functioning of a political society made up of diverse individual and group views of the good.

The concept of public reason denotes the guidelines for inquiry that impose limits on political argument.[10] Since reasonable pluralism is a fact, and an

8. Here Rawls echoes Madison, in Federalist 10. A commitment to political liberty, along with a proper understanding of the workings of the human mind, makes diverse conceptions of the good a fact of social life. As Madison put it, "As long as the reason of man continues fallible, and he is at liberty to exercise it, different opinions will be formed" (*The Federalist Papers*, ed. Clinton Rossiter [New York, 1961], 78).

9. Rawls often vacillates between posing the overlapping consensus as an ideal (*PL*, 154) and using it as a descriptive term. On balance, though, his account seems to indicate that he thinks that an overlapping consensus, if an imperfect one, obtains in mature liberal democracies.

10. Public reason is analogous to Bruce Ackerman's neutrality principle. As Ackerman puts it, "Nobody has the right to vindicate political authority by asserting a privileged insight into the moral universe which is denied the rest of us" (*Social Justice*, 10–11). From a supposedly more receptive position on the acceptability of religious reasoning in public discourse, Kent Greenawalt expresses a similar position. Although in certain cases reliance on religious convictions is "appropriate for ordinary citizens," he argues (and legislators as well, but only occasionally for judges), such reliance is "often an inapt form of public dialogue" (*Religious Convictions*, 12). See note 24.

The literature on public reason more generally—most of it highly critical of Rawls—is immense, intertwined with critiques of neutralist liberalism more generally, and not germane to the narrower focus of this chapter. A useful starting point is Neal, *Liberalism and Its Discontents*, esp. chaps. 5, 6.

overlapping consensus supporting a freestanding conception of justice exists or nearly exists between those with differing comprehensive doctrines, and since legitimate political power is consensual, citizens must constrain themselves in the sort of justifications they offer in support of their proposals for the use of political power. In other words, they must refer solely to political values and/or widely accessible forms of reasoning. In framing political arguments, Rawls asserts, the liberal citizen must appeal solely to elements of society's shared, freestanding political conception of justice. This insistence on political justifications is not merely a strategic counsel offered by Rawls, but a criterion of reciprocity, representing the duty of citizenship and "civic friendship" (*PL*, 217; IPE, li). It recognizes the politics of reasonable pluralism.

DILEMMAS FOR RELIGIOUS OR NON-MAINSTREAM COMPREHENSIVE DOCTRINES

Many of the comprehensive doctrines held by citizens in liberal societies do indeed, as part of an overlapping consensus, promote the Rawlsian view of political justice. The three examples provided by Rawls, however (free faith, philosophical autonomy, and pluralism [*PL*, 145]), all share foundations that could be loosely termed "liberal." Although Rawls disavows claims to "comprehensive" liberalism, he does not attempt to show how marginal philosophical, religious, or political doctrines (e.g., varieties of participatory democracy, religious fundamentalism, or radical skepticism) could affirm the political conception of justice as do those comprehensive views making up the overlapping consensus. If one's comprehensive doctrine is not part of the overlapping consensus, one's ability to affirm such a doctrine in public life will be radically diminished once the limitations of public reason are imposed upon public debate. For example, Rawls rules out, *a priori*, a principled and comprehensive opposition to abortion. An extended quotation here seems necessary to illustrate the nature of this exclusion.

> Suppose . . . that we consider the question [of abortion in adult women] in terms of these three important political values: the due respect for human life, the ordered reproduction of political society over time . . . and finally the equality of women as citizens. (There

are, of course, other important political values besides these.) Now I believe any reasonable balance of these three values will give a woman a duly qualified right to decide whether or not to end her pregnancy during the first trimester. The reason for this is that at this early stage of pregnancy the political value of the equality of women is overriding. . . . Other political values, if tallied in, would not, I think, affect this conclusion. A reasonable balance may allow her such a right beyond this, at least in certain circumstances. . . . [A]ny comprehensive doctrine that leads to a balance of political values excluding that duly qualified right [to abortion] in the first trimester is to that extent unreasonable. . . . Thus, assuming that this question is either a constitutional essential or a matter of basic justice, we would go against the ideal of public reason if we voted from a comprehensive doctrine that denied this right. (*PL*, 243–44)[11]

Rawls's sweeping dismissal of any grounds to dissent on so vital an issue of public policy raises the central issue of the relationship between public reason and comprehensive doctrines. What option does Rawls provide the individual with a marginal comprehensive doctrine—say, religious fundamentalism of a Christian, Jewish, or Islamic variety; even someone holding a humanistic prolife position—in the public sphere? How do these options reflect upon his ambitious claims about completing and extending the movement for liberty of conscience? Rawls seems to leave four possibilities open for such a citizen. I shall consider them in turn.

Option 1. Alter one's comprehensive doctrine. If an individual's comprehensive doctrine falls outside the overlapping consensus and thus fails to affirm the political conception, Rawls might insist that he or she change it. This is in some ways the most straightforward, if most drastic, solution: in other words, to become liberal (one might say, reasonable in the Rawlsian sense), rather than *fundamentalist*, Christian.[12] This option, however, is quite

11. Rawls has since attempted to downplay the significance of this quotation (IPE, lv–lvi, note 31), denying that it represents "an argument for a right to abortion in the first trimester" (lv). Nothing in his disclaimer, however, alters the substance of my argument here.

12. E. A. Goerner accuses Rawlsian liberals of insisting on just this transformation, the adoption of "rationalistic liberal ethics," in his critique of Eamonn Callan's version of liberal political education. See his "Forcing the Free to Be Correctly Free," *Review of Politics* 58 (1996): 38, and Eamonn Callan, "Political Liberalism and Political Education," *Review of Politics* 58 (1996): 5–33.

likely impossible from a psychological point of view. Given the nature of belief, individuals are simply not able to change their comprehensive doctrines at will. Furthermore, this claim about human psychology represents one of the most fundamental arguments utilized in the early modern toleration debates to which Rawls attaches such importance. As we have seen, those seeking religious freedom argued that conscience and belief, the bases upon which religiously-based comprehensive doctrines are built, are functions not of the will but of the *understanding*. Thus it was *a priori* impossible to coerce belief, since belief change is not a voluntary act. Only reflection and persuasion, they argued, could bring about such an alteration.

To be sure, early modern authors were opposing "corporal punishment" and not the philosophical arguments about public reason that Rawls proposes. The option of "altering one's comprehensive doctrine," though, does suggest belief change as the price of inclusion, so to speak, into full membership in political society. For Rawls, as we have seen, early modern toleration debates were instrumental in the historical and conceptual development of political liberalism. Those seeking religious liberty, however, argued that persuasion alone was the way to deal with the divisive issues raised by belief and conscience. If evidence (reason, revelation, or any combination of the two) persuaded one to hold a given belief, one would hold it. But altering one's view on the basis of a command (be it the command of a political ruler or the threat of exclusion from public life more generally) was impossible. One might be forced to act in certain ways, but beliefs themselves are beyond the power of individuals to change: only the persuasion of the senses (reason or revelation) can lead to a moral doctrine worthy of the name.

Perhaps, however, there is another possibility. Perhaps Rawls has rejected this view of conscience and persuasion, what we might call "evidentialism,"[13] in favor of a pure choice model of morality. Indeed, Rawls does say that people may change or revise their conceptions of the good "if they so desire" (*PL*, 30), that "each person is free to plan his life as he pleases" (*TOJ*, 447), and that citizens "regard themselves as self-authenticating sources of valid claims" (*PL*, 32). Michael Sandel argues that Rawls (and other deontological liberals) views comprehensive doctrines as strictly "choosable" like other market goods, and that justifications of morality, for Rawls, essentially boil

---

13. The term is Nicholas Wolterstorff's. See his "Locke's Philosophy of Religion," in *The Cambridge Companion to Locke*, ed. Vere Chappell (New York, 1994).

down to "second-order desire."[14] If this is the case, these historical criticisms might not apply.

If Sandel is correct, if Rawlsian morality is pure desire, then it seems much closer to a will-based faculty. One could, conceivably, change one's doctrine, and the arguments about psychological impossibility would not hold.[15] But would this represent the completion and extension of liberty of conscience? After all, that movement attempted (and continues to attempt) to *increase* the areas of public life in which people were not penalized for the comprehensive doctrines that they did, in fact, hold. If this option is what Rawls has in mind—if he attempts to solve the clash between comprehensive doctrines and public reason by insisting on the eradication of non-mainstream doctrines—then he either requires a psychological impossibility or retreats from the aims of the movement for liberty of conscience.

Option 2. Dissemble. If it is not possible to alter one's comprehensive doctrine at will, and such a doctrine does not make up part of the overlapping consensus, one might dissemble, manufacturing a political reason for one's position when in fact such a position is derived entirely from a comprehensive doctrine. Let me clarify my use of the terms "manufacture" and "dissemble": they apply when an individual either advances a political justification as definitive when in fact her intentions derive from a comprehensive doctrine, or advocates as definitive a justification he either does not believe or believes only marginally. In this case, an individual is not merely offering those who might hold different views *additional* reasons for supporting a given political action, but misrepresenting *his* or *her* reasons for supporting such action. In this case, the problem lies not so much in whether the "manufactured" reason

14. See Sandel, *Liberalism and the Limits of Justice*, 163; more generally, pp. 154–64. Sandel's more specific critique of Rawls on this issue is found in "Freedom of Conscience or Freedom of Choice?" in *Articles of Faith, Articles of Peace: The Religious Liberty Clauses and the American Public Philosophy*, ed. James Davison Hunter and Os Guinness (Washington, D.C., 1990). In "Religion in a Free Society," also in *Articles of Faith, Articles of Peace,* Charles Taylor distinguishes this "liberal freedom" (individual as chooser of private life plan) from a more robust "civic freedom" emphasizing common self-government (94–98).

15. I should add that, in my own view, although Rawls's terminology of pleasing and desiring is oblique in these passages, he does not conceive of comprehensive doctrines purely in terms of the market metaphor imputed to him by Sandel. Even the example of conversion (*PL*, 30) does not prove Sandel's charge, since conversion operates on a persuasion model. Instead, the importance of choice in conceptions of the good seems, for Rawls, to involve safeguarding the working of the human mind and the fact of reasonable pluralism in the social and political realms. Rawls focuses on the political manifestations of belief, at which level the language of choice seems apt.

is a "good" (persuasive, public) reason, but whether it is actually relevant to the individual putting it forward as his or her own. A clear contemporary example would lie in the individual whose opposition to abortion derives from religious doctrine, claiming that the potential citizenship of fetuses entitled them to constitutional protections of the right to life, and that this constitutional claim formed the basis of his or her prolife position.[16]

Now political deliberation has never been, nor need it be, an exercise in transparency. Certainly one might advocate a *number of reasons* for a given political action, some of which are more congenial to that individual than others. Rawls's aim in framing conditions of publicity is in some ways an admirable search for consensus about how political debate should proceed. His commitment to reciprocity and sincerity requires that "we sincerely believe that the reasons we offer for our political action may reasonably be accepted by other citizens as a justification of those actions" (IPE, xlvi). The issue of liberty of conscience arises, I suggest, when certain reasons are excluded *a priori* by the strictures of public reason. Given that we speak politically, not only to bring about public action but also to give voice to the values underlying our political views, Rawls's ambitious claims about completing and extending liberty of conscience must be cast into doubt if individuals feel compelled to advocate as definitive reasons they do not believe or that they find only marginally convincing.

By excluding such views from political debate, Rawls also likely encourages disingenuousness and a tendency toward obfuscation or at least duplicity.[17]

16. I distinguish this manufacturing of reasons from that which occurs when an individual states *outright* his or her comprehensively derived position, and then proceeds to provide public reasons for the same position. This course of action would fall under Rawls's "proviso," what I call option 4, and I discuss it in turn.

17. It seems likely that, as Kenneth A. Strike suggests, the unwillingness or inability of political liberals to distinguish *between* comprehensive doctrines—taking instead the more drastic step of barring all from public debate—contributes to the likelihood of this dissembling. Rawls and others perhaps fear the impact of comprehensive doctrines in politics (which, after all, are all around us in actual political debates) too much and trust too little in the ability of individuals with different comprehensive doctrines to engage in what Strike calls "argumentative reciprocity." As Strike further argues, such a dialogic approach to moral and religious rhetoric in political debate would distinguish (as Rawls apparently does not) between "arguing from the perspective of a comprehensive doctrine and seeking to advantage its adherents."

Without endorsing his approach *in toto*, I am inclined to agree with Strike that such a context-based, dialogic approach to finding an *emergent* overlapping consensus, rather than insisting upon a strictly freestanding (putatively existing) one, better respects freedom of conscience. See Strike, "Must Liberal Citizens Be Reasonable?" *Review of Politics* 58 (1996): 41–51. Fish, on the other hand, provocatively denies the existence of *any* common ground where such divisive issues present themselves: see "Mission Impossible," esp. secs. 1 and 4.

Such dissembling would be contrary to Rawls's intentions, given his commitment to civility and reciprocity on moral, not simply legal, grounds (*PL*, 217); but dissembling or duplicity are clearly possible in Rawlsian politics. If liberty of conscience is a necessary requirement for the exercise of moral powers, it seems difficult to conceive that the completion and extension of such liberty involves masking the moral foundations of one's political reasoning. We might not be surprised to see such masking condoned by theorists of a *modus vivendi* state (as Rawls portrays it), but it sits more awkwardly with Rawls's robust notions of citizenship, reciprocity, and liberty of conscience.[18]

Like that surrounding the nature of belief, this general issue of duplicity and dissembling also animated early modern toleration debates. Unlike calls for the alteration of beliefs, which go against the entire historical trend supporting liberty of conscience in *psychological* terms, the potential for public dissembling drew the ire of proponents of religious freedom on ethical and political grounds, as producing a disingenuous citizenry. Compelling an individual into a state church, participants in these debates argued, forced individuals into hypocrisy by making them perform actions in which they did not believe.

For early modern supporters of religious freedom, compulsion was seen as "the way to increase not the number of converts, but hypocrites."[19] Penn and Locke similarly condemned persecution and compulsory church membership as forcing individuals to profess beliefs that they did not hold. Although seventeenth-century authors saw the more specifically religious consequences of such dissembling as much in other- as in this-worldly terms, the more general point regarding the undesirability of such disingenuous conduct remains. Forcing an individual into a mode of reasoning or public action that he or she does not accept, I suggest, is much like forcing an individual to affirm a religious or philosophical creed. Excluding individuals who refuse to so affirm from participating in the public life of their communities, tolerationists argued, led to dissembling and hypocrisy, and dissemblers and hypocrites were not good citizens.[20] I do not think the term "compelling" is too

18. I stress the words "as Rawls portrays it": I argue in the following chapter that Rawls does not give the *modus vivendi* model enough credit, that the *modus vivendi* model, as he sees it, is (in Patrick Neal's words) "the creation of its critics . . . created for the purpose of allowing them to explain what they are not" (*Liberalism and Its Critics*, 191).

19. *Toleration Justified*, 5.

20. See also Busher, *Religions Peace*, in Underhill, *Tracts*, 22; Walwyn, *A Whisper in the Ear of Mr. Thomas Edwards*, 5; *The Plea of the Harmless Oppressed*, 9; *A Discourse of Toleration*, 6; and Paston, *A Discourse of Penal Laws*, 32–33.

strong or misleading here: acceptance of public reason is, for Rawls, the price of inclusion in political debate. Without accepting its rhetorical constraints on argument, one is not admitted to the table of Rawlsian political dialogue. I return to this point at the conclusion of this essay, noting that Rawls seeks a far more sweeping (and, from the standpoint of religious liberty, trouble-some) self-repression instead of legal prohibition to achieve the exclusion of comprehensive doctrines from public debate.

Option 3. Engage in some sort of demonstrative or confrontational activity to attempt to change the parameters of public debate.[21] Civil disobedience, (and other activities of its sort), attempts to make formerly marginal ideas part of mainstream political discourse. Rawls addresses the important role of civil disobedience and conscientious refusal in *A Theory of Justice* (*TOJ*, 363–91). While supporting the idea of protest to appeal to society's shared sense of justice, Rawls's definition of civil disobedience explicitly rules out action on the basis of comprehensive doctrines: civil disobedience is "a public, nonviolent conscientious yet political act contrary to law usually done with the aim of bringing about a change in the law or policies of the government [in which] one invokes the commonly shared conception of justice that under-lies the political order" (*TOJ*, 365). Conscientious refusal is a broader notion, consisting of "noncompliance . . . not necessarily based on political principles; it may be founded on religious or other principles at variance with the consti-tutional order" (*TOJ*, 369). While supporting the right of individuals to engage in civil disobedience, however, Rawls ignores (or, implicitly, rules out) religiously based conscientious refusal: the single concrete example he pro-vides "assume[s] that this [conscientious refusal] is based upon political and not upon religious and other principles" (*TOJ*, 377).

All mention of civil disobedience or conscientious refusal is absent from *Political Liberalism*. The focus instead is on stability, which constitutes a necessary precondition of political liberalism (*PL*, 38–40; 140–44).[22] The aim of insisting on public reason is largely to remove divisive and irreconcilable issues from politics (*PL*, 157), and the exclusion of highly contentious issues from Rawlsian politics is the price of political (and philosophical) stability.

21. I thank Sam Nelson for suggesting this third possibility to me.
22. Rawls emphasizes in IPE that "stability" refers always to "stability for the right reasons," that is, citizens acting from a conception of justice and not merely participating in *modus vivendi* arrangements (IPE, xxxix–xliii).

The emphasis on stability in *Political Liberalism* represents a departure from Rawls's earlier (if equivocal) support for such activities as civil disobedience or conscientious refusal. In *A Theory of Justice*, Rawls noted that in a well-ordered society one need not worry excessively about the appearance of intolerant sects (*TOJ*, 219). In *Political Liberalism*, from Rawls's first mention of the formative role of sixteenth and seventeenth-century religious wars (xxiv) to his discussion of the importance of securing citizens' compliance with just institutions (141) and the development of "trust and confidence" among citizens (86), one senses Rawls's anxiety about the stability of the political order. His discussion of the overlapping consensus is concerned with "how the well-ordered democratic society of justice as fairness may establish and preserve unity and stability given the reasonable pluralism characteristic of it" (*PL*, 133–34). Rawls's worrisome comments about the collapse of Weimar Germany, the rise of Hitler, and the ensuing Holocaust (IPE, lxi–lxii) further emphasize his concern about the failure of contemporary liberal societies to engage the support of political elites, not to mention their citizens more broadly.

Although political liberalism seeks to "bypass religion and philosophy's profoundest controversies," a major problem always remains "whenever someone insists . . . that certain questions are so fundamental that their being rightly settled justifies civil strife" (*PL*, 152). It seems likely, however, that fomenting a controlled amount of "civil strife," attempting to raise perceived injustices before an often-apathetic populace, is precisely what those engaging in civil disobedience or conscientious refusal are seeking; namely, the deliberate and purposive violation of accepted public standards often on the basis of a comprehensively derived critique of prevailing practices. Just prior to this discussion, Rawls suggests that such individuals are likely to favor "civil war" (*PL*, 151), thus ruling out any possibility of society countenancing their activities. There seems little room for principled resistance, or even symbolic protest, in Rawlsian theory. Here again, the departure from the tradition of conscience-based politics and dissent—which is replete with such principled action and which includes individuals and movements Rawls clearly admires (abolitionists and Martin Luther King, to name just two)—is striking.

Option 4. The Rawlsian Ideal. Restrict the utilization of one's comprehensive doctrine to elements that are in accord with public reason, allowing temporary violations of public reason only so long as they are followed with acceptable noncomprehensive justifications "in due course" (IPE, li). Perhaps the strong claim elaborated in option 1 overstates Rawls's aim. Certainly such a strong form is far from compatible with his claim to political liberalism's place at the pinnacle of three hundred years of liberty of conscience. In his support of abolitionists, Abraham Lincoln, and Martin Luther King, Jr., for example, Rawls seeks a more "inclusive" understanding of the limits of public reason, allowing individuals to violate public reason "provided they do this in ways that strengthen the ideal of public reason itself" (*PL*, 247). Rawls has subsequently formulated this "inclusive" view of public reason as a "proviso" allowing citizens to offer comprehensive reasons for political actions "provided that in due course public reasons, given by a reasonable political conception, are presented sufficient to support whatever the comprehensive doctrines are introduced to support" (IPE, li–lii). Public reason, then, seems simply to require that we *supplement* our comprehensive reasons with public ones.

This fourth option is also problematic, however, in a way that goes to the heart of the disjuncture between comprehensive doctrines that each, in their own way, affirm the political conception and the political conception itself. Rawls assumes that the various components of a comprehensive doctrine are separable in such a way that an individual can draw "freestanding" political stances without the entire process of political justification becoming therefore "comprehensive." He views comprehensive views and political views as "two views . . . [which] can be divided into two parts, suitably related" (*PL*, 140).[23] But it is not clear that any of the individuals Rawls uses as examples saw their political and comprehensive views as separable in the way he claims.[24] He admits that for abolitionists, in their historical context,

23. Greenawalt, despite echoing Rawls on other issues, here departs from his view of belief (*Religious Convictions*, 155).

24. This circular and hypothetical Rawlsian speculation appears in IPE. There, Rawls admits that "I do not know whether the Abolitionists and King ever fulfilled the proviso. But whether they did or not, they could have. And, had they known the idea of public reason and shared its ideal, they would have" (iii, n. 27). This puzzling statement seems to boil down to the claim that if the Abolitionists and King had agreed with Rawls ("known the idea of public reason and shared its ideal"), they would have agreed with Rawls ("fulfilled the proviso"). Such a tautology is echoed by Greenawalt, who after noting that "religious convictions . . . bear pervasively on people's ethical choices, including choices about government policies," goes on to say that "a citizen's reliance on religious convictions is inapt only if . . . 3) they are disqualified by some aspect of liberal democracy or its underlying principles" (*Religious Convictions*, 30).

Defending Rawls, Greenawalt argues that Rawls "does not suggest that religious grounds for accepting [basic political] premises are necessarily irrelevant or inappropriate," but that "what "it was necessary to invoke the comprehensive grounds on which those values were widely seen to rest" (*PL*, 251). The abolitionists did not violate public reason, he claims, "provided they thought, or on reflection would have thought (as they certainly *could* have thought) that the comprehensive reasons they appealed to were required to give sufficient strength to the political conception *to be subsequently realized*" (*PL*, 251, emphasis added). King "could appeal—as the abolitionists could not—to the Constitution *correctly understood*" (*PL*, 250, emphasis added).[25]

But if abolitionists, properly, used comprehensive justifications to advance a political conception not even in existence at the time such justifications were employed, why should Rawls disallow such comprehensive grounds being brought to bear upon our own political debates? The answer seems to be that the contemporary United States is well ordered, or at least far better ordered, than the antebellum United States. Rawls argues that American society was not well ordered into the 1960s, that both the abolitionists and King spoke to "an unjust political society" (IPE, lii). For him to exclude religious rhetoric and justifications in the 1990s, however, raises the obvious question of precisely when during the past three decades American society became well ordered.[26] Rawls realizes the tenuous nature of the argument he is making, admitting that "much more would have to be said to make this suggestion at all convincing" (*PL*, 251).

Certainly the early modern tolerationists whom Rawls sees as building blocks of political liberalism did not restrict themselves to purely political

is inappropriate is reliance on religious grounds to decide political issues within a society that accepts Rawls' conception of justice" (53). Yet despite these claims, Greenawalt clearly sees *himself* as defending religion's role in the public sphere: "If all people must draw from their personal experiences and commitments of value to some degree, people whose experience leads them to religious convictions should not have to disregard what they consider the critical insights about value that their convictions provide" (145). They should not, that is, unless those insights are ruled out by the premises of liberal democracy. This parallel between Greenawalt and Rawls—an underlying similarity despite apparently differing arguments—has been noted by Franklin I. Gamwell, *The Meaning of Religious Freedom: Modern Politics and the Democratic Resolution* (Albany, 1995), 109 n. 6, 111 n. 7.

25. Given that for Rawls "the constitution is not what the Court says it is . . . it is what the people acting constitutionally through the other branches eventually allow the Court to say it is" (*PL*, 237), we are left wondering to what exactly Rawls thinks King was appealing.

26. One might also wonder whether Rawls considers the United States to be "stable for the right reasons" even in 1998, given the extensive criteria for such a designation—public financing of elections, a "decent distribution of income," "society as employer of last resort," and basic health care for all citizens—he lays out in the introduction to the paperback edition of *Political Liberalism* (IPE, lvi–lvii).

reasons in advancing their own agenda, nor did they hasten to add public reasons "in due course." Although the arguments about dissembling and the nature of belief (options 1 and 2) formed an important element of the argument for toleration, such arguments were largely couched in theological language: the argument about the nature of belief, for example, owes much to Paul's comment in Romans 14:23 that "whatever is not of faith is sin." The scriptural argument was central for seventeenth-century tolerationists, who sought a massive reconsideration of what it meant to be a Christian. Early modern thinkers did not bracket off their comprehensive doctrines, nor did they hasten to add public reasons to their comprehensively derived ones. Indeed, the two were considered inseparable, and both were brought to bear on this pressing issue of their day.[27] The entire seventeenth-century argument in favor of toleration aimed to show that such a policy was, not only compatible with, but *commanded* by Christian (and more specifically in the Anglo-American context, Protestant) values.

The comprehensive foundations of individuals' political views and the political views themselves are thus not so neatly separable as Rawls claims. One might more accurately define a comprehensive doctrine as a complex and integrally related (though not necessarily *logically* connected) set of precepts and principles influencing one's views on epistemology, human nature, ethics, and politics. On this view, the relationship between principles of a comprehensive doctrine and the social and political consequences of that doctrine does not resemble that between discrete planks of a political platform; but rather a relationship of meaning and value, intimately related to one's sense of self. Michael J. Perry argues that a citizen attempting to bracket religious convictions in favor of publicly accessible ones "would bracket—indeed . . . annihilate—herself. And doing that would preclude her—the particular person she is—from engaging in moral discourse with other members of the society."[28] To presume that elements compatible with public reason are neatly separable from more "comprehensive" ones misunderstands or misrepresents the nature of moral reasoning and political justification. One's comprehensive foundations may be left unspoken or implied, but they are no less implicated in the process of political decisionmaking.

27. Antitolerationists, for their part, did not object in the least to the use of religious imagery and rhetoric in public debate: they simply had *different* religious imagery and rhetoric.

28. *Morality, Politics, and the Law: A Bicentennial Essay* (New York, 1988), 72–73.

Rawlsian liberalism, of course, commits us to privileging *political* values, appealing solely to public reason, in effect eradicating comprehensive doctrines from the public sphere. Despite his claims, this would likely rule out the theologically laced rhetoric of Lincoln's Second Inaugural, since "public reason . . . always applies to public and government officers in official forums" (*PL*, 252). Much of King's eloquent "Letter from Birmingham Jail," grounded as it is in Thomistic theology, seems unacceptable as well, since the "ideal of public reason hold[s] for citizens when they engage in political advocacy in the public forum" (*PL*, 215). Similarly, the scripturally based rhetoric of early modern tolerationists seems to find no home in Rawls's liberal society. If abolitionists, civil rights marchers, and Lincoln did not violate the "proviso," there seems no defensible argument for excluding prolife activists, which Rawls apparently wants to do (see *PL*, 243–44). The "proviso" makes Rawls's exclusion of comprehensive doctrines from public life kinder and gentler, but no less real.

PUBLIC REASON, COMPREHENSIVE DOCTRINES, AND THE DISTINCTION BETWEEN BELIEF AND ACTION

Rawls's conditions of publicity distinguish between comprehensive doctrines (belief structures) and political actions (action here encompassing political speech and argument). Rawls, after all, describes public reason not as reason itself but as "the reason of citizens as such" (*PL*, 213). In such an understanding, the priority of the political requires individuals to submerge or set aside their comprehensive doctrines when entering the public sphere. Although clearly one retains full liberty to believe any comprehensive doctrine one chooses, political debate must proceed along political lines. Such a distinction between belief and action has a long history in the Anglo-American tradition. Unfortunately for Rawls and his ambitious claims about political liberalism and the culmination of liberty of conscience, this split between belief and action been directly *opposed to* tolerationist impulses, and frequently associated with the suppression of religious minorities. A few examples will clarify this point.

In seventeenth-century Massachusetts, as we have seen, claims of conscience and toleration occasioned a number of protracted debates between defenders of the "New England Way" and those seeking religious liberty. Roger Williams and Anne Hutchinson, most famously, collided with established practice and, in doing so, epitomized the tension between conscience and community that I have elaborated in this study. At one point, Richard Saltonstall, one of the colony's founders, wrote to John Cotton supporting moderation in exacting penalties for religious dissent. He raised these very issues of hypocrisy and dissembling. Cotton's response is instructive, and evokes this distinction between belief and action. "Better hypocrites than profane persons. Hypocrites give God his due in an outward form at least."[29] Clearly, Cotton and many others would admit, the exercise of political power does not change belief. But this psychological admission does not, in itself, justify individual liberty to act upon those beliefs.

Thomas Hobbes, for his part, drew a clear distinction between belief and action, maintaining that although the freedom of private belief is unaffected by sovereign power, a sovereign may (and must) regulate public *behavior*, including religious behavior, in the interests of peace and security. Hobbes admitted that conscience is beyond the reach of the sovereign, and that "no human law is intended to oblige the conscience of a man, but his actions only."[30] Regarding the civil religion and its legitimate determination of scriptural interpretation and other canonical matters, Hobbes stated that a "private man has always the liberty, because thought is free, to believe or not believe in his heart those acts that have been given out for miracles" (*L*, 300). In matters of public profession, though, the sovereign must do all necessary for ensuring the people's security: "We are not every one, to make our own private reason, or conscience, but the public reason, that is, the reason of God's supreme lieutenant, judge; and indeed we have made him judge already, if we have given him a sovereign power, to do all that is necessary for our peace and defense . . . when it comes to confession of that faith, the private reason must submit to the public" (ibid.).

In a sense, we might see the Rawlsian distinction between attachments to comprehensive doctrines and the restrictions of public reason in political debate as analogous to Hobbes's concern about the polarizing influence of private religious belief on political stability.[31] The Hobbesian system is in many ways a coherent response to civil war and the breakdown of sovereignty.

29. In Hutchinson, *The History*, 2:132.
30. *Elements of Law*, 114.
31. Especially, that is, when we consider the emphasis Rawls places on stability and security (see option 3).

Whether it (and the resonances we see in Rawlsian theory) represents an advance in the history of liberty of conscience is another question entirely.

This distinction between belief and action also appears in U. S. Supreme Court jurisprudence. The first significant case dealing with this issue was *Reynolds v. United States* (1879). In *Reynolds*, the Court articulated the distinction between belief and action, ruling that the federal government was free to regulate religiously derived *actions* in the context of insuring social order, provided such regulations did not proscribe *beliefs* or opinions. According to this reasoning, the state could legitimately prohibit polygamy (although it was a practice central to the religious beliefs of Mormons) because this regulation did not touch belief, only action.

Such an understanding did not last. The dichotomy between belief and action was chipped away over the course of the next century: for example, in *Braunfield v. Brown* (1961) the Court recognized that both direct and indirect burdens had to be weighed in assessing the extent to which ability to *practice* a religion could legitimately be impeded by secular law.[32] *Sherbert v. Verner* (1964) brought this change in legal reasoning full circle: states were disallowed from structuring even government benefits programs (in this case, unemployment compensation) in ways that burdened religious exercise. The nonreceipt of government benefits was no longer considered an indirect, but rather a significant and substantial, burden on free exercise, because it penalized an individual for the exercise of his or her conscience. Belief implied action, and punishment of action equaled punishment of belief. Of course, such an evolution in legal reasoning can be reversed as well: the distinction between belief and action reappeared in *Oregon Department of Human Resources v. Smith* (1990) signaling a movement away from the trend of *Braunfield* and *Sherbert*. Indeed, the Court explicitly refers (*Smith* at 1559) to this very distinction in its opinion.[33]

The broader history of Anglo-American toleration debates, so important to Rawls, sheds light on this issue of beliefs and actions. Many proponents of religious liberty argued not only that conscience was impervious to coercion,

32. Of course we must remember that the Court *upheld* the Pennsylvania Sunday closing law in *Braunfield*, making clear that direct or indirect burdens *in and of themselves* would not be dispositive in deciding the legality of a statute. This led to the free exercise "balancing" process, in which the state had to establish compelling interest and show that its proposed course represented the least possible infringement of religious exercise.

33. For a helpful overview of the evolution of religion clause jurisprudence, see Ronald B. Flowers, *The Godless Court? Supreme Court Decisions on Church-State Relationships* (Louisville, Ky., 1994).

according to the aforementioned psychological argument (option 1), but that a true understanding of liberty of conscience entailed *both* belief and action. Such an argument, furthermore, represented not a purely secular or psychological ("public," in Rawlsian terms) understanding, but a religious one, grounded in passages from the book of James and other scriptural sources.

PUBLIC REASON, COMPREHENSIVE DOCTRINES, AND REPRESSION

In *Political Liberalism*, Rawls states his view that "except for certain kinds of fundamentalism, all the main historical religions admit of such an account and thus may be seen as reasonable comprehensive doctrines" (*PL*, 170). He admits that "a society may . . . contain unreasonable and irrational, and even mad, comprehensive doctrines. In their case the problem is to contain them so that they do not undermine the unity and justice of society" (*PL*, xvi–xvii). Of course, Rawls's society protects a free press and religious worship, as do all liberal societies worth the name. Still, he seems to be calling for a vastly more far-reaching system of psychological restraint, suggesting that people ought not to hold certain comprehensive doctrines in the first place.

Rawls's examples of comprehensive doctrines and their relation to the overlapping consensus are illuminating here. In his view, a freestanding political conception of justice may receive support from a number of sources: religious doctrines that incorporate a commitment to toleration (e.g., Locke), philosophical ones emphasizing individual moral autonomy (e.g., Mill, Kant), or a more general commitment to pluralism (*PL*, 145).[34] These three examples are all clearly liberal at root. As I noted, Rawls states outright that fundamentalism does not allow for an independent allegiance to the political order, and is not part of the overlapping consensus. In these scattered remarks, he implies a philosophical and political system far more radical and repressive than Hobbes, whose *modus vivendi* state was satisfied with minimal public activities that conformed to the will of the sovereign.

---

34. Again, Ackerman echoes Rawls's liberal reasoning: one might accept the Neutrality Principle on grounds of skepticism, support for the freedom to experiment with different conceptions of the good, an independent affirmation of "autonomous deliberation" (*Social Justice*, 11), or a concern about the corrupting influence of political power. As with Rawls's three examples, all of Ackerman's possible grounds are, broadly speaking, liberal.

Implicitly, that is, Rawls suggests that to believe or think in certain ways threatens the political order.

The possible role for any nonliberal, nonrational comprehensive doctrine progressively shrinks as a reader proceeds through *Political Liberalism* and Rawls repeatedly expands the scope of public reason. Initially, he claims that it applies only when constitutional essentials or matters of basic justice are at stake (*PL*, 214). Shortly thereafter, we find that the "ideal of public reason hold[s] for citizens when they engage in political advocacy in the public forum" (*PL*, 215). Finally, in a sweeping expansion of the scope of public reason, Rawls claims that *voting* on the basis of one's comprehensive doctrines is illegitimate.

> On fundamental political questions the idea of public reason rejects common views of voting as a private and even personal matter. One view is that people may properly vote their preferences and interests, social and economic, not to mention their dislikes and hatreds. Another view, offhand quite different, is that people may vote what they see as right and true as their comprehensive convictions direct without taking into account public reasons. Yet both views are similar in that neither respects the limits of public reason in voting on matters of constitutional essentials and questions of basic justice. (*PL*, 219)

Public reason also applies, as we have seen, to "public and government officers in official forums" (*PL*, 252). Acting politically on the basis of comprehensive doctrines violates the "duty of civility" (*PL*, 253). In the case of political "stand-offs" such as abortion, "if . . . citizens invoke the grounding reasons of their comprehensive views, then the principle of reciprocity is violated" (IPE, lv).

In essence Rawls seems to insist upon "liberal" comprehensive doctrines or no comprehensive doctrines at all. If one can refer meaningfully to the philosophical and theological bases of one's political views neither in the privacy of the voting booth nor in the public square, it is difficult to see how Rawls's system is compatible with a historically informed understanding of liberty of conscience. If this represents, not merely the completion but the extension of such liberty, it is a truly unorthodox notion of extension.

CONCLUDING REFLECTIONS ON RAWLS'S "COMPLETION AND EXTENSION" OF LIBERTY OF CONSCIENCE

It seems ironic, then, that Rawls's "completion and extension" of liberty of conscience actually involves *constricting* the ability of individuals to affirm publicly and act upon the moral, theological, and ethical foundations of their political stances. Historically, the expansion of liberty of conscience has resulted in a steadily increasing sphere in which religious and conscientious concerns were removed as bases for punishment or the denial of public benefits and civil rights. Such a process was halting and bitterly contested, but has over the past three centuries led to an expansive notion of conscience and the importance of allowing citizens to follow its dictates. Although the English and American strategies for pursuing religious liberty differed (an official church with legal toleration of dissenters versus disestablishment), the aim and historical struggle has involved similar issues: moving from a minimal understanding of the requirements of religious freedom (one compatible with a distinction between belief and action) to the more expansive notions embodied in *Sherbert* and the Religious Freedom Restoration Act of 1993, which sought to address the perceived retreat on religious liberty present in *Smith*.[35]

Were Rawls to defend his liberalism as *modus vivendi, a la* Charles Larmore or Judith Shklar, or as a story among stories, *a la* Richard Rorty,[36] his radical restriction of citizens' private beliefs would perhaps not pose a problem, in that this great disconnection between theoretical or historical claims and practical outcomes would not be so glaring. While disavowing "comprehensive" liberalism, however, Rawls explicitly rejects the idea of a "mere modus vivendi" (*PL*, 146–54), seeks to make the overlapping consensus a moral notion, and makes the ambitious claim noted above about "complet[ing] and extend[ing]" the movement for liberty of conscience dating back to the sixteenth and seventeenth centuries. Rawls's restrictive, repressive system might be justified on the basis of political order, or any number of other

35. The Religious Freedom Restoration Act reinstated the compelling government interest/ least possible infringement standard in free exercise issues. Although portions of the Act were struck down by the Supreme Court, its passage by overwhelming majorities in both houses of the U.S. Congress demonstrates the broad support the Act commanded. For a fuller explication, see Flowers, *The Godless Court?*

36. Larmore, *Patterns of Moral Complexity* (Cambridge, 1987), esp. 69–77; Shklar, *Ordinary Vices* (Cambridge, Mass., 1984); idem, "Liberalism of Fear," 21–38; Rorty, *Contingency, Irony, Solidarity* (Cambridge, 1989).

pressing considerations, and Rawls does imply some of these in his persistent focus on stability. He hardly offers, though, a completion and extension of three hundred years of struggle for liberty of conscience. On those terms, we might reasonably expect something more than the sterile middle ground of political liberalism, purged of all claims to action on the basis of conscience.

8

THE POLITICS OF CONSCIENCE AND THE
POLITICS OF IDENTITY

The Limits and Promise of Liberal Toleration

It may seem that my emphasis on the Reformation and the long controversy about toleration as the origin of liberalism is dated in terms of the problems of contemporary political life. Among our most basic problems are those of race, ethnicity, and gender. These may seem of an altogether different character calling for different principles of justice, which [*A Theory of Justice*] does not discuss. . . .

I still think that once we get the conceptions and principles right for the basic historical questions, those conceptions and principles should be widely applicable to our own problems also. The same equality of the Declaration of Independence which Lincoln evoked to condemn slavery can be invoked to condemn the inequality and oppression of women. I think it a matter of understanding what earlier principles require under changed circumstances and of insisting that they now be honored in existing institutions.

—John Rawls, *Political Liberalism*

[The argument from religious toleration] is the most compelling model for the case for gay rights. . . . The moral empowerment of making claims to one's basic human rights in one domain generalizes, on grounds of rights-based principles, to empowering claims to revise the terms of all identities marred by such structural injustice.

—David A. J. Richards, *Identity and the Case for Gay Rights*

As we have seen, religious toleration has emerged over the past several centuries as a core value in the liberal tradition. But contemporary theorists have also sought to expand toleration far beyond its religion-based origins: not only does the tradition of thought that justified such toleration protect individuals acting on the basis of conscience, Rawls (and others) claims, but it also lends itself to extension to contemporary political issues involving race, gender, ethnicity, sexuality, and culture.[1]

I take issue with such claims, seeking an improved understanding of the broad historical relevance of religious toleration as well as the limits of its applicability. I argue that toleration derived from the historical struggle for liberty of conscience—the paradigm example of toleration in the work of Rawls, for example—secures certain core liberal values. The most vexing contemporary issues in political theory and practice, however, tend to involve identity, which in turn raises more diffuse issues of authenticity and respect. The arguments and evidence historically marshaled in support of freeing belief from political control, I argue, are politically far more restricted in nature and cannot easily be placed into the service of identity politics or multiculturalism. I intend such an admission, not as a sort of defeatism about the contemporary relevance of tolerationist thought, but instead as a call for attention to the *promise* of an articulated politics of conscience for our time as well as the need for new thinking about the issues of identity and difference that confront twenty-first-century societies.

After briefly explicating the close link between conscience-related toleration debates and the liberal tradition in the work of Rawls and David A.J. Richards, the two most prominent exponents of an "expansive" view of toleration, I reiterate the ways in which the idea of conscience itself has been transformed over the past three centuries. I argue that conscience grounds a variety of liberal practices (free speech, press, assembly, principled objection to specific laws) in which individual belief conflicts with established custom or law. While appreciative of the transformed nature of conscience, however, I suggest that a "conscience paradigm" still differs markedly from the principles of social equality and equal respect that undergird the more ambitious agenda

---

1. See the essays in the following collections: Horton and Mendus, *Aspects of Toleration*; Horton and Nicholson, *Toleration: Philosophy and Practice*; idem, eds., *Toleration, Identity, and Difference* (New York, 1999); Richards, *Identity and the Case for Gay Rights*; and William N. Eskridge, "A Jurisprudence of 'Coming Out': Religion, Homosexuality, and Collisions of Liberty and Equality in American Public Law," *Yale Law Journal* 106 (1997): 2411–74.

of contemporary identity politics. I suggest that we ought not minimize the importance of the *modus vivendi* politics that historically accompanied the achievement of religious toleration.[2]

TOLERATION AND LIBERTY OF CONSCIENCE: CONTEMPORARY LIBERAL AND CONSTITUTIONAL PERSPECTIVES

Both historically and conceptually, toleration grounds liberalism for Rawls: David McCabe accurately depicts Rawls as regarding "modern liberalism as the logical extension of religious toleration."[3] In *A Theory of Justice*, Rawls characterizes the principle of equal liberty as representing the "generaliz[ation] of] religious toleration to a social form" (*TOJ*, 206). It is easy to see why liberty of conscience is crucial for Rawls, since the denial of such liberty seems to entail the denial of individual moral agency, creative and religious thought, and voluntarism more generally. But Rawls says very little about how the process of generalization—from conscience to issues of gender, ethnicity, and identity—might take place: the passages at the head of this chapter represent the only attention Rawls gives to his crucial claim about the paradigmatic nature of toleration debates. This lack of attention leads critics such as Michael Sandel to view Rawls's "generalization of religious toleration to a social form" as equating moral and religious values with market choices.[4]

In the field of legal scholarship, the most sophisticated exponent of an expansive view of the legacy of religious toleration has been David A.J. Richards. In a number of important works, Richards has argued for the broad import of conscience-based arguments to American constitutionalism, not only

2. Given the placement of this chapter in a project on the historical development of religious toleration, it should be clear that my argument evolves not from any lack of appreciation of the (historical or contemporary) power of tolerationist arguments. Quite the contrary, the key role played by liberty of conscience in the history of liberal theory, in my view, mandates that we not confuse conscience-based arguments with other justifications for individual or group liberty. I also am not arguing either (a) that liberal toleration is in some way *insufficient* to contemporary concerns because of its Christian or liberal roots, or (b) that toleration dismisses value concerns as mere fictions and diminishes its own scope by constantly adverting to issues of civil peace and sovereignty. For these two (respectively), see Galeotti, "Citizenship and Equality," and Kirstie M. McClure, "Difference, Diversity, and the Limits of Toleration," *Political Theory* 18 (1990): 361–91.

3. David McCabe, "John Locke and the Argument Against Strict Separation," *Review of Politics* 59 (1997): 234 n. 2.

4. See Sandel, "Freedom of Conscience or Freedom of Choice?" and *Democracy's Discontent*, chap. 1.

in First Amendment jurisprudence but also in the equal protection clauses of the Reconstruction Amendments and in contemporary debates over racism, sexism, and gay rights.[5] Indeed, Richards opens his most recent book with the following words: "In American law, the argument for gay rights arises against a shared background of cumulative historical experience of successful struggles for human rights in various domains—religious toleration, racial inequality, and, most recently, gender equality."[6]

For Richards, the "inalienable right to conscience" represents "the central paradigm of the kind of respect for rights that actuates the form and substance of constitutional government," and he echoes Rawls in asserting that "conscience and the social contract rest . . . on an underlying political ideal of the moral sovereignty of the people."[7] For Richards, the philosophy and underlying impulses behind the respect for conscience—the "internal ideals of contractarian thought"—motivate extensive protections for speech and press, privacy rights, contraception, abortion, a variety of forms of sexual expression, and (perhaps) drug use and even a right to die.[8]

Seeking to detach toleration from its (historically) theistic roots, Richards connects it not only with religious belief and actions but, more generally, with individual "theories of life and how to live it well."[9] The notion of a moral conscience underlying the choice of a gay or lesbian identity, he says, operates at "exactly the same level" as religious faith, given its central role in the "reasonable formation of one's moral identity in public and private life."[10] Locke and Pierre Bayle, on whose account of conscience and toleration Richards relies heavily, were "surely wrong in linking ethical independence to theism in general or Protestant theism in particular, as Jefferson and Madison acknowledged."[11]

---

5. *Toleration and the Constitution; Conscience and the Constitution: History, Theory, and Law of the Reconstruction Amendments* (Princeton, 1993); *Women, Gays, and the Constitution: The Grounds for Feminism and Gay Rights in Culture and Law* (Chicago, 1998); and *Identity and the Case for Gay Rights.*

6. *Identity and the Case for Gay Rights,* 1; see also 3, 195.

7. *Toleration and the Constitution,* 68, 98. Richards also suggests Rawls's reasoning from the original position, claiming that "each person would reasonably demand [the inalienable right to conscience] as a protection of freedom and rationality, the highest-order good" (*Toleration and the Constitution,* 101).

8. Ibid., 249, chaps. 6–9, 281.

9. Ibid., 97, 137. Indeed, Richards presumes the "conceptual independence of ethical and religious concepts" (250). Similarly, Rawls discusses such issues by referring to "the good" rather than specifically religious or spiritual phenomena.

10. *Identity and the Case for Gay Rights,* 180, 93.

11. Ibid., 88.

For Richards, given the modern development of moral philosophy and humanistic values, we need not restrict ourselves to traditional theistic notions of conscience. In this he echoes Rawls, who begins with a call for liberals to recognize the importance of "the long controversies over religious toleration in the sixteenth and seventeenth centuries," but ends with extensive discussions of, not religious, but "comprehensive" doctrines of the good more generally (*PL*, xxvi). Thus advocacy of gay rights, like opposition to racism and sexism, represents an "expression of the inalienable right to conscience."[12] For both Rawls and Richards, the expansive view of toleration and conscience involves equating how individuals seek salvation and work out the practical implications of their beliefs about ultimate truths with far more general (and contemporary) notions of personal autonomy and the infinite revisability of views of the good life.

Richards's argument for the power of extension involves an apparent equation between conscience and personal autonomy. For example, he links the right to conscience with a broader notion of the private sphere, which in turn

includes those highly personal relationships and activities whose just moral independence requires special protection from a hostile public interest that compromises the range of thought, self-image, emotional vulnerabilities, sensitivities, and aspirations essential to the role of such relationships in the formation of self expressive of one's moral powers. Intimate relationships—which give play to love, devotion, friendship as organizing themes in self-conceptions of permanent value in living— are among the essential resources of moral independence.[13]

This privacy, which Richards derives from conscience, removes a vast scope of human activity from the purview of the state, moving far beyond the protection of conscientious belief from persecution. The scope of Richards's conscience-derived private sphere becomes apparent when he seems to equate the use of contraception with the right to conscience.[14] Even abortion decisions are defended by Richards on conscientious grounds, "centering [women's] lives in

12. Ibid., 86.
13. *Toleration and the Constitution*, 243–44.
14. Ibid., 259.

a body image and aspirations expressive of their moral powers."[15] The background right of conscience, which Richards sees as buttressing liberal constitutionalism more generally, involves a "respect for moral independence."[16]

THE EVOLUTION OF CONSCIENCE: OBJECTIVE TO SUBJECTIVE

The tradition of religious toleration that both Rawls and Richards portray as central to their approach to liberal theory, as we have seen, is fundamentally bound up with the notion of conscience.[17] This term, of course, originally meant something quite different from its generally accepted contemporary usage, and in order to appreciate its breadth and depth we must appreciate the historical transformation it has undergone. Although early modern proponents of toleration stressed the notion of inward assent rather than imposed religious uniformity, their position was always located firmly within the Christian tradition. In our time, by contrast, conscience tends to be more closely identified with *individual* standards of right and wrong. James F. Childress, for example, takes for granted that "conscience is personal and subjective."[18] According to this view, which I take to be an expression of the predominant contemporary understanding, conscience denotes a faculty by which individuals compare the propriety of a contemplated act to their own standard of morality and arrive at a decision as to the rightness or wrongness of such an act.

15. "In sum, the choice to use contraceptives has been a key exercise of constructive moral powers in the rational and reasonable redefinition of personal and moral relationships. . . . Contraceptive use in marriage has secured for couples a deepened freedom and rationality of sexual expression in the bonding of their intimate lives and greater control over their reproductive histories and other personal aims" (ibid., 268).

16. Ibid., 252. Richards's argument here is echoed by Richard D. Mohr, in his argument for gay rights: "The general right to control one's body has at its core a cluster of specific, bodily-based liberties. . . . Only when one's control of one's body is protected does one have a right to bodily integrity, and only when one has bodily integrity is one a person at all." See Mohr, *A More Perfect Union: Why Straight America Must Stand Up for Gay Rights* (Boston, 1994), 24.

17. The direct connection between conscience and toleration (i.e., that claims of conscience raise political questions of toleration) is made in Bugg, *De Christiana libertate* (London, 1682), chap. 1. See also Bates, *Religious Liberty*, 296–300, 373.

18. "Appeals to Conscience," *Ethics* 89 (1978): 318. Perhaps the most interesting contemporary example of this point is the notion of "Sheilaism," the radically individualistic religion reported by one of Robert Bellah's interviewees. See Bellah et al., *Habits of the Heart*, chap. 9, esp. 221, 235.

Take, for example, the issue of conscientious objection to military service. For many years successful claims to conscientious objector status required membership in a "peace church" (e.g., Amish, Mennonite, Quaker). More recently, however, although Selective Service retains the language of "religious training and belief," such claims are decided on the basis of sincerity and individual philosophical or moral stances. The leading scholars of conscientious objection conclude that

> even when national singularities are taken into account, a consistent pattern characterizes the social and political evolution of conscientious objection in modern Western democracies. Over time the definition of objector status as recognized by the state shifts from membership in historic "peace churches" to include congregants of mainline religious bodies, and finally those who object to military service on moral and ethical reasons not deriving from religious tenets.[19]

Charles Moskos and John Chambers refer to this pattern as "the secularization of conscience," and it is, in my view, an apt term.[20]

I do not claim, however, that this secularization of conscience represents the point at which the history and tradition of religious toleration ceases to provide insights into contemporary issues of toleration and dissent.[21] Neither should my account be read as a criticism of this secularization as a slide into subjectivism, a claim made famously by Allan Bloom.[22] Although it is true that, in one sense, the development of ideas about conscience represents "a

19. Charles C. Moskos and John Whiteclay Chambers III, eds., *The New Conscientious Objection: From Sacred to Secular Resistance* (New York, 1993), 6. See also Robert A. Seeley, *Handbook for Conscientious Objectors* (Philadelphia, 1981), esp. chap. 5, and the U.S. Supreme Court decision in *United States v. Seeger* (380 U.S. 163, 85 S.Ct. 850, 13 L.Ed.2d. 733 [1965]).

20. *The New Conscientious Objection*, 6.

21. Joshua Mitchell (personal communication, November 20, 1998) has suggested that this attempt to secularize an inherently theological concept is doomed: in other words, that one simply *cannot* generalize or secularize conscience without doing violence to the coherence of the original concept. Although this is not my position—I view the argument for a "secularized" conscience as *structurally* analogous, though not identical, to the theological or "objective" sense of the term—Mitchell's point is well taken, and much of this chapter is devoted to disputing what I consider hasty generalizations from conscience to contemporary issues of identity. Mitchell's more general position on the intricate relationship between theological and political concepts in early modern thought may be found in the introduction to his *Not By Reason Alone: Religion, History, and Identity in Early Modern Political Thought* (Chicago, 1993).

22. Bloom, *Closing of the American Mind*.

new subjectivism," it need not (and at its theoretically richest, does not) entail a relativist refusal to countenance any claims of an objective moral order.[23] Although such secularization and subjectivism does divorce conscience from necessarily involving transcendent or objective moral codes, it does not change the fact that liberty of conscience is seen as freeing an individual from penalization for the exercise of sincerely-held beliefs; and that the sincerity of the believer must somehow figure into any account of the belief's significance.

In fact, I argue that we can isolate a core concept that underlies *both* the earlier, theologically driven notion as well as the contemporary one, and I shall refer to "conscience" hereafter as the individual faculty that compares contemplated actions with *any* deeply held standard of morality. Whether that standard is individualistic or based upon a religious tradition, punishment for the sake of belief has traditionally been viewed (by tolerationists) as especially odious, since it involves inflicting punishment for something which an individual could not change even had he wanted to (belief, again, not being under the control of the will). Since individuals arrive at their beliefs on the basis of sensory experience, revelation, intuition, and so on, punishing an individual for nontreasonous beliefs and the actions that follow from them not only smacks of irrational cruelty (due to the extravoluntary nature of the understanding) but also violates the general liberal argument that civil bonds of allegiance suffice for a healthy political society.[24] For all its change over the years, then, conscience remains a term denoting the belief structures (whatever their source or foundation) by which individuals decide upon and judge their actions.

What I shall call "the conscience paradigm," then, attempts to distill a fundamental political aim of tolerationists from early modern times to our own day.[25] Although, as noted, conscience has undergone a remarkable trans-

23. On these points my argument parallels that of Charles Taylor: see his *Ethics of Authenticity* (Cambridge, Mass., 1992), 15, and chaps. 5–7, and, more generally, *Sources of the Self*, chaps. 10–11.

24. As Rawls puts it, "The social union is no longer founded on a conception of the good as given by a common religious faith or philosophical doctrine, but on a shared public conception of justice appropriate to the conception of citizens in a democratic state as free and equal persons" (*PL*, 304).

25. Hegel saw this development as key to understanding modernity: "Man himself has a conscience; consequently the subjection required of him is a free allegiance. . . . The rational no longer meets with contradiction on the part of the religious conscience. . . . [T]he individual must gain the assurance that the Spirit dwells within him." See *The Philosophy of History*, trans. J. Sibree (1840; New York, 1956), 423.

formation, conscience-based politics boils down to the claim that states must recognize individuals' beliefs and values about truth and the good, being extravoluntary and formed by individuals convinced by reason or revelation, as sacrosanct. Considerations of conscience raise issues of ultimate meaning and individual judgment, affecting questions of thought, worship, action, and assembly: hence this most private of faculties injects itself by definition into wrenching public debates. Within the parameters of civil peace and social order, governments must grant the liberty to act upon such values, as a necessary corollary to the free workings of the human mind. The liberal tolerationist state—from Locke and Mill through Rawls and Richards—lays claim to the bodies, not the souls, of its citizens.

WHAT A CONSCIENCE PARADIGM WON'T DO: CONSCIENCE POLITICS AND IDENTITY POLITICS

Whether one views conscience as the individual assent to God's law or the purely subjective standards each of us holds about right and wrong, the concept clearly admits of extension (both historically and conceptually) from its most narrow historical dimension, namely liberty of (Protestant, Christian) worship. In fact, as we have seen throughout this project, early modern thinkers themselves were the first to extend the concept, broadening their concerns from religious belief to include action, and from worship to broader civil protections and involvement in the public life of their community.

More broadly, though, the conscience paradigm has supported a number of practices that contemporary thinkers associate with the liberal tradition. For example, given the importance of acting in accord with one's beliefs and values, especially in the realm of religion (as well as the inability of an individual to change his or her beliefs at will), liberty of conscience implies liberty of speech and assembly. In speech, this extension of conscience originally focused on the right of all Christian believers to preach the word of God without fear of legal or political harassment, while those advocating freedom of assembly claimed the rights of like-minded believers to gather and pursue their own salvation in the way they best perceived it. William Penn's *Peoples Ancient and Just Liberties Asserted* brings together these two arguments: Penn was arrested for unlicensed preaching in a public street and published a (purported) transcript of his trial as a defense of traditional English liberties against a persecuting magistrate.[26] In this sense, Rawls echoes early modern tolerationists when he claims that "freedom of association is required to give effect to liberty of conscience; for unless we are at liberty to associate with other like-minded citizens, the exercise of liberty of conscience is denied" (*PL*, 313).[27]

Early modern thinkers also connected liberty of conscience with liberty of the press, since authorities routinely directed censorship against religious dissidents who were seen as threatening the established order by undermining the established church. In Milton's famous polemic *Areopagitica*, the theory that "truth needs no sword" serves to bolster claims for a free press as well as the liberty of religious proselytization more generally.[28] The seizure of Bradford's press by Pennsylvania Quaker magistrates during the Keithian schism represented a move against a group of religious dissidents who had made themselves a socially divisive force as well. More broadly, tolerationists have historically included principled dissent or disobedience from specific laws—whether this involved a refusal to attend the established church (which traditionally brought fines or jail sentences) or the refusal to perform certain civic actions that violated the dictates of one's conscience[29]—under the rubric of liberty of conscience. All of these "extensions," however, are political, legal, or institutional efforts aimed at broadening the areas in which individuals are not penalized for the exercise of their conscientious beliefs. They go no farther (nor did their historical exponents seek to extend them farther) than the political or institutional realm.

A broad range of contemporary social and political issues, on the other hand—gay rights, cultural and ethnic pluralism, gender and race relations— elevate issues of identity and identity politics to the fore. Although Rawls and Richards, as we have seen, often claim that the history of conscience and religious toleration provides a platform for addressing these issues, multiculturalists and identity theorists (in sharp contrast) have often harshly criticized liberalism's inattention to difference and been more attracted to models of deliberative or pluralist democracy.[30] I should be clear: I do not mean to pose

---

26. London, 1670.
27. See also Hobhouse, *Liberalism*, chap. 2, esp. p. 19.
28. Reprinted in Milton, *Areopagitica and Other Political Writings*.
29. See, e.g., Thoreau's "Essay on Civil Disobedience."
30. See, e.g., Iris Marion Young, *Justice and the Politics of Difference* (Princeton, 1990), and Wendy Brown, "Wounded Attachments: Late Modern Oppositional Political Formations,"

"conscience" and "identity" as dichotomous entities. Certainly one's religious affiliations and/or belief about ultimate truth form a central and foundational part of who one *is*. In this sense, conscience contains within it at least a latent notion of identity. My distinction between the two lies in a matter of emphasis, though a crucial one. It is a difference of emphasis, but a difference of emphasis that carries with it vastly different political and social agendas.

When I use the term "identity politics," I am referring to a general (if diverse) school of thought that, in addressing issues of race, gender, sexuality, and culture, forgoes a simply political strategy of seeking equal treatment before the law (the negative approach of removing barriers to equal opportunity), and instead argues for a positive commitment to equal respect between social groups and even the affirmation and celebration of difference *per se*.[31] Identity politics thus represents "a politics based on the particular life experiences of people who seek to be in control of their own identities and subjectivities and who claim that socially dominant groups have denied them this opportunity."[32]

Identity politics is often inspired by, but differs from, more traditional civil rights agendas in U. S. history in its movement beyond legal and political categories into the more ambitious terrain of social respect and equality. Such earlier movements for racial equality, for example, opposed Jim Crow legislation and separate facilities for blacks and whites as an affront to the equality celebrated in the Declaration of Independence and the Constitution (not to mention the Bible).[33] Supporters of the Equal Rights Amendment

---

in *The Identity in Question*, ed. John Rajchman (New York, 1995). The common rejection of liberal solutions (both theoretically and politically) by identity theorists suggests four possibilities: (1) identity theorists have misunderstood the promise of liberalism; (2) liberalism truly cannot deal with the sorts of diversity and difference that characterize late modern societies; (3) liberal theorists make overly grandiose claims for the conscience paradigm's ability to address identity issues; or (4) liberalism can deal successfully with issues of diversity, but not on conscience-based grounds. I argue the third of these possibilities, and tend to agree with the fourth.

31. See, e.g., Young, *Justice and the Politics of Difference*; also see William Connolly, *Identity/Difference: Democratic Negotiations of Political Paradox* (Ithaca, N.Y., 1991). Connolly advocates a "politics of agonistic respect," or as he frames it, "a conception of the political as the medium through which the interdependent antinomies of identity and difference can be expressed and explored" (33, 92). Richards, *Identity and the Case for Gay Rights*, attempts to limn the differences between liberalism and identity politics on the issue of gay rights through a sympathetic reading of liberalism's potential.

32. Edward E. Sampson, "Identity Politics: Challenge to Psychology's Understandings," *American Psychologist* 48 (1993): 1219.

33. The most famous example of this approach occurs in Martin Luther King, Jr.'s "I Have a Dream" speech.

sought an explicit constitutional recognition of the equal citizenship of men and women. In contrast to these earlier movements, which stressed basic civil rights and equal treatment before the law, contemporary identity politics often uses the language of authenticity and respect.[34] As Cornel West puts it, "The difficult and delicate quest for black identity . . . is not solely a political and economic matter. [It] involves self-respect and self-regard, realms inseparable from, yet not identical to, political power and economic status."[35]

Contemporary issues of identity revolve around heritages of oppression and exclusion based on race, gender, ethnicity, sexual orientation, and so on. Such political or theoretical concerns often have little to do with belief or conscience, though, since historical standards of exclusion have generally depended as much on formal (ascribed status- or category-based) as upon substantive (belief-based) criteria.[36] The paradigm of toleration that Rawls and Richards appropriate simply does not easily lend itself to ascribed characteristics. Blacks were not excluded from American public life because of a purported belief they held, or practice in which they engaged: rather, they were attributed an inferiority on the basis of (ascribed) racial classification, which justified their subordinate status in the eyes of their oppressors. Contemporary feminists do not argue for freedom of belief and action, as such, but against inegalitarian social and political structures that—however insidiously, however subtly—deny them equal standing as members of the community, or make the compromising of an essential element of their identity the "price of admission" to mainstream society.[37]

Such issues of race, gender, and sexuality, then, do not involve the assertion of conscientious belief that political regimes are violating, as did the traditional liberal movements for religious toleration, a free press, and voluntary assembly.

34. Without necessarily agreeing with his claim that the "politics of difference grows organically out of the politics of universal dignity," I find Charles Taylor's distinction between a universalist politics of equal dignity and a politics of difference helpful on the distinction between conscience-based and identity-based politics. See *Multiculturalism and "The Politics of Recognition"* (Princeton, 1992), 39.

35. *Race Matters* (New York, 1994), 97.

36. For a broad sketch of the power of this exclusionary history, see Rogers M. Smith, *Civic Ideals: Conflicting Visions of Citizenship in U. S. History* (New Haven, Conn., 1997).

37. See, e.g., Susan Brownmiller, *Femininity* (New York, 1984); also Iris Young's "five faces of oppression," in *Justice and the Politics of Difference*, chap. 2. Betty Friedan referred to the diffuse existential and identity aspects of women's dilemma as "the problem that has no name" (*The Feminine Mystique* [New York, 1963], chap. 1).

They also transcend legal or political categories and address more amorphous aspects of human existence, evoking a demand for recognition and respect of oneself and one's deepest level of being. As Justice Warren wrote in the Brown decision, segregated school systems foster "feeling[s] of inferiority" in African-American students.[38] Bernard Williams sees stereotypes or prejudice as an obstacle to the fundamental (functional) role of identity, "an aid to living [freely or effectively in a convinced way]."[39] Acceptable social or political arrangements, from the perspective of identity theorists, involve not merely legal guarantees for the practice of certain sincerely held beliefs, or even simply equal treatment before the law (both of which fit easily with the historical and conceptual aims of tolerationists), but rather overcoming the social and political devaluation of one's very being and the erection of barriers to self-respect and self-esteem for both individuals and entire groups. This "threat of annihilation"[40] gives much of the literature on politics and identity its sense of urgency and alarm.

TOLERATION AND THE *MODUS VIVENDI* STATE: THE LIMITS, AND PROMISE, OF LIBERAL TOLERATION

Rawls, as I have noted, views the historical experience of the Reformation and the long debates over religious toleration as paradigmatic in the development of liberal theory and, more specifically, his version of political liberalism. Aiming for something far beyond a mere *modus vivendi* state, in which a balance of power dictates the guarantee of certain political rights, Rawls elaborates a progression by which political (indeed, armed) stalemate leads to acceptance of basic constitutional principles, culminating in an "overlapping consensus" of comprehensive doctrines in which citizens affirm a political conception of justice that provides for the exercise of their moral powers and the attainment of self-respect (*PL*, 318ff.).

Rawls wants this concern and respect from his citizens, since he believes that liberty of conscience is essential in order for individuals to feel a sense

---

38. 347 U.S. 483, 74 S.Ct. 686, 98 L.Ed. 873 (1954).

39. "Identity and Identities," in *Identity: Essays Based on Herbert Spencer Lectures Given in the University of Oxford*, ed. Henry Harris (Oxford, 1995), 8.

40. Etienne Balibar, "Culture and Identity: Working Notes," trans. J. Swenson, in *The Identity in Question*, ed. John Rajchman (New York, 1995), 186.

of self-worth. As he puts it, "Self-respect is rooted in our self-confidence as a fully cooperating member of society capable of pursuing a worthwhile conception of the good over a complete life" (*PL*, 318). This notion of a progression from *modus vivendi* to overlapping consensus suggests that Rawls sees basic toleration and equal respect as occupying a kind of continuum, that the sort of political/legal minimalism represented by basic toleration must inevitably (indeed, almost logically) lead to a more robust sense of principled equal respect between citizens. This claim, however, is never addressed explicitly in regard to his claims about the historical and conceptual centrality of toleration in his political liberalism; indeed, it sits strangely with his repeated invocation of the historical development of toleration, which was characterized by the politics of the *modus vivendi* state. Think of the Toleration Act, Cromwell's carefully created state church, and Penn's continuing attempt to protect the civil rights of various groups in Pennsylvania despite royal interference: attempting to placate a number of different religious and political constituencies, these actors carved out the best space for conscience that their conflict-ridden circumstances would allow. These outcomes were real advances in the history of liberty of conscience, not merely second-best solutions.

I am not arguing here that a *modus vivendi* state, in failing to live up to Rawls's standards of equal respect and shared values, fails to protect the conscientious beliefs of its members. Rather, my claim is that Rawls's standards are too high, and never justified by any historical referent: defining *modus vivendi* as purely interest-based and akin to armed stalemate (*PL*, 146–48) fails to appreciate how effective minimal agreements can be (and, historically, have been) in protecting basic rights.[41] In addition, more crucially, Rawls fails to explain why such respect is necessary to a functioning liberal regime, since tolerationists have rarely focused on such issues, concerning themselves with legal and political guarantees for the exercise of conscience.[42] The actual historical development of religious toleration, as I have elaborated its emergence as a practice and a principle, is littered with *modus vivendi*-like arrangements, in which minimal agreements were fashioned to placate various political and

---

41. For a discussion of the promise of *modus vivendi* arrangements, see M.E.H.N. Mout, "Limits and Debates: A Comparative View of Dutch Toleration in the Sixteenth and Early Seventeenth Centuries," in *The Emergence of Tolerance in the Dutch Republic*, ed. C. Berkvens-Stevelinck, J. Israel, and G. H. M. Posthumus Meyjes (Leiden, 1997).

42. I address the distinction between attitudinal tolerance (the basis, in my view, for the type of equal respect that Rawls wants his liberal citizens to exhibit) and political toleration in "Tolerance, Toleration, and the Liberal Tradition."

religious parties and bring peace out of religious strife. Charles Larmore refers to this approach as "defin[ing] the common good of political association by means of a *minimal moral conception.*"[43]

Early modern tolerationists might agree with Rawls that "a plurality of conceptions of the good [is] a fact of modern life" (*PL*, 304). They would never follow such a statement, however (as Rawls does), with the claim that "a plurality of conceptions of the good is desirable" (*PL*, 304). In this respect, the true heirs of early modern toleration debates are not Rawls, Richards, or Dworkin, but those who seek to carve out protected spaces between often-hostile factions in a much more chastened fashion. Liberalism is, in the words of Charles Larmore, "a theory of politics, not a theory of man," in Judith Shklar's, "a political doctrine, not a philosophy of life."[44] Both Shklar and Patrick Neal point out that such a politics will lean heavily on a minimal, Hobbesian understanding of the value of prudence and the potentially dangerous ways that (political, religious, cultural) differences may lead to broad social conflict.[45] Will Kymlicka distinguishes between the attachment to liberal values (i.e., believing that liberal values are the "right" ones) and the much more difficult question of when and whether to insist that nonliberal minorities be required to abide by those values: the distinction, for Kymlicka, should be guided by *prudential, pragmatic* considerations, not the rigid and

43. *The Morals of Modernity* (Cambridge, 1996), 123, emphasis in original. In my account, I contrast Rawls and Larmore. The two do share a number of theoretical and practical commitments; in my account, I emphasize the areas in which Larmore's politically minimal system departs from Rawls. Neal groups them together in the neutralist camp (*Liberalism and Its Discontents*, chap. 9).

44. Larmore, *Patterns of Moral Complexity* (Cambridge, 1987), 118; Shklar, "The Liberalism of Fear," 21. Larmore describes the liberal political system as "a system of mutual advantage, our adherence to which requires that we abstract from controversial ideals of the good life, but in the political domain only, and not in general" (*Patterns of Moral Complexity*, 123–24). This emphasis on the political domain is related to Larmore's distinction between "substantial ideals" (views of the good life) and "the values of autonomy and experimentalism," which refer to how we live out our substantial ideals. See *Patterns of Moral Complexity*, 70–77.

45. Hobbes, of course, has not been presented in these pages as a tolerationist, because in my view he was not one. Given his historical placement (the influence of which on his political theorizing is difficult to overstate), Hobbes viewed such a course as suicidal. But I mean to identify as crucial and valuable something more generally Hobbesian: as Patrick Neal puts it, "Rather than arguing whether Hobbes . . . is a liberal or not . . . I wish to . . . join the issue of whether the Hobbesian spirit of seeking and relying upon a rough equality of power as the linchpin of a liberal order is superior or inferior to the two rival approaches" (*Liberalism and Its Discontents*, 199). He implies that it is superior, and I agree. Replacing "liberal" with "toleration/tolerationist" in the above quotation, I think, will make my point clearer.

unwavering adherence to "liberal" principles.[46] Out of these insights has developed, as Larmore puts it, an appreciation of "two characteristically modern phenomena—the pluralism of ideals about the good life and the existence of reasonable disagreement about which ideals are preferable."[47]

Tolerationists sought to ensure that individuals would not be punished for exercising their conscientious beliefs. In this sense, toleration is at root a "negative liberty": although the term has evolved to include positive elements undreamt of by earlier generations (receipt of unemployment benefits, for example),[48] toleration essentially demands freedom from punishment, and no more.[49] This claim about toleration going no farther than freedom from punishment, of course, does not preclude protracted political arguments about what *constitutes* such freedom from punishment and negative liberty in the context of late modern welfare states, and we should not expect that our definitions will match those current during the seventeenth century. Still, critics of "mere" toleration have perennially and accurately pointed out that it makes no real demands in terms of attitudinal tolerance or mutual respect.[50]

---

46. *Multicultural Citizenship* (Oxford, 1995), chap. 8.

47. *Patterns of Moral Complexity*, 73. Larmore wishes to distinguish between pluralism (a plurality of equally valid values) and reasonable disagreement about what those values are. I agree with his distinction, but the difference does not affect my discussion here—indeed, as Larmore puts it elsewhere, "What is really of significance . . . is that we recognize the difference between pluralism and reasonable disagreement, whatever we may call them" (*Morals of Modernity*, 154).

48. See, for example, the Supreme Court's decision in *Sherbert v. Verner* (374 U. S. 398, 83 S. Ct. 1790, L. Ed. 2d 965 [1964]). The Court ruled that South Carolina's denial of unemployment benefits to a Seventh-Day Adventist who refused to work on Saturdays (her sabbath) violated the First Amendment's prohibition on interference with the free exercise of religion.

49. See Sinopoli, "Thick-Skinned Liberalism," and my "Tolerance, Toleration, and the Liberal Tradition."

50. These critics are not only contemporary theorists of identity. For some classic critiques of toleration by scholars of religious liberty, see Jordan, *Development of Religious Toleration*, 1:17, and Crick, "Toleration and Tolerance in Theory and Practice," 160. Cranston adds that toleration is "always mere toleration" ("Toleration," 8:143). Edward B. Underhill uses the term "liberty of conscience" in connection with the Baptist tradition, describing Samuel Richardson as seeking "no meagre toleration" but rather "complete liberty of conscience." See *Tracts*, 243. See also Bury, *History of Freedom of Thought*, 72, and St. John, *Contest for Liberty of Conscience*, 6. See also Stokes, *Church and State in the United States,* which calls toleration "a halfway house between an attitude by the state of ecclesiastical exclusiveness . . . and . . . freedom of conscience and equality of different religious organizations before the law" (21).

For more contemporary critiques, see Anne Phillips, "Dealing with Difference: A Politics of Ideas or a Politics of Presence?" *Constellations* 1 (1994), 74–91; idem, *Democracy and Difference* (University Park, Pa., 1993); Connolly, *Identity/Difference*; and Young's discussion of the "five faces of oppression" in *Justice and the Politics of Difference*, chap. 2.

At the same time, what I have been calling a minimal, legalistic toleration is not a static phenomenon. Reifying "toleration" into a discrete set of conditions that, once met, ends political debate fails to do justice to the ongoing quest for liberty of conscience in its many forms and risks ossifying an important political and philosophical principle. What I mean is this: although examining the specifics of early modern toleration debates illuminates more general issues of toleration, defining toleration as a species of negative liberty must be further specified and elaborated when making comparisons to advanced welfare states. As we have seen, proponents of liberty of conscience historically sought to a steadily *expanding* sphere in which religious concerns were removed as bases for punishment, persecution, or denial of public benefits. The nature and contours of that expansion, however, represent a series of specific and local applications rather than the unfolding of a grand Rawlsian principle.

In the difficult historical emergence of this cardinal element of the liberal creed, then, what we find is not the progressive flowering of a preordained progress in the direction of Rawlsian liberal consensus, or a desire for the encouragement of "self-respect by . . . basic public institutions" (*PL*, 319), or a search for "constitutional guarantees of equal respect,"[51] but rather painful compromises, hard-headed political negotiations, and a search for political and legal measures to ensure equal citizenship regardless of individuals' religious beliefs. The *modus vivendi* state does not offer blanket declarations of neutrality, or the pursuit of citizens' self-respect, but instead the promotion of a pacific public space in which citizens can live out their deepest beliefs.

Let me consider, very briefly, one contentious contemporary issue. What insights might the history of religious toleration suggest in the context of homosexuality and debates over gay rights? As William N. Eskridge, Jr., puts it, although the emergence and development of religious toleration has led citizens of liberal polities to accept a notion of "benign religious variation" (i.e., to view religious difference as politically unproblematic), "most Americans reject the idea of benign sexual variation . . . [viewing] significant sexual deviation as strange, shameful, perverse, or even wicked."[52] The analogy to early modern religious toleration, in the eyes of those drawing it, runs thus: in the

51. Richards, *Identity and the Case for Gay Rights*, 170.
52. "A Jurisprudence of Coming Out," 2412. See also Eskridge, *Gaylaw*, introduction and chap. 9.

same way that criminal penalties for religious dissent punished individuals for acting in accordance with their deeply held views, legislation criminalizing homosexual acts (even if largely unenforced) makes one's sexual orientation itself a crime, assuming that we understand orientation to include action as well as thought. Given that these views are long-standing, deeply held, and closely interrelated with religious and moral values, any solution to the issue of gay rights will necessarily involve individuals "putting up with" (in some public sense) others whom they view as engaging in perverse, unnatural, and/or socially subversive practices.

Toleration, at its most basic level, would seem to require only the decriminalization of homosexual acts (in contemporary terms, the reversal of the Supreme Court's decision in *Bowers v. Hardwick*).[53] As I have presented it throughout this study, toleration represents a minimal baseline from which further theorizing and action can proceed. The Toleration Act in England, for example, allowed a number of restrictive practices to remain in place; the story of successive generations of religious minorities in England—*beginning* in 1689, and continuing for over a hundred years—is the story of the gradual, grudging, and hard-fought repeal of restrictions on their fuller incorporation into English public life.

If toleration has historically suggested a minimal standard of nonpunishment, that the group in question escape civil prosecution, I am not claiming that this minimum necessarily represents an acceptable degree of liberty across all the contested issues of our own time. In part this unacceptability reflects a modern notion of authenticity, a "being true to oneself," as part of the working out of what a fully human life entails.[54] Beyond the achievement of the basic standard of decriminalization, I am suggesting that we view toleration as a continuum, to be measured in degrees rather than viewed in black-and-white terms. Basic toleration, as I have represented it, is not an end state of affairs but rather the beginning of much more protracted discussions about the requirements of liberal citizenship. Liberal society requires such a basic standard, but whether such a minimum is sufficient for historically evolving notions of liberty and the aspirations of the groups in question will depend, ultimately, on contextual and political factors specific to each situation. In the case of gay rights, one can foresee debates over the incorporation of sexual

53. 478 U.S. 186.
54. Taylor, *Ethics of Authenticity*, chap. 2. The relationship between authenticity and gay identity is eloquently elaborated in Richards, *Identity and the Case for Gay Rights*, 91–95.

orientation as a protected category in civil rights law (broader equal access to public accommodations, housing, and nondiscrimination in employment, for example), military service, gay marriage and adoption, and so on.[55]

At the same time, the history and analogy of toleration do not seek, nor do they provide, a panacea for all social conflict. Early modern tolerationists and the *modus vivendi* politics to which they gave rise espouse a largely state-centered model, and do not set as their goal the eradication of all social prejudice. Tolerationists saw religious liberty as providing fellow citizens with a way to live together, as Richard Sinopoli puts it, in a "thick-skinned" way.[56] Citizens must be willing to live with each other; they need not approve of each other's commitments, religious or otherwise. This disapproval might—often does—take intolerant forms, truly *ugly* forms; and a *modus vivendi* liberalism would likely permit the expression of more of these than other variants of liberalism.[57]

The achievement of basic toleration—the removal of criminal sanctions on the group in question—ends one process and begins another. Whatever the eventual outcome, it will likely be achieved incrementally, and with as much attention to particular specifics as to overarching principles.[58] What tolerationists sought, gradually and step-by-step, was to carve out basic protections for religious dissenters, and to seek a position from which to reflect more broadly about the requirements of a cohesive and ordered society. Advocates of religious toleration historically advanced minimal notions of the requirements of civil society (jettisoning religious uniformity, a centuries-old assumption about the good society). For example, William Penn's advocacy of civil interest as the cement of civil society called on his audiences to forgo a commonly held presupposition (religious uniformity) about the requirements of ordered society.[59] Cass Sunstein uses the analogy of Lincoln's gradual

55. See Richards, *Identity and the Case for Gay Rights*, 110–70, for the argument about conscience and toleration concerning antigay initiatives, exclusion from military service, and same-sex marriage.

56. "Thick-Skinned Liberalism."

57. Neal, *Liberalism and Its Discontents*, chap. 9; my "Tolerance, Toleration, and the Liberal Tradition," 620–23.

58. Stanley Fish, "Boutique Multiculturalism," in *Multiculturalism and American Democracy*, ed. Arthur M. Melzer, Jerry Weinberger, and M. Richard Zinman (Lawrence, Kans., 1998).

59. Recall that Penn asserted, in his *One Project for the Good of England*, that "civil interest is the foundation and end of civil government" (*Works*, 2:682), and invoked the ship of state metaphor on a number of occasions, arguing that "men embarked in the same vessel, seek the safety of the whole in their own, whatever other differences they may have" (*Works*, 2:727).

approach to slavery in arguing for a continual, incremental process of removing barriers to gays and lesbians in American public life; Charles Taylor, in commenting on the clash of cultures that erupted with the publication of Salman Rushdie's *Satanic Verses*, counsels us to learn to live with "inspired adhoccery."[60]

Identity politics, on the other hand, is animated by the historical quest for social equality, a far more expansive set of goals than the more narrowly political or legal focus of toleration. As many proponents of identity politics point out, toleration is not good enough: the good society is not one that merely "lives and lets live," content to leave pockets of prejudice intact so long as they are not acted upon,[61] but rather one that draws out the many different identities in its midst and fosters an active concern and respect for each of them. Given identity theorists' notions about the experiential nature of identity and its totalizing role in the formation of individual consciousness, many scholars have expressed dissatisfaction with "toleration" (with its implicit condemnation or at least condescending disapproval) as a model for social progress. According to Anne Phillips, "We only tolerate what we do not like or approve of . . . yet, where difference is bound up with identity, this is hard for the tolerated to accept."[62] Advocates of identity politics instead frequently call for equality of respect or recognition rather than the "mere" permission associated with toleration. Cornel West argues that an affirmation of "black humanity . . . speaks to the existential issues of what it means to be a degraded African (man, woman, gay, lesbian, child) in a racist society."[63] Phillips's solution calls for "shared experience . . . [to take] precedence over shared ideas," and suggests "public manifestations in which differences can be confronted and (hopefully) resolved," as opposed to the privatization of difference that liberal toleration purportedly advances.[64]

---

60. Cass R. Sunstein, "Homosexuality and the Constitution," *Indiana Law Journal* 70 (1994): 1–28, esp. sec. 4; Taylor, "The Rushdie Controversy," *Public Culture* 2 (1989): 121. Taylor's term is cited approvingly in Fish, "Boutique Multiculturalism," 76.

61. This notion of "live and let live" is most powerfully articulated by Chandran Kukathas: see "Cultural Toleration," in *Nomos 39: Ethnicity and Group Rights*, ed. Ian Shapiro and Will Kymlicka (New York, 1997). Admittedly, Kukathas's position is not a mainstream one, insofar as he effectively jettisons any notion of a shared public sphere; cf. Michael Walzer's "Response to Kukathas," in the same volume.

62. "Dealing With Difference," 79.

63. *Race Matters*, 97.

64. "Dealing With Difference," 76, 79.

In a sense, these critics of liberal toleration are right. But given that contemporary societies are characterized by seemingly intractable divisions on religious, moral, and philosophical views, we must admit that some citizens will continue to view the practices of others, not merely with suspicion or ignorance, but with well-informed hatred. The alternatives, however, are not always so clear. What would it mean to move "beyond" toleration into the realm of respect for and celebration of the differences that make us different? Are such values and celebrations *necessary*, not to say *sufficient*, for the furtherance of human liberty and/or community? The political implications of attitudinal intolerance are difficult to ascertain *a priori*, and certainly need not include persecution and suppression. In fact, individual intolerance in itself may have few implications for politics at all.[65] As Russell Hanson notes, "Most people refrain from intolerant actions, even though they harbor less-than-tolerant attitudes."[66]

A firm commitment to equal protection of law, equal opportunity, and a structure of basic civil rights might indeed seem minimal against the background of calls for the celebration of difference. But, as Judith Shklar has put it, "The very refusal to use public coercion to impose creedal uniformity and uniform standards of behavior demands an enormous degree of self-control. . . . Far from being an immoral free-for-all, liberalism is, in fact, extremely difficult and constraining."[67] The liberal citizen commits him- or herself to performing certain civil actions, and to little else: this is deeply disturbing to communitarians, second nature to liberals, but worth reiterating nonetheless. We should not underestimate, I suggest, the value of a *modus vivendi*. It is a chastened politics, a politics that realizes that deeply held and fundamentally conflicting values are with us to stay.[68]

---

65. See James Davison Hunter, "Religion and Political Civility: The Coming Generation of American Evangelicals," *Journal for the Scientific Study of Religion* 23 (1984): 364–80, and idem, *Evangelicalism: The Coming Generation* (Chicago, 1987), chap. 5.

66. "Deliberation, Tolerance, and Democracy," in *Reconsidering the Democratic Public*, ed. George E. Marcus and Russell Hanson (University Park, Pa., 1993), 274.

67. Shklar, *Ordinary Vices*, 4–5.

68. Here I agree with Fish ("Boutique Multiculturalism") in viewing multiculturalism as a demographic fact rather than a philosophical problem. The accompanying politics, then, will be pragmatic and situated, not grand and all-encompassing.

CONCLUSION

Over the course of several centuries, religious liberty and the freedoms of press, speech, and assembly have evolved into basic liberal constitutional values. Rawls sees the generalization of religious toleration as the root of the broader principle of equal liberty. Toleration (with its purported underwriting of liberal neutrality) is Rawls's master metaphor, historically and conceptually: recall that, for Rawls, the principle of equal political liberty represents the "generaliz[ation of] religious toleration to a social form" (*TOJ*, 206). Richards echoes Rawls in his search for a principle on which to ground a host of issues: "A plausible theory of suspect classification analysis must unify, on grounds of principle, the claims to such analysis by African-Americans, women, and lesbians and gays."[69] Other liberal theorists invoke Locke and Mill as embodying a sort of historical progression of tolerationist ideas, one that originates in a narrow plea for Protestant Dissenters and expands to incorporate lifestyle differences or more general nonconformity.[70]

Religious toleration is indeed a central liberal commitment, and free conscience has historically grounded a number of core liberal values such as assembly, speech, and press. But we should not ask our concepts to perform impossible tasks. Identity politics poses new and different problems in political theory and practice, and liberal theorists have so far provided far too little argumentation about how conscience can speak to identity issues. Rawls, for example, hastens to systematize the liberal tradition.[71] But claims about master metaphors are ahistorical and illusory, and (although the rhetorical advantages are clear) we would do better to develop appropriate arguments for our own political issues. By attempting to make identity issues fit into the tradition that justified religious toleration, Rawls and Richards misrepresent both present-day issues (since toleration and identity politics seek two quite different aims) and historical figures central to our tradition (since these figures were dealing with debates which do not generalize nearly as easily as Rawls, and others, would like to think).

Perhaps, though, we need not differentiate toleration and identity politics in the ways I have suggested in order to question such ambitious claims about

---

69. *Identity and the Case for Gay Rights*, 10.
70. See Cranston, "Toleration," 8:143–46; Tinder, *Tolerance*.
71. This tendency is markedly diminished in Rawls's *Political Liberalism* in contrast to his earlier *Theory of Justice*, yet the insistence on liberty of conscience as a formative, grounding element of a liberal creed displays a fundamental continuity.

religious toleration and its power to address a range of contemporary issues. Perhaps we need only acknowledge the plurality, heterogeneity, and contingency inherent in the development of the liberal tradition and in the process of historical change itself. There seem to be a number of foundations for liberalism generally: to suggest the two most relevant to this project, what I have called the conscience paradigm and another we might refer to as an equality paradigm. The conscience paradigm, evoking the campaign for liberty of conscience and its attendant institutional and political manifestations—worship, speech, press, and assembly—has played a key role in carving out a gradual and steadily expanding area in which individuals are protected from civil sanctions for their religious or ethical stances.

An equality paradigm, on the other hand, might address the exclusion from citizenship and social life of various ethnic, sexual, or racial groups, whose representatives have historically asserted, not an unjust penalty inflicted on account of creed (and the compatibility of that creed with ordered civil society), but rather a common humanity or at least Americanism, that "the Declaration applies to us, too."[72] Equality as the basis for liberal rights is best represented in the work of Ronald Dworkin, who argues for a "right to equal concern and respect in the design and administration of the political institutions that govern them."[73] I intend these comments—this positing of two different "paradigms" as foundation of something called "liberalism"—as merely suggestive, intended to reinforce an appreciation of the heterogeneity of the liberal tradition and move away from the overemphasis, and consequently the overextension, of one principle among many.[74]

The tradition that gave rise to religious toleration and liberty of conscience will not "buy" a politics of broad respect for identity and authenticity. Contrary to Rawls's claims, there is no single formative liberal virtue or practice that grounds all others and from which all others derive. Liberal values have

72. See, for example, the Seneca Falls Declaration and Martin Luther King, Jr.'s "I Have a Dream" speech. Sometimes those evoking equality blend American and religious overtones, as when King stated flatly, "We have waited for more than 340 years for our constitutional and God-given rights" ("Letter from Birmingham Jail," 768).

73. *Taking Rights Seriously* (Cambridge, Mass., 1977), 180. See also Dworkin, "Liberalism," in *A Matter of Principle*.

74. Others might adduce additional paradigms or building blocks of liberal modernity: for example, Charles Taylor identifies inwardness, the "affirmation of everyday life," and an increased attention to nature as hallmarks of modern life (*Sources of the Self*).

developed over the course of the past three hundred years, often on an ad hoc basis, as liberal thinkers have come to see various political issues as related in one way or another and as vital to the achievement or maintenance of human freedom. This project has been devoted to illuminating the development of one principle in one historically significant period of time. If there is any sort of historical progression, it does not lie in the steady expansion of the principle of toleration from religion to other spheres of human life and the burgeoning equal respect that purportedly follows from such an expansion, but rather in the accumulation of different arguments to deal with the many areas in which individuals seek protection from their governments and each other.

BIBLIOGRAPHY

I. PRIMARY SOURCES

A. Printed Material

Alighieri, Dante. *De monarchia.* Translated and edited by Prue Shaw. Cambridge: Cambridge University Press, 1996.
————. *Inferno.* Translated and with an introduction by Allen Mandelbaum. Berkeley and Los Angeles: University of California Press, 1980.
Allen, James, Joshua Moody, Samuel Willard, and Cotton Mather. *The Principles of the Protestant Religion Maintained.* Boston, 1690.
Ames, William. *Conscience with the Power and Cases Thereof.* London, 1639. Translation of *De conscientia et eius iure vel casibus.* Amsterdam, 1630.
————. *A Fresh Suit Against Human Ceremonies in God's Worship.* Amsterdam, 1633.
The Answer of the Assembly of Divines unto the Reasons of the Seven Dissenting Brethren. London, 1644.
Anti-toleration; or, A Modest Defense of the Letter of the London Ministers. London, 1646.
Aquinas, Thomas. *The Disputed Questions on Truth.* 3 vols. Translated by Robert W. Mulligan, S.J. Chicago: Henry Regnery, 1952.
————. *Summa Theologica.* Translated by Fathers of the English Dominican Province. Westminster, Md.: Christian Classics, 1981.
Ashenden, Thomas. *No Penalty, No Peace.* London, 1682.
Assheton, William. *A Seasonable Discourse Against Toleration.* London, 1685.
Augustine. *The Confessions and Letters of St. Augustine.* Edited by Philip Schaff. Vol. 1 of *A Select Library of the Nicene and Post-Nicene Fathers.* Grand Rapids, Mich.: Eerdmans, 1983.
————. *Letter 185: On the Treatment of the Donatists.* In *St. Augustine's Letters,* vol. 4, trans. Sister Wilfred Parsons. New York: Fathers of the Church, 1955.
Baillie, Robert. *The Letters and Journals of Robert Baillie, A.M., Principal of the University of Glasgow.* Edited by David Laing. 3 vols. Edinburgh, 1842.
Barclay, Robert. *Theologiae vere Christianae apologia.* Amsterdam, 1675. Published in English as *An Apology for the True Christian Divinity.* London, 1678.
Baxter, Richard. *Reliquae Baxterianae.* London, 1696.
Bethel, Slingsby. *The Present Interest of England Stated.* London, 1671.
Bishop, George. *New England Judged.* London, 1661.
Blount, Charles. *An Appeal from the Country to the City.* London, 1679.

Bohun, Edmund. "Preface." In Robert Filmer, *Patriarcha*. London, 1685.

The Book of the General Laws and Liberties Concerning the Inhabitants of the Massachusetts. 1647. Reprint. San Marino, Calif.: Huntington Library Press, 1975.

Brooke, Lord (Robert Greville). *Discourse Opening the Nature of That Episcopacy, Which Is Exercised in England*. London, 1642.

Buckingham, duke of (George Villiers). *A Short Discourse on the Reasonableness of Men Having a Religion*. 2d ed. London, 1685.

Budd, Thomas. *A Just Rebuke to Several Calumnies, Lies, and Slanders*. Philadelphia, 1692.

———. *A True Copy of Three Judgments . . . Against George Keith and His Friends*. Philadelphia, 1692.

Bugg, Francis. *De Christiana libertate*. London, 1682.

———. *News from Pennsylvania*. London, 1703.

Burnet, Gilbert. *The Case of Compulsion in Matters of Religion, Stated*. London, 1688.

———. *A Letter, Containing Some Reflections on His Majesties Declaration for Liberty of Conscience*. London, 1689.

[Burthogge, Richard]. *Prudential Reasons for Repealing the Penal Laws Against All Recusants, and for a General Toleration*. London, 1688.

Busher, Leonard. *Religion's Peace; or, A Plea for Liberty of Conscience*. London, 1614.

[Care, George]. *Liberty of Conscience Asserted; or, A Looking-Glass for Persecutors*. London, 1687.

———. *Liberty of Conscience Asserted and Vindicated*. London, 1689.

Care, Henry. *English Liberties*. London, 1682.

———. *Liberty of Conscience, Asserted*. London, 1687.

The Case of Protestants in England Under a Popish Prince. London, 1681. In Scott, *Somers Tracts*, 8:147–66.

Certain Additional Reasons to Those Presented [by the London Ministers] Against the Toleration of Independency. London, 1645.

"The Charge of the Scottish Commissioners." In Scott, *Somers Tracts*, 4:415–31.

Chillingworth, William. *Mr. Chillingworths Letter Touching Infallibility*. London, 1662.

———. *The Religion of Protestants a Safe Way to Salvation*. London, 1638.

Church of Scotland. *A Solemn Testimony Against Toleration*. Edinburgh, 1649.

Clarendon, earl of (Edward Hyde). *History of the Rebellion and Civil Wars in England*. Edited by W. Dunn Macray. Oxford: Oxford University Press, 1888.

Clarke, John. *Ill Newes from New England*. London, 1652. Reprinted in *Massachusetts Historical Society Collections*, ser. 4, vol. 2. Boston: Massachusetts Historical Society, 1854.

Cobbett, Thomas. *The Civil Magistrates Power in Matters of Religion*. London, 1653.

Coleman, Thomas. *Hopes Deferred and Dashed*. London, 1645.

[Comber, Thomas]. *Christianity No Enthusiasm*. London, 1678.

———. *Three Considerations Proposed to Mr. William Penn, Concerning . . . His New Magna Charta for Liberty of Conscience*. London, 1688.

Cotton, John. *An Abstract of the Laws of New England*. London, 1641.

———. *The Bloudy Tenent, Washed and Made White in the Blood of the Lambe*. London, 1647.

———. *The Controversie Concerning Liberty of Conscience in Matters of Religion.* London, 1646.

———. *A Discourse About Civil Government in a New Plantation Whose Design Is Religion.* Cambridge, Mass., 1663.

———. John Cotton's Letter to Samuel Skelton." Edited by David D. Hall. *WMQ* 23 (1965): 478–85.

———. *A Letter of Mr John Cottons Teacher of the Church in Boston.* London, 1643. In volume 1 of *The Complete Writings of Roger Williams*, ed. Samuel L. Caldwell. New York: Russell and Russell, 1963.

———. *A Reply to Mr. Williams His Examination.* London, 1647. In volume 2 of *The Complete Writings of Roger Williams*, ed. Samuel L. Caldwell. New York: Russell and Russell, 1963.

———. *The Way of the Churches of Christ in New England.* London, 1645.

The Danger and Unreasonableness of a Toleration. London, 1685.

Davis, William. *Jesus, the Crucified Man.* Philadelphia, 1700.

Defoe, Daniel. *A Letter to a Dissenter from His Friend at the Hague.* London, 1688.

Delaune, Thomas. *Compulsion of Conscience Condemned.* London, 1683.

Dell, Willam. *Right Reformation.* London, 1646.

Directory for the Publique Worship of God Throughout the Three Kingdomes. London, 1646.

A Discourse of Toleration. London, 1691.

The Dissenting Ministers Vindication of Themselves from the . . . Murder of King Charles I. London, c. 1660. In Scott, *Somers Tracts*, 5:258–62.

Divine Observations upon the London Ministers Letter Against Toleration. London, 1645.

Edwards, Thomas. *Antapologia; or, A Full Answer to the Apologeticall Narration.* London, 1646.

———. *The Casting Down of the Last and Strongest Hold of Satan; or, A Treatise Against Toleration and Pretended Liberty of Conscience.* London, 1647.

———. *Gangraena.* London, 1646.

———. *Reasons Against the Independent Government of Churches.* London, 1641.

The Excellent Priviledge of Liberty and Property. Philadelphia, 1687.

An Expedient for Peace. London, 1688.

Fagel, Gasper. *A Letter, Writ by Mijn Heer Fagel, Pensioner of Holland.* Amsterdam, 1688.

Falkland, Viscount (Lucius Cary). *A Discourse of Infallibility.* London, 1660.

Falkner, William. *Christian Loyalty.* London, 1684.

Ferguson, Robert. *A Brief Justification of the Prince of Orange's Descent into England.* London, 1689.

A Few Short Arguments Proving That Tis Every Englishman's Interest as Well as Duty . . . to Endeavor the . . . Repeal of All the Religious Penal Laws and Tests. London, 1687.

F[i]eld, John. *Light and Truth Discovering Sophistry and Deceit.* London, 1701.

———. *The Weakness of George Keith's Reasons for Renouncing Quakerism.* London, 1700.

Filmer, Robert. *Patriarcha and Other Writings.* Edited by Johann Sommerville. Cambridge: Cambridge University Press, 1991.

Fleming, Robert. *A Survey of Quakerism*. London, 1677.

[Forbes, Alexander]. *An Anatomy of Independency; or, A Brief Commentary on the Apologeticall Narration*. London, 1644.

Four Grand Questions Proposed. London, 1689.

Fox, George. *A Journal or Historical Account of the Life, Travels, Sufferings, Christian Experiences and Labor of Love in the . . . Ministry of . . . George Fox*. London, 1694.

Foxe, John. *Acts and Monuments of the English Martyrs*. London, 1583.

Fraser, James. *King William's Toleration, Being an Explanation of That Liberty of Religion Which May Be Expected from His Majesty's Declaration*. London, 1689.

A Friendly Debate upon the New Elections of Parliament, and the Settlement of Liberty of Conscience. London, 1688.

G. T. *A Letter in Answer to Two Main Questions*. London, 1687.

Gillespie, George. *Wholesome Severity Reconciled with Christian Liberty*. London, 1644.

Goodwin, John. *Anti-Cavalierism*. London, 1642.

——. *Independency Gods Verity*. London, 1647.

——. *Right and Might Well Met*. London, 1649.

——. *Theomachia; or, The Grand Impudence of Men Running the Hazard of Fighting Against God*. London, 1644.

——. *Truth and Innocency Triumphing Together*. London, 1648.

Goodwin, Thomas, Philip Nye, Sidrach Simpson, Jeremiah Burroughes, and William Bridge. *An Apologeticall Narration*. London, 1643.

Gorton, Samuel. *Simplicities Defence Against Seven-Headed Policy*. London, 1646. In *Collections of the Rhode Island Historical Society* 2 (1835).

The Great Case of Toleration Stated. London, 1688.

Halifax, marquis of (George Savile). *A Letter from a Clergy-Man in the City, to His Friend*. London, 1688.

——. *A Letter to a Dissenter: Upon Occasion of His Majesties Late Gracious Declaration of Indulgence*. London, 1687.

The Harmonious Consent of the Ministers . . . of Lancaster. London, 1648.

Harrington, James. *The Commonwealth of Oceana and A System of Politics*. Edited by J.G.A. Pocock. Cambridge: Cambridge University Press, 1992.

[Henderson, Alexander]. *Reformation of Church-Government in Scotland Cleared from Some Mistakes and Prejudices*. London, 1644.

Hobbes, Thomas. *Behemoth, or the Long Parliament*. 1682. Edited by Ferdinand Tonnies. 2d ed. London: Frank Cass, 1969.

——. *De Cive [Philosophical Rudiments Concerning Government and Society]*. 1651. Edited by Howard Warrender. Oxford: Oxford University Press, 1983.

——. *Elements of Law*. 1650. Edited by Ferdinand Tonnies. 2d ed. New York: Barnes and Noble, 1969.

——. *Elements of Philosophy, The First Section, Concerning Body*. 1656. Edited by William Molesworth. London, 1839.

——. *Leviathan*. 1651. Edited by Edwin Curley. Indianapolis: Hackett, 1994.

Holdsworth, Richard. *An Answer Without a Question*. London, 1649.

Howgill, Francis. *The Popish Inquisition Newly Erected in New England*. London, 1659.

The Humble Petition of Many Well-Affected Freemen and Citizens of the City of London. London, 1646.
The Humble Petition of the Ministers of the Counties of Suffolk and Essex. London, 1646.
The Humble Request. London, 1630.
H[umfrey], J[ohn]. *The Authority of the Magistrate, About Religion, Discussed.* London, 1672.
Hunt, Thomas. *Mr. Hunts Argument for the Bishops Right.* London, 1682.
Hutchinson, Thomas. *The History of the Colony and Province of Massachusetts-Bay.* 1756–58. Edited by Lawrence Shaw Mayo. Cambridge: Harvard University Press, 1936.
Jacob, Henry. *An Attestation of Many Learned . . . Divines.* London, 1613.
———. *A Christian and Modest Offer.* London, 1606.
———. *To the Right High and Mighty Prince, James . . . an Humble Supplication for Toleration.* London, 1609.
Jefferson, Thomas. "Bill for Establishing Religious Freedom." In *The Portable Thomas Jefferson,* ed. Merrill D. Peterson. New York: Penguin, 1977.
Jennings, Samuel. *The State of the Case.* London, 1694.
John the Baptist, Forerunner of Christ Jesus; or, A Necessity of Liberty of Conscience. London, 1644.
Johnson, Edward. *Wonder-Working Providence of Sion's Saviour in New England.* 1658. Edited by J. Franklin Jameson. Original Narratives of Early American History. New York: Charles Scribner's Sons, 1910.
Johnson, Samuel. *Julian the Apostate.* London, 1682.
[Jurieu, Pierre.] *A Letter of Several French Ministers Fled into Germany upon the Account of the Persecution in France.* London, 1688.
Kant, Immanuel. "An Answer to the Question: What Is Enlightenment?" In *Perpetual Peace and Other Essays,* trans. Ted Humphrey. Indianapolis: Hackett, 1983.
Keith, George. *An Account of the Great Divisions Amongst the Quakers in Pennsylvania.* London, 1692.
———. *The Anti-Christs and Sadducees Detected.* London, 1696.
———. *An Appeal from the Twenty-Eight Judges to the Spirit of Truth and True Judgment.* Philadelphia, 1692.
———. *Bristol Quakerism Exposed.* London, 1700.
———. *The Causeless Ground of Surmises, Jealousies and Unjust Offenses Removed.* London, 1694.
———. *An Exhortation and Caution to Friends, Concerning the Buying and Keeping of Negroes.* New York, 1693.
———. *The Fundamental Truths of Christianity.* London, 1688.
———. *A Further Discovery of the Spirit of Falsehood and Persecution in Samuel Jennings.* London, 1694.
———. *Gross Error and Hypocrisy Detected.* London, 1695.
———. *The Heresy and Hatred That Was Falsely Charged upon the Innocent, Justly Returned upon the Guilty.* Philadelphia, 1693.
———. *New England's Spirit of Persecution Transmitted to Pennsylvania.* Philadelphia, 1693.
———. *A Plain Short Catechism for Children and Youth.* Philadelphia, 1690.

————. *The Presbyterian and Independent Visible Churches in New-England*. Philadelphia, 1689.

————. *The Pretended Antidote Proved Poyson*. Philadelphia, 1690.

————. *A Seasonable Information and Caveat Against . . . Thomas Ellwood*. London, 1694.

————. *A Serious Appeal to All the More Sober, Impartial, and Judicious People in New-England*. Philadelphia, 1692.

————. *Some Reasons and Causes of the Late Separation That Hath Come to Pass at Philadelphia*. Philadelphia, 1692.

————. *A Testimony and Caution*. Philadelphia, 1693.

————. *The Trials of Peter Boss, George Keith, Thomas Budd, and William Bradford, Quakers*. London, 1693.

————. *The True Christ Owned*. London, 1679.

Keith, George, and Thomas Budd. *False Judgments Reprehended*. Philadelphia, 1692.

Kidder, Richard. *The Judgment of Private Discretion in Matters of Religion, Defended*. London, 1687.

Langhorne, Richard. *Considerations Touching the Great Question of the King's Right in Dispensing with the Penal Laws*. London, 1687.

A Late Dialogue Between a Civilian and a Divine. London, 1644.

Laud, William. *Speech Delivered in the Star-Chamber, at the Censure of John Bastwick, Henry Burton, and William Prynne*. London, 1637.

Leeds, Daniel. *News of a Strumpet Cohabiting in the Wilderness*. New York, 1701.

————. *News of a Trumpet Sounding in the Wilderness*. New York, 1697.

L'Estrange, Roger. *The Case Put, Concerning the Succession of His Royal Highness the Duke of York*. 2d ed. London, 1679.

A Letter from a Gentleman in the Country to His Friend in London. London, 1687.

A Letter from an Independent to His Honoured Friend, a Presbyterian in London. London, 1645.

A Letter in Answer to a City Friend. London, 1687.

A Letter of the Ministers of the City of London. London, 1645.

A Letter to a Member of Parliament, for Liberty of Conscience. London, 1689.

Liberty and the Weal Public Reconciled. London, 1637.

Liberty of Conscience Confuted. London, 1648.

Liberty of Conscience Explicated and Vindicated. London, 1689.

Locke, John. *An Essay Concerning Human Understanding*. London, 1690.

————. *A Letter Concerning Toleration*. 1689. Edited by James Tully. Indianapolis: Hackett, 1983.

————. *A Letter from a Person of Quality to His Friend in the Country*. London, 1675. Also in *State Tracts: Being a Collection of Several Treatises Relating to the Government* (London, 1693), 41–56.

————. *Political Writings of John Locke*. Edited by David Wootton. New York: Mentor/New American Library, 1993.

————. *The Reasonableness of Christianity, as Delivered in the Scriptures*. London, 1695. Edited by George M. Ewing. (Chicago: Henry Regnery, 1965).

————. *Scritti Editi e Inediti Sulla Tolleranza*. Edited by C. A. Viano. Turin: Taylor, 1961.

————. *Second Treatise of Government*. 1690. Edited by Peter Laslett. Cambridge: Cambridge University Press, 1988.

———. *Two Treatises of Government.* 1690. Edited and with an introduction by Peter Laslett. Cambridge: Cambridge University Press, 1963.

Luther, Martin. *Address to the Christian Nobility.* 1520.

———. *Commentary on Galatians.*

Makemie, Francis. *An Answer to George Keith's Libel.* Boston, 1694.

Mather, Richard. *Church-Government and Church-Covenant Discussed.* London, 1643.

[Maurice, Henry]. *The Antithelemite.* London, 1685.

Melanchthon, Phillip. *The Loci Communes of Philip Melanchthon.* 1555. Translated and with an introduction by Charles Leander Hall. Boston: Meador, 1944.

Mill, John Stuart. *On Liberty.* 1859. Edited by Elizabeth Rapaport. Indianapolis: Hackett, 1978.

Milton, John. *Areopagitica.* London, 1644.

———. *Areopagitica and Other Political Writings of John Milton.* Edited by John Alvis. Indianapolis: Liberty Fund, 1999.

———. *Of Reformation, and the Causes Which Have Hindered It.* London, 1641.

———. "On the Forcers of Conscience." In *The Complete Poetry of John Milton,* ed. John T. Shawcross. Garden City, N.Y.: Doubleday, 1971.

———. *The Tenure of Kings and Magistrates.* London, 1649.

———. *A Treatise of Civil Power in Ecclesiastical Causes.* London, 1659.

A Most Humble Supplication of Many of the King's Majesty's Loyal Subjects. London, 1620.

Musgrave, John. *The Conscience Pleading for Its Own Liberty.* London, 1647.

Nalson, John. *The Complaint of Liberty and Property, Against Arbitrary Government.* Edinburgh, 1681.

Newcomen, Matthew. *The Duty of Such as Would Walk Worthy of the Gospel: To Endeavour Union, Not Division Nor Toleration.* London, 1646.

[Norris, John]. *The Charge of Schism Continued.* London, 1691.

Norton, John. *The Heart of New England Rent at the Blasphemies of the Present Generation.* Cambridge, Mass., 1659.

———. *Three Choice and Profitable Sermons.* Cambridge, Mass., 1664.

[Overton, Richard]. *The Arraignment of Mr. Persecution.* London, 1645.

———. *A Remonstrance of Many Thousand Citizens.* [The Large Petition of the Levellers.] London, 1646.

Owen, John. *Indulgence and Toleration Considered: In a Letter unto a Person of Honour.* In *The Works of John Owen,* vol. 13, ed. Rev. William Gould. London and Edinburgh, 1851.

———. *Of Toleration: And the Duty of the Magistrate About Religion.* In *The Works of John Owen,* vol. 8, ed. Rev. William Gould. London and Edinburgh, 1851.

———. "Propositions Humbly Tendered to the Committee for Propagating the Gospel." *Perfect Diurnall,* 25 March 1652, 1776–77.

———. *Righteous Zeal Encouraged by Divine Protection.* In *The Works of John Owen,* vol. 8, ed. Rev. William Gould. London and Edinburgh, 1851.

Papers Given in to the [Committee for Accommodation]. London, 1644.

Parker, Samuel. *A Discourse of Ecclesiastical Polity.* London, 1669.

———. *Religion and Loyalty.* London, 1684.

Paston, James. *A Discourse of Penal Laws in Matters of Religion.* London, 1688.

Penn, William. *A Collection of the Works of William Penn*. 2 vols. London, 1726. Reprint. New York: AMS Press, 1974.

———. *Considerations Moving to a Toleration, and Liberty of Conscience*. London, 1685.

———. *A Letter from a Gentleman in the Country . . . upon the Penal Laws and Tests*. London, 1687.

———. *The Reasonableness of Toleration*. London, 1687.

———. *Some Sober and Weighty Reasons Against Punishing Protestant Dissenters*. London, 1682.

Persecution for Religion Judged and Condemned. London, 1615.

Phillips, John. *The Character of a Popish Successor*. London, 1681. Also in *State Tracts: Being a Collection of Several Treatises Relating to the Government* (London, 1693), 148–64.

Platform of Church Discipline. [Cambridge Platform.] Boston, 1649.

The Plea of the Harmless Oppressed. London, 1688.

The Popish Plot, Taken out of Several Depositions. London, c. 1680. In Scott, *Somers Tracts*, 7:54–56.

A Protestant dissenter. *One Wonder More, Added to the Seven Wonders of the World. Verified in the Person of Mr. George Keith, Once a Presbyterian, Afterwards About Thirty Years a Quaker, Then a Noun Substantive at Turners-Hall, and Now an Itinerant Preacher (upon His Good Behavior) in the Church of England.—and All Without Variation (as Himself Says) in Fundamentals*. London, c. 1701.

Proud, Robert. *The History of Pennsylvania . . . 1681–1742*. 2 vols. Philadelphia: Zachariah Poulson, Jr., 1797.

Prynne, William. *Anti-Arminianism*. London, 1630.

———. *Diotrephes Catechised*. 2d ed. London, 1646.

———. *Independency Examined*. London, 1644.

———. *Twelve Considerable and Serious Considerations Touching Church-Government*. London, 1644.

Pusey, Caleb. *A Modest Account from Pennsylvania*. London, 1696.

———. *Satan's Harbinger Encountered*. Philadelphia, 1697.

Pym, John. "A Declaration of the Grievances of the Kingdom, c. 1640." In Scott, *Somers Tracts*, 4:390–404.

The Reasons of the Dissenting Brethren Against the Third Proposition, Concerning Presbyterial Government. London, 1645.

Richardson, Samuel. *The Necessity of Toleration in Matters of Religion*. London, 1647.

[Robinson, Henry]. *Liberty of Conscience*. London, 1644.

[Rous, Francis]. *The Ancient Bounds, or Liberty of Conscience*. London, 1645.

Rutherford, Samuel. *A Free Disputation Concerning Pretended Liberty of Conscience*. London, 1649.

———. *Joshua Redivivus, or Mr. Rutherford's Letters*. Rotterdam, 1664.

———. *A Peaceful and Temperate Plea*. London, 1642.

Saltmarsh, John. *Dawnings of Light*. London, 1646.

———. *A New Quaere*. London, 1646.

———. *The Smoke in the Temple*. London, 1646.

Sanderson, Robert. *Complete Works*. 6 vols. Edited by William Jacobson. Oxford: Oxford University Press, 1854.

A Serious and Faithfull Representation. London, 1649.

Shaftesbury, earl of (Anthony Ashley Cooper). "Speech to Parliament, November 1678." In Scott, *Somers Tracts*, 8:48–50.

Sharp, John. *A Discourse Concerning Conscience*. London, 1684.

Shepard, Thomas. "Thomas Shepard's Election Sermon, in 1638." *New England Historical and Genealogical Register* 24 (1870): 361–66.

Shewen, William. *A Brief Testimony for Religion*. London, 1688.

Sidney, Algernon. *Discourses Concerning Government*. 1698. Edited by Thomas G. West. Indianapolis: Liberty Fund, 1990.

A Solemn League and Covenant, for Reformation, and Defense of Religion. Edinburgh, 1643.

Some Queries Concerning Liberty of Conscience, Directed to William Penn and Henry Care. London, 1688.

[Steuart, Adam]. *Some Observations and Annotations upon the Apologeticall Narration*. London, 1643.

Stillingfleet, Edward. *The Mischief of Separation*. London, 1680.

———. *The Unreasonableness of Separation*. London, 1682.

Stoughton, William. *An Assertion for True and Christian Church-Policy*. 1604. London, 1642.

Taylor, Jeremy. *Theologike Eklektike; or, A Discourse on the Liberty of Prophesying*. London, 1647.

Three Queries, and Answers to Them. London, 1688.

Thucydides. *The Peloponnesian War*. Translated by Thomas Hobbes. 1628. Chicago: University of Chicago Press, 1989.

Toleration Justified. London, 1645.

Twelve Weighty Queries of Great Concernment. London, 1646.

Tyrrell, James. *Patriarcha non Monarcha*. London, 1681.

Vernon, John. *The Swords Abuse Asserted*. London, 1648.

de Vitoria, Francisco. "On Civil Power." c. 1528. In *Political Writings*, ed. Anthony Pagden and Jeremy Lawrance. Cambridge: Cambridge University Press, 1991.

Walker, Clement. *Anarchia Anglicana; or, The History of Independency*. London, 1649.

Walwyn, William. *The Compassionate Samaritane*. London, 1644.

———. *A Help to the Right Understanding of a Discourse Concerning Independency*. London, 1645.

———. *The Power of Love*. London, 1643.

———. *A Prediction of Mr. Edwards His Conversion and Recantation*. London, 1646.

———. *A Still and Soft Voice from the Scriptures*. London, 1647.

———. *A Whisper in the Ear of Mr. Thomas Edwards, Minister*. London, 1646.

Ward, Nathaniel. *The Simple Cobbler of Aggawwam in America*. 1647. Edited by P. M. Zall. Lincoln: University of Nebraska Press, 1969.

The Western Rebel. London, 1685.

Wetenhall, Edward. *The Protestant Peace-Maker*. London, 1682.

Wheelwright, John. "Sermon Preached at Boston in New England upon a Fast Day, the 16th of January 163[7]." In *John Wheelwright: His Writings*. Boston: The Prince Society/John Wilson and Son, 1876.

Whitelock, Bulstrode. *Memorials of the English Affairs from the Beginning of the Reign of Charles the First, to the Happy Restoration of King Charles the Second*. 4 vols. 1682. Oxford: Oxford University Press, 1853.

Williams, Roger. *The Bloudy Tenent of Persecution*. London, 1644. In volume 3 of *The Complete Writings of Roger Williams*, ed. Samuel L. Caldwell. New York: Russell and Russell, 1963.

———. *The Bloudy Tenent Yet More Bloudy*. London, 1652.

———. *Mr Cottons Letter Lately Printed, Examined, and Answered*. London, 1644. In volume 1 of *The Complete Writings of Roger Williams*, ed. Samuel L. Caldwell. New York: Russell and Russell, 1963.

———. *Queries of Highest Consideration*. London, 1647.

Winslow, Edward. *Hypocrisie Unmasked*. London, 1646.

Winthrop, John. *A Short Story of the Rise, Reign, and Ruine of the Antinomians, Familists and Libertines*. London, 1644.

———. *Winthrop's Journal: History of New England, 1630–1649*. Edited by James Kendall Hosmer. Original Narratives of Early American History. New York: Charles Scribner's Sons, 1908.

de Witt, Cornelius. *A Letter from Holland, Touching Liberty of Conscience*. London, 1688.

B. Manuscripts and Unpublished Documents

"An Answer to Certain Proposals Presented to Several of Us." SW Keithian controversy MSS, 1693 4 mo 8.

[Blair, Harold.] "Novations in Religion. . . ." HL Manuscript EL 7001.

Bucks County Meeting. Condemnation of George Keith. Historical Society of Pennsylvania, Etting Collection (Early Quakers), p. 79.

[Burhope, George]. *A Seasonable Discourse to the Clergy and Laity in a Visitation Sermon* (1680). HL Manuscript EL 8388 (35/B/38).

Cooper, James, and Esther Cooper. "Acknowledgment of Having Followed George Keith." SW Misc. MSS, 1695 11 mo 9.

Downing, Calibut. Sermon extract. HL Manuscript EL 6874.

England's Congratulation, for Its Happy Condition Under the Glorious Reign of William and Mary. [1690.] HL Manuscript EL 8770 (35/B/43).

"An Epitaph on Passive Obedience." HL Manuscript EL 8780.

"George Keith's Articles of Church Fellowship, or Gospel Order and Discipline Improved." SW Proud MSS, Folder C.

Hitchcock, Robert. *A Sermon on Law, Nature, and Conscience*. HL Manuscript EL 8389, n.d.

———. *The Thankful Leper, or Samaritan*. HL Manuscript EL 8178 (35/B/29).

"The Humble Answer of Edward Randolph to His Majesties Question in Council; viz, What Disadvantage Doth Arise to Persons Inhabiting the Massachusetts Colony Who Are Conformable to the Church of England?" HL Manuscript EL 9605.

The Humble Remonstrance of His Majesty's Most Loyal Subjects of His Majesty's Province of Pennsylvania. May 26, 1694. HL Manuscript EL 9596.

The Lawes of England. HL Manuscript EL 1182a (1620s or 1630s).

Lloyd, Thomas. *Philadelphia's Tears*. SW Misc. MSS, 1693.

Maryland Yearly Meeting, 1692. "To George Keith." October 4, 1692. SW Keithian controversy MSS, 1692 8 mo 4.

Meeting of Public Friends. Condemnation of George Keith. SW Keithian controversy MSS, 1692 4 mo 20.

Meeting of Public Friends. Minutes. HV Reel 2.

"New Interpreter." HL Manuscript EL 7801.

Pennsylvania Yearly Meeting at Burlington, to the Yearly Meeting in London. September 7, 1692. HV reel 7X.

Pennsylvania Yearly Meeting at Burlington, to Monthly and Quarterly Meetings in Pennsylvania and Jersey. September 7, 1692. HV Reel 7X.

Pennsylvania Yearly Meeting of Women Friends at Burlington, to Yearly Meeting of Women Friends in London. September 7, 1692. HV Reel 136A.

Pennsylvania Yearly Meeting, 1692. Minutes. HV Reel 7X.

Pennsylvania Yearly Meeting, 1693. Minutes. HV Reel 7X.

Pennsylvania Yearly Meeting, 1694. Minutes. HV Reel 7X.

Public Friends to Friends in England. 4 mo 1692. HV Reel 2.

Public Friends to Friends in London. June 9, 1693. SW Keithian controversy MSS, 1693 4 mo 9.

Sermon on Acts 24:16. HL Manuscript EL 34/B/62.

Shaftesbury, earl of (Anthony Ashley Cooper). *The Lord Shaftesbury His Speech to the House of Lords* (24 March 1679). HL Manuscript EL 8422.

Six Weeks Meeting at Bridgetown, Barbados. "To George Keith and the Rest of the Separate Company in Pennsylvania." September 12, 1692. SW Keithian controversy MSS, 1692 7 mo 12.

Snead, Robert. Letter, 6 May 1698. HL Manuscript EL 9598.

"Some of Our Principles to Which If You Agree We Are the More Like to Agree with You in Other Things." SW Keithian controversy MSS, n.d.

"Some Propositions in Order to Heale the Breach That Is Amongst Us." SW Keithian controversy MSS, 1692 2 mo 18.

C. Anthologies, Collections, Compilations, Records

Armstrong, Edward, and Deborah Logan, eds. *Correspondence Between William Penn and James Logan, 1700–1750*. Philadelphia: J. B. Lippincott, 1870.

Bartlett, John Russell, ed. *Records of the Colony of Rhode Island and Providence Plantations, in New England*. Providence, R.I.: A. C. Greene and Brother, 1856–64.

Browning, Andrew, ed. *English Historical Documents*. Vol. 8, *1660–1714*. New York: Oxford University Press, 1953.

Clarke, William. *The Clarke Papers: Selections from the Papers of William Clarke, Secretary to the Council of the Army, 1647–1649, and to General Monck and the Commanders of the Army in Scotland, 1651–1660*. 2 vols. 1891, 1894. Edited by C. H. Firth. London: Royal Historical Society, 1992.

Colonial Records. Vol. 1, *Minutes of the Provincial Council of Pennsylvania*. Philadelphia: Joseph Stevens and Company, 1852.

Cotton, John. *John Cotton on the Churches of New England*. Edited by Larzer Ziff. Cambridge: Harvard University Press, 1968.

Cressy, David, and Lori Anne Ferrell, eds. *Religion and Society in Early Modern England: A Sourcebook*. London: Routledge, 1996.

Cromwell, Oliver. *The Writings and Speeches of Oliver Cromwell*. 4 vols. Edited by W. C. Abbott. Cambridge: Harvard University Press, 1937–47.

Emerson, Everett, ed. *Letters from New England: The Massachusetts Bay Colony, 1629–1638*. Amherst: University of Massachusetts Press, 1976.

Gardiner, Samuel Rawson, ed. *Constitutional Documents of the Puritan Revolution, 1625–1660*. 2d ed. Oxford: Oxford University Press, 1906.

Hall, David D., ed. *The Antinomian Controversy, 1636–1638: A Documentary History*. 2d ed. Durham: Duke University Press, 1990.

Haller, William, ed. *Tracts on Liberty in the Puritan Revolution, 1638–1648*. 3 vols. New York: Columbia University Press, 1934.

Haller, William, and Godfrey Davies, eds. *The Leveller Tracts, 1647–1653*. New York: Columbia University Press, 1944.

Hooker, Thomas. *Thomas Hooker: Writings in England and Holland, 1626–1633*. Edited by George H. Williams, Norman Pettit, Winfried Herget, and Sargent Bush, Jr. Cambridge: Harvard University Press, 1975.

Kenyon, J. P., ed. *The Stuart Constitution: Documents and Commentary*. 2d ed. Cambridge: Cambridge University Press, 1986.

Lightfoot, John. *Journal of the Proceedings of the Assembly of Divines*. In *The Whole Works of the Rev. John Lightfoot*, vol. 13, ed. John Rogers Pitman. London, 1824.

Malcolm, Joyce Lee, ed. *The Struggle for Sovereignty: Seventeenth-Century Political Tracts*. Indianapolis: Liberty Fund, 1999.

Miller, Perry, and Thomas H. Johnson, eds. *The Puritans*. New York: American Book Company, 1938.

Mitchell, Rev. Alex F., and Rev. John Struthers, eds. *Minutes of the Sessions of the Westminster Assembly of Divines*. Edinburgh and London, 1874.

Moody, Robert E., ed. *Saltonstall Papers*. Boston: Massachusetts Historical Society, 1972.

Morgan, Edmund S., ed. *Puritan Political Ideas, 1558–1794*. New York: Bobbs-Merrill, 1965.

Myers, Albert Cook, ed. *Narratives of Early Pennsylvania, West New Jersey, and Delaware*. Original Narratives of Early American History. New York: Charles Scribner's Sons, 1912.

Penn, William. *The Papers of William Penn*. 5 vols. Edited by Mary Maples Dunn, Richard S. Dunn, Richard A. Ryerson, and Scott M. Wilds. Assisted by Jean R. Soderlund. Philadelphia: University of Pennsylvania Press, 1981–86.

Scott, Walter, ed. *Somers Tracts. A Collection of Scarce and Valuable Tracts, But Chiefly Such as Relate to the History and Constitution of These Kingdoms*. 2d ed. 13 vols. London, 1809–15.

Shurtleff, Nathaniel B., M.D., ed. *Records of the Governor and Company of the Massachusetts Bay in New England, 1628–1686*. 5 vols. Boston, 1853–54.

Soderlund, Jean R., ed. *William Penn and the Founding of Pennsylvania, 1680–1684: A Documentary History*. Philadelphia: University of Pennsylvania Press, 1983.

Underhill, Edward B., ed. *Tracts Concerning Liberty of Conscience and Persecution, 1614–1661*. London, 1846.

Williams, Roger. *The Correspondence of Roger Williams*. Edited by Glenn W. Lafantasie. Hanover: University Press of New England, 1988.

Winstanley, Gerrard. *The Works of Gerrard Winstanley*. Edited by George Sabine. New York: Russell and Russell, 1965.

Winthrop Papers. 5 vols. Boston: Massachusetts Historical Society, 1929–47.
Woodhouse, A.S.P., ed. *Puritanism and Liberty.* Chicago: University of Chicago Press, 1950.

II. SECONDARY SOURCES

Ackerman, Bruce. *Social Justice in the Liberal State.* New Haven: Yale University Press, 1980.
Adair, John. *Founding Fathers: The Puritans in England and America.* London: J. M . Dent, 1982.
Adams, Brooks. *The Emancipation of Massachusetts.* New York: Houghton Mifflin, 1887.
Adams, James Truslow. *The Founding of New England.* Boston: Little, Brown, 1921.
Adeney, W. F. "Toleration." In *The Encyclopedia of Religion and Ethics*, vol. 12, ed. James Hastings. New York: Charles Scribner's Sons, 1925.
Allen, C. Leonard. "Roger Williams and 'the Restauration of Zion.'" In *The American Quest for the Primitive Church*, ed. Richard T. Hughes. Urbana: University of Illinois Press, 1988.
Allen, David. "The Role of the London Trained Bands in the Exclusion Crisis, 1678–1681." *English Historical Review* 87 (1972): 287–303.
Altholtz, Josef L. *Anatomy of a Controversy: The Debate over "Essays and Reviews," 1860–1864.* Aldershot: Scolar Press/Ashgate, 1994.
Ashcraft, Richard. "Faith and Knowledge in Locke's Philosophy." In *John Locke: Problems and Perspectives*, ed. John W. Yolton. New York: Cambridge University Press, 1969.
———. "Latitudinarianism and Toleration: Historical Myth vs. Political History." In *Philosophy, Science, and Religion in England, 1640–1700*, ed. Richard Kroll, Richard Ashcraft, and Perez Zagorin. Cambridge: Cambridge University Press, 1992.
———. *Revolutionary Politics and Locke's "Two Treatises of Government."* Princeton: Princeton University Press, 1986.
Ashcraft, Richard, and M. M. Goldsmith. "Locke, Revolution Principles, and the Formation of Whig Ideology." *Historical Journal* 26 (1983): 773–800.
Ashley, Maurice. *The Glorious Revolution of 1688.* London: Hodder and Stoughton, 1966.
Ashton, Robert. *Counter-Revolution: The Second Civil War and Its Origins, 1646–1648.* New Haven: Yale University Press, 1994.
———. *The English Civil War: Conservation and Revolution, 1603–1649.* 2d ed. London: Weidenfeld and Nicolson, 1989.
Balibar, Etienne. "Culture and Identity: Working Notes." Translated by J. Swenson. In *The Identity in Question*, ed. John Rajchman. New York: Routledge, 1995.
Bancroft, George. *History of the United States.* 6 vols. Boston: D. Appleton, 1834.
Barbour, Hugh. "William Penn, Model of Protestant Liberalism." *Church History* 48 (1979): 156–73.
Barbour, Hugh, and J. William Frost. *The Quakers.* New York: Greenwood Press, 1988.
———. *The Quakers in Puritan England.* New Haven: Yale University Press, 1964.
Barker, Arthur E. *Milton and the Puritan Dilemma.* Toronto: University of Toronto Press, 1942.

Barker, Ernest. "The Achievement of Oliver Cromwell." In *Cromwell: A Profile*, ed. Ivan Roots. London: Macmillan, 1973.

Bates, M. Searle. *Religious Liberty: An Inquiry*. New York: Harper and Brothers, 1945.

Baumgold, Deborah. "Hobbes' Political Sensibility: The Menace of Political Ambition." In Dietz, *Thomas Hobbes and Political Theory*.

Beatty, Edward C.O. *William Penn as Social Philosopher*. New York: Columbia University Press, 1939.

Beddard, Robert. "The Unexpected Whig Revolution of 1688." In *The Revolutions of 1688: The Andrew Browning Lectures, 1988*, ed. Robert Beddard. Oxford: Clarendon Press, 1991.

Beer, Samuel H. *To Make a Nation: The Rediscovery of American Federalism*. Cambridge: Harvard University Press, 1994.

Behrens, B. "The Whig Theory of the Constitution in the Reign of Charles II." *Cambridge Historical Journal* 7 (1941): 42–71.

Beiner, Ronald. *What's the Matter with Liberalism?* Berkeley and Los Angeles: University of California Press, 1992.

Bellah, Robert N., Richard Madsen, William M. Sullivan, Ann Swidler, and Steven M. Tipton. *Habits of the Heart: Individualism and Commitment in American Life*. New York: Harper and Row, 1985.

Bennett, G. V. "The Seven Bishops: A Reconsideration." In *Religious Motivation: Biographical and Sociological Problems for the Church Historian*, ed. Derek Baker. Oxford: Basil Blackwell, 1978.

Bercovitch, Sacvan. *The Puritan Jeremiad*. Madison: University of Wisconsin Press, 1978.

Berlin, Isaiah. *Four Essays on Liberty*. New York: Oxford University Press, 1969.

Blitzer, Charles. *An Immortal Commonwealth: The Political Thought of James Harrington*. New Haven: Yale University Press, 1960.

Bloom, Allan. *The Closing of the American Mind: How Higher Education Has Failed Democracy and Impoverished the Souls of Today's Students*. New York: Simon and Schuster, 1987.

Bonomi, Patricia U. *Under the Cope of Heaven: Religion, Society, and Politics in Colonial America*. New York: Oxford University Press, 1986.

Boyer, Richard E. *English Declarations of Indulgence, 1687 and 1688*. The Hague: Mouton, 1968.

Bozeman, Theodore Dwight. "Biblical Primitivism: An Approach to New England Puritanism." In *The American Quest for the Primitive Church*, ed. Richard T. Hughes. Urbana: University of Illinois Press, 1988.

———. "The Puritans' 'Errand into the Wilderness' Reconsidered." *NEQ* 59 (1986): 231–51.

———. "Religious Liberty and the Problem of Order in Early Rhode Island." *NEQ* 45 (1972): 44–64.

———. *To Live Ancient Lives: The Primitivist Dimension in Puritanism*. Chapel Hill: University of North Carolina Press, 1988.

Braithwaite, William C. *The Beginnings of Quakerism*. London: Macmillan, 1912.

Breen, T. H. *The Character of the Good Ruler: A Study of Puritan Political Ideas in New England, 1630–1730*. New Haven: Yale University Press, 1970.

Brockunier, Samuel Hugh. *The Irrepressible Democrat, Roger Williams*. New York: The Ronald Press Company, 1940.

Bronner, Edwin B. "The Failure of the 'Holy Experiment' in Pennsylvania, 1684–1699." *Pennsylvania History* 21 (1954): 83–108.

———. *William Penn's "Holy Experiment": The Founding of Pennsylvania, 1681–1701.* Philadelphia: Temple University Publications, 1962.

Brooks, Phillips. *Tolerance: Two Lectures.* New York: E. P. Dutton, 1887.

Brown, Wendy. "Wounded Attachments: Late Modern Oppositional Political Formations." In *The Identity in Question,* ed. John Rajchman. New York: Routledge, 1995.

Brownmiller, Susan. *Femininity.* New York: Simon and Schuster, 1984.

Buranelli, Vincent. "William Penn and the Socinians." *PMHB* 82 (1959): 369–81.

Burgess, Glenn. *The Politics of the Ancient Constitution: An Introduction to English Political Thought, 1603–1642.* University Park: Pennsylvania State University Press, 1992.

———. "Thomas Hobbes: Religious Toleration or Religious Indifference?" In Nederman and Laursen, *Difference and Dissent.*

Burke, Peter. "Tacitism, Scepticism, and Reason of State." In Burns and Goldie, *Cambridge History of Political Thought.*

Burns, J. H., and Mark Goldie, eds. *The Cambridge History of Political Thought, 1450–1700.* Cambridge: Cambridge University Press, 1991.

Bury, J. B. *A History of Freedom of Thought.* 1913. Oxford: Oxford University Press, 1952.

Butler, Jon. "'Gospel Order Improved': The Keithian Schism and the Exercise of Quaker Ministerial Authority in Pennsylvania." *WMQ* 31 (1974): 431–52.

———. "Into Pennsylvania's Spiritual Abyss: The Rise and Fall of the Later Keithians." *PMHB* 101 (1977): 151–70.

Butterfield, Herbert. *The Whig Interpretation of History.* London: G. Bell and Sons, 1931.

Cadbury, Henry J. "Persecution and Religious Liberty, Then and Now." *PMHB* 68 (1944): 359–71.

Callan, Eamonn. "Political Liberalism and Political Education." *The Review of Politics* 58 (1996): 5–33.

Canup, John. *Out of the Wilderness: The Emergence of an American Identity in Colonial New England.* Middletown: Wesleyan University Press, 1990.

Capp, Bernard S. *The Fifth Monarchy Men: A Study in Seventeenth-Century English Millenarianism.* London: Faber, 1972.

Carroll, Peter N. *Puritanism and the Wilderness: The Intellectual Significance of the New England Frontier, 1629–1700.* New York: Columbia University Press, 1969.

Carter, Stephen L. *The Culture of Disbelief: How American Law and Politics Trivialize Religious Devotion.* New York: Anchor/Doubleday, 1993.

Casino, Joseph J. "Anti-Popery in Colonial Pennsylvania." *PMHB* 105 (1981): 279–309.

Chabot, Dana. "Thomas Hobbes: Skeptical Moralist." *APSR* 89 (1995): 401–10.

Champion, J.A.I. *The Pillars of Priestcraft Shaken: The Church of England and Its Enemies, 1660–1730.* New York: Cambridge University Press, 1992.

Childress, James F. "Appeals to Conscience." *Ethics* 89 (1978): 315–35.

Christianson, Paul. *Reformers and Babylon: English Apocalyptic Visions from the Reformation to the Eve of the Civil War.* Toronto: University of Toronto Press, 1978.

Clarkson, Thomas. *Memoirs of the Private and Public Life of William Penn.* 2 vols. Philadelphia: Bradford and Innskeep, 1814.

Claydon, Tony. *William III and the Godly Revolution.* Cambridge: Cambridge University Press, 1996.

Clifton, Robin. *The Last Popular Rebellion: The Western Rising of 1685.* London: M. T. Smith, 1984.

————. "The Popular Fear of Catholics during the English Revolution." *Past and Present* 52 (1971): 23–55.

Cody, Edward J. "The Price of Perfection: The Irony of George Keith." *Pennsylvania History* 39 (1972): 1–19.

Cohen, Charles Lloyd. *God's Caress: The Psychology of Puritan Religious Experience.* New York: Oxford University Press, 1986.

Collingwood, R. G. *The Idea of History.* Oxford: Oxford University Press, 1946.

Collinson, Patrick. *The Elizabethan Puritan Movement.* New York: Oxford University Press, 1989.

Comfort, William Wistar. *William Penn: A Tercentenary Estimate.* Philadelphia: University of Pennsylvania Press, 1944.

————. "William Penn's Religious Background." *PMHB* 68 (1944): 341–58.

Connolly, William. *Identity/Difference: Democratic Negotiations of Political Paradox.* Ithaca: Cornell University Press, 1991.

Cook, Sarah Gibbard. "The Congregational Independents and the Cromwellian Constitutions." *Church History* 46 (1977): 335–57.

Cotton, A.N.B. "Cromwell and the Self-Denying Ordinance." *History* 62 (1977): 211–31.

Coulton, G. G. "A Protestant View of Toleration." *The Contemporary Review* 138 (1930): 310–19.

Cragg, Gerald R. *Freedom and Authority: A Study of English Thought in the Early Seventeenth Century.* Philadelphia: Westminster Press, 1975.

Cranston, Maurice. "Toleration." In *The Encyclopedia of Philosophy*, ed. Paul Edwards. New York: Macmillan, 1967.

Cressy, David. "'The vast and Furious Ocean': The Passage to Puritan New England." *NEQ* 57 (1984): 511–32.

Crick, Bernard. "Toleration and Tolerance in Theory and Practice." *Government and Opposition* 6 (1971): 144–71.

Crisp, Roger. "Communitarianism and Toleration." In Horton and Nicholson, *Toleration: Philosophy and Practice.*

Curry, Thomas J. *The First Freedoms: Church and State in America to the Passage of the First Amendment.* New York: Oxford University Press, 1986.

Davidson, Robert L.D. *War Comes to Quaker Pennsylvania, 1682–1756.* New York: Columbia University Press/Temple University Publications, 1957.

Davis, J. C. "Cromwell's Religion." In *Oliver Cromwell and the English Revolution*, ed. John Morrill. London: Longman, 1990.

DeBeer, Esmond S. "Locke and English Liberalism: The *Second Treatise of Government* in Its Contemporary Setting." In *John Locke: Problems and Perspectives*, ed. John W. Yolton. New York: Cambridge University Press, 1969.

DeKrey, Gary S. "Rethinking the Restoration: Dissenting Cases for Conscience, 1667–1672." *Historical Journal* 38 (1995): 53–83.

Delbanco, Andrew. *The Puritan Ordeal.* Cambridge: Harvard University Press, 1989.

Deutsch, Kenneth L., and Walter Soffer, eds. *The Crisis of Liberal Democracy: A Straussian Perspective*. Albany: State University of New York Press, 1987.

Dickens, A. G. *The English Reformation*. New York: Schocken, 1964.

Dietz, Mary G., ed. *Thomas Hobbes and Political Theory*. Lawrence: University Press of Kansas, 1990.

Dixon, William Hepworth. *William Penn: An Historical Biography*. Philadelphia: Blanchard and Lea, 1851.

Dow, F. D. *Radicalism in the English Revolution*. Oxford: Basil Blackwell, 1985.

Dunn, John. "'Bright Enough for All Our Purposes': John Locke's Conception of a Civilized Society." *Notes and Records of the Royal Society of London* 43 (1989): 133–53.

———. *The Political Thought of John Locke: An Historical Account of the Argument of the "Two Treatises of Government."* London: Cambridge University Press, 1969.

Dunn, Mary Maples. *William Penn: Politics and Conscience*. Princeton: Princeton University Press, 1967.

Dworkin, Ronald. *A Matter of Principle*. Cambridge: Harvard University Press, 1985.

———. *Taking Rights Seriously*. Cambridge: Harvard University Press, 1977.

Earle, Peter. *Monmouth's Rebels: The Road to Sedgmoor, 1685*. London: Weidenfeld and Nicholson, 1977.

Eisenach, Eldon J. "Hobbes on Church, State, and Religion." *History of Political Thought* 3, no. 2 (1982): 215–43.

———. *Two Worlds of Liberalism: Religion and Politics in Hobbes, Locke, and Mill*. Chicago: University of Chicago Press, 1981.

Endy, Melvin B., Jr. "Puritanism, Spiritualism, and Quakerism: An Historiographical Essay." In *The World of William Penn*, ed. Richard S. Dunn and Mary Maples Dunn. Philadelphia: University of Pennsylvania Press, 1986.

———. "Theology in a Religiously Plural World: Some Contributions of William Penn." *PMHB* 105 (1981): 453–68.

———. *William Penn and Early Quakerism*. Princeton: Princeton University Press, 1973.

Erikson, Kai T. *Wayward Puritans: A Study in the Sociology of Deviance*. New York: John Wiley and Sons, 1966.

Eskridge, William N. *Gaylaw: Challenging the Apartheid of the Closet*. Cambridge: Harvard University Press, 1999.

———. "A Jurisprudence of 'Coming Out': Religion, Homosexuality, and Collisions of Liberty and Equality in American Public Law." *Yale Law Journal* 106 (1997): 2411–74.

Farr, James. "Atomes of Scripture: Hobbes and the Politics of Biblical Interpretation." In Dietz, *Thomas Hobbes and Political Theory*.

Figgis, J. N. *The Divine Right of Kings*. Cambridge: Cambridge University Press, 1914.

Firth, C. H. *Cromwell's Army*. London: Methuen, 1902.

Fish, Stanley. "Boutique Multiculturalism." In *Multiculturalism and American Democracy*, ed. Arthur M. Melzer, Jerry Weinberger, and M. Richard Zinman. Lawrence: University Press of Kansas, 1998.

———. "Mission Impossible: Settling the Just Bounds Between Church and State." *Columbia Law Review* 97 (1997): 2255–333.

Flowers, Ronald B. *The Godless Court? Supreme Court Decisions on Church-State Relationships*. Louisville: Westminster/John Knox Press, 1994.

Foster, Stephen. "English Puritanism and the Progress of New England Institutions, 1630–1660." In *Saints and Revolutionaries: Essays on Early American History*, ed. David Hall, John M. Murrin, and Thad W. Tate. New York: W. W. Norton, 1984.

——. *Notes from the Caroline Underground: Alexander Leighton, the Puritan Triumvirate, and the Laudian Reaction to Nonconformity*. Hamden, Conn.: Archon 1978.

Fowler, Robert Booth. *Unconventional Partners: Religion and Liberal Culture in the United States*. Grand Rapids, Mich.: Eerdmans, 1989.

Frank, Joseph. *The Levellers: A History of the Writings of Three Seventeenth-Century Social Democrats, John Lilburne, Richard Overton, William Walwyn*. Cambridge: Harvard University Press, 1955.

Friedan, Betty. *The Feminine Mystique*. New York: W. W. Norton, 1963.

Friedman, Milton. *Capitalism and Freedom*. Chicago: University of Chicago Press, 1962.

Frost, J. William. "The Affirmation Controversy and Religious Liberty." In *The World of William Penn*, ed. Richard S. Dunn and Mary Maples Dunn. Philadelphia: University of Pennsylvania Press, 1986.

——. *The Keithian Schism in Early Pennsylvania*. Norwood, Pa.: Norwood Press, 1980.

——. "Pennsylvania Institutes Religious Liberty." *PMHB* 113 (1988): 323–48.

——. *A Perfect Freedom: Religious Liberty in Pennsylvania*. Cambridge: Cambridge University Press, 1990.

——. "Religious Liberty in Early Pennsylvania." *PMHB* 105 (1981): 419–52.

——."Unlikely Controversialists: Caleb Pusey and George Keith." *Quaker History* 64 (1975): 16–36.

Furley, O. W. "The Whig Exclusionists: Pamphlet Literature in the Exclusion Campaign, 1679–1681." *Cambridge Historical Journal* 13 (1957): 19–36.

Galeotti, Anna Elisabetta. "Citizenship and Equality: The Place for Toleration." *Political Theory* 21 (1993): 585–605.

Galston, William. *Liberal Purposes: Goods, Virtues, and Diversity in the Liberal State*. Cambridge: Cambridge University Press, 1991.

Gamwell, Franklin I. *The Meaning of Religious Freedom: Modern Politics and the Democratic Resolution*. Albany: State University of New York Press, 1995.

Gardner, Peter. "Propositional Attitudes and Multicultural Education, or Believing Others Are Mistaken." In Horton and Nicholson, *Toleration: Philosophy and Practice*.

Gaustad, Edwin S. *Liberty of Conscience: Roger Williams in America*. Grand Rapids, Mich.: Eerdmans, 1991.

——. *A Religious History of America*. New revised edition. San Francisco: Harper and Row, 1990.

Geach, Peter. "The Religion of Thomas Hobbes." *Religious Studies* 17 (1981): 549–58.

Gentles, Ian. *The New Model Army in England, Ireland and Scotland, 1645–1653*. Oxford: Basil Blackwell, 1992.

Gillespie, Michael. "Descartes and the Question of Toleration." In Levine, *Early Modern Skepticism*.

Gilpin, W. Clark. *The Millenarian Piety of Roger Williams*. Chicago: University of Chicago Press, 1979.

Goerner, E. A. "Forcing the Free to Be Correctly Free." *The Review of Politics* 58 (1996): 35–40.

Goldie, Mark. "John Locke and Anglican Royalism." *Political Studies* 31 (1983): 61–85.

———. "The Political Thought of the Anglican Revolution." In *The Revolutions of 1688: The Andrew Browning Lectures, 1988,* ed. Robert Beddard. Oxford: Clarendon Press, 1991.

———. "The Reception of Hobbes." In Burns and Goldie, *Cambridge History of Political Thought.*

———. "The Theory of Religious Intolerance in Restoration England." In Grell, Israel, and Tyacke, *From Persecution to Toleration.*

Goodin, Robert, and Andrew Reed, eds. *Liberal Neutrality.* London: Routledge, 1989.

Gough, J. W. *John Locke's Political Philosophy.* 1950. 2d ed. Oxford: Oxford University Press, 1973.

Gray, John. "Toleration: A Post-Liberal Perspective." In *Enlightenment's Wake: Politics and Culture at the Close of the Modern Age.* London: Routledge, 1995.

Gray, Stanley. "The Political Thought of John Winthrop." *NEQ* 3 (1930): 681–705.

Greaves, Richard L. *Secrets of the Kingdom: British Radicals from the Popish Plot to the Revolution of 1688–1689.* Stanford: Stanford University Press, 1992.

Green, James N. "The Book Trades in the Middle Colonies, 1680–1720." In *A History of the Book in America. Volume One: The Colonial Book in the Transatlantic World,* ed. Hugh Amory and David D. Hall. New York: Cambridge University Press; Worcester, Mass.: American Antiquarian Society, 1998.

Grell, Ole Peter, and Roy Porter, eds. *Toleration in Enlightenment Europe.* Cambridge: Cambridge University Press, 1999.

Grell, Ole Peter, Jonathan I. Israel, and Nicholas Tyacke, eds. *From Persecution to Toleration: The Glorious Revolution and Religion in England.* New York: Oxford University Press, 1991.

Greenawalt, Kent. *Religious Convictions and Political Choice.* New York: Oxford University Press, 1988.

Gregg, Pauline. *Free-Born John: A Biography of John Lilburne.* 1961. London: Dent, 1986.

Gura, Philip F. *A Glimpse of Sion's Glory: Puritan Radicalism in New England, 1620–1660.* Middletown: Wesleyan University Press, 1984.

———. "Samuel Gorton and Religious Radicalism in England, 1644–1648." *WMQ* 40 (1983): 121–24.

———. "The Radical Ideology of Samuel Gorton: New Light on the Relation of English to American Puritanism." *WMQ* 36 (1979): 78–100.

Halbertal, Moshe. "Autonomy, Toleration, and Group Rights." In Heyd, *Toleration: An Elusive Virtue.*

Hall, Timothy L. *Separating Church and State: Roger Williams and Religious Liberty.* Urbana: University of Illinois Press, 1998.

Haller, William. *Liberty and Reformation in the Puritan Revolution.* New York: Columbia University Press, 1955.

Hallowell, Richard P. *The Quaker Invasion of Massachusetts.* 4th ed. Boston: Houghton Mifflin, 1887.

Hanson, Russell L. "Deliberation, Tolerance, and Democracy." In *Reconsidering the Democratic Public,* ed. Russell L. Hanson and George E. Marcus. University Park: Pennsylvania State University Press, 1993.

Harris, Tim, Paul Seaward, and Mark Goldie, eds. *The Politics of Religion in Restoration England.* Cambridge: Harvard University Press, 1990.

Haydon, Colin. "'I Love My King and My Country, But a Roman Catholic I Hate': Anti-Catholicism, Xenophobia, and National Identity in 18th Century England." In *Protestantism and National Identity: Britain and Ireland, c. 1650–c.1850,* ed. Tony Claydon and Ian McBride. Cambridge: Cambridge University Press, 1998.

Hegel, G.W.F. *The Philosophy of History.* Translated by J. Sibree. 1840. New York: Dover, 1956.

Heimert, Alan. "Puritanism, the Wilderness, and the Frontier." *NEQ* 26 (1953): 361–82.

Hetherington, W. M. *History of the Westminster Assembly of Divines.* Ed. Robert Williamson. 4th ed. Edinburgh: James Gemmell, 1878.

Heyd, David, ed. *Toleration: An Elusive Virtue.* Princeton: Princeton University Press, 1996.

Hibbard, Caroline. *Charles I and the Popish Plot.* Chapel Hill: University of North Carolina Press, 1983.

Hildreth, Richard. *History of the United States.* 3 vols. New York: Harper and Brothers, 1849.

Hill, Christopher. *The Century of Revolution, 1603–1714.* 2d ed. New York: Norton, 1980.

———. *The English Bible and the Seventeenth-Century Revolution.* London: Penguin, 1994.

———. *God's Englishman: Oliver Cromwell and the English Revolution.* New York: Harper and Row, 1970.

———. *Intellectual Origins of the English Revolution Revisited.* Oxford: Oxford University Press, 1997.

———. *Society and Puritanism in the Pre-Revolutionary England.* 2d ed. New York: Schocken, 1967.

———. *Some Intellectual Consequences of the English Revolution.* Madison, Wisconsin: University of Wisconsin Press, 1989.

———. *The World Turned Upside Down: Radical Ideas During the English Revolution.* New York: Temple Smith, 1972.

Hoak, Dale, and Mordechai Feingold, eds. *The World of William and Mary: Anglo-Dutch Perspectives on the Revolution of 1688–89.* Stanford: Stanford University Press, 1996.

Hobhouse, L. T. *Liberalism.* 1911. New York: Oxford University Press, 1964.

Holmes, Stephen. *The Anatomy of Antiliberalism.* Cambridge: Harvard University Press, 1993.

Hood, F. C. *The Divine Politics of Thomas Hobbes: An Interpretation of Leviathan.* Oxford: Oxford University Press, 1964.

Horle, Craig W. *The Quakers and the English Legal System, 1660–1688.* Philadelphia: University of Pennsylvania Press, 1988.

Horton, John. "Toleration." In *The Blackwell Encyclopedia of Political Thought,* ed. David Miller. Oxford: Basil Blackwell, 1991.

———. "Toleration as a Virtue." In Heyd, *Toleration: An Elusive Virtue.*

Horton, John, and Peter Nicholson, eds. *Toleration: Philosophy and Practice*. Brookfield, Vt.: Avebury, 1992.

Horton, John, and Susan Mendus, eds. *Aspects of Toleration: Philosophical Studies*. London: Methuen, 1985.

———, eds. *Toleration, Identity, and Difference*. New York: St. Martin's Press, 1999.

Horton, John T. "Two Bishops and the Holy Brood: A Fresh Look at a Familiar Fact." *NEQ* 26 (1953): 361–82.

Houston, Alan. *Algernon Sidney and the Republican Heritage in England and America*. Princeton: Princeton University Press, 1991.

———. "Monopolizing Faith: The Levellers, Rights, and Religious Toleration." In Levine, *Early Modern Skepticism*.

Hudson, Winthrop S. *Religion in America*. 4th ed. New York: Macmillan, 1987.

Hunter, James Davison. *Evangelicalism: The Coming Generation*. Chicago: University of Chicago Press, 1987.

———. "Religion and Political Civility: The Coming Generation of American Evangelicals." *Journal for the Scientific Study of Religion* 23 (1984): 364–80.

Illick, Joseph E. *Colonial Pennsylvania: A History*. New York: Charles Scribner's Sons, 1976.

———. "The Pennsylvania Grant: A Re-evaluation." *PMHB* 86 (1962): 375–96.

Israel, Jonathan. "The Intellectual Debate About Toleration in the Dutch Republic." In *The Emergence of Tolerance in the Dutch Republic*, ed. C. Berkiens-Stevelinck, J. Israel, and G.H.M. Posthumus Meyjes. Leiden: Brill, 1997.

———. "Toleration in Seventeenth-Century Dutch and English Thought." In *The Exchange of Ideas: Religion, Scholarship, and Art in Anglo-Dutch Relations in the Seventeenth Century*, ed. Simon Groenveld and Michael Wintle. Zutphen: Walburg Institute, 1994.

———. "William III and Toleration." In Grell, Israel, and Tyacke, *From Persecution to Toleration*.

———, ed. *The Anglo-Dutch Moment: Essays on the Glorious Revolution and Its World Impact*. Cambridge: Cambridge University Press, 1991.

Jackson, Jennifer. "Intolerance on the Campus." In Horton and Nicholson, *Toleration: Philosophy and Practice*.

James, Margaret. "The Political Implications of the Tithes Controversy in the English Revolution, 1640–1660." *History* 26 (1941): 1–18.

Janney, Samuel M. *The Life of William Penn*. Philadelphia: Hogan, Perkins, 1852.

Johns, David L. "'Convincement and Disillusionment: Printer William Bradford and the Keithian Controversy in Colonial Philadelphia." *Journal of the Friends Historical Society* 57 (1994): 21–32.

Johnson, Paul J. "Hobbes' Anglican Doctrine of Salvation." In *Thomas Hobbes in His Time*, ed. Ralph Ross, Herbert W. Schneider, and Theodore Waldman. Minneapolis: University of Minnesota Press, 1974.

Johnston, David. *The Idea of a Liberal Theory: A Critique and Reconstruction*. Princeton: Princeton University Press, 1994.

Jones, J. R. *The First Whigs: The Politics of the Exclusion Crisis*. London: Oxford University Press, 1961.

———. "The Revolution in Context." In Jones, *Liberty Secured?*

————, ed. *Liberty Secured? Britain Before and After 1688*. Stanford: Stanford University Press, 1992.

Jordan, W. K. *The Development of Religious Toleration in England*. 4 vols. Cambridge: Harvard University Press, 1932–1940.

Kamen, Henry. *The Rise of Toleration*. London: Weidenfeld and Nicholson, 1967.

Kaplan, Lawrence. *Politics and Religion During the English Civil War: The Scots and the Long Parliament, 1643–1645*. New York: New York University Press, 1976.

Kaufman, Peter Iver. *Redeeming Politics*. Princeton: Princeton University Press, 1990.

Kautz, Steven. *Liberalism and Community*. Ithaca: Cornell University Press, 1995.

————. "Liberalism and the Idea of Toleration." *American Journal of Political Science* 37 (1993): 610–32.

Keith, Charles P. *Chronicles of Pennsylvania from the English Revolution to the Peace of Aix-la-Chappelle*. 2 vols. Philadelphia: Patterson and White, 1917.

Kelly, Kevin T. *Conscience: Dictator or Guide? A Study in Seventeenth-Century English Protestant Moral Thought*. London: G. Chapman, 1967.

Kenyon, J. P. *The Popish Plot*. London: Heinemann, 1972.

Kessler, Sanford. "Locke's Influence on Jefferson's 'Bill for Establishing Religious Freedom.'" *Journal of Church and State* 25 (1983): 231–52.

King, Martin Luther, Jr. "Letter from Birmingham Jail." *The Christian Century*, June 12, 1963, pp. 768–69.

King, Preston. *Toleration*. New York: St. Martin's Press, 1976.

Kirby, Ethyn Williams. *George Keith*. New York: D. Appleton-Century, 1942.

————."The Quakers' Efforts to Secure Civil and Religious Liberty, 1660–1696." *Journal of Modern History* 7 (1935): 401–21.

Kishlansky, Mark. "The Army and the Levellers: The Roads to Putney." *Historical Journal* 22 (1979): 795–824.

————. *The Rise of the New Model Army*. Cambridge: Cambridge University Press, 1979.

Knight, Janice. *Orthodoxies in Massachusetts: Rereading American Puritanism*. Cambridge: Harvard University Press, 1994.

Knights, Mark. *Politics and Opinion in Crisis, 1678–1681*. Cambridge: Cambridge University Press, 1994.

Koehler, Lyle. "The Case of the American Jezebels: Anne Hutchinson and Female Agitation During the Years of Antinomian Turmoil, 1636–1638." *WMQ* 31 (1974): 55–78.

Kraynak, Robert P. *History and Modernity in the Thought of Thomas Hobbes*. Ithaca: Cornell University Press, 1992.

————."John Locke: From Absolutism to Toleration." *APSR* 74 (1980): 53–69.

Kukathas, Chandran. "Cultural Toleration." In *Nomos 39: Ethnicity and Group Rights*, ed. Ian Shapiro and Will Kymlicka. New York: New York University Press, 1997.

Kymlicka, Will. *Liberalism, Community, and Culture*. Oxford: Oxford University Press, 1989.

————. *Multicultural Citizenship*. Oxford: Clarendon Press, 1995.

————. "Two Models of Freedom and Tolerance." In Heyd, *Toleration: An Elusive Virtue*.

Labaree, Benjamin W. *Colonial Massachusetts: A History*. Millwood, N.Y.: KTO Press, 1979.

Lamont, William. "Arminianism: The Controversy That Never Was." In *Political Discourse in Early Modern Britain*, ed. Nicholas Phillipson and Quentin Skinner. Cambridge: Cambridge University Press, 1993.

Larmore, Charles. *The Morals of Modernity*. Cambridge: Cambridge University Press, 1996.

——. *Patterns of Moral Complexity*. Cambridge: Cambridge University Press, 1987.

Lasch, Christopher. *The Culture of Narcissism: American Life in an Age of Diminishing Expectations*. New York: W. W. Norton, 1979.

Laslett, Peter. "The English Revolution and Locke's 'Two Treatises of Government.'" *Cambridge Historical Journal* 22 (1956): 40–55.

Laursen, John Christian, and Cary Nederman, eds. *Beyond the Persecuting Society: Religious Toleration Before the Enlightenment*. Philadelphia: University of Pennsylvania Press, 1998.

Lecler, Joseph. *Toleration and the Reformation*. Translated by T. L. Westow. 2 vols. New York: Association Press, 1960.

Letwin, Shirley. "Skepticism and Toleration in Hobbes' Political Thought." In Levine, *Early Modern Skepticism*.

Levine, Alan. "Skepticism, Self, and Toleration in Montaigne's Political Thought." In Levine, *Early Modern Skepticism*.

——, ed. *Early Modern Skepticism and the Origins of Toleration*. Lanham, Md.: Lexington, 1999.

Lockhart, William B., Yale Kamisar, Jesse H. Choper, and Steven H. Shiffrin. *Constitutional Law: Cases—Comments—Questions*. 7th ed. St. Paul, Minn.: West, 1991.

Lottin, D. Odon. *Psychologie et Morale aux XIIe et XIIIe Siècles*. 6 vols. Louvain: Abbaye du Mont Cesar, 1942–49.

Lovejoy, David S. *Religious Enthusiasm in the New World*. Cambridge: Harvard University Press, 1985.

——. "Roger Williams and George Fox: The Arrogance of Self-Righteousness." *NEQ* 66 (1993): 199–225.

Macedo, Stephen. *Liberal Virtues: Citizenship, Virtue, and Community in Liberal Constitutionalism*. Oxford: Oxford University Press, 1990.

——. "Toleration and Fundamentalism." In *A Companion to Contemporary Political Philosophy*, ed. Robert E. Goodin and Philip Pettit. Cambridge, Mass.: Basil Blackwell, 1993.

MacIntyre, Alasdair. *After Virtue: A Study in Moral Theory*. Notre Dame: University of Notre Dame Press, 1981.

——. *Whose Justice? Which Rationality?* Notre Dame: University of Notre Dame Press, 1988.

Maclear, James Fulton. "Anne Hutchinson and the Mortalist Heresy." *NEQ* 54 (1981): 74–103.

——. "'The Heart of New England Rent': The Mystical Element in Early Puritan History." *Mississippi Valley Historical Review* 42 (1955–56): 621–52.

Madison, James. "Federalist 10." In *The Federalist Papers*, ed. Clinton Rossiter. New York: Mentor, 1961.

Malcolm, Noel. "Hobbes and Spinoza." In Burns and Goldie, *Cambridge History of Political Thought*.

Manschreck, Clyde L. "The Role of Melanchthon in the Adiaphora Controversy." *Archiv für Reformationsgeschichte* 48 (1957): 165–81.

Marcus, George E., John L. Sullivan, Elizabeth Theiss-Morse, and Sandra L. Wood. *With Malice Toward Some: How People Make Civil Liberties Judgments.* Cambridge: Cambridge University Press, 1995.

Marcuse, Herbert. "Repressive Tolerance." In Robert Paul Wolff, Barrington Moore, Jr., and Herbert Marcuse, *A Critique of Pure Tolerance.* Boston: Beacon, 1967.

Marshall, John. "The Ecclesiology of the Latitude-Men, 1660–1689: Stillingfleet, Tillotson, and 'Hobbism.'" *JEH* 36 (1985): 407–27.

———. *John Locke: Resistance, Religion and Responsibility.* Cambridge: Cambridge University Press, 1994.

Martinich, A. P. *The Two Gods of Leviathan: Thomas Hobbes on Religion and Politics.* Cambridge: Cambridge University Press, 1992.

McCabe, David. "John Locke and the Argument Against Strict Separation." *Review of Politics* 59 (1997): 233–58.

McClure, Kirstie M. "Difference, Diversity, and the Limits of Toleration." *Political Theory* 18 (1990): 361–91.

McDowell, Gary L. "Private Conscience and Public Order: Hobbes and *The Federalist.*" *Polity* 25 (1993): 421–44.

McGregor, J. F. "Seekers and Ranters." In McGregor and Reay, *Radical Religion in the English Revolution.*

McGregor, J. F., and B. Reay, eds. *Radical Religion in the English Revolution.* Oxford: Oxford University Press, 1984.

McLoughlin, William G. *New England Dissent, 1630–1833: The Baptists and the Separation of Church and State.* Cambridge: Harvard University Press, 1971.

———. *Soul Liberty: The Baptists' Struggle in New England, 1630–1833.* Hanover: University Press of New England, 1991.

Megone, Christopher. "Truth, the Autonomous Individual, and Toleration." In Horton and Nicholson, *Toleration: Philosophy and Practice.*

Mendle, Michael. "Parliamentary Sovereignty: A Very English Absolutism." In *Political Discourse in Early Modern Britain*, ed. Nicholas Phillipson and Quentin Skinner. Cambridge: Cambridge University Press, 1993.

Mendus, Susan. *Toleration and the Limits of Liberalism.* Atlantic Highlands, N.J.: Humanities Press International, 1989.

———, ed. *Justifying Toleration: Historical and Conceptual Perspectives.* New York: Cambridge University Press, 1988.

Miller, John. "Crown, Parliament, and People." In Jones, *Liberty Secured?*

———. "James II and Toleration." In *By Force or By Default? The Revolution of 1688–1689*, ed. Eveline Cruickshanks. Edinburgh: John Donald, 1992.

———. *Popery and Politics in England, 1660–1688.* Cambridge: Cambridge University Press, 1973.

———. "The Potential for 'Absolutism' in Later Stuart England." *History* 69 (1984): 187–207.

———. *Restoration England: The Reign of Charles II.* New York: Longman, 1985.

Miller, Perry. *The New England Mind: The Seventeenth Century.* 1939. Cambridge: Harvard University Press, 1954.

———. *Orthodoxy in Massachusetts, 1630–1650.* Boston: Beacon, 1933.

————. "'Preparation for Salvation' in Seventeenth-Century New England." In *Nature's Nation*. Cambridge: Harvard University Press, 1967.

————. "Roger Williams: An Essay in Interpretation." In *The Complete Writings of Roger Williams*, vol. 7. New York: Russell and Russell, 1963.

————. *Roger Williams: His Contribution to the American Experience*. Indianapolis: Bobbs-Merrill, 1953.

Milton, Anthony. *Catholic and Reformed: The Roman and Protestant Churches in English Protestant Thought, 1600–1640*. New York: Cambridge University Press, 1995.

Mitchell, Joshua. "Hobbes and the Equality of All Under the One." *Political Theory* 21 (1993): 78–100.

————. *Not By Reason Alone: Religion, History, and Identity in Early Modern Political Thought*. Chicago: University of Chicago Press, 1993.

Mohr, Richard D. *A More Perfect Union: Why Straight Americans Must Stand Up for Gay Rights*. Boston: Beacon, 1994.

Mood, Fulmer. "William Penn and English Politics, 1680–81: New Light on the Granting of the Pennsylvania Charter." *Journal of the Friends Historical Society* 32 (1935): 3–19.

Moore, Rosemary. *The Light in Their Consciences: The Early Quakers in Britain, 1646–1666*. University Park: Pennsylvania State University Press, 2000.

Morgan, Edmund S. "The Case Against Anne Hutchinson." *NEQ* 10 (1937): 635–49.

————. *The Puritan Dilemma: The Story of John Winthrop*. Boston: Little, Brown, 1958.

————. *Roger Williams: The Church and the State*. New York: Harcourt, Brace, and World, 1967.

————. *Visible Saints*. New York: New York University Press, 1963.

Morison, Samuel Eliot. *Builders of the Bay Colony*. New York: Houghton Mifflin, 1930.

Morrill, John. "The Attack on the Church of England in the Long Parliament, 1640–1642." In *History, Society and the Churches: Essays in Honour of Owen Chadwick*, ed. Derek Beales and Geoffrey Best. Cambridge: Cambridge University Press, 1985.

————. "The Church in England, 1642–9." In *Reactions to the English Civil War, 1642–1649*, ed. John Morrill. London: Macmillan, 1982.

————. "The Religious Context of the English Civil War." *Transactions of the Royal Historical Society*, ser. 5, no. 33 (1984): 155–78.

Moskos, Charles C., and John Whiteclay Chambers III, eds. *The New Conscientious Objection: From Sacred to Secular Resistance*. New York: Oxford University Press, 1993.

Mout, M.E.H.N. "Limits and Debates: A Comparative View of Dutch Toleration in the Sixteenth and Early Seventeenth Centuries." In *The Emergence of Tolerance in the Dutch Republic*, ed. C. Berkvens-Stevelinck, J. Israel, and G.H.M. Posthumus Meyjes. Leiden: Brill, 1997.

Mullett, Charles F. "Toleration and Persecution in England, 1660–1689." *Church History* 18 (1949): 18–43.

Murphy, Andrew R. "Augustine and English Protestants: Authority and Order, Coercion and Dissent in the Earthly City." In *Augustine and Liberal Education*, ed. Kevin Hughes and Kim Paffenroth. Aldershot: Ashgate, 2000.

————. "Rawls and a Shrinking Liberty of Conscience." *Review of Politics* 60 (Spring 1998): 247–76.

————."Tolerance, Toleration, and the Liberal Tradition." *Polity* 29 (1997): 593–623.

————. "The Uneasy Relationship Between Social Contract Theory and Religious Toleration." *The Journal of Politics* 59 (1997): 368–92.

Myers, Albert Cook. *Immigration of the Irish Quakers into Pennsylvania, 1682–1750.* Swarthmore, 1902. Reprint. Baltimore: Genealogical Publishing Company, 1985.

Nash, Gary B. "The Framing of Government in Pennsylvania: Ideas in Contact with Reality." *WMQ* 23 (1966): 183–209.

————. *Quakers and Politics: Pennsylvania, 1681–1726.* Princeton: Princeton University Press, 1968.

Neal, Patrick. *Liberalism and Its Discontents.* New York: New York University Press, 1997.

Nederman, Cary J. *Worlds of Difference: European Discourses of Toleration, c.1100–c.1550.* University Park: Pennsylvania State University Press, 2000.

Nederman, Cary J., and John Christian Laursen, eds. *Difference and Dissent: Theories of Toleration in Medieval and Early Modern Europe.* New York: Rowman and Littlefield, 1996.

Nenner, Howard. *By Colour of Law: Legal Culture and Constitutional Politics in England, 1660–1689.* Chicago: University of Chicago Press, 1977.

————. "Liberty, Law, and Property: The Constitution in Retrospect from 1689." In Jones, *Liberty Secured?*

Neuhaus, Richard John. *The Naked Public Square: Religion and Democracy in America.* Grand Rapids, Mich.: Eerdmans, 1984.

Niebuhr, H. Richard. *Christ and Culture.* New York: Harper and Brothers, 1951.

Nozick, Robert. *Anarchy, State, and Utopia.* New York: Basic, 1974.

Paine, Thomas. *Rights of Man.* 1792. Edited by Eric Foner. New York: Penguin, 1984.

Palfrey, John Gorham. *History of New England During the Stuart Dynasty.* 5 vols. Boston: Little, Brown, 1858–90.

Park, Charles E. "Puritans and Quakers." *NEQ* 27 (1954): 53–74.

Parrington, Vernon L. *Main Currents in American Thought.* Vol. 1, *The Colonial Mind, 1620–1800.* New York: Harcourt, Brace, and World, 1927.

Paul, Robert S. *The Assembly of the Lord: Politics and Religion in the Westminster Assembly and the "Great Debate."* Edinburgh: T. and T. Clark, 1985.

Perry, Michael J. *Love and Power: The Role of Religion and Morality in American Politics.* New York: Oxford University Press, 1991.

————. *Morality, Politics, and the Law: A Bicentennial Essay.* New York: Oxford University Press, 1988.

Pestana, Carla Gardina. *Quakers and Baptists in Colonial Massachusetts.* New York: Cambridge University Press, 1991.

Pettit, Norman. *The Heart Prepared: Grace and Conversion in Puritan Spiritual Life.* 2d ed. Middletown: Wesleyan University Press, 1989.

Phillips, Anne. "Dealing with Difference: A Politics of Ideas or a Politics of Presence?" *Constellations* 1 (1994): 74–91.

————. *Democracy and Difference.* University Park: Pennsylvania State University Press, 1993.

Phillips, Kevin. *The Cousins' Wars: Religion, Politics, and the Triumph of Anglo-America.* New York: Basic Books, 1999.

Pincus, Steven. "From Butterboxes to Wooden Shoes: The Shift in English Popular Sentiment from Anti-Dutch to Anti-French in the 1670s." *Historical Journal* 38 (1995): 333–61.

———. " 'To Protect English Liberties': The English Nationalist Revolution of 1688–1689." In *Protestantism and National Identity: Britain and Ireland, c.1650–c.1850*, ed. Tony Claydon and Ian McBride. Cambridge: Cambridge University Press, 1998.

Pocock, J.G.A. *The Ancient Constitution and the Feudal Law: A Study of English Historical Thought in the Seventeenth Century.* Cambridge: Cambridge University Press, 1957.

Polizzotto, Carolyn. "Liberty of Conscience and the Whitehall Debates of 1648–9." *JEH* 26 (1975): 69–82.

Popkin, Richard H. *The History of Scepticism from Erasmus to Descartes.* New York: Humanities Press, 1964.

———. "Skepticism about Religion and Millenarian Dogmatism: Two Sources of Toleration in the Seventeenth Century." In Laursen and Nederman, *Beyond the Persecuting Society.*

Porterfield, Amanda. *Female Piety in New England: The Emergence of Religious Humanism.* New York: Oxford University Press, 1992.

Potts, Timothy C. "Conscience." In *The Cambridge History of Later Medieval Philosophy*, ed. Norman Kretzmann, Anthony Kenny, and Jan Pinborg. Cambridge: Cambridge University Press, 1982.

Prall, Stuart E. *The Bloodless Revolution: England, 1688.* Madison: University of Wisconsin Press, 1972.

Rawls, John. "Kantian Constructivism in Moral Theory." *Journal of Philosophy* 77 (1980): 515–72.

———. *Political Liberalism.* New York: Columbia University Press, 1993.

———. *A Theory of Justice.* Cambridge: Harvard University Press, 1971.

Raz, Joseph. *The Morality of Freedom.* Oxford: Oxford University Press, 1986.

Reay, Barry. "The Quakers, 1659, and the Restoration of the Monarchy." *History* 63 (1978): 193–213.

———. *The Quakers and the English Revolution.* New York: St. Martins Press, 1985.

Remer, Gary. "Hobbes, the Rhetorical Tradition, and Toleration." *Review of Politics* 54 (1992): 5–33.

———. *Humanism and the Rhetoric of Toleration.* University Park: Pennsylvania State University Press, 1995.

Richards, David A.J. *Conscience and the Constitution: History, Theory, and Law of the Reconstruction Amendments.* Princeton: Princeton University Press, 1993.

———. *Identity and the Case for Gay Rights: Race, Gender, Religion as Analogies.* Chicago: University of Chicago Press, 1999.

———. *Toleration and the Constitution.* New York: Oxford University Press, 1986.

———. *Women, Gays, and the Constitution: The Grounds for Feminism and Gay Rights in Culture and Law.* Chicago: University of Chicago Press, 1998.

Robertson, D. B. *The Religious Foundations of Leveller Democracy.* New York: Columbia University Press, 1951.

Ronalds, Francis Spring. *The Attempted Whig Revolution of 1678–1681*. 1937. Totowa, N.J.: Rowman and Littlefield, 1974.

Rorty, Richard. *Contingency, Irony, Solidarity*. New York: Cambridge University Press, 1989.

Rose, Craig. *England in the 1690s: Revolution, Religion, and War*. Oxford: Basil Blackwell, 1999.

Rosenmeier, Jesper. "'New England's Perfection': The Image of Adam and the Image of Christ in the Antinomian Crisis, 1634 to 1638." *WMQ* 27 (1970): 435–59.

Russell, Conrad. "Arguments for Religious Unity in England, 1530–1650." *JEH* 18 (1967): 201–26.

———. *The Causes of the English Civil War*. Oxford: Oxford University Press, 1990.

Ryan, Alan. "Hobbes, Toleration, and the Inner Life." In *The Nature of Political Theory*, ed. David Miller and Larry Siedentop. New York: Oxford University Press, 1983.

———. "Hobbes and Individualism." In *Perspectives on Thomas Hobbes*, ed. G.A.J. Rogers and Alan Ryan. Oxford: Clarendon Press, 1988.

———. "A More Tolerant Hobbes?" In Mendus, *Justifying Toleration*.

Sabine, George. *A History of Political Theory*. Revised edition. New York: Henry Holt, 1950.

Sampson, Edward E. "Identity Politics: Challenge to Psychology's Understandings." *American Psychologist* 48 (1993).

Sandel, Michael J. *Democracy's Discontent: America in Search of a Public Philosophy*. Cambridge: Harvard University Press, 1996.

———. "Freedom of Conscience or Freedom of Choice?" In *Articles of Faith, Articles of Peace: The Religious Liberty Clauses and the American Public Philosophy*, ed. James Davison Hunter and Os Guinness. Washington, D.C.: Brookings Institution, 1990.

———. *Liberalism and the Limits of Justice*. Cambridge: Cambridge University Press, 1982.

Sandler, S. Gerald. "Lockean Ideas in Thomas Jefferson's 'Bill for Establishing Religious Freedom.'" *Journal of the History of Ideas* 21 (1961): 110–16.

Schlatter, Richard B. *The Social Ideas of Religious Leaders, 1660–1688*. New York: Oxford University Press, 1940.

Schlesinger, Arthur M. *The Birth of the Nation: A Portrait of the American People on the Eve of Independence*. New York: Knopf, 1968.

Schochet, Gordon J. "The Act of Toleration and the Failure of Comprehension: Persecution, Nonconformity, and Religious Indifference." In Hoak and Feingold, *The World of William and Mary*.

———. "From Persecution to 'Toleration.'" In Jones, *Liberty Secured?*

———. "John Locke and Religious Toleration." In *The Revolution of 1688–1689: Changing Perspectives*, ed. Lois G. Schwoerer. Cambridge: Cambridge University Press, 1992.

———. "Toleration, Revolution, and Judgment in the Development of Locke's Political Thought." *Political Science* 40 (1988): 84–96.

Schwartz, Sally. *"A Mixed Multitude": The Struggle for Toleration in Colonial Pennsylvania*. New York: New York University Press, 1987.

Schwoerer, Lois G. *"No Standing Armies!" The Antiarmy Ideology in Seventeenth-Century England*. Baltimore: Johns Hopkins University Press, 1974.

Scott, Jonathan. "England's Troubles: Exhuming the Popish Plot." In Harris, Seaward, and Goldie, *Politics of Religion*.

Seaward, Paul. *The Cavalier Parliament and the Reconstruction of the Old Regime, 1661–1668*. New York: Cambridge University Press, 1988.

———. *The Restoration, 1660–1688*. New York: St. Martin's Press, 1991.

Seeley, Robert A. *Handbook for Conscientious Objectors*. Philadelphia: Central Committee for Conscientious Objectors, 1981.

Seligman, Adam. *Innerworldly Individualism: Charismatic Community and Its Institutionalization*. New Brunswick, N.J.: Transaction Publishers, 1994.

Shapiro, Barbara J. *Probability and Certainty in Seventeenth-Century England: A Study of the Relationships Between Natural Science, Religion, History, Law, and Literature*. Princeton: Princeton University Press, 1983.

Shaw, Harold. *The Levellers*. London: Longmans, Green, 1968.

Shaw, William. *A History of the English Church During the Civil Wars and Under the Commonwealth, 1640–1660*. 2 vols. New York: Longmans, Green, 1900.

Shils, Edward. "The Antinomies of Liberalism." In *The Relevance of Liberalism*, ed. Research Institute on International Change. Boulder, Colo.: Westview Press, 1978.

Shklar, Judith. "The Liberalism of Fear." In *Liberalism and the Moral Life*, ed. Nancy Rosenblum. Cambridge: Harvard University Press, 1989.

———. *Ordinary Vices*. Cambridge: Harvard University Press, 1984.

Simpson, Alan. "The Covenanted Community." In *Religion in American History: Interpretive Essays*, ed. John M. Mulder and John F. Wilson. Englewood Cliffs, N.J.: Prentice-Hall, 1978.

———. "How Democratic Was Roger Williams?" *WMQ* 13 (1956): 53–67.

Sinopoli, Richard. "Liberalism and Contested Conceptions of the Good: The Limits of Neutrality." *Journal of Politics* 55 (1993): 644–63.

———. "Thick-Skinned Liberalism: Redefining Civility." *APSR* 89 (1995): 612–20.

Skinner, Quentin. "Conquest and Consent: Thomas Hobbes and the Engagement Controversy." In *The Interregnum: The Quest for Settlement*, ed. G. E. Aylmer. Hamden, Conn.: Archon, 1972.

———. *The Foundations of Modern Political Thought*. 2 vols. New York: Cambridge University Press, 1978.

———. *Liberty Before Liberalism*. Cambridge: Cambridge University Press, 1998.

———. "Meaning and Understanding in the History of Ideas." *History and Theory* 8 (1969): 3–53.

———. *Reason and Rhetoric in the Philosophy of Hobbes*. Cambridge: Cambridge University Press, 1996.

———. "Thomas Hobbes et la defense du pouvoir 'de facto.'" *Revue philosophique* 99 (1973): 131–54.

———. "Thomas Hobbes on the Proper Signification of Liberty." *Transactions of the Royal Historical Society*, 5th ser., 40 (1990): 121–51.

Smith, David L. *Constitutional Royalism and the Search for Settlement, c. 1640–1649*. Cambridge: Cambridge University Press, 1994.

Smith, Rogers M. *Civic Ideals: Conflicting Visions of Citizenship in U. S. History*. New Haven: Yale University Press, 1997.

———. *Liberalism and American Constitutional Law*. Cambridge: Harvard University Press, 1985.

Smith, Steven B. "Toleration and the Skepticism of Religion in Spinoza's *Tractatus Theologico-Politicus*." In Levine, *Early Modern Skepticism*.

Sommerville, Johann P. "Oliver Cromwell and English Political Thought." In *Oliver Cromwell and the English Revolution*, ed. John Morrill. London: Longman, 1990.

———. *Politics and Ideology in England, 1603–1640*. New York: Longman, 1986.

———. *Thomas Hobbes: Political Ideas in Historical Context*. New York: St. Martin's, 1992.

Sommerville, Margaret R. "Independent Thought, 1603–1649." Ph.D. diss., Cambridge University, 1982.

Speck, W. A. *Reluctant Revolutionaries: Englishmen and the Revolution of 1688*. Oxford: Oxford University Press, 1988.

Spurr, John. "The Church of England, Comprehension, and the Toleration Act of 1689." *English Historical Review* 104 (1989): 927–46.

———. *The Restoration Church of England, 1646–1689*. New Haven: Yale University Press, 1991.

St. John, Wallace. *The Contest for Liberty of Conscience in England*. Chicago: University of Chicago Press, 1900.

Staloff, Darren. *The Making of an American Thinking Class: Intellectuals and Intelligentsia in Puritan Massachusetts*. New York: Oxford University Press, 1998.

Stille, Charles J. "Religious Tests in Colonial Pennsylvania." *PMHB* 9 (1885): 365–406.

Stoever, William K.B. *"A Faire and Easie Way to Heaven": Covenant Theology and Antinomianism in Early Massachusetts*. Middletown: Wesleyan University Press, 1978.

Stokes, Anson Phelps. *Church and State in the United States*. New York: Harper and Brothers, 1950.

Stout, Harry S. *The New England Soul: Preaching and Religious Culture in Colonial New England*. New York: Oxford University Press, 1986.

Strauss, Leo. *The Political Philosophy of Hobbes: Its Basis and Genesis*. Oxford: Oxford University Press, 1936.

Strike, Kenneth. "Must Liberal Citizens Be Reasonable?" *Review of Politics* 58 (1996): 41–51.

Sullivan, John L., James Piereson, and George E. Marcus. *Political Tolerance and American Democracy*. Chicago: University of Chicago Press, 1982.

Sullivan, William M. *Reconstructing Public Philosophy*. Berkeley and Los Angeles: University of California Press, 1986.

Sunstein, Cass R. "Homosexuality and the Constitution." *Indiana Law Journal* 70 (1994): 1–28.

Tarcov, Nathan. "John Locke and the Foundations of Toleration." In Levine, *Early Modern Skepticism*.

Taylor, Charles. "Atomism." In *Powers, Possessions, and Freedom*, ed. Alkis Kontos. Toronto, 1979.

———. *The Ethics of Authenticity*. Cambridge: Harvard University Press, 1992.

———. *Multiculturalism and "The Politics of Recognition."* Princeton: Princeton University Press, 1992.

———. "Religion in a Free Society. " In *Articles of Faith, Articles of Peace: The Religious Liberty Clauses and the American Public Philosophy*, ed. James Davison Hunter and Os Guinness. Washington, D.C.: Brookings Institution, 1990.

———. "The Rushdie Controversy." *Public Culture* 2 (1989): 118–22.

———. *Sources of the Self: The Making of the Modern Identity.* Cambridge: Harvard University Press, 1989.

Thomas, Keith. "Cases of Conscience in Seventeenth-Century England." In *Public Duty and Private Conscience: Essays Presented to G. E. Aylmer,* ed. John Morrill, Paul Slack, and Daniel Woolf. Oxford: Oxford University Press, 1993.

———. *Religion and the Decline of Magic.* New York: Charles Scribner's Sons, 1971.

Thomas, Roger. "Comprehension and Indulgence." In *From Uniformity to Unity, 1662–1962,* ed. Geoffrey F. Nuttall and Owen Chadwick. London: Society for Promoting Christian Knowledge, 1962.

———. "The Seven Bishops and Their Petition, 18 May 1688." *JEH* 12 (1961): 56–70.

Tinder, Glenn. *Tolerance: Toward a New Civility.* Amherst: University of Massachusetts Press, 1976. Reissued as *Tolerance and Community* (Columbia: University of Missouri Press, 1995).

de Tocqueville, Alexis. *Democracy in America.* 1848. Revised by Francis Bowen, edited by Phillips Bradley. New York: Vintage, 1945.

Trevor-Roper, Hugh. "Archbishop Laud in Retrospect." In *From Counter-Reformation to Glorious Revolution.* Chicago: University of Chicago Press, 1992.

———. *Catholics, Anglicans, and Puritans.* London: Secker and Warburg, 1987.

Tuck, Richard. "The Civil Religion of Thomas Hobbes." In *Political Discourse in Early Modern Britain,* ed. Nicholas Phillipson and Quentin Skinner. Cambridge: Cambridge University Press, 1993.

———. "Hobbes and Locke on Toleration." In Dietz, *Thomas Hobbes and Political Theory.*

———. "Optics and Sceptics: The Philosophical Foundations of Hobbes' Political Thought." In *Conscience and Casuistry in Early Modern Europe,* ed. Edmund Leites. New York: Cambridge University Press, 1988.

———. *Philosophy and Government, 1572–1651.* Cambridge: Cambridge University Press, 1993.

———. "Scepticism and Toleration in the Seventeenth Century." In Mendus, *Justifying Toleration.*

Tulloch, John. *Rational Theology and Christian Philosophy in England in the Seventeenth Century.* 2 vols. Edinburgh and London, 1874.

Tully, James. "Governing Conduct." In *Conscience and Casuistry in Early Modern Europe,* ed. Edmund Leites. New York: Cambridge University Press, 1988.

———. "Locke." In Burns and Goldie, *Cambridge History of Political Thought.*

Tyacke, Nicholas. *Anti-Calvinists: The Rise of English Arminianism, 1590–1640.* New York: Oxford University Press, 1986.

Underdown, David. *Pride's Purge: Politics in the Puritan Revolution.* Oxford: Clarendon Press, 1971.

Vann, Richard T. *The Social Development of English Quakerism, 1655–1755.* Cambridge: Harvard University Press, 1969.

Verkamp, Bernard J. *The Indifferent Mean: Adiaphorism in the English Reformation to 1554.* Studies in the Reformation, vol. 1. Athens: Ohio University Press, 1977.

Vernon, Richard. *The Career of Toleration: John Locke, Jonas Proast, and After.* Montreal and Kingston: McGill-Queen's University Press, 1997.

Waldron, Jeremy. *Liberal Rights: Collected Papers, 1981–1991.* New York: Cambridge University Press, 1993.

———."Locke: Toleration and the Rationality of Persecution." In Mendus, *Justifying Toleration.*

Walker, William. "Force, Metaphor, and Persuasion in Locke's *Letter Concerning Toleration.*" In Nederman and Laursen, *Difference and Dissent.*

Wall, Robert Emmett. *Massachusetts Bay: The Crucial Decade, 1640–1650.* New Haven: Yale University Press, 1972.

Walzer, Michael. *On Toleration.* New Haven: Yale University Press, 1997.

———. "Response to Kukathas." In *Nomos 39: Ethnicity and Group Rights.* New York: New York University Press, 1997.

———. *The Revolution of the Saints: A Study in the Origins of Radical Politics.* Cambridge: Harvard University Press, 1965.

Warden, G. B. "The Rhode Island Civil Code of 1647." In *Saints and Revolutionaries: Essays on Early American History,* ed. David D. Hall, John M. Murrin, and Thad W. Tate. New York: W. W. Norton, 1984.

Way, H. Frank. "The Problem of Toleration in New Israel: Religious Communalism in Seventeenth-Century Massachusetts." In Laursen and Nederman, *Beyond the Persecuting Society.*

Webb, R. K. "From Toleration to Religious Liberty." In Jones, *Liberty Secured?*

Webster, Tom. *Godly Clergy in Early Stuart England: The Caroline Puritan Movement, c. 1620–1643.* Cambridge: Cambridge University Press, 1997.

Weinstein, Kenneth R. "Pierre Bayle's Atheist Politics." In Levine, *Early Modern Skepticism.*

Wellenreuther, Herman. *Glaube und Politik in Pennsylvania, 1681–1776: Die Wandlungen der Obrigkeitsdoktrin und des Peace Testimony der Quaker.* Cologne: Bohlau, 1972.

West, Cornel. *Race Matters.* New York: Vintage, 1994.

Westerkamp, Marilyn. "Anne Hutchinson, Sectarian Mysticism, and the Puritan Order." *Church History* 59 (1990): 482–96.

White, Peter. "The Twilight of Puritanism in the Years Before and After 1688." In Grell, Israel, and Tyacke, *From Persecution to Toleration.*

———. "The *Via Media* in the Early Stuart Church." In *The Early Stuart Church, 1603–1642,* ed. Kenneth Fincham. Stanford: Stanford University Press, 1993.

Williams, Bernard. "Identity and Identities." In *Identity: Essays Based on Herbert Spencer Lectures Given in the University of Oxford,* ed. Henry Harris. Oxford: Oxford University Press, 1995.

———. "Toleration: An Impossible Virtue?" In Heyd, *Toleration: An Elusive Virtue.*

Williams, Selma R. *Divine Rebel: The Life of Anne Marbury Hutchinson.* New York: Holt, Rinehart, and Winston, 1981.

Wingenbach, Ed. "Unjust Context: The Priority of Stability in Rawls' Contextualized Theory of Justice." *AJPS* 43 (1999): 213–32.

Withington, Anne Fairfax, and Jack Schwartz. "The Political Trial of Anne Hutchinson." *NEQ* 51 (1978): 226–40.

Wolfson, Adam. "Two Theories of Toleration." *Perspectives on Political Science* 25, no. 4 (1996): 192–202.

Wolterstorff, Nicholas. "Locke's Philosophy of Religion." In *The Cambridge Companion to Locke,* ed. Vere Chappell. New York: Cambridge University Press, 1994.

Woolrych, Austin. *Commonwealth to Protectorate.* Oxford: Oxford University Press, 1982.

———. "Oliver Cromwell and the Rule of the Saints." In *Cromwell: A Profile,* ed. Ivan Roots. London: Macmillan, 1973.

Wootton, David. "Leveller Democracy and the Puritan Revolution." In Burns and Goldie, *Cambridge History of Political Thought.*

Worden, Blair. "Providence and Politics in Cromwellian England." *Past and Present* 109 (1985): 55–99.

———. "Toleration and the Cromwellian Protectorate." In *Persecution and Toleration,* ed. W. J. Sheils. Oxford: Basil Blackwell, 1984.

Wykes, David L. "Quaker Schoolmasters, Toleration, and the Law, 1689–1714." *Journal of Religious History* 21 (1997): 178–92.

Young, Iris Marion. *Justice and the Politics of Difference.* Princeton: Princeton University Press, 1990.

Zakai, Avihu. *Exile and Kingdom: History and Apocalypse in the Puritan Migration to America.* Cambridge: Cambridge University Press, 1992.

———. "Religious Toleration and Its Enemies: The Independent Divines and the Issue of Toleration During the English Civil War." *Albion* 21 (1989): 1–33.

———. *Theocracy in Massachusetts: Reformation and Separation in Early Puritan New England.* Lewiston: Mellen University Press, 1994.

Ziff, Larzer. *The Career of John Cotton: Puritanism and the American Experience.* Princeton: Princeton University Press, 1962.

Zook, Melinda S. *Radical Whigs and Conspiratorial Politics in Late Stuart England.* University Park: Pennsylvania State University Press, 1999.

Zuckerman, Michael. *An Almost Chosen People: Oblique Essays in the American Grain.* Berkeley and Los Angeles: University of California Press, 1993.

———. "Pilgrims in the Wilderness: Community, Modernity, and the Maypole of Merry Mount." *NEQ* 50 (1977): 255–77.

INDEX